Title Withdrawn

ED-R

Writers for Young Adults

Writers for Young Adults

Ted Hipple

Editor

VOLUME 2

CHARLES SCRIBNER'S SONS
Macmillan Reference USA
Simon & Schuster Macmillan
New York

Simon & Schuster and Prentice Hall International
London   Mexico City   New Delhi   Singapore
Sydney   Toronto

Copyright © 1997 Charles Scribner's Sons

Library of Congress Cataloging-in-Publication Data
Writers for young adults / Ted Hipple, editor.
    p.   cm.
    Summary: Contains articles on writers whose works are popular with
young adults, including contemporary authors, such as Francesca Lia
Block and Maya Angelou, and classic authors, such as Sir Arthur
Conan Doyle and Louisa May Alcott.
    ISBN 0-684-80475-1 (v. 1 : hardcover). — ISBN 0-684-80476-X (v. 2
: hardcover). — ISBN 0-684-80477-8 (v. 3 : hardcover). — ISBN
0-684-80474-3 (set : hardcover)
    1. Young adult literature, American—Bio-bibliography—
Dictionaries.   2. Young adult literature, English—Bio-
bibliography—Dictionaries.   3. Authors, American—Biography—
Dictionaries.   4. Authors, English—Biography—Dictionaries.
[1. Authors, American.   2. Authors, English.   3. Young adult
literature.]   I. Hipple, Theodore W.
PS490.W75   1997
810.9'9283'03
[B]—DC21

        97-6890
        CIP
        AC

5 7 9 11 13 15 17 19 20 18 16 14 12 10 8 4

Printed in the United States of America. The paper used in this publication meets the minimum
requirements of the American National Standard for Information Sciences—Permanence of Paper
for Printed Library Materials, ANSI Z39.48–1984.

Contents

VOLUME 1

VOLUME 2

Writers for Young Adults

Russell Freedman

(1929-   )

by Richard F. Abrahamson

Russell Freedman was born in San Francisco on 11 October 1929 to a mother who was an actress and a father who was a salesman and gifted storyteller. At the age of fourteen, his father, Louis Garbowitz, wanted so much to join the army and fight during World War I that he lied about his age and his last name, adopting the last name of his best friend, Freedman.

A Writer's Apprenticeship

Russell, one of two children, grew up in a home where he was surrounded by books and authors. As Freedman recalls, "In fact, my parents met in a bookshop. She was a sales clerk, and he was a sales representative for Macmillan. They held their first conversation over a stack of best-sellers, and before they knew it, they were married. I had the good fortune to grow up in a house filled with books and book talk" ("Newbery Medal Acceptance," p. 446).

1

There is an article about John Steinbeck in volume 3.

William Saroyan (1908–1981) was an American writer of short stories, plays, and novels. **John Masefield** (1878–1967) was an English poet, novelist, critic, and playwright. He served as England's poet laureate for 37 years.

"Whenever [my mother] came home from the butcher with a leg of lamb, I knew another author was coming for dinner."

Some of the book talk Freedman remembers came from many of America's greatest writers who were invited to the Freedman house for dinner. John Steinbeck, William Saroyan, and John Masefield all dined at the Freedman house, "and they all had leg of lamb," Freedman remembers, "since that was the one thing my mother trusted herself to cook. Whenever she came home from the butcher with a leg of lamb, I knew another author was coming for dinner" ("Russell Freedman," p. 453).

From 1951 to 1953, Freedman served as an infantryman in the Korean War. When he returned from Korea, he took a job as a reporter and editor for the Associated Press that served as his real training as a writer. From San Francisco and the Associated Press, he headed for New York and a job with an advertising agency, where he wrote publicity pieces for some of the most popular television shows of the time – *Kraft Television Theatre, Father Knows Best,* and *The Real McCoys.* Of this period Freedman says, "Many people thought I had one of the most glamorous jobs in the world, but I didn't think so. I wanted to write about people and things that I cared about" ("Russell Freedman," p. 454).

Teenagers: The Subject of Freedman's First Book

The career Freedman was searching for was uncovered one day when he was reading an article in the *New York Times* about a sixteen-year-old blind boy who had invented the Braille typewriter. "That seemed remarkable, but as I read on, I learned something even more amazing: the Braille system itself, as used today all over the world, was invented by another sixteen-year-old boy who was blind, Louis Braille. That newspaper article inspired my first book, a collection of biographies called *Teenagers Who Made History*" ("Newbery Medal Acceptance," p. 446).

After *Teenagers Who Made History* (1961) came out, Freedman published several other books including *Jules Verne: Portrait of a Prophet* (1965) and *Thomas Alva Edison* (1966). Then he discovered the subject that would be his specialty for dozens of books—animals and animal behavior. His first series of animal books, co-authored with James Morriss, included *How Animals Learn* (1969), *Animal Instincts,*

(1970), and *The Brains of Animals and Man* (1972). The books were highly praised by critics but left Freedman dissatisfied with writing such definitive, comprehensive books. "I wondered, does anyone really sit down and read a book like this from beginning to end? Or do they just dip into it and use it to write reports?" ("Pursuing the Pleasure Principle," p. 29).

Photographs: A Hallmark of Freedman's Work

Worried that readers were not really reading these books, Freedman started to experiment with format and approach. He began to think about making the books more narrow in subject focus and more visually appealing by adding striking photographs.

> One day I was browsing through a book on bats, and I came upon a close-up photograph of a mother bat flying past the camera. Clutching her furry chest was a scrawny, helpless baby. Its eyes were closed, and it was hanging on with its teeth and claws as its mother flew about, hunting for insects. She was a bat, to be sure, but the photo presented a timeless and powerful image of a mother and her infant. The photograph was an enormously affecting one and fascinating because the infant's very life depended on its ability to hang on to its mother.
>
> Hanging on, I thought. That's a terrific title for a book. ("Pursuing the Pleasure Principle," p. 29)

Since the 1970s, and the publication of *Hanging On: How Animals Carry Their Young* (1977), a hallmark of Russell Freedman's nonfiction books on animals or biographies of famous Americans is the visual appeal brought to the books by wonderful, engaging photos that help bring his subjects alive.

It was in 1980 that Freedman's interest in photographs moved him away from animal books back into books about people. The occasion was a visit to an exhibit of old photographs, "New York Street Kids," celebrating the 125th anniversary of the Children's Aid Society. Freedman recollects, "Many of the photographs in the show dated back to the nineteenth century and showed children, primarily poor children, playing, working, and just hanging out on the teeming New York City streets of that era. What impressed me most of all was the way that those old photographs seemed to defy the passage of time" ("Pursuing the Pleasure Principle," p. 31). Coupled with the haunting power of the photos was Freedman's own connection to the way of life the photographs depicted. His grandparents were immigrants who came to New York City, and his father had played in the same city streets as shown in those photographs. From that exhibit experience came Freedman's *Immigrant Kids* (1980). Presenting photographs of immigrant children in the late 1800s and early 1900s, Freedman describes their lives at home, school, work, and play.

immigrants people who come to a country, from another country, in order to take up permanent residence

Freedman had found a way to blend his love of research, writing, and photographs to create appealing books that helped adolescent readers see what life was like for youngsters a hundred years ago. Not surprisingly, *Immigrant Kids* was met with critical praise, and other Freedman books with a similar format followed: *Children of the Wild West* (1983), *Cowboys of the Wild West* (1985), and *Kids at Work: Lewis Hine and the Crusade Against Child Labor* (1994). All four were named American Library Association Notable Books.

Putting It All Together: Freedman's Biographies for Young Adults

In many ways, all that Freedman learned in the writing of the animal books and the photographic essays on immigrant children and cowboys come together in his most acclaimed works—biographies for young adults. In fact, Russell Freedman's biography *Lincoln: A Photobiography* (1987) won the most coveted prize in the world of books for children and young adults, the John Newbery Medal. Let's take a look at what makes this book and Freedman's biographies of Franklin Delano Roosevelt and Eleanor Roosevelt so special.

Even though Freedman is writing biography and dealing with the facts of a person's life, he sees himself as a storyteller first. In fact, pinned above his typewriter is this quotation from noted nonfiction writer John McPhee: "Whatever you're writing, your motive is always to tell a good story while you're sitting around the cave, in front of the fire, before going out to club another mastodon" (quoted in "Fact or Fiction," p. 3).

In "Bring 'Em Back: Writing History and Biography for Young People" (1994), Freedman describes what he means by storytelling in his work:

> By storytelling, I do not mean making things up, of course. I don't mean invented scenes, or manufactured dialogue, or imaginary characters. As a writer of nonfiction, I have a pact with the reader to stick to the facts, to be as factually accurate as human frailty will allow. What I write is based on research, on the documented historical record. And yet, there are certain storytelling techniques that I can use without straying from the straight and narrow path of factual accuracy. (Pp. 138-139)

Pinned above Freedman's typewriter is this quotation: "Whatever you're writing, your motive is always to tell a good story while you're sitting around the cave, in front of the fire, before going out to club another mastodon."

One of the storytelling techniques Freedman employs to great success is "creating vivid word pictures of people, places, and events" (p. 139). He uses such "vivid word pictures" in his biography of Lincoln to help readers capture the character of the president. In discussing how he accomplished this in the writing of *Lincoln,* Freedman says, "There are plenty of small details that provide glimpses of Abraham Lincoln's life in the White House. He said, 'Howdy' to visitors, and invited them to 'stay a spell.' He greeted diplomats while wearing carpet slippers. . . . He mended his gold-rimmed spectacles with a piece of string" (p. 139).

Many readers of *Lincoln* come away with a vivid picture of the president simply by reading Freedman's inventory of what was in the president's pockets the morning he died.

> Lincoln had in his pockets a pair of small spectacles folded into a silver case; a small velvet eyeglass cleaner, a large linen handkerchief with *A. Lincoln* stitched in red; an ivory pocketknife trimmed with silver; and a brown leather wallet lined with purple silk. The wallet contained a Confederate five-dollar bill

bearing the likeness of Jefferson Davis and eight news-paper clippings that Lincoln had cut out and saved. All the clippings praised him. As president he had been denounced, ridiculed, and damned by a legion of critics. When he saw an article that complimented him, he often kept it. (P. 130)

In addition to using storytelling techniques in his biographies, Freedman also develops his famous subjects through quotations from their own writings. In *Lincoln,* Freedman quotes from the writings of Lincoln himself and uses quotations from others who knew the president. For example, Lincoln was a devoted father who seldom disciplined his children. William Herndon, Lincoln's law partner, describes what Lincoln's sons were like when they accompanied their father to the law office on Sundays. "The boys were unrestrained in their amusement. If they pulled all the books from the shelves, bent the points of all the pens, overturned the spittoon, it never disturbed the serenity of their father's good nature. I have felt many and many a time that I wanted to wring the necks of those little brats and pitch them out the windows" (*Lincoln,* p. 41). What you won't find in Freedman's biographies are examples of any invented dialogue, made-up scenes, or imaginary characters.

Another thing that makes Freedman's biographies special is found in the subtitle of *Lincoln,* which describes the book as *A Photobiography.* A meticulous researcher who made trips to Lincoln's Kentucky birthplace, to his home in Indiana, and to Ford's Theater for the text of the Lincoln book, Freedman always had his eyes open for the second part of the research—photos and other visual images that would help make his text and his subject come to life. Learning about the importance of visual images from his early books on animal behavior, Freedman makes sure that his biographies are also visually exciting. The text of the Lincoln biography is broken up and enhanced with scores of photographs and prints the author selected from archives across the United States. Posters announcing Lincoln's election as president, photos of plantations and slave families, and images of dead soldiers on Civil War battlefields add a power to his biographies not often found in such books for teen readers.

The hallmarks of storytelling techniques, quotations, and historically accurate prints and photos also can be found in

Ford's Theater, located in Washington, D.C., is the theater in which Lincoln was shot by the actor John Wilkes Booth. Lincoln died in the house across the street, where he was carried after the shooting.

archives places in which public records or historical documents are stored

Freedman's biographies of President Franklin Delano Roosevelt, and of Eleanor Roosevelt. With so many people he could write about, Freedman is often asked why he chooses the famous people he has. He explains,

> I wanted to write about Lincoln because I knew very little about the Civil War or about Lincoln himself. He seemed to be an impossible mythological figure, filled with contradictions, and I was curious.
>
> Learning about FDR, on the other hand, gave me a chance to go back and relive my own childhood. Roosevelt elicited such powerful feelings from the people I knew; I can remember the bread lines, the Hoovervilles around San Francisco. . . . I wanted to write about this period in order to understand what was happening around me when I was growing up.
>
> While I was working on FDR, Eleanor emerged as a unique and fabulous character who deserved a book of her own. Her story is an aspect of American social history that wasn't appropriate to cover in my biography of FDR. . . . I was irresistibly drawn to her as a subject, and I had already done half the research! ("An Interview with Russell Freedman," p. 2)

Hoovervilles towns of temporary, substandard dwellings created in the U.S. during the Great Depression in the 1930s; so called after President Herbert Hoover, whom many blamed for the Depression

Conclusion

Russell Freedman is one of the best writers of nonfiction for young adults working in the 1990s. Whether he is writing about the lives of cowboys in the Wild West or chronicling the life of Abraham Lincoln or Eleanor Roosevelt, you can be sure the books will be filled with interesting true stories, accurate quotations, and carefully selected photographs and prints that help make his subjects live again for today's young adult readers.

If you enjoy biographies and other nonfiction books like Russell Freedman's, also take a look at the work of Milton Meltzer.

Selected Bibliography

WORKS BY RUSSELL FREEDMAN

Nonfiction for Young Adults

Teenagers Who Made History (1961)

Two Thousand Years of Space Travel (1963)

Thomas Alva Edison (1966)

How Animals Learn, with James E. Morris (1969)

Animal Instincts, with James E. Morris (1970)

Animal Architects (1971)

The Brains of Animals and Man, with James E. Morris (1972)

The First Days of Life (1974)

Growing up Wild: How Young Animals Survive (1975)

Animal Fathers (1976)

Animal Games (1976)

Hanging On: How Animals Carry Their Young (1977)

How Birds Fly (1977)

Getting Born (1978)

How Animals Defend Their Young (1978)

Immigrant Kids (1980)

Tooth and Claw: A Look at Animal Weapons (1980)

They Lived with the Dinosaurs (1980)

Animal Superstars: Biggest, Strongest, Fastest, Smartest (1981)

Farm Babies (1981)

When Winter Comes (1981)

Can Bears Predict Earthquakes? Unsolved Mysteries of Animal Behavior (1982)

Killer Fish (1982)

Killer Snakes (1982)

Children of the Wild West (1983)

Dinosaurs and Their Young (1983)

Rattlesnakes, illustrated by the author (1984)

Sharks, illustrated by the author (1984)

Cowboys of the Wild West (1985)

Indian Chiefs (1987)

Lincoln: A Photobiography (1987)

Buffalo Hunt (1988)

The Wright Brothers: How They Invented the Airplane (1991)

An Indian Winter (1992)

Nonfiction for Adults

Holiday House: The First Fifty Years (1985)

Biographies for Young Adults

Jules Verne: Portrait of a Prophet (1965)

Scouting with Baden-Powell (1967)

Franklin Delano Roosevelt (1990)

Eleanor Roosevelt: A Life of Discovery (1993)

Kids at Work: Lewis Hine and the Crusade Against Child Labor (1994)

Articles

"Bring 'Em Back: Writing History and Biography for Young People." In *School Library Journal,* March 1994, pp. 138–141.

"Fact or Fiction." In *Using Nonfiction Trade Books in the Elementary School: From Ants to Zepplins,* 1992, pp. 2–10.

"Newbery Medal Acceptance." *Horn Book,* July/August 1988, pp. 444–451.

"Pursuing the Pleasure Principle." *Horn Book,* January/February 1986, pp. 27–32.

WORKS ABOUT RUSSELL FREEDMAN

Book

Carter, Betty, and Richard Abrahamson. *Nonfiction for Young Adults: From Delight to Wisdom.* Phoenix: Oryx Press, 1990.

Articles

"An Interview with Russell Freedman." *Clarionnews,* fall 1990, pp. 1–3.

Dempsey, Frank J. "Russell Freedman." *Horn Book,* July/August 1988, pp. 452–456.

Videotape

"A Video Visit with Russell Freedman." Burlington, Mass.: Houghton Mifflin, 1990.

How to Write to the Author
Russell Freedman
280 Riverside Drive, 10K
New York, NY 10025-9028

Michael French

(1944-   )

by Pam B. Cole

Michael French was born into a middle-class family in Los Angeles, the second of two sons. His father was a medical doctor and his mother was a housewife. As a child, French led an inventive and fantastic life. He created imaginary pets (such as a gopher) and wrote to people who had either died or never existed. He also created stories in his head and acted out heroic roles.

introspection examination of one's own thoughts and feelings

French's Life and Influences

Like many adolescents, French was keenly interested in sports, particularly basketball, and through sports made many friends in his neighborhood. During his teenage years he also experienced periods of intense introspection and loneliness. In *Speaking for Ourselves, Too,* French describes these years as a time in which he felt "a not untypical antagonism toward the world" (p. 68). He retreated to the typewriter, where he often

Quotations from Michael French that are not atributed to a publshed source are from personal correspondence with the author of this article during the summer of 1995 and are published here by permission of Michael French.

> *"I suppose my motivation for writing," French says, "comes from a lonely adolescence where my typewriter became my port from the storm."*

wrote for days. "I suppose my motivation for writing," French says, "comes from a lonely adolescence where my typewriter became my port from the storm."

As a youth, French had strong religious convictions. Heavily influenced by his church (Methodist), good teachers, and the discipline and idealism of his father, he developed an exaggerated sense of doing what was right. In *Speaking for Ourselves, Too,* he says, "I always had an untested sense of trying to improve myself or the world. Like Don Quixote, I thought there was no wrong I could not right" (p. 68). This strong sense of idealism has found its way into much of his work.

After completing high school, French attended Stanford University, where he majored in creative writing and received a bachelor's degree in English in 1966. He went on to Northwestern University, where he completed a master's degree in journalism a year later. The day after French graduated from Northwestern, he received his draft notification in the mail—an announcement with which he was not thrilled. With much apprehension, however, he served two years in the army during the Vietnam War. This experience became the basis for his young adult novel *Soldier Boy* (1985).

In December 1969, French married Patricia Goodkind, a real estate developer, whom he had met at Northwestern. The couple settled in New York City, where they lived for seven years. French first worked for a public relations firm as a financial writer and then for a large corporation as an economics writer, specializing in annual reports. During these years in New York, French wrote part-time, publishing *Club Caribe* (1977) and *Abingdon's* (1979)—two novels for adults—and his first novel for young adults, *The Throwing Season* (1980), a story about corruption in high school athletics. In 1976 French's first child, Timothy, was born, and the couple moved to Santa Fe, New Mexico, where their daughter Alison was born two years later and where French began devoting more time to his fiction writing.

French and his wife own and manage a large real estate company in northern New Mexico. His interests include spending time with his teenagers, mountain climbing, and armchair archaeology. He and his wife purchased an "archaeological ranch," containing extensive historic and prehistoric pueblo ruins, pit houses, kivas, and similar items of

archaeology the scientific study of material remains of past human life and activities

archaeological interest, and began restoring the ruins in the 1990s. Amid these activities, French still finds time to write. In the mid-1990s he was writing a screenplay for Fred Roos based on Jack Schaffer's novella *Old Ramon,* a story about a thirteen-year-old white boy who apprentices for a summer with an old Hispanic sheepherder in northern New Mexico.

Most of French's ideas for writing come from his own childhood: "I think there are primarily two types of YA [young adult] writers, those who draw their characters from memories of their own adolescence, and those who write from current observations of young people around them. I tend to fall into the former camp." Although French's stories are contemporary, his characters are similar to people he knew as a young adult. Some of them are drawn from facets of French's own personality, particularly his strong sense of righteousness.

Although French writes to entertain, he also tries to convey a message or, as he says, provide "at least some nuggets of thought that a reader can chew on and digest, even if he doesn't agree with them." Thus, in writing for a young adult audience, French strives to make readers aware of the moral dilemmas that they will one day face. In virtually all his novels for young adults, French says, "there is at least one protagonist who is haunted about trying to do the right thing while somebody—his parents, his friends, a teacher, or some antagonist—challenges that idealism by arguing in some way that it is inappropriate or selfishly one-sided or just naive. Moral growth is achieved only by that kind of challenge."

Many of French's themes are existential, and his novels, often characterized as psychological thrillers, are usually suspenseful. French often writes about alienation from the mainstream—in his words, "the price one pays to be an individual, a maverick, a renegade." This theme is fundamental to his writing. French says, "One can be a very quiet, inconspicuous maverick for most of his life. Then, in a moment of truth, when one least wants or expects it, something happens, a choice has to be made, and one's character is defined." Thus, strong, well-drawn characters who make sudden decisions in illuminating moments are essential to his work. Self-reliance, trust, relationships, manipulation, exploitation, power, and triumph over adversity are also recurrent themes.

existential relating to or affirming existence

alienation separation of a person from a position of former attachment, such as within a particular society

French's Novels for Young Adults

Pursuit

The seed for *Pursuit* (1982), French's second novel for young adults, came from a dream. In the middle of the night, French was awakened by the novel's death scene, in which Roger cuts Martin's safety rope, causing Martin to plunge to his death. The novel grew from there, the plot developing around four male friends on a sociable hiking excursion in the Sierras.

Pursuit has a number of themes, including survival, overcoming adversity, and coming to terms with one's own sense of morality. Martin's brother Gordy, having seen Roger cut Martin's rope, turns against Roger and vows he will expose the truth. A game of cat and mouse ensues. Gordy sets out alone for help (Luke, the other member of the hiking team, is afraid to oppose Roger), and Roger stalks him, looking for the right moment to kill him. Gordy, a righteous, idealistic young man, is a less experienced hiker than Roger is and has a completely different perspective of right and wrong. Thus, Gordy struggles alone in the wilderness without food, proper clothing, or travel gear, swearing he will reach help.

The story is also about alienation from the mainstream. Roger is the campus hero in school, trying to impress everyone and thriving on attention; he is also different from all his classmates. No one really knows him. As French describes him, "Roger kept a distance from other kids, even friends. He didn't like to talk about his feelings" (p. 15). Roger's difference becomes more distinctive in the Sierras, even before he causes Martin's death: "They all laughed except Roger, who kept dragging a stick through the timothy grass. His letterman's jacket looked out of place, and the white leather sleeves were soiled from starting the fire. His face was distant" (p. 12).

Luke, the fourth member of the hiking party who fears opposing Roger, likewise is alienated. Overweight, clumsy, unpopular, and with low self-esteem, he both admires and fears Roger. Instead of becoming involved in sports, Luke immerses himself in his schoolwork and in helping his parents at home. After Martin's death, Luke will never forget his own alienation. He contemplates the loneliness in his life and the fact that he has no real friends. Although alienated from oth-

Sierras the Sierra Nevada, a huge mountain range in eastern California

ers his age, Luke yearns to belong; it is this yearning that prevents him from being self-reliant and causes him to side with Roger after Martin's death instead of standing up for the truth.

Pursuit is a psychological thriller. In one sense it can be read as a story of manipulation and mind control. Although Roger's friends see him as a natural leader who is ambitious and always working to prove himself, Roger reveals his negative side: he is impatient, indifferent, and manipulative. He thinks he needs no one and is completely self-reliant. Once he cuts Martin's rope, he rationalizes the entire incident, convincing Luke to side with him. Roger's arguments are: neither Luke nor Gordy saw him cut the rope; the entire incident was a mere accident because the rope was weak; there is nothing any of them could do; and, besides, they're friends, and friends stick together, and so on. Gordy, however, is not easily manipulated by Roger and leaves to find help. Roger begins a mad pursuit, tracking Gordy, teasing and tantalizing him, playing on Gordy's mind and his sanity, testing Gordy's own sense of morality and waiting for the right moment to murder him.

tantalizing teasing by repeatedly frustrating

Soldier Boy

Drawn somewhat from French's experiences as a soldier during the Vietnam War, *Soldier Boy* is a story about four teenagers who are trying to come to grips with their own identities and their relationships with those around them.

Central to this story is the theme of self-reliance. Melanie and Nina are high school seniors and best friends, but they have very different personalities. Nina is plodding, predictable, and obedient. Nina's parents have planned her future: she will marry a local well-to-do boy and settle down in her hometown. Nina feels comfortable with her parents controlling her life because she fears making decisions for herself. Melanie, however, is independent, spontaneous, and adventurous. She does not believe in conformity or passivity. Although she is not rebellious toward her single mom, she lives "a peaceful if delicate coexistence" with her (p. 44). Melanie wants nothing more than to leave her small town—even if she has to marry a soldier boy to do it. In short, she appears to be the direct opposite of Nina. She is self-assured and self-reliant.

When the girls meet and begin dating two privates in training at the nearby army base, both girls come to know themselves in a new way. Melanie falls in love with B. J. and realizes that behind her "facade of confidence" lies a "trembling sea of insecurity" (p. 46). When she falls in love with him, her self-reliant exterior crumbles. She begs B. J. to marry her. She pleads, "I may act strong, but I'm really not. I need somebody. I need you" (p. 166). She realizes that she needs people and that she needs stability in her life.

foil a character who, by contrast, makes clear the qualities of another character

Nina is a perfect foil for Melanie. While Melanie is outwardly carefree and self-sufficient, Nina is docile and dependent upon others. Every movement of her life is carefully orchestrated for her. Yet as her relationship with Cliff develops, Nina becomes more independent and self-reliant. Cliff takes her out of her small, narrow world and gives her a different perspective on life. Although she chides Cliff for living a safe life and not taking risks, she comes to understand her own sheltered and guarded life through her relationship with him. Having acquired this understanding, she ends her relationship with her fiancé, Billy, determined to make her own decisions about her future.

Us Against Them

bucking resisting

Us Against Them (1987) explores peer pressure; that is, the conflict between allegiance to friends and loyalty to one's own sense of what is right. In this novel, sixteen-year-old Reed, the leader of a teenage club who is well-known for bucking adult authority, discovers that the club house is going to be torn down. Thus, as an act of defiance, he leads his club members into the Adirondack Mountains on a camping excursion, where the club members confront situations of peer pressure. Dissension and violence occur while the group is in the Adirondacks, and the teenagers must decide whether to remain loyal to one another and their club or stay true to their individual consciences.

Us Against Them deals with one of French's most popular themes: the price one pays for being an individual and a renegade, and for bucking society's rules and alienating oneself from the mainstream. Although the club members choose to isolate themselves in the mountains and plan to return within a week to their town, they are unaware of the price they will pay for their rebellious behavior. Reed, an independent, indifferent, and inconsiderate personality much like Roger in *Pursuit,* wants more than the others to prove his independence to the adult population; thus, he convinces the other club members to prolong their stay in the Adirondacks. When Reed becomes involved in a shooting, the club members learn how unreliable faith in one person can be. They then must choose between their loyalty to Reed and their own values.

Split Image

French repeats the theme of independence, or self-reliance, in *Split Image* (1990), a psychological thriller in which the main character finds himself in an almost impossible moral dilemma. Abandoned by his father as a small child, Garrett has been reared by his mother and his uncle. When his mother dies, Garrett's father, Clarence Murchinson, sends word to the small, sleepy Arizona town in which Garrett grew up that he wants Garrett to live with him in Los Angeles. When Garrett first moves in with his father, he is seduced by the man's lifestyle and the future he envisions for himself.

Clarence Murchinson works for the government, and Garrett learns that his father's work is top secret; in fact, his father is a spy. Garrett becomes infatuated with his father's career, and his father lures him into an espionage scheme. Believing that the work he does with his father is for the United States, Garrett is thrilled by his new sense of power; however, when he discovers that his father has involved him in espionage against his own country, Garrett faces a moral dilemma: Does he remain loyal to his father, or does he report his father to the government?

espionage spying or using spies to obtain information

In his creation of the character Clarence Murchinson, French echoes the indifferent, inconsiderate, manipulative characters portrayed in his earlier two novels. Like Roger in *Pursuit,* who appears to have no reason for killing Martin other than his own impatience to travel faster through the Sierras, Murchinson exploits his own son, using him as a pawn in the dangerous game of espionage. Like Reed in *Us Against Them,* who uses his charm to manipulate his fellow club members into defying adult authority, Murchinson preys upon Garrett's sense of insecurity, guilt, and responsibility to manipulate him.

Circle of Revenge

Described by critics as a psychological thriller, *Circle of Revenge* (1988) intricately weaves the lives of two young boys, both loners who are alienated from their peers. Robbie, who has low self-esteem and no real friends, becomes a naive participant in a science experiment conducted by Dr. Edward Salazar, an indifferent and coldhearted scientist from a local college—an experiment designed to control and manipulate Robbie's thinking. Carlos, the son of a former Central American dictator who lives a secret life of exile in the United States, befriends Robbie. Their friendship is challenged, however, when Robbie discovers that Dr. Salazar has programmed him to murder Carlos, an act of vengeance against Carlos's father—a man responsible for the death of his own family.

exploitation the use of someone or something unjustly for one's own advantage

Exploitation is one of the main themes in this work. Robbie, looking for a few easy dollars and diversion from an otherwise dull life, becomes a victim of Salazar's ploy, a pawn in the scientist's wild game of vengeance. Ironically, Carlos is also a victim of exploitation: his father, a Central American totalitarian ruler, forces Carlos to identify his best friend and the friend's family as traitors against the government. As a result, Carlos's father has Carlos's best friend and mother assassinated.

totalitarian relating to a political regime in which the government has strict control over the lives of the citizens, especially by coercive measures

Conclusion

French's novels for young adults place well-drawn teenage characters in moral predicaments, wherein they must make decisions that will shape their future as adults. In *Pursuit,* Luke struggles with the question of whether to remain loyal to Roger or tell the truth about Martin's death; Gordy struggles between doing the obvious—reporting the death of his brother—and adopting Roger's warped values. Melanie and Nina both struggle with their identities in *Soldier Boy*. Both discover that they are not the people they imagined themselves to be and must gain courage to face the future. All the club members in *Us Against Them* must define themselves either in terms of the group or in terms of their own individual morals. In *Split Image,* Garret must choose between maintaining allegiance to his father and defending his country. Finally, Robbie, in *Circle of Revenge,* must decide whether to commit murder for the scientist or follow his own conscience.

Selected Bibliography

If you like stories by Michael French, you might also like the works of Robert Cormier.

WORKS BY MICHAEL FRENCH

Novels for Young Adults

The Throwing Season (1980)

Pursuit (1982)

Flyers (1983)

Indiana Jones and the Temple of Doom (1984)

Lifeguards Only Beyond This Point (1984)

Soldier Boy (1985)

Us Against Them (1987)

Circle of Revenge (1988)

Split Image (1990)

NOVELS FOR ADULTS

Club Caribe (1977)

Abingdon's (1979)

Rhythms (1980)

Texas Bred (1986)

Family Money (1990)

AUTOBIOGRAPHY

Speaking for Ourselves, Too: More Autobiographical Sketches by Notable Authors. Edited by Donald R. Gallo. Urbana, Ill.: National Council of Teachers of English, 1993, pp. 68–69.

WORKS ABOUT MICHAEL FRENCH

Commire, Anne, ed. *Something about the Author: Facts and Pictures about Authors and Illustrators of Books for Young People.* Detroit: Gale Research, 1985, vol. 38, p. 79.

How to Write to the Author
Michael French
c/o Bantam Doubleday Dell
Publishing Group, Inc.
1540 Broadway
New York, NY 10036

Commire, Anne, ed. *Something About the Author: Facts and Pictures About Authors and Illustrators of Books for Young People*. Detroit: Gale Research, 1987, vol. 49, pp. 99–100.

Locher, Francis C., ed. *Contemporary Authors*. Detroit: Gale Research, 1980, vols. 89–92, pp. 180–182.

Robert Frost

(1874-1963)

by Philip Gerber

Readers fond of Robert Frost like to picture him as the ideal poet of the Northeast, the poet "born" to write of life in states such as Vermont, Massachusetts, and New Hampshire. These readers are surprised to hear that their favorite poet actually was born in California. And not only was he born in San Francisco, on 26 March 1874, but he continued living there until he reached the age of ten. Very few clues to these ten years exist in Frost's poems. The most notable instance may be these lines about "life in the Golden Gate" from his poem "A Peck of Gold":

> Dust always blowing about the town,
> Except when sea fog laid it down,
> And I was one of the children told
> Some of the blowing dust was gold.
> (*The Poetry of Robert Frost*, p. 249)

The **Golden Gate** is a strait connecting San Francisco Bay with the Pacific Ocean.

Beginnings

But Frost came by his New England connections honestly, a legacy from his parents, who moved west across the continent from Massachusetts in 1873. Following the untimely death of Robert's father, William Prescott Frost Jr., in 1885, Isabelle Moodie Frost returned to the East, taking with her the two children, Robert, then ten, and his nine-year-old sister, Jeanie. Their destination was Lawrence, Massachusetts. There the bereaved family was taken in by Robert's grandparents, William Prescott Frost, and his wife, Judith, and there the future poet grew into his young manhood.

By the time that Robert Frost completed his first year at Lawrence High School, he stood at the head of his class and had taken an interest in creative writing. As a sophomore, Robert published a long poem in *The Bulletin,* the student publication. Entitled "La Noche Triste," this poem retold in verse the story of the Spanish conquest of the Aztecs at the Mexican lake city of Tenochtitlán. As a junior, Frost was experimenting with blank verse, the unrhymed pentameter lines used in English since Shakespeare's time and a form that would be used for a good deal of Frost's mature poetry. During his senior year, Frost became chief editor of *The Bulletin,* continued to write poems, and most importantly, fell in love with his fellow student and future wife, Elinor White, whose interest in poetry matched his own.

There is an article about Shakespeare in volume 3.

In 1892, Elinor White and Robert Frost served as co-valedictorians of their graduating class and were secretly engaged to be married. But for the time being they parted, he traveling east to enter Dartmouth College, she west to attend St. Lawrence University in upstate New York. The separation was not a happy time for either of them, and even before the first semester was completed, Robert had left Dartmouth hoping to marry Elinor and begin their married life together. The marriage did not take place until December 1895, but during the previous November a magazine called *The Independent* had printed "My Butterfly: An Elegy," Robert's first professionally published poem. He was hoping to establish himself as a writer and to earn a living by his pen. That was not to become a reality until quite some time in the future.

Meanwhile, once married, the Frosts found life difficult. Robert tried schoolteaching and farming, neither seemingly his calling. Steadily, the children arrived: Elliott in 1896, Lesley in 1899, Carol in 1902, Irma in 1903, and Marjorie in 1905. Elinor, another daughter, was born and died in 1907, and Elliott also died, a toll not altogether unexpected in those times of heavy child mortality. During the interim, Frost had tried college again, entering Harvard University; again he left, without completing the full 1898–1899 academic year. From 1900 to 1909, the Frost family lived on a farm near Derry, New Hampshire, where Robert tried to establish a livelihood in the poultry business. Another spell of teaching followed, this time at Pinkerton Academy. Wherever and whenever possible, Frost was writing poems. But he was publishing very few of them.

Flight to England

In 1912, Robert Frost stood on the brink of total discouragement. Much of what he had already written would some day help to create his fame. But right now poem after poem was being rejected by the prominent periodicals that printed verse. American poetry itself, in fact, stood at a strange crossroads. Caught between a powerful nineteenth-century tradition and restless new forces that might encourage change, the poetic art was not making much progress. No new major career had emerged in decades, although Emily Dickinson, unpublished during her lifetime, was being allowed a posthumous chance at fame. Whitman, the freshest new voice, was long dead and, besides, had been rejected by the poetry establishment as "disgraceful." Stephen Crane's attempt to gain ground with a revolutionary free verse had come to a sad end with Crane's death at age twenty-nine in 1900. Edwin Arlington Robinson was breaking new ground, especially by way of incorporating new psychological insights with poems of character—a path that Frost was beginning to follow and would excel at—but Robinson remained unappreciated, forced to publish his books at his own expense.

No one seemed to be encouraging the development of American poetry; the editors in the book- and magazine-publishing world seemed frozen in place. Any number of skilled imitators were busy producing poems that looked like and sounded like the poems of the influential generation just passed: Henry Wadsworth Longfellow, James Russell Lowell,

There are articles about Emily Dickinson and Stephen Crane in volume 1.

free verse poetry that does not follow traditional forms, meters, or rhyme schemes.

Edwin Arlington Robinson (1869–1935) was an American poet. He was best known for his poems in which he presented strong characters, such as "Richard Cory" and "Miniver Cheevy."

John Greenleaf Whittier, and the like. But no one could write Longfellow, Lowell, or Whittier poems better than the great originals. The works of the imitators were doomed to become extinct, and the timidity of the editors was holding them back from taking chances with newcomers whose work seemed too revolutionary, too "different" from the safe and expected. Fresh new writers were waiting in the wings— Carl Sandburg, Vachel Lindsay, and Robert Frost were only three of many. But none was being given recognition, and all were rapidly approaching their forties. Frost himself in 1912 was thirty-eight and, even though poetry was conceded to be a young man's game, he had not published a single book of verse.

Frost's apparent "silence" was not for lack of trying. He continued to send his poems to the magazines, here and there gaining an acceptance. The *Atlantic Monthly* was—as it had been for years—America's most prestigious literary periodical. Ellery Sedgwick was its editor. Frost took a chance, sending six poems for Sedgwick to consider. Sedgwick read the poems, made his decision, and returned them to Frost, writing: "We are sorry that we have no place in the *Atlantic Monthly* for your vigorous verse" (*Robert Frost: The Early Years,* p. 389). Frost by now had come to a decision of his own. His grandfather having left him a modest annuity, he was planning to leave the United States for England, where he hoped to find a less hidebound publishing world, one more open to the new. On 23 August 1912, the Frost family, parents and children together, boarded the steamship SS *Parisian* out of Boston Harbor bound for Glasgow.

Somewhat amazingly, Frost's great gamble paid off handsomely. Within a year's time he had published his first book of poems. Thanks were due to assistance from the American poet Ezra Pound, then residing in London, who helped him locate a publisher. Soon afterward, another American poet, Amy Lowell, carried back to Boston the news of Robert Frost's English triumph. The first book, *A Boy's Will* (1913), was composed largely of poems that Frost had been unable to place with American editors. A handful, such as "Storm Fear" and "Mowing," have remained favorites through the years, as has "The Tuft of Flowers," with its optimistic message and memorable theme-lines: "'Men work together,' I told him from the heart / 'Whether they work together or apart.'" (*The Poetry of Robert Frost,* p. 23).

Vachel Lindsay (1879–1931) was an American poet. His poems were noted for their strong rhythms and vivid images. Many show his love of nature and democracy.

Ezra Pound (1885–1972) was an American poet and essayist. He was one of the most influential literary figures of his time. **Amy Lowell** (1874–1925) was an American poet, critic, and biographer. She became a leader of the movement known as imagism. The imagists stressed a precise treatment of images.

Before another year had passed, Robert Frost's London publisher, David Nutt, brought out his second book, one that had an even more phenomenal reception than the first. It was *North of Boston* (1914) by all odds the single best book overall of Frost's lifetime. He declared that any poet's ambition was "to lodge a few poems where they would be hard to get rid of" (introduction to *King Jasper*, p. x). If that aim is a proper basis for judgment, then *North of Boston* has proved to be perhaps the best single book of poems ever published by any American.

The number of poems that lodged—and have remained lodged—in the minds of readers of *North of Boston* includes a very high percentage of Frost favorites. The list leads off with "Mending Wall," a dialogue in which two New England neighbors contemplate the stone wall separating their properties, one man raising the question of what purposes might be served by walls of any kind at all, the other only reiterating the adage: "Good fences make good neighbors." Much depends upon whether the word "good" has reference to a good, solidly constructed wall or to the wall that has a good, beneficial purpose.

Robert Frost was a superb writer of dramatic poems, little playlets in verse. In *North of Boston* that note is struck first in "Mending Wall" and then continued in a series of "people poems" such as "A Hundred Collars." The series is capped by a pair of masterworks. One, "Home Burial," is the superb study of death, grief, and consolation, in which a young couple find their marriage cracking under the strain of their first child's death. Of equal quality and better known is "The Death of the Hired Man," another disquisition between husband and wife; this one concerns the responsibilities people owe to other people and contains the memorable but hardnosed definition offered by the husband, Warren:

> "Home is the place where, when you have to go there,
> They have to take you in."
> (*The Poetry of Robert Frost*, p. 38)

Ironically, "The Death of the Hired Man," composed in 1905, was among those Frost poems considered by American editors to be unpublishable.

Another masterpiece from *North of Boston,* "After Apple-Picking," is a philosophical poem noted for its aggregation of

---

Robert Frost's London publisher, David Nutt, declared that any poet's ambition was "to lodge a few poems where they would be hard to get rid of."

disquisition formal discussion of a subject

symbol anything that stands for or represents something else, for example, "The dove is a symbol of peace"

symbols for life and death gathered from the age-old analogy between the parts of the day, the seasons of the year, and the successive stages of human life:

> My long two-pointed ladder's sticking through the tree
> Toward heaven still,
> And there's a barrel that I didn't fill
> Beside it, and there may be two or three
> Apples I didn't pick upon some bough,
> But I am done with apple-picking now.
> (*The Poetry of Robert Frost*, p. 68)

metaphor a figure of speech in which one thing is referred to something else, for example, "My love is a rose"

Apple-growing and the harvest serve as a metaphor for life itself. The poem contains Frost's thought-provoking rumination on the nature of death, that final sleep, "whatever sleep it is," whether it is like a woodchuck's hibernation, looking toward spring and resurrection, or whether it's like "just some human sleep."

Triumph in America

By 1915, both of Frost's books had been printed in America, *North of Boston* reaching the status of a bestseller. With the inception of *Poetry* and other magazines that opened their pages to new fashions in verse, a renaissance in poetry was underway. Ellery Sedgwick, no longer blind to Frost's excellence, in 1915 proudly presented a collection of Frost poems in his *Atlantic Monthly*. The poet had returned to America in triumph.

verse here, the term means poetry

Frost rapidly capitalized on his newly won recognition. If he was reaching forty before he published a first book, he was fortunate in having that many years—and more— remaining in which to pursue a career. Book followed book in regular succession. *Mountain Interval* (1916), *New Hampshire* (1923), *West-Running Brook* (1928), *A Further Range* (1936), *A Witness Tree* (1942), *A Masque of Reason* (1945), *Steeple Bush* and *A Masque of Mercy* (1947), and *In the Clearing* (1962).

The fame that had eluded the poet for so long now poured in upon him. He was awarded the Pulitzer Prize four times between 1923 and 1943 and, at one time or another, garnered just about every other prize available to poets. He was elected to membership in both the National Institute of Arts and Letters (1916) and the American Academy of Arts and Letters (1930), was highly sought after as a reader of his own poems, and served on the faculties of Amherst College, the University of Michigan, and Harvard University. Innumerable honorary degrees were conferred by these and other universities across the length and breadth of the land. He was famous, honored like no other twentieth-century American poet before or since.

The list of Frost's outstanding poems waxed longer with each book. "An Old Man's Winter Night," the nostalgic "Birches," and the psychological scare-piece "The Hill Wife" appeared in *Mountain Interval,* along with his searing and unforgettable poem-story of a young boy whose hand is hacked off by a buzz saw, causing him to die before he has lived, its grim title "Out, Out—" borrowed from the empty lament of the defeated Macbeth in Shakespeare's drama:

> MACBETH: Out, out, brief candle!
>
> Life's but a walking shadow, a poor player,
>
> That struts and frets his hour upon the stage
>
> And then is heard no more. It is a tale
>
> Told by an idiot, full of sound and fury,
>
> Signifying nothing.
>
> (*Macbeth,* Act V, scene v, ll. 23–28)

waxed grew

Macbeth, a Scottish general, is the protagonist, or main character, in Shakespeare's tragedy *Macbeth*.

No volume failed to add to Frost's luster as a poet. He excelled at poems depicting an intimate and very positive relationship between people and nature. His volume *West-Running Brook* contributed a pair of the best of these: "Tree at My Window" and "Acquainted with the Night"; *A Further Range* gave us something different, the humorous "Departmental" as well as the somber "Desert Places"; *Steeple Bush* the philosophical "Directive." And from the single slim volume *New Hampshire* came a series of short lyrics of unsurpassed poetic splendor that included "Fire and Ice," "Dust of Snow," "Nothing Gold Can Stay," and "For Once, Then, Something," as well as the work that many critics consider to be Frost's masterpiece—and which the poet himself called "my heavy-duty poem" (*Robert Frost,* p. 108)—"Stop-

ping by Woods on a Snowy Evening," with its haunting conclusion:

> The woods are lovely, dark, and deep,
> But I have promises to keep,
> And miles to go before I sleep,
> And miles to go before I sleep.
> (*The Poetry of Robert Frost,* p. 224)

Last Days

President John F. Kennedy—born in 1917 just as Frost was
basking in his first wave of American enthusiasm—formed a
habit of using those finish-lines to close his campaign
speeches in 1960. As he moved from podium to wings, he
would give a farewell wave to his audience and say, "I'd love
to stay, but I have promises to keep—and miles to go before
I sleep." Invariably, the applause was deafening.

In gratitude for providing this poem, perhaps, and surely
for Robert Frost's lifetime achievement as a poet, President
Kennedy invited the aging Frost to appear on the platform
with him at the presidential inauguration and read a poem
especially written for the occasion. And so, on 20 January
1961, Robert Frost, now eighty-seven, his familiar thatch of
hair as white as the snow that drifted down upon the cele-
brants, stood up to read. But the wind's suddenly whipping
his manuscript from his hands forced Frost to improvise. The
old man, quick-witted as ever, launched into a substitute
poem long held fast in memory: "The Gift Outright."

In some ways, that event marked Frost's passage from
the public scene, a final high point surely. Yet, even though
ill, in 1962 he found the energy to travel to the Soviet Union
where, in Moscow, he read his "Mending Wall," now loaded
with global political implications concerning the highly controversial wall erected by the Russians to divide East Berlin
from West Berlin. Later that year, just as his final volume, *In
the Clearing,* was published, Robert Frost entered Peter Bent
Brigham Hospital in Boston, and there, on 29 January 1963,
having just been awarded the Bollingen Prize in Poetry, he
died at age eighty-eight. President Kennedy, himself soon off
to Berlin to stand defiantly before the Berlin wall and deliver

his "Ich bin ein Berliner!" speech, said of Frost: "[He] was one of the granite figures of our time in America. He was supremely two things—an artist and an American" (Thompson and Winnick, *Robert Frost: The Later Years,* p. 347).

Selected Bibliography

WORKS BY ROBERT FROST

Poetry

A Boy's Will (1913; 1915)

North of Boston (1914; 1915)

Mountain Interval (1916)

New Hampshire (1923)

West-Running Brook (1928)

A Further Range (1936)

A Witness Tree (1942)

A Masque of Reason (1945)

A Masque of Mercy (1947)

Steeple Bush (1947)

In the Clearing (1962)

Collected Works: Poetry

The Poetry of Robert Frost. Edited by Edward Connery Lathem. New York: Holt, Rinehart and Winston, 1969.

Prose Works

Introduction to *King Jasper: A Poem,* by Edwin Arlington Robinson. New York: Macmillan, 1935.

Selected Prose of Robert Frost. Edited by Hyde Cox and Edward Connery Lathem. New York: Holt, Rinehart and Winston, 1966.

Robert Frost on Writing. Edited by Elaine Barry. New Brunswick, N.J.: Rutgers University Press, 1973.

Collected Works: Letters

Family Letters of Robert and Elinor Frost. Edited by Arnold Grade. Albany: State University of New York Press, 1972.

The Letters of Robert Frost to Louis Untermeyer. Edited by Louis Untermeyer. New York: Holt, Rinehart and Winston, 1963.

President Kennedy said of Frost: "[He] was one of the granite figures of our time in America. He was supremely two things—an artist and an American."

An interesting contemporary, Carl Sandburg, moved through the same historical period as Robert Frost, but wrote poems dedicated almost entirely to the American industrial city and its people. His *Chicago Poems* (1916), for example, provide a fascinating contrast with Frost's poems of rural New England.

Robert Frost and John Bartlett: The Record of a Friendship. Edited by Margaret Bartlett Anderson. New York: Holt, Rinehart and Winston, 1963.

Robert Frost and Sidney Cox: Forty Years of Friendship. Edited by William R. Evans. Hanover, N.H.: University Press of New England, 1981.

Selected Letters of Robert Frost. Edited by Lawrence Thompson. New York: Holt, Rinehart and Winston, 1964.

Interviews with Robert Frost

Interviews with Robert Frost. Edited by Edward Connery Lathem. New York: Holt, Rinehart and Winston, 1966,

WORKS ABOUT ROBERT FROST

Biographical and Critical Studies

Cady, Edwin H., and Louis J. Budd, eds. *On Frost: The Best from American Literature.* Durham, N.C.: Duke Univ. Press, 1991.

Cook, Reginald L. *The Dimensions of Robert Frost.* New York: Rinehart, 1958.

Cox, Sidney. *A Swinger of Birches.* New York: New York University Press, 1957.

Francis, Robert. *Frost: A Time to Talk.* Amherst, Mass.: University of Massachusetts Press, 1972.

Gerber, Philip. *Robert Frost,* rev. ed. Boston: Twayne, 1982.

Gould, Jean. *Robert Frost: The Aim Was Song.* New York: Dodd, Mead and Company, 1964.

Isaacs, Elizabeth. *An Introduction to Robert Frost.* Denver: Alan Swallow, 1962.

Kemp, John C. *Robert Frost and New England.* Princeton: Princeton University Press, 1979.

Lynen, John F. *The Pastoral Art of Robert Frost.* New Haven: Yale University Press, 1960.

Mertins, Louis. *Robert Frost: Life and Talk-Walking.* Norman: University of Oklahoma Press, 1965.

Morrison, Kathleen. *Robert Frost: A Pictorial Chronicle.* New York: Holt, Rinehart and Winston, 1974.

Nitchie, George W. *Human Values in the Poetry of Robert Frost.* Durham, N.C.: Duke University Press, 1960.

Poirer, Richard. *Robert Frost: The Work of Knowing*. New York: Oxford University Press, 1977.

Pritchard, William. *Frost: A Literary Life Reconsidered*. New York: Oxford University Press, 1984.

Sergeant, Elizabeth Shepley. *Robert Frost: The Trial by Existence*. New York: Holt, Rinehart and Winston, 1960.

Thompson, Lawrence. *Robert Frost: The Early Years, 1874–1915*. New York: Holt, Rinehart and Winston, 1966.

————. *Robert Frost: The Years of Triumph, 1915–1938*. New York: Holt, Rinehart and Winston, 1970.

Thompson, Lawrence, and R. H. Winnick. *Robert Frost: The Later Years, 1938–1963*. New York: Holt, Rinehart and Winston, 1976.

Wilcox, Earl J., ed. *Robert Frost: The Man and the Poet*. Conway, Ark.: University of California Press, 1990.

You can visit the Robert Frost Farm at:
N.H. Route 28
Derry, NH 03038.
You can also write to the farm for information at:
P.O. Box 1075
Derry, NH 03038

Leon Garfield

(1921-1996)

by Ken Donelson

lmost all Leon Garfield's novels are set in eighteenth-century England—a robust, adventurous, rowdy, and dangerous setting. Readers who skim through reviews of Garfield's novels are sure to find certain words used over and over to describe the way Garfield portrays that time and place: *blood-and-thunder, daring deeds, sinister characters, orphans, danger, piracy, treasure, villains, gore, complex plots, thrilling action, violence, and murder.* Two other words, which describe virtually everything Garfield writes but are sometimes ignored by reviewers, are *strangeness* and *humor.*

These two moods—danger and thrills mixed with the weird and ironic and funny—describe Garfield as a writer, but they also help to explain some things about Garfield as a man. He jokes that he was born ten days after his birth. Although he was born on 14 July 1921, his birth date was not registered for another ten days because his somewhat happy-go-lucky father forgot. As Garfield tells us in *Speaking*

irony a situation in which the actual outcome is opposite or contrary to what was expected

Garfield wrote throughout his life—as a child, a schoolboy, and an adult.

for Ourselves, Too, his family was made up of some strange people he could later use in his novels. One scowling uncle, a sour aunt, and their home gave Garfield an early introduction to hell. "They lived in a tall dark house in North London," he recalls, "inhabited by funereal furniture, camphor balls, and Lithuanian rabbis, who seemed to lurk behind every plum-colored velvet curtain. . . . I was sent there on holidays, as a punishment, I suppose" (p. 73).

Garfield wrote throughout his life—as a child, a schoolboy, and an adult. When he was a young man, he took art lessons, convinced that an artist's life was for him. But his art was interrupted when he was taken into military service during World War II and assigned to the medical corps. He spent most of the war hating the sergeant of his platoon, who had a loud voice and teeth "like bayonets." He enlisted as a private and emerged at the end of the war still a private, something of a major accomplishment for five years in the service.

The First Two Novels

There is an article about Robert Louis Stevenson in volume 3.

Out of the service and married to Vivien Alcock, also a writer, Garfield wrote to find out if he was truly a writer himself. He had been reading Robert Louis Stevenson's *The Master of Ballantrae,* set in eighteenth-century Scotland, and he was fascinated by the story of two brothers. So he set out to write about two brothers, found he needed a way to focus on his subject, and decided to tell the story through a young boy's eyes. The book that emerged, *Jack Holborn,* was about the sea and pirates, although Garfield knew almost nothing about these subjects.

Jonathan Swift
(1667–1745) was an Irish writer, who wrote *Gulliver's Travels*, a satirical memoir about an adventurous man who visits a number of strange and fantastic places.

Daniel Defoe
(1660–1731) was an English novelist, who wrote *Robinson Crusoe*, a realistic memoir about a resourceful man who is shipwrecked on an island.

Garfield had long admired the works of Jonathan Swift and Daniel Defoe, particularly their love of the sea and their knowledge of ships. After some discouragement about what he could do to make up for his ignorance, Garfield discovered a truth: that writers like Swift and Defoe, or even like himself, do not need to know everything. They can steal from other sources. As he ruefully says in his December 1968 article in *Horn Book* magazine, "I was very depressed . . . until I discovered that both had got their information straight out of an old sailing manual from which, in places, they had copied word for word. They knew no more about the sea than I did" (p. 670).

By the time Garfield had investigated enough about piracy and shipping laws and living conditions on land and sea to write his novel, five years had elapsed and the story was now a grotesque monster. No publisher wanted it, but Grace Hogarth at Constable publishers in London was interested *if* Garfield would cut it in half. Would he cut it? Of course he did not want to, but he did, and the book was published in 1964.

Jack Holborn suffers from many of the faults of Garfield's first novels. It sounds more like a novel written under the influence of another novel than a book that stands on its own merits. The theme of finding one's identity and potential is awkwardly handled. Garfield seems intent on reminding us of the theme and repeating variations of it (Jack must save the captain's life three times) rather than letting us find what Garfield has obviously placed before us. Garfield's preachiness seems terribly heavy-handed, and what he wants readers to get from the novel is too obviously pointed out. Although Garfield continues to preach in later novels, he learns to be less obvious and intertwines his message with more thrills, irony, and fun.

Despite its flaws, *Jack Holborn* is a marvelous adventure tale, but Garfield's second novel written two years later, *Devil in the Fog,* is a disappointment. *Jack Holborn* was too long and apparently needed cutting, but *Devil in the Fog* was too short and needed padding. The story, again set in eighteenth-century England, is about young George Treet, the son of traveling actors, who is suddenly discovered to be the son and heir of Sir John—and then just as suddenly discovered not to be the son of nobility. This novel repeats many of the same themes found in Garfield's first novel and adds little to his reputation.

Lessons from His First Two Books

Garfield learned more than he probably realized at the time. He learned that the eighteenth century was going to be the setting for his novels for several good reasons. In his introduction to his history, *The House of Hanover: England in the*

Eighteenth Century (1976), Garfield lists the defining characteristics of London in the eighteenth century: ordure was left lying in the streets; rubbish lay everywhere; cellar doors were left open, and stone steps projected out into the streets; broken pavements and ruinous houses could be seen all over; streets were blocked with sheds and stalls; newly built houses stuck out into the middle of streets; bullocks and other animals were driven through the streets; mad dogs, beggars, and profanity abounded; and lighting in the streets was almost nonexistent.

The author might also have added a number of other fascinating facts about the eighteenth century. Crime was rampant. In the country, highwaymen ruled the roads, robbing and raping. In London, pickpockets and thieves were everywhere, especially in the narrow streets. Murders were common. Criminals were condemned to death for trivial reasons—stealing a handkerchief was a capital crime—and hanged at Tyburn before jeering mobs that delighted in the free entertainment. Prostitution was rampant, and so were drunkenness, madness, cruelty to humans, and even more horrible cruelty to animals, especially dogs and cats. The world seemed to be full of orphans seeking any means to survive. Eighteenth-century England—particularly London—may not have been a perfect world, but it was an almost perfect setting for Garfield's fiction.

Garfield had learned that he could effectively convey a social message through fiction about illusions and reality and the human need to distinguish one from the other. He also had learned, or been told by his editor, that he needed to find ways of telling stories other than through the eyes of the main character. He was beginning to master an important skill, that of writing first paragraphs that grabbed and held readers. Finally, he had begun to learn the art of writing the

picaresque novel a novel that depicts the eposodic adventures of a clever scoundrel who finds himself in predicament after predicament

picaresque novel, in which the central character is a poor young man who lives by his wits and becomes involved with lower levels of society, usually criminals, and who ultimately proves that he is essentially good and worth saving. Writers of picaresque novels tend to take a cynical view of society, just as they tend to moralize about society's failings. Henry Fielding's *Tom Jones* and Tobias Smollett's *Roderick Random* were popular eighteenth-century picaresque novels, and both are still worth reading today.

Garfield's Next Three Novels: Two Winners and a Dubious One

Smith (1967), *Black Jack* (1968), and *The Drummer Boy* (1969) are superior in many ways to Garfield's first two novels. *Smith* lures readers in with its first lines:

> He was called Smith and was twelve years old which, in itself, was a marvel; for it seemed as if the small-pox, the consumption, brain-fever, gaol-fever, and even the hangman's rope had given a wide berth for fear of catching something. Or else they weren't quick enough. (P. 7)

Smith may be young, but he is already a gifted professional pickpocket, and as the book opens, he has an eye on his target, an old gentleman with money. Smith follows his mark, waiting patiently for the time to strike. When the time comes, Smith brushes against the old man and cleans out his pockets. But the reader is not done with the old man, nor is Smith. He sees two men: "curious fellows of a very peculiar aspect—which Smith knew well. Uneasily, he scowled—and wished he might vanish through the crumbling bricks." The men move closer to their target, the old gentleman, but their game is more sinister than Smith's:

> They moved very neat, and with no commotion. They were proficient in their trade. The taller came at the old man from the front; the other took on his back—and slid a knife into it.
>
> The old gentleman's face was fatefully towards a certain dark doorway. He seemed to peer anxiously round the heavy shoulder of the man who was holding him—as if for a better view. His eyes flickered with pain at the knife's quick prick. Then he looked surprised—amazed, even—as he felt the cold blade slip into his warm heart. (P. 11)

The murderers search the old man's pockets but do not find what Smith already has. As soon as a crowd forms, Smith flees, knowing that whatever he has taken is a source of danger to himself. Worse yet, Smith cannot read and has no idea what awful thing he now possesses.

Black Jack is even more frightening and powerful. Unlike Smith, young Bartholomew Dorking is only on the innocent edge of the criminal world. He agrees to "baby-sit" a convict just hanged at Tyburn, watching the body for Mrs. Gorgandy to make sure that none of the late criminal's clothes or possessions are taken while she pops out for a moment. But this dead criminal is not the usual variety. Black Jack, for that is his name, is certainly a criminal, but as Bartholomew learns soon enough, Black Jack is not dead. He had wedged a silver tube an inch wide and four inches long down into his throat and had not been strangled by the rope. He is alive, and he takes Bartholomew with him for protection. So begins the adventure. A beautiful but mad young girl joins the plot, and everything is sorted out by the earthquake scare of 1750.

The Drummer Boy is both a lesser novel and something new for Garfield, a book-length symbolic study of moral bankruptcy. It opens with a magnificent description of a mighty battle with the inevitable carnage but with no clear victor. Charlie Samson, the drummer boy, leads the troops but is wounded and goes down, only to rise again as the battle ends. Charlie has only contempt for a surgeon named Mr. Shaw, who goes from corpse to corpse gathering teeth to sell; but he has only admiration for the dead James Digby, who leaves behind a note for Sophia Lawrence. Even though it is discovered that Digby is not dead (though, ironically, he is killed shortly thereafter), he still has Charlie's admiration. Charlie and Shaw go to London to visit Sophia, and Charlie is smitten. Although it takes some time, Charlie learns about Sophia's coldness and the horrors that can sometimes be caused by beautiful people.

Readers are seldom indifferent about *The Drummer Boy*. In his 1990 book, *What Do Draculas Do. Essays on Contemporary Writers of Fiction for Children and Young Adults,* David Rees calls *The Drummer Boy* a "total failure, almost unbelievably bad." It is hard not to agree with him. The book is a study in nonaction, nonadventure, and unrealistic symbolism. Garfield has not repeated this form again.

Garfield's Favorite Book

Garfield says that *The Strange Affair of Adelaide Harris* (1971) is his favorite book, and it is easy to see why. This story is funny and complicated enough to please any reader. The premise is simple, if weird. Harris and Bostock, two inattentive schoolboys at Dr. Bunnion's Academy in Brighton, England (Garfield was born in Brighton; is he telling us something about his education?) learn for the first time something that excites them. Their teacher tells them ancient stories of babies abandoned on mountaintops who are saved by suckling she-wolves. Harris and Bostock question whether such a feat is possible; but to help their education along, they leave Harris' baby sister, Adelaide, in the wilderness.

What happens becomes a typical eighteenth-century comic plot of mistaken identities, misunderstandings, coincidences, and intrigues. Waiting for the she-wolf to take Adelaide away, Bostock and Harris see their math teacher's daughter, Tizzy Alexander, and the headmaster's son, Ralph Bunnion, walking without a chaperone nearby. Tizzy's father challenges Ralph to a duel. Adelaide is found by church officials and taken to a poorhouse. Bostock and Harris find a Gypsy baby, assume it is Adelaide even though it is a boy, and take it home to Mrs. Harris, who loathes it on sight. Eventually, things get sorted out. Even the Gypsy baby comes out well. Near the end of the book, Garfield tells what will happen to the boy, and it provides an inside joke to anyone who knows Emily Brontë's *Wuthering Heights*.

Wuthering Heights (1847) is a romantic masterpiece that was made into a classic movie in 1939. The simple summary of the boy's life at the end of *Adelaide Harris* is the plot of glorious and complex *Wuthering Heights*.

So the infant grew and grew in all his darkly passionate mystery. He grew until he was between five and six years old, when, early one summer, he ran away from Mrs. Bonney's care. By degrees he made his way northward, until one day he was found in the streets of Liverpool by a kindly old gentleman by the name of Earnshaw. This old gentleman took him home and brought him up, and after an early disappointment in love, he ended his days in prosperous circumstances in a remote part of Yorkshire. Considering his unfavorable beginnings, he ended up rather well. (P. 223)

Novels for Slightly Older Readers

Garfield's next three novels have been almost universally praised. *The Sound of Coaches* (1974), *The Prisoners of September* (1975), and *The Pleasure Garden* (1976) are all safely locked into the eighteenth century. They are also more somber books about young men who have trouble recognizing who they are and what they wish to be.

The Sound of Coaches has flashes of humor and wit, but essentially it is the story of a young boy born to an uncertain father—there is no question about his mother—who longs for more than he finds at home. He finds his future, at least for the moment, on the stage. This setting allows Garfield, who loves Shakespeare and the theater, the opportunity to show both the good and the bad about the world of drama. The novel begins with a long and powerful paragraph that provides Garfield all the room he could want for various metaphors and descriptive images:

> Once upon a winter's night . . . a coach came thundering down the long hill outside of Dorking. Its progress was wild, . . . the passing landscape conspired to increase the terror of the journey, and the fleeting sight of a gibbet—its iron cage swinging desolately against the sky—turned the five passengers' thoughts towards the next world. (P. 9)

Almost immediately thereafter, a baby is born to a "spiritless creature, with a pale, unhealthy face and sick eyes." The entire coachload of people adopt the tiny boy in spirit, if not in the eyes of the law, and the mother lives long enough to kiss the baby and leave it her shabby old box.

The boy, Sam, is adopted by the coachman and his wife and lives happily enough for a time, glad to be driving his father's coach. But there comes that time, as it must in novels—and maybe once in a while in life—when Sam must know his roots. So off to London he goes, where he discovers the alcoholic man who is his father. Sam also finds love in this lovely book.

The Prisoners of September is a darker story, perhaps less satisfying but still good Garfield. The focus is less on the London of the time and more on Paris and the French Revolution, particularly a massacre in a Paris prison in September 1792. Lewis Boston sets out to free every Frenchman he can find, but instead he rescues three swindlers and thieves. Lewis' longtime friend, Richard Mortimer, is so passionately involved in freeing prisoners that he is taken in by every Frenchman in sight and goes mad out of frustration.

The Pleasure Garden, set in one of London's many public gardens of the time, tells of blackmail, immorality, and other ethical issues. Mainly it is about a young clergyman caught up in intrigue and murder. The plot keeps readers going, but it is a dark tale, leaving more questions unanswered than answered.

A Few Other Books

Garfield has written several other novels (see the bibliography). He has also written, with Edward Blishen, two good books about ancient myths. *The God Beneath the Sea* (1970) begins and ends with the myth of Hephaestus, the first son of Zeus, thrown out of Olympus because of his ugliness and ultimately helped into the city of the gods by his brother. *The Golden Shadow* (1973) follows with stories of the gods who came before the Trojan War.

The House of Hanover: England in the Eighteenth Century (1976) retells the history of an era by using portraits in the National Portrait Gallery near Trafalgar Square. It is wonderful history and a funny read, but possibly only to readers who are already familiar with its subject.

Garfield's love of drama in general and Shakespeare in particular are obvious in two books summarizing some of Shakespeare's plays. *Shakespeare Stories* (1985) covers nine plays, and the later *Shakespeare Stories II* (1994) covers a dozen plays. During the 1990s people who subscribed to Home Box Office (HBO) on cable television had the opportunity to see the half-hour animated productions of *Hamlet, Macbeth, A Midsummer Night's Dream, Romeo and Juliet, The Tempest,* and *Twelfth Night.* Each was done in striking colors by Russian animators, and Garfield abridged the plays. Six more plays using Garfield's abridgments were released in film and print versions in 1994. Having built a long and distinguished career from his varied forms of writing, Garfield died on 2 June 1996 in London.

There is an article on William Shakespeare in volume 3.

abridgement a shortened or condensed version

When we put down one of Garfield's novels, particularly something as powerful as Smith *or* Black Jack *or* The Sound of Coaches, *we are as likely to remember the villains as we are the protagonist.*

If you like Leon Garfield, you will probably enjoy novels by Robert Louis Stevenson, Charles Dickens, and Robert Westall. You might also enjoy the stories and spectacle that make up William Shakespeare's plays.

Garfield's Villains

When we put down one of Garfield's novels, particularly something as powerful as *Smith* or *Black Jack* or *The Sound of Coaches*, we are as likely to remember the villains as we are the protagonist. Catherine Storr, in "Things That Go Bump in the Night," points out how brilliantly Garfield handles villains and villainy:

> [Leon Garfield] involves his readers in a situation where, identified with the hero, they see the forces of evil moving to engulf them and then, suddenly, by a delicate twist of phrase, he shows not the wickedness of the villain but his weakness and above all, his vanity.

Selected Bibliography

WORKS BY LEON GARFIELD

Novels for Young Adults

Jack Holborn, illustrated by Anthony Maitland (1964; 1965)

Devil-in-the-Fog, illustrated by Anthony Maitland (1966)

Smith, illustrated by Anthony Maitland (1967)

Black Jack, illustrated by Anthony Maitland (1968; 1969)

The Drummer Boy, illustrated by Anthony Maitland (1969; 1970)

The Strange Affair of Adelaide Harris, illustrated by Fritz Wegner (1971)

The Sound of Coaches, illustrated by John Lawrence (1974)

The Prisoners of September (1975)

The Pleasure Garden, illustrated by Fritz Wegner (1976)

The Confidence Man (1978; 1979)

Bostock and Harris: Or, The Night of the Comet, illustrated by Martin Cottam (1979); retitled as *The Night of the Comet: A Comedy of Courtship Featuring Bostock and Harris* (1979)

John Diamond, illustrated by Anthony Maitland (1980); retitled as *Footsteps* (1980)

The December Rose, written from Garfield's television series in England (1987)

The Empty Sleeve (1988)

Short Stories

The Apprentices, stories about apprentices published individually from 1976 to 1978 (1978; 1982)

Ghost Stories

Mr. Corbett's Ghost, illustrated by Alan E. Cober (1969)

Mr. Corbett's Ghost, and Other Stories, illustrated by Anthony Maitland (1972)

The Wedding Ghost, illustrated by Charles Keeping (1985; 1987)

Novels for Adults

The Mystery of Edwin Drood, the completion of Charles Dickens' novel (1980; 1983)

The House of Cards (1982; 1983)

Mythology

The God Beneath the Sea, with Edward Blishen, illustrated by Charles Keeping (1970); illustrated by Zevi Blum (1971)

The Golden Shadow, with Edward Blishen, illustrated by Charles Keeping (1973)

History

The House of Hanover: England in the Eighteenth Century (1976)

Shakespeare Abridgments

Shakespeare Stories, illustrated by Michael Foreman (1985)

Shakespeare Stories II, illustrated by Michael Foreman (1994)

Shakespeare Abridgments Edited by Garfield

Hamlet, illustrated by Natalia Orlova, Peter Kotov, and Natasha Demidova (1993)

Macbeth, illustrated by Nikolai Serebriakov (1993)

A Midsummer Night's Dream, illustrated by Elena Prorokova (1993)

Romeo and Juliet, illustrated by Igor Makarov (1993)

The Tempest, illustrated by Elena Livanova (1993)

Twelfth Night, illustrated by Ksenia Prytkova (1993)

As You like It, illustrated by Valentin Olschwang (1994)

Julius Caesar, illustrated by Victor Chuguyevski, Yuri Kulakov, and Galina Melko (1994)

King Richard III, illustrated by Peter Kotov (1994)

Othello, illustrated by Nikolai Serebriakov (1994)

The Winter's Tale, illustrated by Elena Livanova and Stanislav Sokolov (1994)

Articles

"And So It Grows." *Horn Book,* December 1968, pp. 668–672.

"Writing for Children." *Children's Literature in Education,* 2 July 1970, pp. 56–63.

"Is There a Boundary Between Children's Literature and Adult Literature?" *Children's Libraries Newsletter,* May 1974, pp. 31–36.

"An Evening with Leon Garfield." In *One Ocean Touching: Papers from the First Pacific Rim Conference on Children's Literature.* Edited by Sheila Egoff. Metuchen: Scarecrow, 1979, pp. 110–120.

"Historical Fiction for Our Global Times." *Horn Book,* November/December 1988, pp. 736–742.

"The Outlaw." *Horn Book,* March/April 1990, pp. 164–170.

Adaptations of Garfield's Work

Black Jack. Film. Directed by Kenneth Loach, 1979.

John Diamond. Television movie. Also known as *Footsteps.* BBC, 1981.

The Ghost Downstairs. Television movie, 1982.

The Restless Ghost. Television movie, 1983.

The December Rose. Six-part television series. BBC, 1986–1987.

Mr. Corbett's Ghost. Television movie, 1978.

Awards

Boys' Club of America Award for *Jack Holborn,* 1966; Guardian Award for *Devil-in-the-Fog,* 1967; *Boston Globe* book award for *Smith,* 1987; Carnegie Medal for *The God Beneath the Sea,* 1970, and *Boston Globe* citation for *Footsteps,* 1981.

Works About Leon Garfield

Bryfonski, Dedria, ed. *Contemporary Literary Criticism.* Detroit: Gale Research, 1980, vol. 12, pp. 215–242.

Collins, Laurie, ed. *Authors and Artists for Young Adults.* Detroit: Gale Research, 1992, vol. 8, pp. 51–59.

Eyre, Frank. *British Children's Books in the Twentieth Century.* New York: Dutton, 1973, esp. pp. 98–105.

Gallo, Donald R., ed. *Speaking for Ourselves, Too.* Urbana: National Council of Teachers of English, 1993, pp. 73–76.

Holland, Philip. "Shades of the Prison House: The Fiction of Leon Garfield." In *Children's Literature in Education,* Winter 1978, pp. 159–172.

Jones, Rhodri. "Writers for Children: Leon Garfield." In *The Use of English,* Summer 1972, pp. 293–299.

Natov, Roni. "Not the Blackest of Villains . . . Not the Brightest of Saints: Humanism in Leon Garfield's Adventure Novels." In *The Lion and the Unicorn,* Fall 1978, pp. 44–71.

———. *Leon Garfield.* New York: Twayne, 1994.

Rees, David. *What Do Draculas Do: Essays on Contemporary Writers of Fiction for Children and Young Adults.* Metuchen, N.J.: Scarecrow, 1990, pp. 126–143.

Senick, Gerard J., ed. *Children's Literature Review.* Detroit: Gale Research, 1990, vol. 21, pp. 82–122.

Storr, Catherine. "Things That Go Bump in the Night." In *Suitable for Children: Controversies in Children's Literature.* Edited by Nicholas Tucker. Berkeley, Calif.: University of California Press, 1976, pp. 143–152.

Sucher, Mary Wadsworth. "Recommended: Leon Garfield." *English Journal,* September 1983, pp. 73–74.

Townsend, John Rowe. *A Sounding of Storytellers: New and Revised Essays on Contemporary Writers for Children.* New York: Lippincott, 1979, pp. 66–79.

Wintle, Justin, and Emma Fisher. "Interview by Justin Wintle." In *The Pied Pipers: Interviews with the Influential Creators of Children's Literature.* New York: Paddington, 1974, pp. 192–207.

Jean Craighead George

(1919-   )

by Lorraine Mary Leidholdt

From the barren North Slope of Alaska, where winds scream, where no roads exist, and where temperatures dip well below zero, to the island of Bimini in the warm waters of the Atlantic Ocean, where colorful fish swim, Jean Craighead George leads her readers through adventures with young people and animals. George, a naturalist, shows her concern about the destruction of wildlife and her knowledge of specific ecosystems in all her works. As she says about herself, "All I wish to do is tell the story of our North American animals and plants, hoping my readers will come to love them as I do in all their magnificence."

Indeed, this is what happens when readers find George's books. For those who already feel a kinship to animals, her works will reinforce their love and awe of them. For those who perhaps have never thought of a dog, a crow, or a weasel as a relative, George's works may awaken these feelings.

George was born on 2 July 1919 into a family of naturalists who taught her "the mysteries of sky and waterways,

Quotations from Jean Craighead George that are not attributed to a published source are from a telephone interview conducted by the author of this article on 20 February 1995 and are published here by permission of Jean Craighead George.

> *So that readers are given correct information about the people and places about which she writes, George always visits them.*

how to climb trees, fish, and camp." As a child—along with her father, who is an entomologist (scientist who studies insects) and botanist, and her twin brothers, who are falconers—George experienced wilderness living and grew to respect the earth and all it has to offer.

When George married and became a mother of three children, Twig, Craig and Luke, she traveled across America with them, looking for nature stories. Her travels took her into unique ecosystems, where her children helped find animal and insect characters for her works. Eventually, George's travels, observations, and creative mind helped her win the 1973 John Newbery Medal—the most prestigious award given to American writers of literature for children and youth—for *Julie of the Wolves* (1972).

She is probably best known for her wilderness survival stories. These include *Julie of the Wolves, My Side of the Mountain* (1959), a Newbery Honor book, its sequel *On the Far Side of the Mountain* (1990), and *The Talking Earth* (1983).

The Julie Novels

Before writing *Julie of the Wolves,* George first researched wolf behavior and then visited Barrow, Alaska, in 1970. So that readers are given correct information about the people and places about which she writes, George always visits them. In Barrow, she experienced the weather, observed the Eskimos, felt the push and pull of two cultures, and most important, learned about wolf communication firsthand. At the Naval Arctic Research Laboratory in Alaska, scientists were studying wolf communication, and from these scientists George learned to give the submissive grin, to grunt-whine to gain attention in a friendly way, and to say "hello" with an open-mouthed smile. She used this language to communicate with a beautiful female silver wolf in Alaska at that time.

In *Julie of the Wolves,* illustrated by John Schoenherr, readers find thirteen-year-old Julie Miyax Kapugen, an Eskimo, caught in a struggle between a traditional Eskimo way of life and a new way brought about by the influence of *gussacks,* or white-faced people. Julie loves her people's traditional values and way of life and cannot accept the thought of changing and adapting. At thirteen, following a disastrous marriage to a young Eskimo, Julie runs away. She becomes lost on the North Slope of Alaska. There, alone on the tundra, she relies on her intelligence and her knowledge of traditional Eskimo skills to survive the harsh Arctic winter.

While lost, Julie also uses her knowledge of wolf behavior to communicate with the wolves she encounters on the tundra. One day, surprised by the pack leader, or alpha male, whom she names Amaroq (the Eskimo word for "wolf"), Julie is caught off guard and struggles to find the right communication signals:

> **The hairs on her neck rose and her eyes widened. Amaroq's ears went forward aggressively and she remembered that wide eyes meant fear to him. It was not good to show him she was afraid. Animals attacked the fearful. She tried to narrow them, but that was not right either. Narrowed eyes were mean. (P. 24)**

Because the book is filled with factual, believable wolf lore and at the same time presents a riveting story, *Julie of the Wolves* has become a classic.

riveting interesting and exciting; holding one's attention

In 1994, twenty-two years after *Julie of the Wolves* was published, George wrote its sequel, *Julie*. This book, illustrated by Wendell Minor, begins exactly where the other one ended. Julie, at the end of *Julie of the Wolves,* had pointed her boots toward her father, Kapugen, and had decided to live with him even though he had changed.

Julie's decision to live with her father is difficult for her to make, for it means that she must leave her beloved wolf pack and live in the Kangik village with her father and his gussack (white) wife. *Julie,* however, is not a tense wilderness survival tale like the first "Julie" book. In this work, Julie struggles to adjust to a rapidly changing Eskimo way of life and to a white stepmother. At the same time, she strives to save her wolf pack from being hunted and shot. Julie also finds that a young Siberian Eskimo, Peter, is romantically interested in her. With these new issues, George again takes readers into the pristine wilderness of Alaska that is under assault by gussacks and their ways and machines.

The Sam Gribley Novels

From the unique ecosystem of the Alaskan tundra, we travel southward to the Catskill Mountains of New York, the setting for yet another excellent survival tale: *My Side of the Moun-*

tain, illustrated by George herself. In this story, Sam Gribley, like most teenagers, decides he needs to be on his own. Although he loves his family, he thinks they restrict his freedom and independence. Therefore, Sam runs away to the wilderness of the Catskill Mountains, where he plans to live alone with very little equipment:

> I left New York in May. I had a penknife, a ball of cord, an ax, and forty dollars, which I had saved from selling magazine subscriptions. I also had some flint and steel, which I had bought at a Chinese store in the city. The man in the store had showed me how to use it. He had also given me a little purse to put it in, and some tinder to catch the sparks. (P. 15)

Equipped with these few tools, knowledge gained from books, and a driving need to be on his own, Sam begins his year alone. As nature challenges Sam's courage, intelligence, and stamina, and as he experiences life on his own terms, Sam comes to accept and understand himself. This extraordinary adventure is filled with information on wilderness survival, which comes directly from George's own experiences. In her personal narrative in the *Horn Book,* she explains:

> *My Side of the Mountain* is a novel from my girlhood outdoors with my father and twin brothers. We made fish hooks from thorns and rope from vine fibers. We built shelters and hunted with falcons. We cooked wild plants in turtle shells and boiled water in leaves. I did and ate everything in that book. (P. 171)

My Side of the Mountain became a Newbery Honor book. The movie producer Robert B. Radnitz honored it in another way, making it into a Paramount Pictures film in 1969.

Thirty years after *My Side of the Mountain* was published, George wrote and illustrated its sequel, *On the Far Side of the Mountain.* In this work, Sam is on his own in the Catskills for the second year, with his tree home, his falcon, and his weasel. But now he is joined by his younger sister, Alice. As the story begins, a conservation officer confiscates Frightful, Sam's falcon, and takes him away from Sam. Sam despairs.

He not only loves Frightful but counts on the falcon to help him hunt for food for himself and Alice. Shortly after Frightful is taken, Alice disappears. Sam uses all his knowledge to track his sister through the wilderness while Alice uses her own survival knowledge to leave clues along the way.

The Talking Earth

George has also written about the Florida Everglades ecosystem, which provides the setting for another survival tale, *The Talking Earth* (1983). Billie Wind, a thirteen-year-old Seminole girl, doubts the truth and value of her Native American people's beliefs. Because of her doubts, the councilmen of her tribe think she should be punished. Billie, not taking them seriously, jokingly offers to go into the Everglades and "stay until I hear the animals talk, see the serpent and meet the little people who live underground" (p. 3). To Billie's surprise, the councilmen agree that this is what she should do and that she should stay one night and two days. Alone in a dugout canoe with a little food, a machete, a magnifying glass with which to start fires, a string hammock, a penknife, and a fishing hook, Billie sets off.

Billie's plan to be home the next day, however, changes abruptly when a fire sweeps through the Everglades. Forced to find a safe place to avoid the fire, she abandons her dugout and hides in a cave with other creatures seeking safety. When Billie finally leaves this refuge, she finds her dugout burned beyond repair. At this point, her real survival adventure begins. Throughout the next twelve weeks, Billie, facing daily hunger and a hurricane, learns that she, like all living things, is part of a delicately balanced ecosystem. George's descriptions of the sights, sounds, and smells of the Everglades allow readers to experience the setting as though they were in the dugout with Billie.

> **ecosystem** an ecological community and its environment, functioning as a unit

> *George's descriptions of the sights, sounds, and smells of the Everglades allow readers to experience the setting as though they were in the dugout (canoe) with Billie.*

Ecological Whodunits

Not only does George write survival tales, but she also writes ecological mysteries that include information about the relationship of animals and other organisms to their environment. Three such mysteries, *Who Really Killed Cock Robin?* (1991), *The Missing 'Gator of Gumbo Limbo* (1992), and *The*

Fire Bug Connection (1993), will appeal once again to young naturalists and ecologists.

Who Really Killed Cock Robin? features two teenagers, Tony Isidoro and Mary Alice Lamberty, who want to discover the cause of death of their town's mascot, a robin. Through this work, readers discover the harmful effects of pollutants while learning how nature's complicated food chain works.

Liza K., a homeless teen, and her mother are living in a hammock in the Florida Everglades when a twelve-foot alligator named Dajun disappears in *The Missing 'Gator of Gumbo Limbo*. A collection of interesting homeless people live on this rich piece of land and its surrounding Gumbo Limbo Hole, sharing it with alligators, turtles, ducks, and other living creatures. Dajun is being hunted by an official who is to shoot him because he has grown beyond the eight-foot limit, supposedly making him a danger to people. The woods people, as the homeless group is called, band together to try to find Dajun before the hunter does. Through the woods people's search, readers come to realize that alligators play an important part in their ecosystem and that without them, the delicate balance of nature is upset.

When asked how long it takes to complete the research for a book such as *The Missing 'Gator of Gumbo Limbo,* George states that this work covered about twenty years of research by her and her father, Frank Craighead, Sr., a scholar of the Everglades. The actual writing of the work took seven months.

The Fire Bug Connection (1993) is set in Maine at a "bug camp," as twelve-year-old Maggie Mercer calls the Biological Research Center. As a birthday gift, Maggie receives a batch of fire bugs that mysteriously die. Maggie and her mischievous friend Mitch work together to investigate the causes, which include global warming and the fire bug's natural predators.

Our Winged Friends

For young ornithologists (those who study birds), George has two very special books: *The Cry of the Crow* (1980) and *The Summer of the Falcon* (1962). In *The Cry of the Crow,* which George dedicates to all the pet crows she has had or known, we meet Mandy Tressel, who lives near the Florida

Everglades where her family raises strawberries. Mandy loves crows; her father and brothers hate them and shoot them because they threaten the family's strawberry crops and livelihood. Unbeknown to her father and brothers, Mandy befriends a motherless crow. She names it Nina Terrance and she tames, trains, and comes to love the creature. This book is filled with information about crows and their unique intelligence.

In *The Summer of the Falcon,* George uses the knowledge she gained from watching her twin brothers train falcons to create a story about thirteen-year-old June Pritchard and her sparrow hawk, Zander. For three summers, June trains Zander, helping him to develop the hunting instincts that he will need as an adult. As Zander grows and matures, so does June. In the end, June comes to understand the responsibility that growing into adulthood requires.

Adventures Under Water

George's works not only take readers into the realm of winged animals but also into the realm of those that live under water.

Water Sky (1987), set in Alaska, gives readers an intimate and contemporary look at bowhead whaling with the Inuit (Eskimo). This book is filled with fascinating information gained from George's visits with her son, Craig, a naturalist who studies whales in the Arctic. A young teen, Lincoln Noah Stonewall, the main character in this work, travels from Boston to Barrow to participate in a bowhead whaling expedition with the Eskimo. During this adventure, he learns how dependent the Eskimos are upon the whale.

> *George's works not only take readers into the realm of winged animals but also into the realm of those that live underwater.*

In *Shark Beneath the Reef* (1989), readers meet fourteen-year-old Tomas Torres, who lives on the island of Coronados in the Sea of Cortez (the Gulf of California, which separates Baja California from the rest of Mexico). Tomas daydreams about killing the shark that ruined his grandfather's fishing nets. This act, he thinks, will make him a hero to all the fishermen and prove that he is ready to accept adult responsibilities.

Tomas, like Julie in *Julie of the Wolves,* is also caught between the push and pull of two worlds. For years, Tomas and his family have relied on the plentiful supply of fish for a living; however, the fish supply has dwindled because

Mexican government officials have allowed Japanese factory fishing boats to over-fish in the Sea of Cortez. Tomas and his family, without fishing to sustain them, face a crisis: finding an entirely new way of life.

Talking with Animals

For readers who own cats or dogs, there are two special books that will help them communicate with their pets. *How to Talk to Your Dog* and *How to Talk to Your Cat,* written and illustrated by George in 1986, are full of information about animal behavior, the area that she believes is her main area of expertise as a naturalist. Readers of these books will find specifics about communicating with dogs and cats, but they also will find short stories about other animals that George has known and lived with.

Jean Craighead George, the Person

George lives in Chappaqua, New York, near New York City, with her dog, Qimmig (Inuit for "dog") and an African gray parrot. Each day, beginning after breakfast and continuing until around three o'clock in the afternoon, George writes. She has always loved words and writing. Since childhood, she has used writing as a way to share her knowledge and ideas. As a naturalist, she is most interested in animal behavior, as readers of her works soon learn.

George is hopeful about the future of our planet. She believes that humans are becoming more and more aware of the need to preserve and protect the earth and the beautiful animals and plants that live on it.

If you like the works of Jean Craighead George, you might also like the works of Scott O'Dell and Gary Paulsen.

Selected Bibliography

WORKS BY JEAN CRAIGHEAD GEORGE

Novels for Young Adults Illustrated by George
Vulpes, the Red Fox, with John L. George (1948)
Vision, the Mink, with John L. George (1949)
Masked Prowler: The Story of a Raccoon, with John L. George (1950)

Memph, the pet Skunk, with John L. George (1952)
Bubo, the Great Horned Owl, with John L. George (1954)
Dipper of Copper Creek, with John L. George (1956)
The Hole in the Tree (1957)
Snow Tracks (1958)
My Side of the Mountain (1959)
The Summer of the Falcon (1962)
Red Robin, Fly Up! (1963)
Gull Number 737 (1964)
Hold Zero! (1966)
Water Sky (1987)

Novels for Young Adults

Coyote in Manhattan, illustrated by John Kaufman (1968)
All upon a Stone, illustrated by Don Bolognese (1971)
Julie of the Wolves, illustrated by John Schoenherr (1972)
All Upon a Sidewalk, illustrated by Don Bolognese (1974)
Hook a Fish, Catch a Mountain (1975)
Going to the Sun (1976)
The Wentletrap, illustrated by Symeon Shimin (1978)
The Wounded Wolf, illustrated by John Schoenherr (1978)
River Rats, Inc. (1979)
The Cry of the Crow (1980)
The Grizzly Bear with the Golden Ears, illustrated by Tom Catania (1982)
The Talking Earth (1983)
Shark Beneath the Reef (1989)
On the Far Side of the Mountain (1990)
Dear Rebecca, Winter Is Here, pictures by Loretta Krupinski (1993)
The First Thanksgiving (1993)
Julie, illustrated by Wendell Minor (1994)
There's an Owl in the Shower (1995)
To Climb a Waterfall, illustrated by Thomas Locker *(1995)*

Children's Books

Who Really Killed Cock Robin? (1991)
The Missing 'Gator of Gumbo Limbo (1992)
The Fire Bug Connection (1993)

Nonfiction

Spring Comes to the Ocean (1965)

Beastly Inventions: A Surprising Investigation into How Smart Animals Really Are (1970)

Everglades Wildguide: The Natural History of the Everglades, with drawings by Better Fraser (1972)

New York in Maps, 1972/73, with Toy Lasker (1974)

New York in Flashmaps, 1974/75, with Toy Lasker (1976)

The American Walk Book: An Illustrated Guide to the Country's Major Historic and Natural Walking Trails from New England to the Pacific Coast (1978)

How to Talk to Your Cat (1986)

How to Talk to Your Dog (1986)

The Big Book for Our Planet, edited with Ann Durell and Katherine Paterson (1993)

Animals Who Have Won Our Hearts (1994)

Acorn Pancakes, Dandelion Salad, and 38 Other Wild Dishes (1995)

"Thirteen Moon" Young adult Series

The Moon of the Bears, illustrated by Ron Parker (1967)

The Moon of the Owls, illustrated by Wendell Minor (1967)

The Moon of the Salamanders, illustrated by Marlee Werner (1967)

The Moon of the Chickarees, illustrated by Don Rodell (1968)

The Moon of the Fox Pups, illustrated by Norman Adams (1968)

The Moon of the Monarch Butterflies, illustrated by Kam Mak (1968)

The Moon of the Mountain Lions, illustrated by Ron Parker (1968)

The Moon of the Wild Pigs, illustrated by Paul Mirocha (1968)

The Moon of the Alligators, illustrated by Michael Rothman (1969)

The Moon of the Deer, illustrated by Sal Catalano (1969)

The Moon of the Gray Wolves, illustrated by Sal Catalano (1969)

The Moon of the Moles, illustrated by Michael Rothman (1969)

The Moon of the Winter Bird, illustrated by Vincent Nasta (1969)

"One Day" Young adult Series

One Day in the Desert, illustrated by Fred Brenner (1983)

One Day in the Alpine Tundra, illustrated by Walter Gaffney-Kessell (1984)

One Day in the Prairie, illustrated by Bob Marstall (1986)

One Day in the Woods, illustrated by Gary Allen (1988)

One Day in the Tropical Rain Forest, illustrated by Gary Allen (1990)

Autobiography

Journey Inward (1982)

Articles

"Taking Care of Our Planet Through Books." *Horn Book,* March/April 1994, pp. 170–176.

George has been a contributor to *Audubon, Reader's Digest, National Wildlife,* and *International Wildlife.*

Adaptations

My Side of the Mountain. Film, 1969.

Julie of the Wolves. Audio recording, 1977.

One Day in the Woods. Musical video, 1989.

Julie of the Wolves, The Talking Earth, and *One Day in the Desert* have been translated into Spanish.

How to write to the Author

Jean Craighead George
c/o HarperCollins Publishers
10 East 53rd Street
New York, NY 10022

(1934-   )

by Lynne Alvine

I n her novels for young readers, Bette Greene presents characters who deal with child abuse and with discrimination against homosexuals and Jews. When asked why she takes on such "risky subjects," Greene is quick to respond:

> I am offended by injustice in any form. Young people need for adults to say, "Injustice is wrong. It is wrong to bother people, to hurt people who are minding their own business—just because they may be different from us." We adults must understand that the young people are going to be our leaders. We must encourage them to develop moral courage.

Throughout her novels, Greene's characters face challenges that demand moral courage. Patty Bergen in *Summer of My German Soldier* (1973) is burdened with an abusive father, a

> *"My roots, my memories are all of Arkansas."*

rejecting mother, and a hostile community. In *The Drowning of Stephan Jones* (1990), a gay young man is brutalized by a popular high school boy and his friends, while the popular boy's girlfriend Carla struggles to decide whether she will stand up against their unjust actions. Pressures on Beth Lambert to conform to the behavior of her peers in *Philip Hall Likes Me. I Reckon Maybe* (1974) and *Get on Out of Here, Philip Hall* (1981) are very subtle, but they are no less real.

The Author's Early Life and Memories of Arkansas

Although she has lived much of her adult life in Brookline, Massachusetts, Bette Greene was born in Memphis, Tennessee, and grew up in Parkin, Arkansas. Her books draw heavily on her early life experiences. Her readers would not be surprised to hear her say, "My roots, my memories are all of Arkansas" (Holtze, *Fifth Book of Junior Authors and Illustrators,* p. 136).

Greene broke into print as a high school student when she sold a news story to the *Memphis Commercial Appeal.* After working as a stringer, gathering news stories for the Memphis newspaper (1950–1952), she wrote for the Memphis bureau of United Press International (1953–1954) and served with the Memphis chapter of the American Red Cross (1958–1959). She also worked as public information officer for the Boston State Psychiatric Hospital (1959–1961).

stringer part-time reporter

Greene's college study included courses she took at the University of Alabama (1952) and Memphis State (1953–1954). She also studied at Columbia University (1955–1956) and at Harvard (1965). In 1959, she married Donald Sumner Greene, a Boston doctor with whom she has raised two children, Carla and Jordan Joshua.

It was, however, those early years of her childhood in rural Arkansas during World War II that gave Greene the memories of people, places, and events that later found their way into her novels. While at Columbia, she developed the ambition to "write a book so real, so intensely emotional that every single reader would be compelled to see what I saw and feel what I felt" (Gallo, *Speaking for Ourselves,* pp. 80–81). She realized that goal in 1973. With the publication of *Summer of My German Soldier,* Greene knew that she had become what she had always wanted to be—a writer.

The Author in the Schools

Bette Greene has spoken to many groups of students who have read one or more of her books prior to her visit. She begins her presentation by talking about her books and their characters. Then students are encouraged to ask questions. They nearly always want to know how she began her career. Greene credits one teacher who believed in her, who helped her believe that she could be anything she set out to be.

She also tells about a teacher who did not believe in her but who still played a part in motivating her to be successful. After winning first prize in a school writing contest, Greene was stripped of the honor by a teacher who thought she had copied her story from a magazine. The first prize—a very fancy fountain pen—was taken away from her. She had not plagiarized the story. It had been entirely her own work. A few months later, when she sold her first news story to the *Memphis Commercial Appeal,* she used her earnings to buy herself a fountain pen similar to the one that had been taken from her.

plagiarize to steal the ideas or words of someone else and pretend they are one's own

Readers of all ages have responded positively to Greene's novels. After speaking to a group of ninth graders, one of the teachers commented during the question and answer session:

> I don't want to ask a question, but I do want to thank you. I never had read *The Summer of My German Soldier* before, but did so when I learned you would be speaking here at our school. I cried throughout the reading because it touched me so deeply. When I was a girl, I had a friend who was abused by her father as Patty Bergen was. Last night I called that friend and told her about the book. I've mailed her my copy. Thank you for the book that stimulated me to get back in touch with my high school friend. After all of these years, I now understand what she was going through with her abusive father and how that affected our friendship.

According to an interview with me in *ALAN Review,* a reader of *The Drowning of Stephan Jones* told Greene, "Your book gave me a whole new way of looking at gay people. Thank you for stretching the mind and heart of a sixty-four-year-old

> *The emotional connection that people have with Greene's characters may indeed be what has caused her books to be popular with such a wide range of readers.*

country woman" (p. 8). The emotional connection that people have with Greene's characters may indeed be what has caused her books to be popular with such a wide range of readers.

Summer of My German Soldier

In Greene's first novel, *Summer of My German Soldier,* Patty Bergen, a twelve-year-old Jewish girl, befriends twenty-two-year-old Anton, a German soldier who is being held as a prisoner of war in a small town in Arkansas during World War II. Patty seeks from Anton the affection she does not receive from her domineering mother and cruel father. When it is learned that Patty has helped the Nazi prisoner escape, she is scorned by the Protestant townspeople and further rejected by her Jewish parents. Anton is pursued and killed as he attempts to return to Germany, and Patty is sent to reform school for her "treasonous" crime.

This intensely emotional book has captured the attention of readers and critics alike. In more than twenty years, it has not once gone out of print. In 1973, *Summer of My German Soldier* received the Golden Kite Award of the Society of Children's Book Writers and was on the *New York Times* List of Outstanding Books. In 1974, it was named a Notable Book by the American Library Association and was nominated for the National Book Award.

Although most readers would agree that *Summer of My German Soldier* is "unforgettable because of the genuine emotion it evokes," as it was appraised by Mary Burns in the February 1974 *Horn Book,* reviewers are divided in their opinions on the quality of Greene's writing. A common concern is the credibility and depth of the characters. In a 1973 *New York Times Book Review,* critic Peter Sourian suggested that "her characters could easily have come out of an ordinary movie melodrama. Along with the loving black maid, there's a nasty minister's wife, a hard-boiled girl reporter, a bigoted businessman, a town gossip, and a chicken-soup grandma." In a 1975 issue of *Junior Bookshelf,* the reviewer was disappointed with the characterization of Patty, noting that she "has many enemies, and suffers much abuse, but unfortunately she fails to become a sympathetic character." A reviewer in a 1973 issue of *Kirkus Reviews* praised the portrayal of Ruth but criticized the credibility of Anton, the German soldier, saying that Ruth is "so much truer and more important than the thin, escapist fantasies she spins around thin, escapist Anton."

If Ruth, the African American family servant, is the most real character, perhaps it is because Greene lifted her "whole cloth" from her own Arkansas childhood. She describes her family's housekeeper as "not a subservient person" but a person who "protected her dignity at a time when it was not popular or even safe to do so" (Alvine, *ALAN Review,* p. 6).Characterization may be problematic to some critics, but Greene has been highly praised for the overall effect of *Summer of My German Soldier.* It has been called "more than a mirror of reality" because it "offers no panaceas for loneliness, no easy solutions for problems" (Burns, 1974). Finally, reviewer C. S. Hannabuss wrote in *Children's Book Review* that, "The issues raised, and the characters who raise them, are proof of the book's integrity."

> **characterization** method by which a writer creates and develops the appearance and personality of a character

Summer of My German Soldier has been banned in some school communities as anti-Semitic because of its portrayal of Patty's Jewish father as a child abuser. When I asked Greene about this issue in March 1993, she dismissed the charge as incomprehensible. "How could I, a Jew, write an anti-Semitic novel?" she said. "Patty Bergen's father doesn't represent all Jews just because he is the only Jewish man in town. He is an evil man, but he is certainly not a prototype of all Jewish people."

Greene is also author of the screenplay of *Summer of My German Soldier,* which was produced as a television movie. Many books have received a mixed reception from reviewers, but few of them stay in print continuously for more than twenty years, as this book has done.

Morning Is a Long Time Coming

Morning Is a Long Time Coming, the sequel to *Summer of My German Soldier,* was first published in 1978. In this book, Patty goes to Europe to search for her lost Anton's family. Her love affair with Roger, a young teacher in Paris, is interrupted by her need to find a connection with the love she has lost. She finds Anton's mother in Germany, but more important, she finds herself and a renewed capacity to love and to forgive.

Although the sequel did not receive the recognition bestowed upon *Summer of My German Soldier,* it had a similar mixed response from reviewers, again centering on Patty's character. In the April 1978 *New York Times Book Review,* Peter Sourian wrote, "Bette Greene excels at depicting the process by which Patty arrives at each moral insight along the way of her literal and figurative journey, first to Paris and then to Germany." Later that year, in the *Times Educational Supplement,* Geoffrey Fox assessed Greene's accomplishment with the main character in this way: "Since Patty is the narrator, the journey is charted with wit and energy. . . . She is characterized with subtlety and even tenderness."

In the April 1978 issue of *School Library Journal,* Jack Forman noted that "Greene's portrayal of a southern Jewish family in the 1940s is strong and honest, but the depiction of Patty's relationship with Roger is strangely forced and detached. Despite this central flaw, however, the novel will attract teens because of its sensitive treatment of the loosening of familial bonds." Again, it is often Greene's subject matter that evokes such powerful emotional responses from readers. *Morning Is a Long Time Coming* was made into a full-length television movie in 1978. It was reprinted by Bantam Books, along with a twentieth-anniversary edition of *Summer of My German Soldier,* in 1993.

literal factual or exact

figurative symbolic

The Philip Hall Books

In contrast to the Patty Bergen books with their serious, often disturbing issues, Greene's two novels for younger readers are light and airy. The two titles reveal much of the content: *Philip Hall Likes Me. I Reckon Maybe* and *Get on Out of Here, Philip Hall* (1981). The focus of these two books is on Beth Lambert, a young black girl who has a crush on her classmate Philip Hall and who is confused by his mixed response to her. Philip is Beth's friend when they are alone and her nemesis when they are around his peers.

Criticism of the Philip Hall books is also divided but generally positive. Of *Philip Hall Likes Me. I Reckon Maybe,* Betsy Byars wrote, "There is a nice sort of timeliness about the book too, perhaps because the author has caught something unchanging in young people, and I think the book will retain its warm appeal for a long while." Critics frequently disagree about how effectively a white author handles the language of black characters. Zena Sutherland, in writing about *Philip Hall Likes Me. I Reckon Maybe,* credits Greene: "The writing style is deceptively casual, characterization and dialogue are sound, and the protagonist . . . [is] a resourceful, lively girl whose charm and vitality come through clearly."

In 1974, *Philip Hall Likes Me. I Reckon Maybe* was recognized as a *New York Times* Outstanding Book, a *New York Times* Outstanding Title, and an American Library Association Notable Book. It was also selected for the Kirkus Choice Award. In 1975, it was a Newbery Honor Book and a Junior Literary Guild selection.

Them That Glitter and Them That Don't

Bette Greene's next novel, *Them That Glitter and Them That Don't* (1981), is the story of another young girl whose family lacks the capacity to appreciate her good qualities. It has been less widely read than the Patty Bergen and Philip Hall books. Its central character, Carol Ann Delaney, draws on her Gypsy heritage to summon the courage to leave home and go to Nashville to become a singing star. Reviewers tended to be positive. Susan F. Marcus said that Carol Ann "will keep her readers turning the page (pulling for her) as she honestly faces, and overcomes, her painful situation."

The Drowning of Stephan Jones

Bette Greene returned once again to a small town in Arkansas for the setting of her 1991 book, *The Drowning of Stephan Jones,* which is perhaps her most controversial novel for young adults. When a high school senior, Andy Harris, learns that the two young men who have begun attending his church are gay, he begins a homophobic campaign against them. Though she knows that he is wrong, his girlfriend Carla remains unable to stand up to Andy until it is too late. In a tragic prom night incident, Andy and his friends throw Stephan into the river, unaware that he cannot swim.

homophobic hostile toward gay, lesbian, or bisexual people

The Drowning of Stephan Jones is a fictionalized account of a true incident. In her 1994 interview with me in *ALAN Review,* Greene told of her additional research for the novel. She interviewed hundreds of people—including gays who had been the victims of hate crimes, their brutalizers, and the ministers the brutalizers pointed her toward. She is outspoken about the damage created by fundamentalist Christian views toward homosexuality and the ways in which many ministers encourage hatred among their members. "They send people out to kill the sin, but they don't know where the sin is—so they kill the sinner," Greene says (p. 7).

Reviewers tend to agree that the characters in this novel lack credibility. By portraying the gay characters stereotypically, Greene fails to challenge some of her readers' beliefs about gays. She does draw with sensitivity her gay characters' close friendships and genuine love for each other, however. Thus the reader is offered a positive perspective on a gay relationship, a view that is generally unavailable to some young readers. However, *The Drowning of Stephan Jones* has been banned in some school communities for having subject matter that officials regard as too mature for their students. In several communities, Greene has been invited to speak to students and then cautioned after she arrived that she should talk about her other books but not about *The Drowning of Stephan Jones*.

stereotype a character that is not original or individual because it conforms to a preconceived category

Greene's stories challenge her young readers to examine their own capacity for moral courage as it is needed in their lives.

If you like the works of Bette Greene, you might also enjoy *I Know Why the Caged Bird Sings* by Maya Angelou, *Permanent Connections* by Sue Ellen Bridgers, *Staying Fat for Sarah Byrnes* by Chris Crutcher, *Roll of Thunder, Hear My Cry* by Mildred Delois Taylor, and *Dicey's Song* by Cynthia Voigt.

The Capacity for Moral Courage

Bette Greene's novels offer emotional connections to one or more characters facing difficult situations that call forth their moral courage. Her stories also challenge her young readers to examine their own capacity for moral courage as it is needed in their lives. Despite the critics' questions about the depth of her characterization, her books remain extremely popular with a wide range of readers.

Selected Bibliography

WORKS BY BETTE GREENE

Summer of My German Soldier (1973, 1988)
Philip Hall Likes Me. I Reckon Maybe (1974, 1983)
Morning Is a Long Time Coming (1978, 1988)
Get On Out of Here, Philip Hall (1981, 1984)
A Writer's Survivor Kit (1981)
Them That Glitter and Them That Don't (1981)
The Drowning of Stephan Jones (1990)

WORKS ABOUT BETTE GREENE

Biography and General Criticism

Alvine, Lynne. "Understanding Adolescent Homophobia: An Interview with Bette Greene." In *ALAN Review,* Winter 1994, pp. 5–9.

Campbell, Patty. "The Sand in the Oyster." In *Horn Book,* September/October 1993, pp. 568–572.

Commire, Anne, ed. *Something About the Author.* Detroit: Gale Research, 1976, vol. 8, p. 73.

Evory, Ann, ed. *Contemporary Authors, New Revision Series.* Detroit: Gale Research, 1981, vol. 4, pp. 80–81.

Gallo, Donald, ed. *Speaking for Ourselves: Autobiographical Sketches by Notable Authors of Books for Young Adults.* Urbana, Ill.: National Council of Teachers of English, 1990.

Holtze, Sally Holmes, ed. *Fifth Book of Junior Authors and Illustrators.* New York: Wilson, 1983.

Immel, Myra, ed. *The Young Adult Reader's Advisor: The Best in Literature and Language Arts, Mathematics, and Computer Science.* New Providence, N. J.: R. R. Bowker, 1992, vol. 1.

Kirkpatrick, D. L., ed. *Twentieth-Century Children's Writers.* 2d ed. New York: St. Martin's, 1983.

Osa, Osayimwense. "Adolescent Girls' Need for Love in Two Cultures—Nigeria and the United States." In *English Journal,* vol. 78, no. 8, 1983, pp. 35–37.

Riley, Carolyn, ed. *Children's Literature Review.* Detroit: Gale Research, 1976, vol. 2, pp. 85–86.

Solin, Sabrina. "Do Not Read This." In *Seventeen,* September 1994, p. 98.

Stine, Jean C., and Daniel G. Marowski, eds. *Contemporary Literary Criticism.* Detroit: Gale Research, 1984, vol. 30, pp. 169–171.

Short Reviews

Burns, Mary M. Review of *Summer of My German Soldier.* In *Horn Book,* February 1974, p. 56.

———. Review of *Them That Glitter and Them That Don't.* In *Horn Book,* August 1983, p. 453.

Byars, Betsy. *New York Times Book Review,* 8 December 1974, p. 8.

Forman, Jack. Review of *Morning Is a Long Time Coming.* In *School Library Journal,* April 1978, p. 93.

Fox, Geoffrey. "Parents and Lovers." In *Times Educational Supplement,* 24 November 1978, p. 48.

Hannabuss, C. S. *Children's Book Review,* spring 1975, p. 19.

Heins, Ethel L. *Horn Book,* April 1975, p. 149.

Junior Bookshelf, February 1975, p. 62.

Kirkus Reviews, 15 October 1973, p. 1170.

Laski, Audrey. "Partridge in a Pear Tree." In *Times Educational Supplement,* 9 December 1977, p. 21.

Marcus, Susan F. *School Library Journal,* 8 April 1983, pp. 122–123.

Sourian, Peter. *New York Times Book Review,* 4 November 1973, p. 29.

————. "The Nazi Legacy: Undoing History in *Morning Is a Long Time Coming.*" In *New York Times Book Review,* 30 April 1978, p. 30.

Sutherland, Zena. *Bulletin of the Center for Children's Books,* April 1975, p. 130.

Wilson, Kevin. *Best Sellers,* December 1978, p. 291.

Zvirin, Stephanie. "Drowned by Good Intentions." *Booklist,* 1 February 1992, p. 1018.

How to write to the Author
Bette Greene
338 Clinton Road
Brookline, MA 02146

Lynn Hall

(1937-   )

by Susan Stan

"A happy childhood is not always the best preparation for a productive adulthood," Lynn Hall says. Although an observer might consider Hall's childhood as a model one, Hall would not agree. True, she grew up in a stable family environment in a solidly middle-class home, but she always felt like the proverbial square peg in a round hole. She never felt that she fit in with the rest of her family or with any of the groups at school. Like many children, she even harbored the idea—for a while, at least—that she was adopted.

proverbial well-known or expressed in a popular saying

Growing Up

Hall was the middle of three children, all girls. Her older and younger sisters had no difficulties making friends or becoming part of the popular group at school. Lynn was more inclined to spend her time alone, reading horse and dog stories

Quotations from Lynn Hall that are not attributed to a published source are from a personal interview conducted by the author of this article on 28 July 1992 and are published here by permission of Lynn Hall.

69

> *"I did not give a hoot about children in faraway lands unless they had horses."*

that she got from the library and yearning for animals of her own. She read the same books over and over—stories by Marguerite Henry, Betty Cavanna, and others—and remembers one librarian who chided her for not checking out some of the many other books available, books that might broaden her mind and teach her about how children lived in other times and places.

"I did not give a hoot about children in faraway lands," Hall writes in *Something About the Author Autobiography Series,* "unless they had horses." Similarly, she had no interest in the romance stories or teen magazines filled with fashion and makeup tips that other girls her age were reading. The few friends she did have were friends almost by default—a small group of girls who went places together for lack of anyone else to go with. Although her classmates and even the adults around her might have seen Lynn as ordinary, she saw herself as someone who "had things to prove to people."

Born on 9 November 1937 in Lombard, Illinois, Hall grew up during the 1940s and early 1950s. By the standards of that time, her family could not have been more conventional. As with many families during that generation, her mother stayed home and kept house while her father worked to support the family. Although her father may not have been perfect—he was restrained and did not express his emotions—there was neither substance abuse nor violence in her family. When Hall was nine, the family moved back to Iowa, where her father and mother had been raised. They settled in West Des Moines, a suburb not much different, at least in Hall's eyes, from Lombard. She would much have preferred to live in a smaller town or in the country, where she might have a chance to realize her ongoing fantasy of owning her own horse.

For a brief period, when Hall's family moved to the smaller town of Webster City, Iowa, this dream came true, and she became the proud owner of Lady Day. Sadly, her family moved back to the Des Moines area shortly thereafter, and she had to give up her horse. The ensuing years in high school were torture for her. She did what little schoolwork she needed to earn average grades, but her heart was not in it. She began to live for the day she would graduate from high school and be on her own. Neither her parents nor her teachers could persuade Hall to attend college; she told herself that someday, if she found the right reasons, she would get a college degree. The day after her high school graduation, Hall left for Denver and a life of her own.

Leaving Home

The desire for independence is a strong theme throughout Hall's books. Like her, her characters Roxanne Armstrong in *The Leaving* (1980), Jane Cahill in *The Solitary* (1986), and Ariel Brecht in *Flyaway* (1987) all make plans to leave home as soon as they graduate from high school. In writing these books, Hall draws heavily on the feelings she had during adolescence, but her fictional characters' family circumstances are not the same as her own.

In *The Leaving,* Roxanne is the only child of parents who married for the wrong reasons and who are now bound in a situation they cannot seem to escape. Their isolation from one another has extended to Roxanne; the three of them may live under the same roof, but their lives rarely intersect. By rotating the point of view from chapter to chapter, Hall allows readers to see what has brought each of these characters to their unhappy situation.

point of view the position or perspective from which the story is told

Jane Cahill's situation in *The Solitary* is even more extreme. Her mother is in prison for having killed Jane's abusive father, and Jane is living in a prison of another sort: her uncle's house. He demeans her constantly and never lets her forget how his brother died. Jane's goal is to graduate early and move into the abandoned backwoods cabin that was her family's home, and she spends her high school years saving every penny from part-time jobs and studying library books to learn the survival skills she will need in her new environment. When at last she does carve out a new life for herself, she encounters something else that is unfamiliar: self-respect.

The Brecht family in *Flyaway* seems downright perfect by comparison. But appearances can be deceiving, and Ariel's father, Frank Brecht, cares for appearances above everything. He buys his daughters and his wife nice clothes, not to make them happy but to show the community that Frank Brecht is a good provider. He chauffeurs Ariel to her friend's house, not to save her the walk but to control her comings and goings.

For Ariel, there is only one way out. Because the women of the family are not allowed to have their own money, she must sell her precious skis to pay her way. Only after Ariel's escape route is in place does her father realize that he has lost control of her. What Ariel has in common with Roxanne and Jane—and the person who created them—is the desire to have charge of her own life.

Becoming a Writer

Hall's move to Denver was the first in a series of moves that took her throughout the West and Midwest in an effort to find the kind of life and work that would make her happy. Marriage was not the answer, as she learned after a short-lived attempt at the age of twenty-two. She tried out several kinds of jobs, but nothing seemed like the right fit. Office work was confining, and too often she ended up doing her boss's work on a secretary's salary. She knew she wanted to be around animals, but a stint working at a pet hospital taught her that she did not want to be a veterinarian. She had tried her hand at painting portraits of people's pets, but this occupation did not provide enough income for her to live on. She also took a job in a show kennel but found it lacking in mental stimulation.

Hall was still searching when she passed a bookstore one day and noticed a new book displayed in the window. Intrigued, she went in and picked up the book, a horse story written by a local author. As she paged through the book, she realized that the author was neither a good writer nor an expert on horses. And then it hit her—she could write the kind of books she had loved reading as a child. From that moment on, Hall knew what she wanted to do and also what she had to do to achieve that goal. Undaunted by the prospect of hard work, she kept her day job and began working toward her goal at night and on weekends. She reread all the old books from her childhood and used them as models for her own writing.

When she finished her first manuscript, she gave it to Henry Gregor Felsen, a local writer, to critique. Too old-fashioned, he pronounced. Hall went back to her typewriter and started all over again. This time, when she finished, she submitted her manuscript to a publisher, who rejected it. She sent it off to another publisher and meanwhile went to work on a second book. This process continued until the glorious

> *She reread all the old books from her childhood and used them as models for her own writing.*

day when Hall received an acceptance letter. By the time she became a published author, she had several more books ready for publication.

Most of Hall's early books were for younger readers, and almost all can be classified as dog or horse stories. The quartet that began with *A Horse Called Dragon* in 1971 and ended with *Dragon's Delight* in 1980 recounts the life of a mustang from the time it is captured in the Mexican mountains to its final days on a Michigan stud farm. Some of her books for elementary school-age children are mysteries, some are standard dog and horse stories, and others tell stories of exceptional animals.

In all, Hall has written almost ninety books, twenty-four of which are for young adults. Although animals make an appearance in many of these books, they no longer dominate her work in the way they did at the beginning of her career. Over the years, Hall has grown in her ability to create believable human characters who stand on their own, not simply in relation to dogs, horses, or other animals. A few young adult books focus on other issues entirely, with nary an animal in sight. *If Winter Comes* (1986), for example, presents a fictionalized scenario in which the United States is under threat of nuclear attack. The event provides the impetus for the two main characters, boyfriend and girlfriend, to sort out their feelings about one another and their relationships with the members of their families.

Exploring Relationships

Family relationships (and not just the unsatisfying sort that we find in *Flyaway, The Solitary,* and *The Leaving*) are the focus of several of Hall's books. *Letting Go* (1987) is the study of a mother-daughter relationship within the framework of a happy family. The tension here comes in the form of Mrs. Crouse's overwhelming love for her youngest child, her daughter Casey. Unintentionally, her love has become needy and smothering. Mrs. Crouse is a marked contrast to Jennifer Dean's mother in *Fair Maiden* (1990), who, twice divorced, has thrown herself into the dating scene, making it difficult at times to tell who is mothering whom.

The Dean family's troubles stem from a further problem: the erratic and troubled behavior of Jennifer's brother. In this book, readers see the power that one sibling can exert on a whole family. Similarly, in *The Soul of the Silver Dog* (1992), Cory has a chronically ill sister who has become the family focus; when she eventually dies, Cory's parents are unable to cope with their loss together. They subsequently divorce, leaving Cory more isolated than ever. Although the plot lines and characters of these two books do not resemble Hall's life and family in the least, her childhood feelings of being overlooked certainly emerge in the characters' feelings.

plot deliberate sequence of events in a literary work

Some of the characters in Hall's books look to love and romance as a way of escaping from unpleasant family situations; in others, romance is cast as a natural part of adolescence. In *Flyaway,* for instance, Ariel Brecht has to consult with her father before being able to date Jens. She hopes for a chance to be like other teenage girls and maybe she is. Unfortunately, the young man turns out to be much like her father in his desire to control her.

The Giver, published in 1985, (not to be confused with Lois Lowry's 1993 book of the same name) portrays awakening feelings of romance in fifteen-year-old Mary McNeal, feelings that are directed at her homeroom teacher, a bachelor about forty years old. Hall uses the same technique she used in *The Leaving* to tell the story from both Mary's perspective and Mr. Flicket's. Through Mary's eyes, we see a caring teacher who always has a ready compliment for her, and we also understand her lack of confidence in her own attractiveness, which is rooted in the uncomfortable knowledge that her father is cheating on her mother. If her mother, a vivacious and caring woman, could not keep her husband's love, Mary reasons, "then what hope was there for *her* to be loved?" The reader would naturally assume that Mary is fantasizing, were it not for the chapters told from Mr. Flicket's point of view. There we see that he is deliberately favoring Mary and knows the effect it has on her. This dual perspective sets up the suspense. Which way will the story go?

The situation of a teenage girl becoming involved with an older man occurs several times in Hall's books. In *Denison's Daughter* (1983), teenager Sandy Denison's need for male attention leads her to entertain the overtures of an older married man; in *Fair Maiden,* Jennifer Dean has an affair with an older musician whom she meets at the Renaissance Fair. This plot line is perhaps most successfully carried out in *Flying Changes* (1991), which the critic Hazel

Rochman, in her 15 March 1985 review for *Booklist,* described as "Hall at her best."

Flying Changes opens shortly after Denny Browner has spent the night with her father's rodeo partner, who is staying at their house. (Her father is away, but one senses that his presence might not have made much difference.) From the first page to the last, the story is one of adjusting to changes—Denny's changed status from virgin to nonvirgin, her father's return in a wheelchair as a result of a rodeo accident, the reappearance of her mother, and her grandmother's subsequent move out of Denny's house into an apartment. Throughout the book, Denny spends her time training a horse to make the flying lead change—getting it to change direction without breaking its lope. The book's title describes this effort and also becomes a metaphor for Denny's growing ability to handle the many changes in her life.

lope steady and easy movement, especially with springing, energetic steps

By far, the majority of Hall's leading characters are female, but she has also created some interesting male characters. The most prominent is Tom Naylor in *Sticks and Stones* (1972), one of the first books for young adults to confront the subject of homosexuality. As Judy Blume remarks in the 28 May 1972 *New York Times Book Review,* this book is less about homosexuality than about "injustice through the power of gossip." Newcomers in their small Iowa town, Tom and his mother are not privy to town gossip and therefore have not heard that Ward Alexander is gay. When Tom and Ward become friends, Tom finds himself shunned by the townspeople with no idea that the rumors have stretched to include him. When he finally does find out, he turns inward, questioning himself. Could he be gay and not know it? Is there something about the way he looks or acts? He gains a new perspective on the situation when a car accident occurs, injuring him and killing another person. Given a new chance at life, Tom decides to live it not on his neighbors' terms but on his own. Just what those terms will be Hall leaves readers to determine for themselves.

No one should think that Hall knows only how to tackle tough subjects and deal with dysfunctional families in her writing; she is also an entertaining writer. Her wry sense of humor, apparent in scenes throughout her work, is given free rein in *Murder in a Pig's Eye* (1990), one of several mysteries she has written. The whole premise of *Pig's Eye,* painted with broad strokes and almost slapstick in places, turns on a joke—but the joke is on the main character. Other mysteries are equally fun, packed with adventure and action and set against backdrops of horse racing and dog shows.

The Author's Life

Were it not for the entertaining stories she read as a child, Hall herself might never have been a writer. For her, writing has become a means of living the kind of life she dreamed about as a child. Solitary by nature, today she lives in a home in the Iowa countryside, surrounded by rolling hills and bordering on woods. Far from lonely, her one-time fantasy of raising and breeding dogs has become a reality, and she has any number of Bedlington terriers to keep her company. For a while, a horse named Tazo was also part of the picture.

Hall's time is consumed by her many interests. She travels to dog shows, works with 4H Club members and their dogs on an agility course set up near her house, answers letters from readers, is invited to speak to groups of adults and young people, and occasionally writes, although not as much as she used to. As Hall is the first to point out, she is living proof that hard work can make dreams come true.

A **4-H Club** is a recreational association for young adults devoted to the cultivation of the "four Hs"— head, hand, heart, and health.

If you like stories by Lynn Hall, you might also like the works of Gary Paulsen.

Selected Bibliography

WORKS BY LYNN HALL

Novels for Young Adults

Too Near the Sun (1970)

The Siege of Silent Henry (1972)

Sticks and Stones (1972)

Flowers of Anger (1976)

The Leaving (1980)

Half the Battle (1982)

Tin Can Tucker (1982)

Denison's Daughter (1983)

Uphill All the Way (1984)

The Giver (1985)

Just One Friend (1985)

If Winter Comes (1986)

The Solitary (1986)

Flyaway (1987)

Letting Go (1987)

Ride a Dark Horse (1987)

A Killing Freeze (1988)

Murder at the Spaniel Show (1988)

Where Have All the Tigers Gone? (1989)

Fair Maiden (1990)

Halsey's Pride (1990)

Murder in a Pig's Eye (1990)

Flying Changes (1991)

The Soul of the Silver Dog (1992)

Windsong (1992)

Original Manuscripts

Some of Lynn Hall's works are included in the Kerlan Collection at the University of Minnesota, Minneapolis.

WORKS ABOUT LYNN HALL

Blume, Judy. Review of *Sticks and Stones. New York Times Book Review,* 28 May 1972, p. 8.

Brown, Joanne. "An Adolescent's Best Friend: The Role of Animals in Lynn Hall's Fiction." In *ALAN Review,* Spring 1994, pp. 27–31.

Commire, Anne, ed. "Lynn Hall." In *Something About the Author.* Detroit: Gale Research, 1987, vol. 47, pp. 97–104.

Holtze, Sally Holmes, ed. "Lynn Hall." In *Fifth Book of Junior Authors and Illustrators.* New York: H. W. Wilson, 1983, pp. 145–147.

Kirkpatrick, D. L., ed. "Lynn Hall." In *Twentieth-Century Children's Writers,* 2d ed. New York: St. Martin's, 1983, pp. 351–353.

Rochman, Hazel. Review of *Flying Changes. Booklist,* 15 March 1985, p. 1050.

Sarkissian, Adele, ed. "Lynn Hall." In *Something About the Author Autobiography Series.* Detroit: Gale Research, 1987, vol. 4, pp. 181–196.

Stan, Susan. *Presenting Lynn Hall.* New York: Twayne, 1996.

Wilson, Ann K. "Lynn Hall: Solitary and Secure." In *Signal,* Fall 1992, pp. 11–14.

How to Write to the Author

Lynn Hall
Route 2
Elkader, IA 52043

Virginia Hamilton

(1936-)

by Nina Mikkelsen

D o you like reading mysteries? Stories about people your age visiting strange and distant worlds? Ghost stories? Do you like history? Coming-of-age stories? Science fantasy? Teen romances? Or maybe you like reading about stories set in places such as the Kentucky hills, a small river town in the Midwest, or Africa? If any of these stories sound appealing or intriguing, you might like the books of Virginia Hamilton, who has produced more than thirty books of all kinds. Some are realistic; some employ fantasy; some are what we might describe as psychic—or magical—fantasy.

Hamilton has worked in nearly every genre. Her most popular books, *The House of Dies Drear* (1968) and its sequel *The Mystery of Drear House* (1987), blend mystery, ghost story, history, realism, and surrealism. *The House of Dies Drear* won the prestigious Edgar Allan Poe Award for Juvenile Mystery in 1968. Both books are set in a small town in the Midwest where the Underground Railroad plays an im-

surrealism the art of producing fantastic imagery through the use of unnatural combinations

The **Underground Railroad** was an informal system in which free blacks and some whites helped slaves escape to the North during the mid-1800s. The helpers, or "conductors," provided the slaves with food, clothing, directions, and places to hide.

portant role, a town very much like the one in which Hamilton grew up: Yellow Springs, Ohio. And both books focus on a strange old house in which escaped slaves were once hidden during Civil War days.

The Drear Mysteries

In *The House of Dies Drear,* thirteen-year-old Thomas Small suddenly finds himself transplanted to Ohio. His father, a history professor in North Carolina, has taken a job at a college; it is similar in many ways to Antioch, the college that Hamilton had attended in her home town. Arriving in Ohio, Thomas, his parents, and his younger twin brothers discover that the house they have rented has secret passages, hidden stairways, underground passages, puzzling legends—and ghosts. The house of the story is based on a house in Yellow Springs owned by a family named Dies. As a child, Hamilton passed the house each day on her way to school and it always frightened her.

Thomas learns that Dies Drear was an abolitionist, one who did not believe in slavery and who helped slaves escape their condition. He was also a collector of tapestries, carved glass, and Indian crafts, all of which he kept hidden in a secret "room" in the hillside behind his house to help pay for the freedom of escaped slaves if they were caught.

Thomas and his family soon discover accidents happening, and objects moved around or rearranged when they are not watching. When Thomas reads about the legends of the house, he begins wondering if the house is haunted. In the legend, Dies Drear and two slaves were killed by bounty hunters during the Civil War. But there were actually three slaves involved in the chase. So the mystery of what happened to the third slave who escaped that day is important. It seems that he may be the ancestor of someone who is still a part of the local setting. It may be a man named Pluto, who now serves as the caretaker for the house—and who is the secret guardian of the treasure. (Years before, he stumbled upon the treasure that Drear left buried in the hillside.) Or it may be Pluto's neighbor, River Lewis Darrow.

As Pluto tells the story, River Lewis is the direct descendant of River Thames Darrow, a member of the Mohegan tribe who came down from the North with Dies Drear. Pluto and River Swift Darrow (the grandson of River Thames) had heard the legend when they were boys. Each imagined himself the descendant of the third slave, and each hunted for the treasure—but for a different reason. River Swift wanted wealth (or quick money). Pluto wanted heritage. He hoped the treasure would reveal an unknown history and some feeling of who he really was, since slavery had robbed him— and all descendants of slaves—of this knowledge.

Now Pluto is a solitary old man, befriended only by Pesty Darrow, Swift's great-granddaughter, and Mac Darrow, her brother. Thomas gradually comes to know both Darrow children, as well as Pluto and his grown son, Mayhew Skinner, an actor from a nearby city who comes to visit and, with his father, helps them all sort out some of the mysteries of the Drear house. *The House of Dies Drear* dramatizes three major themes woven throughout Hamilton's work, and it reveals her favorite setting and character types, as well as her storytelling purpose.

Major Themes

Coming to know yourself or trying to find out who you are is a central theme in each of Hamilton's novels. "I write about children who struggle to define their own selves," Hamilton has said in her essay "Everything of Value" (1993). Here the sense of self-discovery is seen as the search for heritage, Pluto's quest through both *Drear* books. (The past is shown to be important to identity: no past, no identity.)

A related theme is the African American as a wanderer who must always hide a true self, as Pluto's son says, in order to escape prejudice and oppression and to create a survival pattern within the family or community. African Americans must always wear a mask, Mayhew exclaims, to survive in a bigoted culture. They can never really be themselves. Characteristically, the trickster in Hamilton's fantasies is the mask-wearer who outsmarts his oppressor.

A third theme is the power of the human imagination to create change in the world, the human capacity to make choices that can transform reality and shape cultural learning. In Hamilton's work, cultural learning commonly results from a character's ability to sort out the world through story. Storytelling is one of the strongest forces for producing growth in self-identity. A many-layered structure of "inner

theme central message about life in a literary work

setting the general time and place in which the events of a literary work take place

heritage cultural traditions or knowledge handed down from previous generations

stories" is, in fact, Hamilton's favorite storytelling strategy. In all her books, a main story is filled with many embedded "inner stories" that characters tell one another or themselves in order to make sense of things. Pluto, Mayhew, and Pesty's stories all help Thomas learn more about his African American heritage, for example.

Setting and Characters

Hamilton's favorite characters, like herself, come from a rural midwestern background. Her favorite setting is a small town in the Midwest, a place in which nuclear or extended families provide a strong support system for her main characters, most of whom are twelve or thirteen years old. By the end of both *Drear* books, Thomas's "family" includes his grandmother from the South, who eventually moves North with them; Pluto, who is invited to live with them also at the end of both books; and the Darrow clan, who finally resolve their differences and learn to live in peace with all the others when Walter Small, as final guardian of the Drear treasure, extends a helping hand to them. Hamilton's range of characters is wide: from quiet, unassuming characters such as Thomas and his father to the more dramatic, spunky characters such as Mayhew and Pesty. Whether retiring or spirited, however, Hamilton's characters are all descendants of the author herself, gifted African American storytellers. "I'm all the characters in a sense; I created them all," she says in "Virginia Hamilton: The Continuing the Conversation" (p. 71). And the characters all serve to remind us of Hamilton's reason for writing: "to help reveal and define a people," as she said when accepting the Hans Christian Andersen Award.

> *"I'm all the characters in a sense; I created them all."*

Storytelling Purpose

Creole a white person descended from early French or Spanish settlers of the Gulf states, who has preserved his or her speech and culture

The "people" for Hamilton are almost always African Americans, but at times the term includes those of American Indian ancestry. Sometimes ethnic influence is a subtle part of the story, yet it always has crucial underlying meanings. In *The House of Dies Drear*, the Darrows have more than one ethnic identity—like Hamilton herself, whose mother's mother was part Cherokee and whose father was of black and Creole ancestry. Mattie Darrow, Mac and Pesty's mother, is black, but she may also have Indian ancestry, and her stories of an Indian maiden who escorts slave children along the Underground Railroad are an important part of the book. At one point, Thomas even sees the ghost of this maiden.

And, as Hamilton explains, geography plays as strong a part in identity as ethnicity: "I grew up in Ohio and in Southern Ohio," she says, "[where] black people are black and Indian, black and other things, and they don't talk like anyone else and they don't look like anyone else and they don't act like anyone else. . . . I'm a rural writer . . . a rural black American" (Mikkelsen, 1995, pp. 78–79).

One of Hamilton's most memorable rural characters appears in the book *M. C. Higgins the Great* (1974), which she wrote seven years after *The House of Dies Drear*. This book depicts the values and feelings of the many different groups of African Americans within the larger American culture.

M. C. Higgins the Great

Hamilton's most famous novel, thought by some to be her best, is set in the mountains of eastern Kentucky and southeastern Ohio, a region not far from her home in Yellow Springs. The rural life of M. C., the main character, and his friend Ben, as they roam freely through the woods near his hillside home, is not unlike the life Hamilton and her brothers and sisters had as children.

M. C.'s story takes place during a forty-eight-hour span when a "dude" from Chicago—"some new kind of black fellow . . . all slicked down and dressed to kill" (p. 10), as M. C. says—wanders into this sleepy mountainous area to record folk songs for his taped collection. M. C. decides that James K. Lewis (the dude) might also help his mother become a famous singer. Hamilton was herself a professional singer in New York City for a short time before marrying Arnold Adoff, a teacher and poet. The couple returned with their two children to live in Yellow Springs.

But Lewis, as M. C. eventually discovers, is not in the recording business; he is merely collecting folk songs before they are lost for all time. By the end of the book, M. C.'s hopes for his mother's fame and an exciting life outside the mountains are flattened. The novel emphasizes that M. C. must ultimately come to terms with home, family, and heritage. M. C.'s mother never wanted fame or a city life anyway, nor would his father have ever left the mountain that his own mother, an escaped slave, had purchased years before. The mountain is the family heritage.

Yet resting easy with his setting is what M. C. cannot do. A slag heap hangs over the Higgins home. Outsiders have strip-mined the mountain, leaving a disastrous land "spoil" that threatens to come slipping down and bury them all at any moment. M. C. believes that either they leave or they die. In contrast, his father thinks that to leave the family heritage is to die.

M. C. Higgins the Great is a coming-of-age book in which the main character searches for a sense of self and place in the world, rebels against the constrictions of family life and his father's prejudice toward his Merino neighbors, and finally takes charge of things to save his family's home—and their lives—from the disastrous slag heap.

A farmer's daughter herself, Hamilton has always had a strong concern for the land and keeping it safe. Many of her books reflect this interest, including especially a trilogy of science fantasy that she produced in 1980–1981: *Dustland, The Gathering,* and *Justice and Her Brothers.*

slag the waste left after a metal is separated from its ore during the smelting process

The Justice Books

Leaving their rural midwestern home, Justice and her twin brothers, Thomas and Levi, time travel to a place of the future that serves as a refuge for people who survive environmental disasters on earth. Discovering important methods with which to help the species survive—before it is too late—they return home at last, forewarned and enlightened, to be "just kids" once again. But this does not happen before Thomas has placed them all in serious jeopardy, the result of his destructive sibling jealousy of Justice and Levi.

Justice proves to be courageous, resourceful, intelligent—and, most of all, caring—in dealing with the beings of extraterrestrial places, as well as with her troublesome brother. Hamilton was herself the youngest of five children (two boys and three girls). Hers was a very traditional household: "My mother had very definite ideas in what a girl did, and I resented that. So if you notice, I get even with the boys in the Justice books!" (*Virginia Hamilton,* p. 52).

Of her family, Hamilton says, "My mother had very definite ideas in what a girl did, and I resented that. So if you notice, I get even with the boys in the Justice books!"

Hamilton says she created Justice and her brothers as "spaceships" carrying the "genetic giftedness" of those strong "black people who survived the Middle Passage," the journey across the Atlantic from Africa to America. "And they survived for a reason," she adds. "There is something in them that makes them survive."

Hamilton always focuses on slavery with pride, not with shame or despair. Often in her books, she dramatizes her belief in African American people as being descended from extraordinary people. Only the most gifted humans could have survived the Middle Passage, she feels. Slaves as extraordinary people is also the subject of the book she considers to be her greatest achievement, *The Magical Adventures of Pretty Pearl* (1983), a blending of fantasy, history, legend, creation story, and coming-of-age novel.

The Magical Adventures of Pretty Pearl

Referring to Pearl, the main character of *The Magical Adventures of Pretty Pearl,* Hamilton says she could find "no famous black American women legends," and so, "that's why I created her" (*Virginia Hamilton,* p. 127). As the story opens, Pearl, a goddess living on Mount Kenya, decides she must go to America to help free the slaves. Her oldest brother—and the best god—John de Conquer (a trickster from African American folk tales that Hamilton transplants to her novel) decides to accompany her on her quest. Disguised as birds, they perch on the mast of a slave ship making its way across the ocean. (The image of the flying African is one that Toni Morrison also uses, in *Song of Solomon.*)

But soon after their arrival in the Deep South (Georgia), Pearl fails to pass one of the tests of her quest. Losing her goddess-power, she becomes human. Pearl never returns to Africa; she remains in North America, becoming a storyteller for her people, telling the story of her own life, in fact, as myth, because in her human state, she forgets that she was once a god-child in Kenya.

The interconnectedness of human and spirit worlds is also important in *Sweet Whispers, Brother Rush* (1982). In this novel, a ghost-uncle of a young girl's past arrives to help her discover more about her heritage and family history, when her mother is often absent and her father is missing. Parental

Toni Morrison (1931–) is an African American novelist who won the 1988 Pulitzer Prize for fiction for her novel *Beloved.* Her novel **Song of Solomon** was published in 1977.

absence or neglect is also the subject of several more recent novels by Hamilton.

A Little Love, A White Romance, and Plain City

In three novels of the 1980s and 1990s, Hamilton focuses on the main character's sense of loneliness and isolation because a parent is missing, homeless, or dead. As a result, friends comprising a surrogate family take the place of traditional family relationships. In all her books, says Hamilton, "even though there may not be a total family, there is always the longing for one" (*Virginia Hamilton,* p. 93).

Other issues addressed by these books include: teen depression, obesity, and sexual freedom in *A Little Love* (1984); interracial dating, romance versus realism in male-female relationships, and drug dealing in *A White Romance* (1987); and mixed-race heritage causing confusion of identity in *Plain City* (1993).

In her 1984 article in *New Directions for Women,* Susan Griffith called Sheema, the heroine of *A Little Love,* "one of the most original characters to spring to life in a young adult novel." Betsy Hearne, in her 1984 review of the book in *Booklist,* described it as a "rhythmic narrative in Black English," and Hamilton's exceptional creativity, especially in the areas of invented language and wordplay, is worth noting as a major strength of her books.

Literary Strengths

Hamilton's books have enriched the field of young adult literature artistically and culturally, to the extent that she was chosen in 1992 to receive the Hans Christian Andersen Award, an international medal of recognition for the entire collection of her work. In 1995 she received the Laura Ingalls Wilder Medal for lasting contribution to the field of children's and young adult literature.

Artistically, Hamilton is an image maker, playing with conventional words and phrases to produce new ways of seeing. Her gracefully turned, rhythmical phrases reflect her musical background as well as her talent for shaping talk into

surrogate one that acts as a substitute

melody or prose poems. Here is Buhlaire of *Plain City* as the book ends, "storying" to herself about the future as she watches frogs hopping out of the floodwaters of her town: "Water running. You can't stop it. You can't stop rain or fishes running. . . . Little frogs me. Hop. Blop. You can't stop me" (p. 193).

Cultural learning is an equal strength. Each book reveals the practices, beliefs, history, and traditions of a group of people as the path to self-knowledge for young adult characters. And cultural learning occurs most often for these characters as they tell stories to themselves or among themselves to explore and share insights about family, friends, community, and culture.

Selected Bibliography

WORKS BY VIRGINIA HAMILTON

Fiction

Zeely (1967)

The House of Dies Drear (1968)

The Planet of Junior Brown (1971)

M. C. Higgins the Great (1974)

Arilla Sun Down (1976)

Dustland (1980)

The Gathering (1981)

Justice and Her Brothers (1981)

Sweet Whispers, Brother Rush (1982)

The Magical Adventures of Pretty Pearl (1983)

Willie Bea and the Time the Martians Landed (1983)

A Little Love (1984)

Junius Over Far (1985)

The Mystery of Drear House (1987)

A White Romance (1987)

The Bells of Christmas (1989)

Cousins (1990)

Drylongso (1992)

Plain City (1993)

Jaguarundi (1994)

Readers who enjoy reading the works of Virginia Hamilton might also enjoy reading Molly Hunter, Joyce Carol Thomas, and Laurence Yep.

Biography

W. E. B. Du Bois (1972)

Paul Robeson: The Life and Times of a Free Black Man (1974)

Anthony Burns: The Defeat and Triumph of a Fugitive Slave (1988)

Folklore Collections

The Time-Ago Tales of Jahdu (1969)

Time-Ago Lost: More Tales of Jahdu (1973)

The People Could Fly (1985)

In the Beginning (1988)

The Dark Way (1990)

The All Jahdu Storybook (1991)

Many Thousand Gone: African Americans from Slavery to Freedom (1993)

Her Stories (1995)

Essays and Articles

"Portrait of the Author as a Working Writer." In *Elementary English,* April 1971, pp. 237–240.

"Thoughts on Children's Books, Reading, and Ethnic America." In *Reading Children's Books, and Our Pluralistic Society.* Edited by Harold Tanyzer and Jean Karl. Newark, Del.: International Reading Association, 1972, pp. 61–64.

"The Knowledge." In *Paul Robeson: The Life and Times of a Free Black Man.* New York: Harper, 1974, pp. x–xvi.

"High John Is Risen Again." In *Horn Book,* April 1975, pp. 113–121.

"Newbery Award Acceptance." In *Horn Book,* August 1975, pp. 337–343.

"Writing the Source: In Other Words." In *Horn Book,* December 1978, pp. 609–619.

"Ah, Sweet Rememory!" In *Horn Book,* December 1981, pp. 633–640.

"Changing Woman, Working." In *Celebrating Children's Books: Essays on Children's Literature in Honor of Zena Sutherland.* Edited by Betsy Hearne and Marilyn Kaye. New York: Lothrop, Lee & Shepard, 1981.

"The Mind of a Novel: The Heart of the Book." In *Children's Literature Association Quarterly,* winter 1983, vol. 8, pp. 10–14.

"Boston Globe–Horn Book Acceptance." In *Horn Book,* February 1984, 24–28.

"Introduction." In *The Newbery Award Reader.* Edited by Charles Waugh and Martin Greenberg. New York: Harcourt, Brace, Jovanovich, 1984, pp. xi–xiii.

"On Being a Black Writer in America." In *Lion and the Unicorn,* 1986, vol. 10, 15–17.

"The Known, the Remembered, and the Imagined: Celebrating Afro-American Folktales." In *Children's Literature in Education* 1987, vol. 18, pp. 67–75.

"Anthony Burns." In *Horn Book,* March/April 1989, pp. 183–185.

"Hagi, Mose, and Drylongso." In *The Zena Sutherland Lectures, 1983–1992.* Edited by Betsy Hearne. New York: Clarion Books, 1992.

"Hans Christian Andersen Award Acceptance." In *USSBBY Newsletter,* fall 1992, vol. 18, pp. 6–8.

"Everything of Value: Moral Realism in the Literature for Children." May Hill Arbuthnot Honor Lecture, Richmond, Virginia, 4 May 1993; published in *Journal of Youth Services in Libraries,* summer 1993, pp. 363–377.

"Laura Ingalls Wilder Medal Acceptance." *Horn Book,* July–August 1995, pp. 436–441.

WORKS ABOUT VIRGINIA HAMILTON

Books

Mikkelsen, Nina. *Virginia Hamilton.* New York: Twayne, 1994.

Interview Articles

Apseloff, Marilyn. "A Conversation with Virginia Hamilton." In *Children's Literature in Education,* winter 1983, vol. 14, pp. 204–213.

Mikkelsen, Nina. "A Conversation with Virginia Hamilton." In *Journal of Youth Services in Libraries,* spring 1994, vol. 7, pp. 392–405.

———. "Virginia Hamilton: Continuing the Conversation." In *The New Advocate,* spring 1995, vol. 8, pp. 67–82.

Nicholson, George. "The Trumpet Club Authors on Tape." Holmes, Pa.: Trumpet Club, 1989.

"Planting Seeds." In *Horn Book,* November 1992, pp. 674–680.

Rochman, Hazel. "The Booklist Interview." In *Booklist,* 1 February 1992, pp. 1020–1021.

Ross, Jean. "CA Interview." In *Contemporary Authors,* n.s., vol. 20. Edited by Linda Metzger and Deborah Straub, pp. 208–212.

Articles and Parts of Books

Apseloff, Marilyn. "Creative Geography in the Ohio Novels of Virginia Hamilton." In *Children's Literature Association Quarterly,* spring 1983, vol. 8, pp. 17–20.

Bishop, Rudine Sims. "Books from Parallel Cultures: Celebrating a Silver Anniversary." In *Horn Book,* March–April 1993, pp. 175–181.

———. "Virginia Hamilton." In *Horn Book,* July–August 1995, pp. 442–445.

Dressel, Janice Hartwick. "The Legacy of Ralph Ellison on Virginia Hamilton's Justice Trilogy." In *English Journal,* November 1984, vol. 73, pp. 42–48.

Garrett, Jeffrey. "Reflections of a Jurist." In *USBBY Newsletter,* spring 1992, vol. 17, p. 3.

Glistrup, Eva. "Awarding the Hans Christian Andersen Medal." In *USBBY Newsletter,* fall 1992, vol. 18, pp. 4–6.

Griffith, Susan. "Novel Depicts Black Teens." In *New Directions for Women,* November–December 1984, vol. 13, p. 19.

Harris, Violet. "Contemporary Griots: African-American Writers of Children's Literature." In *Teaching Multicultural Literature.* Edited by Violet Harris. Norwood, Mass.: Christopher Gordon, 1993, pp. 76–77.

Hearne, Betsy. "Booklist Review: A Little Love." In *Booklist,* 1 June 1984, vol. 80, no. 19. Cited in *Children's Literature Review.* Edited by Gerald J. Senick. Detroit: Gale Research, 1986, vol. 11, p. 64.

————. "Introduction to Virginia Hamilton." In *The Zena Sutherland Lectures, 1983–1992.* Edited by Betsy Hearne. New York: Clarion Books, 1992, pp. 71–74.

————. "*Booklist* Review: Junius Over Far." In *Booklist,* 15 May 1985. Cited in *Children's Literature Review,* volume 11. Edited by Gerald J. Senick. Detroit: Gale Research, 1986, p. 64.

————. "Virginia Hamilton." In *Twentieth-Century Children's Writers,* 2nd ed. Edited by D. L. Kirkpatrick. Chicago: St. James, 1985, pp. 353–354.

Heins, Paul. "Virginia Hamilton." In *Horn Book,* August 1975, pp. 344–348.

Mikkelsen, Nina. "Dilemmas of Censorship and the Black Child." In *The Leaflet,* winter 1984, vol. 83, pp. 15–28.

————. "Insiders, Outsiders, and African American Traditions: The Question of Authenticity." In *African American Review,* fall 1997.

————. "A Place to Go To: International Fiction for Children." In *Canadian Children's Literature,* 1984, vols. 35–36, pp. 64–68.

————. "Virginia Hamilton." In *Children's Literature Review.* Edited by Gerald J. Senick. Detroit: Gale Research, 1986, vol. 11, p. 64.

Moore, Opal, and Donnarae MacCann. "The Uncle Remus Travesty, Part II: Julius Lester and Virginia Hamilton." In *Children's Literature Association Quarterly,* Winter 1986–1987, vol. 11, pp. 205–210.

Moss, Anita. "Mythical Narrative: Virginia Hamilton's *The Magical Adventures of Pretty Pearl.*" In *Lion and the Unicorn,* 1985, vol. 9, pp. 50–57.

————. "Gothic and Grotesque Effects in Virginia Hamilton's Fiction." In *ALAN Review,* winter 1992, vol. 19, pp. 16–20.

Nodelman, Perry. "Balancing Acts: Noteworthy American Fiction." In *Touchstones: Reflections on the Best in Children's Literature.* Edited by Perry Nodelman. West Lafayette, Ind.: Children's Literature Association, 1989, pp. 164–171.

————. "The Limits of Structure." In *Children's Literature Association Quarterly,* fall 1982, vol. 7, pp. 45–48.

Rees, David. "Long Ride Through a Painted Desert." In *Painted Desert, Green Shade.* Boston: Horn Book, 1984, pp. 168–184.

Russell, David. "Virginia Hamilton's Symbolic Presentation of Afro-American Sensibility." In *Cross-Culturalism in Children's Literature.* Edited by Susan Gannon and Ruth Anne Thompson. Pleasantville, N.Y.: Pace University Press, 1988, pp. 71–75.

Silvey, Anita. "Editorial: The Problem with Trends." In *Horn Book,* September/October 1994, vol. 70, p. 516.

Sobat, Gail Sidonie. "If the Ghost Be There, Then Am I Crazy? Ghosts in *Sweet Whispers, Brother Rush* and *Beloved.*" In *Children's Literature Association Quarterly,* winter 1995–1996, vol. 20, pp. 168–174.

Townsend, John Rowe. "Virginia Hamilton." In *A Sounding of Storytellers.* New York: Lippincott, 1979, pp. 97–110.

Trites, Roberta Seelinger. "Nesting: Embedded Narratives as Maternal Discourse in Children's Novels." In *Children's Literature Association Quarterly,* winter 1993–1994, vol. 18, pp. 165–170.

White, Mary Lou. "The 1992 Hans Christian Andersen Awards Ceremony: A Personal Reminiscence." In *USBBY Newsletter,* fall 1992, vol. 18, p. 9.

How to Write to the Author
Virginia Hamilton
c/o Elizabeth Meyer
Scholastic, Inc.
555 Broadway
New York, NY 10012-3999

Ernest Hemingway

(1899-1961)

by Ira Elliott

Ernest Hemingway was born to Dr. Clarence E. Hemingway and Grace Hall Hemingway on 21 July 1899 in Oak Park, Illinois, a Chicago suburb. He died of a self-inflicted gunshot wound on 2 July 1961 in Ketchum, Idaho, a small town outside of Sun Valley, the famous ski resort. Word of his death made front-page news around the world.

At the time of his death, Hemingway was one of the most famous men in the world and one of the foremost writers of his time. In his sixty-two years, he had lived in or traveled extensively throughout the United States, Europe, and Africa. He had witnessed or participated in World Wars I and II, the Spanish Civil War, the Greco-Turkish War, and the Sino-Japanese War. He was known worldwide as a big game hunter, a deep-sea fisherman, a bullfight aficionado (enthusiast), and an all-around sportsman and athlete. He had been married four times and had fathered three sons.

Writer, Sportsman, Celebrity

Some movies that were made from Hemingway's novels and short stories include *A Farewell to Arms* (1932), *Islands in the Stream* (1977), *The Killers* (1964), *The Old Man and the Sea* (1958), *The Snows of Kiliman-jaro* (1952), and *To Have and Have Not* (1944).

Most of Hemingway's novels, and several of his short stories, have been made into feature films. He has inspired several full-length biographies, scores of personal remembrances by family and friends, and many books of criticism. During his life, Hemingway was a public figure whose every move was reported in the newspapers and magazines of his day. Even more than thirty years after his death, he remains a powerful presence in the world. It is difficult to think of the Spanish bullfight or the African safari without also thinking of Hemingway. Writing awards and contests bear his name. His own former high school in Oak Park has been renamed Ernest Hemingway High. Monuments erected in his honor stand in Spain, Cuba, and the United States. He sometimes appears as a character in books and films. And Hemingway's former homes in Key West, Florida, and San Francisco de Paula, Cuba, are now museums dedicated to his memory.

But if not for the writing itself, none of this fame and notoriety would matter. Hemingway's phrases have enriched our language. You will often hear references to "grace under pressure," "a moveable feast," "to have and have not," "winner take nothing," "the snows of Kilimanjaro," "death in the afternoon," or "a clean well-lighted place," all phrases coined or popularized by Hemingway. And scenes in his fiction live in the mind long after you stop reading: the bullfight fiesta in Pamplona, Spain; lion hunting in Africa; duck shooting near Venice, Italy; fishing in Michigan; wartime battles in Italy and Spain.

Nick Adams and the Hemingway Hero

style a distinctive manner of expression

When Hemingway won the Nobel Prize for Literature in 1954, the Nobel Foundation said that he had "created a new style in modern literature." This new style was plain and simple. It employed everyday language and realistic dialogue. It marked a break with the "literary" language that many nineteenth-century writers had used. His style set the pattern for generations of authors and spawned countless imitators.

Hemingway's subject matter was also new and bold. He wrote frankly about love, war, and death. He believed that a person's true character came out in the face of a violent death, when you can tell if a person is courageous or cowardly, strong or weak, honest or dishonest. This is one reason that he wrote often about war and bullfighting.

Hemingway created what is often called the Hemingway hero or the code hero: a man who faces danger head-on, who looks at the harsh realities of life without blinking, and who never cracks or complains. No matter how tough things get, the Hemingway hero always exhibits "grace under pressure." This figure defined for a generation of men what it means to be a man and how manhood was achieved. On the other hand, many readers find Hemingway's female characters unreal and claim that his work puts down women. Yet in the 1980s and 1990s, Hemingway scholars have been taking another look at this element of his work. Many of these scholars have concluded that his attitude toward men and women both is far more complicated than we used to think. His work has much to say about male and female roles in society.

A central theme in Hemingway's work is how the individual fits into society, and how one should live in what often seems to be a crazy and difficult world. This issue is explored in many of Hemingway's early short stories that focus on Nick Adams, Hemingway's young alter ego. Some stories portray Nick as a child, others as a teenager in love, and still others as a young man in war. They show Nick struggling to find his own identity and his place in the world. They are stories that nearly everyone can relate to, for everyone must answer the same questions: Who am I? Where do I fit in?

From Kansas City to Paris

Hemingway began to write in high school for the student newspaper. Immediately after graduation in 1917, he joined the *Kansas City Star* as a junior reporter. Like most newspapers, the *Star* had what is called a stylebook, which provides reporters with advice on how to write. At the *Star*, Hemingway learned to write short, clear sentences. He would later call this the "true simple declarative sentence" in *A Moveable Feast* (1964). In *Death in the Afternoon* (1932), his nonfiction book on the Spanish bullfight, Hemingway wrote about his own "greatest difficulty" as a young writer. The problem, he said, was to find "the sequence of motion and fact which made the emotion." He meant that a good writer has to be

Hemingway wrote frankly about love, war, and death. He believed a person's true character came out in the face of a violent death, when you can tell if a person is courageous or cowardly, strong or weak, honest or dishonest.

theme central message about life in a literary work

Hemingway's stories are stories that nearly everyone can relate to, for everyone must answer the same questions: Who am I? Where do I fit in?

honest with himself or herself. The good writer must understand his or her own feelings and what led to those feelings. Then, and only then, can the reader experience the same emotion.

Hemingway did not stay in Kansas City for long. War had broken out in Europe and he wanted to be where the action was. A bad eye kept him out of the armed forces, and so he signed up with the Red Cross as an ambulance driver. He was subsequently wounded in Italy while rescuing a comrade, received medals from the Italian and U.S. governments, and returned to Oak Park in 1919. He soon found work at the *Toronto Star* and with his first wife, Hadley Richardson, got just what he had hoped for: passage to Paris in 1920 as a European correspondent for the paper.

In Paris, Hemingway met other American writers, whom Gertrude Stein called members of the lost generation. This was the generation that had gone through World War I. The war had brought about so many changes in society that they were "lost" in a topsy-turvy world, what the poet T. S. Eliot called a "waste land." The question for these men and women was, how does one live in a world without stability, without security? Hemingway's answer was the code hero: men and women must be true to their own values, their personal code.

Gertrude Stein (1874–1946) was an experimental writer and poet. She had a profound influence on modern literature.

T. S. Eliot (1888–1965) wrote *The Waste Land,* which is a long, bleak poem about modern life after World War I.

Love and War

The Sun Also Rises, Hemingway's first full-length novel, appeared in 1926 and confirmed the promise of his earlier short story collection, *In Our Time* (1925). *The Sun Also Rises* is now widely regarded as one of the most important works of twentieth-century literature. The novel tells the story of Jake Barnes, an American journalist wounded in World War I, and the woman he loves but cannot marry, Lady Brett Ashley. In the novel, Hemingway depicts the chaos of postwar Europe and deals openly with sex, a largely forbidden subject before he and other "lost generation" writers first explored it. *The Sun Also Rises* fixed the characters of Jake and Brett in the public mind. After its publication, young men and women on college campuses modeled their speech, actions, and attire on the characters in the novel.

Hemingway's second collection of stories, *Men Without Women,* was published in 1927, the year that he divorced his first wife in order to marry Pauline Pfeiffer. This was also the year in which his father committed suicide. In 1928, the Hemingways purchased a large house in Key West, where his second and third sons were born. This is also where he completed the work on his second novel, *A Farewell to Arms*.

Published in 1929, *A Farewell to Arms* tells the story of the doomed romance between an American ambulance driver and an English nurse. Hemingway's novel is regarded as one of the major works to have come out of the war, and as one of Hemingway's best. The teenage ambulance driver, Frederic Henry, narrates the story. When he falls in love with Catherine Barkley, the war keeps them apart. They soon reject the war, however, and they also reject society. They make "a separate peace" for themselves and escape the war in Italy and Switzerland. It is unfortunately a short-lived peace, for Hemingway shows how those who rebel against society are ultimately punished for their actions.

The famous opening paragraph of the novel reveals Hemingway at the height of his artistic powers:

> In the late summer of that year we lived in a house in a village that looked across the river and the plain to the mountains. In the bed of the river there were pebbles and boulders, dry and white in the sun, and the water was clear and swiftly moving and blue in the channels. Troops went by the house and down the road and the dust they raised powdered the leaves of the trees. The trunks of the trees too were dusty and the leaves fell early that year and we saw the troops marching along the road and the dust rising and the leaves, stirred by the breeze, falling and the soldiers marching and afterward the road bare and white except for the leaves.

Notice Hemingway's simple language and direct style. Also note his expert use of rising and falling rhythm and of repetition. He manages to get the reader to look with the narrator "across the river and the plain to the mountains," and the sentences seem to move with the river's moving and with the soldiers's marching. The paragraph ends on a dying fall, which mimics the falling leaves. Hemingway creates an overall sense of movement and of passing time. He holds the reader in suspense as well, not saying right away who "we" are or where exactly the house is located. And if you read the whole novel, you will see how this paragraph hints at some of its major themes.

Africa, Spain, and the Novel

In the fall of 1933, Hemingway and Pauline left for a five-month African safari. Hemingway recounted their experiences in *Green Hills of Africa* (1935). While the book is about Africa, Hemingway discusses writing and writers in the early chapters. Here Hemingway makes his famous declaration that "all modern American literature comes from one book by Mark Twain called *Huckleberry Finn*." He probably said this because Twain was one of the first to use authentic, regional American speech in a work of literature. Huck Finn speaks like a real boy from Missouri, not like a character in a book. In fact, he is not so different from Nick Adams. Both are young men who rebel against society in order to find themselves and their own code.

Two short story masterpieces also came from Hemingway's African adventure: "The Snows of Kilimanjaro" and "The Short Happy Life of Francis Macomber." Both are stories of courage, betrayal, failure, and redemption.

To Have and Have Not (1937), Hemingway's third novel, and the only one set entirely in the Americas, attempts to show how the individual is easily corrupted in a world dominated by money. The theme of the novel is expressed by its hero: "A man alone ain't got no . . . chance." A similar theme is struck in Hemingway's immensely popular 1940 novel, *For Whom the Bell Tolls,* which takes place in Spain during the Spanish Civil War. Hemingway covered the war as a reporter, and it was in Spain that he met his third wife, the writer and journalist Martha Gellhorn.

The war was between those who favored a democratic republic and those who followed the fascist general Francisco Franco. Franco's side won and he ruled the country for more than forty years. Hemingway, like most American writers and intellectuals, was on the side of the republicans, also called the loyalists or the partisans. Hemingway's novel of the war centers on the American Robert Jordan and his love affair with a Spanish girl. The title of the book is taken from the writings of the seventeenth-century English poet John

Huckleberry Finn (1884) was a sequel to *Tom Sawyer*. It is a story about a runaway boy and a runaway slave who become friends as they encounter adventures together.

There is an article about Mark Twain in volume 3.

Donne. So is the theme of the book. Like the main character in *To Have and Have Not,* Robert Jordan comes to understand that all of us are "involved in mankind," and that "no man is an island."

Those who saw in the Spanish conflict forebodings of a second world war were right. Hemingway also covered World War II as a reporter. He is said to have helped Allied forces liberate Paris from Nazi control. During World War II, Hemingway met the journalist Mary Welsh. They were married and settled in Cuba, in a big house that Hemingway dubbed *Finca Vigia,* meaning "Lookout Farm." Here Hemingway enjoyed fishing from his boat *Pilar,* watching games of jai alai, and writing.

In 1954, Hemingway won the Pulitzer Prize for his short novel *The Old Man and the Sea* (1952). The old man of the title is a fisherman who struggles with, and learns to love, the marlin he chases for three days. The theme of the novel, "a man can be destroyed but not defeated," points to the nobility of all human beings. This short novel may also be one of Hemingway's best known. The Nobel Prize for literature went to the man by then known the world over as "Papa" Hemingway.

When Donne and Hemingway say that **"no man is an island,"** they mean that all human beings are connected. When Donne writes, "never send to know **for whom the bell tolls;** it tolls for thee" (*Devotions upon Emergent Occasions,* Meditation 17), he is stating the same idea more dramatically: when one person dies and a church bell tolls, or rings, to announce the death, the bell is also ringing for all human beings, who suffer together and must eventually die.

foreboding an uneasy feeling that something bad is going to happen

A Rough Decade

But the 1950s were a rough time for America's most famous author. His health was in serious decline. Battered by two successive plane crashes in Africa and a life of heavy drinking, Hemingway suffered from a variety of physical problems over the next several years. But he continued to work on another book on bullfighting, *The Dangerous Summer,* his recollection of his years in Paris, *A Moveable Feast,* and a novel, *The Garden of Eden.* All were published after his death.

Following Fidel Castro's revolution, Cuba proved too unstable a country for Hemingway to live in. He and Mary moved to Idaho in 1960. Suffering from physical ailments and severe depression, Hemingway twice was secretly hospitalized in the Mayo Clinic in Rochester, Minnesota, where he received electroshock therapy.

He returned to Idaho but was unable to find relief from his depression. He felt that he could no longer write or par-

> *"Hemingway reminds us that to engage in literature one has first to engage life."*

ticipate in all the activities he used to enjoy. At seven o'clock in the morning of 2 July 1961, the Hemingway voice that had thrilled millions of readers was silenced forever by a self-inflicted gunshot.

Whatever flaws the man and the writer may have had, Hemingway was still able to influence the course of twentieth-century literature and culture. As the British critic and writer Anthony Burgess says, "Hemingway reminds us that to engage literature one has first to engage life."

Selected Bibliography

BOOKS BY ERNEST HEMINGWAY

In Our Time (1925), a collection of short stories, many of which focus on the character Nick Adams

The Sun Also Rises (1926), a novel of the "lost generation"

Men Without Women (1927), a second volume of stories, several featuring Nick Adams

A Farewell to Arms (1929), a World War I romance

Winner Take Nothing (1933), more stories about Nick Adams and others; includes the famous "A Clean, Well-Lighted Place"

Death in the Afternoon (1932), Hemingway's fully illustrated book on the Spanish bullfight

Green Hills of Africa (1935), Hemingway on African safari

To Have and Have Not (1937), an honest man gets himself involved in illegal activities in Bimini

The Fifth Column (1938), Hemingway's only play, which takes place in Madrid during the Spanish Civil War

For Whom the Bell Tolls (1940), love and death with the guerrillas in the mountains of Spain

Across the River and into the Trees (1950), an aging colonel's love affair with a beautiful Venetian woman; generally considered to be Hemingway's weakest novel

The Old Man and the Sea (1952), the Pulitzer Prize–winning classic

A Moveable Feast (1964), a portrait of the artist as a young man in Paris; published posthumously

Islands in the Stream (1970), the life of a good painter and his three sons on the island of Bimini; published posthumously

The Nick Adams Stories (1973), all the Nick Adams stories compiled in one volume by the critic Philip Young

The Dangerous Summer (1985), the Spanish bullfight revisited during the "dangerous summer" of 1959; published posthumously

The Garden of Eden (1986), a sophisticated psychological novel centering on a honeymoon couple in the South of France; published posthumously

"The Snows of Kilimanjaro" and "The Short Happy Life of Francis Macomber" can be found in the excellent collection *The Snows of Kilimanjaro and Other Stories* (1970). Like most of Hemingway's work, this volume is published by Scribners and is available at most book stores.

BOOKS ABOUT ERNEST HEMINGWAY

Baker, Carlos. *Ernest Hemingway: A Life Story*. New York: Bantam, 1969.

Burgess, Anthony. *Ernest Hemingway and His World*. New York: Scribners, 1985.

Lynn, Kenneth S. *Hemingway*. New York: Fawcett Columbine, 1987.

Mellow, James R. *Hemingway: A Life Without Consequences*. New York: Houghton Mifflin, 1992.

Meyers, Jeffrey. *Hemingway: A Biography*. New York, Perennial-Harper and Row, 1985.

This is a highly selective list but a good place to begin. All these books include bibliographies that can point you to other books about Hemingway.

BOOKS OF SPECIAL INTEREST

If you are interested in a novel about World War I similar to Hemingway's *A Farewell to Arms,* you may wish to pick up a copy of Erich Maria Remarque's *All Quiet on the Western Front*. Often called a companion novel to *A Farewell to Arms,* the Remarque book is narrated by a soldier fighting on the side of the Germans. For more on one of Hemingway's favorite authors, Mark Twain, see the essay on Twain in this collection.

Hemingway was often asked by his friends to suggest books for them to read, and his recommendations always

Today Ernest Hemingway's house in Key West is a museum open to the public. You can see Hemingway's study where he wrote *A Farewell to Arms* and *For Whom the Bell Tolls*, among other stories, there.

included the following novels: Stendhal's *The Red and the Black*, Gustave Flaubert's *Madame Bovary*, Marcel Proust's *Remembrance of Things Past*, Thomas Mann's *Buddenbrooks*, Nikolai Gogol's *Taras Bulba*, Fyodor Dostoyevsky's *The Brothers Karamazov*, Leo Tolstoy's *Anna Karenina* and *War and Peace*, Mark Twain's *The Adventures of Huckleberry Finn*, Herman Melville's *Moby Dick*, Nathaniel Hawthorne's *The Scarlet Letter,* and Stephen Crane's *The Red Badge of Courage.*

Most of these are nineteenth-century novels, and many of them are long and perhaps difficult, but *Taras Bulba, Huckleberry Finn,* and *The Red Badge of Courage* are good, quick, and exciting reads. See the essay on Crane in this collection for more information about *The Red Badge of Courage* and Crane's other works.

Nat Hentoff

(1925-   )

by Harold M. Foster

Many Americans take for granted the idea of freedom. Most of us do not wake up every morning and think about how the Bill of Rights will be a silent guarantor of our safety, health, speech, movement, work, education, and play. Nat Hentoff is different from most of us. He has almost never spent a day of his adult life without thinking about the essential freedoms that are guaranteed to all Americans. Born on 10 June 1925, Hentoff has lived long enough to experience many events in American and world affairs that challenged the most essential freedoms and, in places outside America, eradicated them completely.

Hentoff claims that three major formative experiences helped create his love of freedom. First, Hentoff's Jewish roots gave him a belief in social justice and a fear of any type of xenophobic behavior. After all, Hentoff was a teenager when European Jews were systematically denied the very right to live in Germany, which afforded to all its citizens none of the protections found in our Bill of Rights. The second formative

xenophobic
marked by fear and hatred of foreigners and strangers

103

influence on Hentoff was jazz, a musical form defined by free-dom—the freedom to improvise and to experiment. Hentoff characterizes jazz as expression where there is no room to run from direct emotions.

Hentoff credits high school as his third major life-forming experience. He graduated from Boston Latin School, which is the oldest public school in America. "The faculty has high expectations of every student and will give no student an excuse not to meet those expectations," wrote Hentoff (*Speaking for Ourselves*, p. 93).

Jazz Country

The themes of *Jazz Country*, Hentoff's first young-adult novel, are not so surprising. After all, Hentoff's love of jazz and intense interest in civil liberties and freedom have been lifelong concerns of his. The 1965 publishing date of *Jazz Country* is what is so surprising. So many novelists for young adults credit S. E. Hinton with publishing the first thematically modern young-adult novel, *The Outsiders*, in 1967. It is true that *The Outsiders* reached a much larger audience than *Jazz Country*. Now, *The Outsiders* is taught in schools all over the country as a classic text, whereas *Jazz Country* is merely a selection on a library shelf in most schools.

Yet *Jazz Country* was incredibly daring for a teenage audience in 1965. And ironically, the first chapter of *Jazz Country* is titled "The Outsiders." Obviously this novel is about jazz. To describe music must be one of the most difficult tasks in writing. Yet, Hentoff gets extremely close to creating a musical experience with words. For instance, Hentoff writes this passage about a jazz rehearsal:

> *To describe music must be one of the most difficult tasks in writing. Yet, Hentoff gets extremely close to creating a musical experience with words.*

As Moses had wanted, the main story line was always set by Burke. His eyes closed, his cheeks puffed out, Burke made the trumpet speak. I mean there were times when it actually did talk—or rather—chuckle, snort, snarl, razz, rage, whimper, bray, and whisper. And he invented melody lines I'd never heard before, and yet once I did hear them, they sounded immediately familiar. Some soared and dipped like a long football pass. Others were like talking in the dark when you were supposed to be asleep. (P. 64)

Any reader interested in music will find *Jazz Country* to be a fascinating chronicle of a musical idiom. But although jazz may be the setting of this book, the themes emanating from the music are what make this book so daring and contemporary. *Jazz Country* is about a teenage white male, Tom Curtis, who is fascinated by the music of an African American artist, Moses Godfrey. The novel chronicles their mentor-student relationship, which centers on racial differences as well as on musical development. Tom's central dilemma is whether to go to college or to devote himself to his burning desire to play jazz on his trumpet. As Tom becomes more involved in the jazz world, he develops an understanding of the hardships, particularly among black jazz musicians, that are so influential to the music. Tom, whose father is a successful lawyer, sees how his own comfortable life makes real jazz difficult for him.

idiom form of artistic expression characteristic of a medium

As the book ends, Tom not only learns to accept who he is but also realizes that not all Americans experience the same level of freedom that he enjoys. Tom, like his creator Nat Hentoff, recognizes the need to make sure that American freedom and justice are truly as blind to race and social class as they are supposed to be.

How different this book was from other young adult books published in the early 1960s. Yet, even compared to today's young adult novels, this book is still fresh. It has a simplicity, yet it gives serious treatment to the issues of freedom, race, poverty, and growth. And the descriptions of music are remarkable. A reader interested in any music should appreciate *Jazz Country*. As the jazz musician Bill Hitchcock says, "but Charlie Parker told the whole story in less than thirty seconds. He said, 'Music is your own experience, your thoughts, your wisdom. If you don't live it, it won't come out of your horn'" (p. 10).

The 1960s

The turmoil of the 1960s provided Hentoff with the source of many themes for the young adult novels he wrote after *Jazz Country*. This was a period of great confusion and unrest. Protest over the Vietnam War led to major tests of civil liberties. The meaning of freedom was constantly questioned during this period roughly dating from the late 1960s into the early 1970s.

In the **Vietnam War** (1957–1975), Communist-ruled North Vietnam fought to take over South Vietnam. From 1965 to 1969, the United States tried to stop the advancement of North Vietnam but failed. In 1975, South Vietnam surrendered to North Vietnam.

It was the culture of the 1960s that emerged most directly in *I'm Really Dragged Out but Nothing Gets Me Down,* published in 1968. This book deals with how Jeremy, a high school senior, decides what to do about military service. Should he allow himself to be drafted, or should he go with his conscience and resist the military? What Jeremy—and millions of other young men facing the same dilemma—should do was a vibrant, nation-dividing question during the Vietnam era. Today, with an all-volunteer army, the intensity of this dilemma may escape young readers, but back then, all able-bodied young men of eighteen faced the very real possibility of being killed in a war many people thought was wrong. This book gives a sense of the enormous social and moral problems encountered by people who grew up in the 1960s, and *I'm Really Dragged but Nothing Gets Me Down* is an excellent supplement to understanding the history of that very painful era.

In the Country of Ourselves also has a 1960s feel. The book, published in 1971, centers on a high school whose administrator attempts to deal with student groups and their series of demands. The issues raised in this book include freedom of speech and racial tension. Although issues do get resolved, Hentoff does not present easy answers, and he portrays a revolutionary teacher, whose views Hentoff must share to some extent, as opportunistic and self-centered.

Huck Finn

There is an article about Mark Twain in volume 3.

Hentoff's understanding of the complexity of most issues is clearly seen in his 1982 novel, *The Day They Came to Arrest the Book.* The major event of this book is an attempt by an angry black parent to have Mark Twain's *The Adventures of Huckleberry Finn* removed as a history class's required reading. The rather spineless principal tries not only to bully the teacher into eliminating this classic book but also to coerce the librarian into taking *Huck Finn* off the shelves. Hentoff throws in a mystery about the previous librarian and ends the book with a provocative school board meeting at which the issues surrounding the problems with *Huck Finn* are debated. The school board makes a decision about the use of the book, but Hentoff makes it clear that no story like this really has a neat Hollywood movie–like ending. The threat of censorship is ongoing.

This book is still relevant. The controversy over *Huckleberry Finn* continues to haunt American schools. At the time of the writing of this essay, the elite National Cathedral School in Washington had dropped the use of *Huck Finn* from its tenth-grade curriculum and allowed its use only in upper-level electives. Schools throughout the country continue to wage the very same battle described in *The Day They Came to Arrest the Book*. The only problem with Hentoff's account is that his characters are mostly upset with the use of the "N word" in *Huck Finn*. Real-world critics of *Huck Finn* seize upon the portrayal of a weak Jim and his mistreatment, particularly by Tom Sawyer, as the central problem with the book. Yet, *The Day They Came to Arrest the Book* presents strong arguments on both sides of this issue. Hentoff does a good job of bringing life to the censors. For instance:

The "N word" is "nigger." Today it is often considered racist, but in Mark Twain's time it was the most common way of referring to an African American.

> Kate, blazing, jumped up. "Yes, our freedoms must be protected. We have the right to be *free* of racism in our schools. We have a right to be *free* of sexism in our schools. And this book is both racist and sexist. Does the First Amendment really mean that schools should be free to warp the minds of their students *in the name of the First Amendment?*" (P. 104)

As this clever argument shows, Hentoff deals with the central issue of book banning, in a timely and all-too-relevant way.

True Stories About Freedom

The American Library Association's 1994 list of the most influential young adult books turned up a Nat Hentoff work that is not a novel. Rather it is a collection of true stories published in 1987, titled *American Heroes In and Out of School.* This is a collection of portraits of people, many of them young, who risk punishment and ridicule to stand up for the rights guaranteed by the Bill of Rights. Some of these true stories are harrowing. One young, proud ninth-grade girl refuses to drop a lawsuit against a school for strip-searching her for drugs. She takes the suit to the Supreme Court and loses, but her courage is awesome. Then there is the young

harrowing disturbing, distressing

woman who refuses to pledge allegiance to the flag because it is her right not to. She continues to fight for her legal right, even though her home is bombed.

Hentoff devotes a great deal of space to describing the great risks that folk singer Joan Baez has undertaken for her pacifist and egalitarian views. Hentoff tells how Baez faced American bombers in Hanoi during the Vietnam War and yet, after the war, condemned the Vietnamese for human-rights violations.

Not all these stories are about liberal causes. One of the vignettes deals with a San Bernardino High School student who has to fight for her right to pass out antiabortion literature on school grounds.

In many ways *American Heroes In and Out of School* represents the best of Hentoff. The heroism of these real people is captured beautifully in this short book. This is the heroism of character—not physical courage, but rather an inspiring moral courage. The last episode in this book describes a Bill of Rights Day held in Charleston, West Virginia, in 1974. Hentoff was there and witnessed these West Virginian teenagers discussing issues of civil rights and freedom. Through the description of this day, Hentoff makes it clear that Americans will remain free by allowing, and participating in, open discussion about the most vexing issues that face us all. Considering how all sides of the political spectrum sometimes seem to have shut down discussion, it is important to have Nat Hentoff remind us of the duty of Americans to remain open to differences in a very complex world.

Other Works by Hentoff

Two other Hentoff works that should not be overlooked are *Does This School Have Capital Punishment?* (1983) and *This School Is Driving Me Crazy* (1978). Both books deal with private schools and the problems of the main character, Sam Davidson. In *This School Is Driving Me Crazy,* Sam attends Bronson Alcott School, where his father is headmaster. Slowly Sam and his father develop a relationship that is more father and son than headmaster and student. In the sequel, *Does This School Have Capital Punishment?,* jazz enters the picture as an older Sam develops a relationship with an elderly trumpeter, Major Kelley. These books, although somewhat more light-

pacifist marked by an opposition to war as a means of settling disputes

egalitarian characterized by a belief in social, political, and economic equality

vexing agitating, troubling

hearted than his other books, are timeless novels about growing up.

More About Hentoff

Nathan Irving Hentoff was born in Boston, Massachusetts, and educated at Northeastern University, a school he characterized as a working-class college. After graduating with highest honors in 1945, he worked at WMEX Radio in Boston until 1953. Also during this time, he studied at Harvard University (1946) and at the Sorbonne in Paris on a Fulbright Fellowship (1950).

After his radio stint, Hentoff became associate editor of *Downbeat* magazine and cofounding editor of *Jazz Review.* Hentoff has been a staff writer for the *New Yorker* magazine and has written a weekly column for the *Washington Post* which was syndicated nationally. He has worked for the *Village Voice* since 1958. His books have won numerous awards.

Boston Boy

If you want to know more about Nat Hentoff, read *Boston Boy* (1986). This autobiography is written in a lively and very readable style. Hentoff discusses, at length, growing up Jewish in the Roxbury section of Boston. He describes his life through college and beyond and gives the reader insights into how he gained his commitments to jazz and civil rights. Hentoff's early experiences were filled with rebelliousness against the rules of his religion on the one hand, and the anti-Semitism of his neighbors on the other.

However, for people who love to read and write, a favorite passage in *Boston Boy* may be this one:

> **I was addicted to books. Both the reading of them and the physical possession of them. On the way home from Boston Latin School, I would sometimes stop at an astonishing building that had nothing but used books, four floors of them. And while hunting for jazz records in other parts of the city, I would often find some in the backrooms of bookshops. And every time**

my father took me for a ride to the railroad station to make the last mail connection to New York, it was understood that I would not return home without at least one book. Soon the books burst out of my bedroom and took over nearly all the wall space in the front hall of our apartment as well as the living room. (P. 32)

The Final Words

Nat Hentoff has lots to say about himself as a writer, including the following:

Having written a good many books for adults, I particularly enjoy the responses of young readers, who write to authors far more often than adults, and often quite trenchantly. I fall behind in all the rest of my correspondence, but my ironclad rule is that a letter from a kid gets answered—right away. If there is a heaven, that might get me a shot at the waiting list. (Gallo, p. 94)

trenchantly articulately; perceptively

If you like the works of Nat Hentoff, you might also enjoy the works of Robert Cormier, Chris Crutcher, and Paul Zindel.

Selected Bibliography

WORKS BY NAT HENTOFF

Novels for Young Adults
Jazz Country (1965; 1986)
I'm Really Dragged but Nothing Gets Me Down (1968)
Journey into Jazz (1968)
In the Country of Ourselves (1971)
This School Is Driving Me Crazy (1975)
Does This School Have Capital Punishment? (1981)
The Day They Came to Arrest the Book (1982)

Nonfiction for Young Adults
American Heroes: In and Out of School (1987)

Autobiography
Boston Boy (1986)

Novels for Adults

Call the Keeper (1966)

Onwards! (1968)

Blues for Charlie Darwin (1982)

The Man from Internal Affairs (1985)

Nonfiction for Adults

Hear Me Talking to Ya: The Story of Jazz by the Men Who Made It. Edited by Nat Hentoff with Nat Shapiro (1955).

The Jazz Makers: Essays on the Greats of Jazz. Edited by Nat Hentoff with Nat Shapiro (1957; 1958).

Jazz: New Perspectives on the History of Jazz by Twelve of the World's Foremost Jazz Critics and Scholars. Edited by Nat Hentoff with Albert McCarthy (1959; 1960).

Jazz Street, photography by Dennis Stouk (1960)

The Jazz Life (1961; 1962)

Peace Agitator: The Story of A. J. Muste (1963)

The New Equality (1964)

Our Children Are Dying (1964)

The Essays of A. J. Muste. Edited by Nat Hentoff (1967)

A Doctor Among the Addicts (1968)

A Political Life: The Education of John V. Lindsay (1969)

State Secrets: Police Surveillance in America, with Paul Crown and Nick Egelson (1974)

Does Anybody Give a Damn? Nat Hentoff on Education (1977)

Jazz Is (1978)

The First Freedom: The Tumultuous History of Free Speech in America (1980)

The 1984 Calendar: An American History, with Tim Keefe and Howard Levine (1983)

John Cardinal O'Connor: At the Storm Center of a Changing American Catholic Church (1988)

Free Speech for Me—But Not For Thee: How the American Left and Right Relentlessly Censor Each Other (1992)

WORKS ABOUT NAT HENTOFF

Carter, Betty. "Best of the Best." *ALAN Review,* fall 1994, pp.67–69.

Contemporary Authors Autobiography Series. Detroit: Gale Research, 1988, pp. 165–174.

Third Book of Junior Authors. New York: A. W. Wilson, 1972, p. 124.

Gallo, Donald R., ed. *Speaking for Ourselves*. National Council of Teachers of English, Urbana, 1990, pp. 93–94.

Spencer, Albert F. "Hentoff, Nat(han Irving)," *Twentieth-Century Young Adult Writers*. Edited by Laura Berger. Detroit: St. James, 1994, pp. 280–282.

How to write to the Author
Nat Hentoff
c/o HarperCollins Publishers
10 East 53rd Street
New York, NY 10022

S. E. Hinton

(1948-   )

by Marjorie Hipple

S. E. Hinton is recognized as the originator and grande dame of the modern young adult literature genre. Ever since the publication of her mold-breaking novel *The Outsiders* (1967), her realistic fiction has dominated the market and led the way for other novelists for young adults.

Hinton's first novel succeeded because she, too, was an outsider. In the literary landscape of the 1960s, there were few stories for adolescents, and those few often portrayed rather benign and romantic teen lives. *The Outsiders* was neither benign nor romantic. Hinton was also an outsider by virtue of her age and sex: she was only fifteen when she began the novel and seventeen when it was published, and she was a woman writing a story about young men. Yet neither her youth nor her sex hindered her. Indeed it is testimony to her skill and understanding that three decades later *The Outsiders* continues to connect with readers and is a yearly bestseller.

benign favorable, wholesome

Quotations from S. E. Hinton that are not attributed to a published source are from a personal interview conducted by the author of this article on 12 March 1995 and appear here by permission of S. E. Hinton.

113

The Outsiders initially elicited mixed feelings from adults, some of whom were disturbed by the stark realism of the gang violence, drinking, and sex it depicts; they deemed it too realistic for its teen audience. But there were not then and are not now any mixed feelings among the youth for whom the novel was intended. It has sold over five million copies.

The Writer

"I was one of those horse-crazy young nuts, running around whinnying in grade school and stuff."

Susan Eloise Hinton was born on 22 July 1948 in Tulsa, Oklahoma, and has spent most of her life in or around that city. It is small wonder that it has become the backdrop for all but one of her novels.

She wrote *The Outsiders* at an age when many teens are struggling to write a theme for English. But she had had lots of practice. She began writing stories when she learned to read and love books, especially books about horses. Growing up in Tulsa during the 1950s and 1960s, she fell in love with cowboys and horses—"I was one of those horse-crazy young nuts," she says, "running around whinnying in grade school and stuff"—and those became the subjects of many of her early writings. Her interest in horses and cowboys reemerged decades later in her novels *Tex* (1979) and *Taming the Star Runner* (1988).

She attended Will Rogers High School, where, in her junior year, she began writing *The Outsiders,* the riveting story of gang rivalry that would launch her career as a writer. Though she wrote much of gangs in her novels, she was never a member of any gang or other social group in high school, including the nonconformists. She made friends with classmates from different groups.

A keen observer of the cruelties and class tensions that framed social relationships among her peers, Hinton could find little of those realities in the books she read. As she recalls, "there weren't any teen books except the 'Mary Goes to the Prom' stuff." So she decided to write about real teenagers herself. She began writing *The Outsiders* in her creative writing class, in which—unbelievably—she earned a D!

The Outsiders was published two years later. By then Hinton had entered the University of Tulsa where she soon switched her major from journalism to education—not surprising in view of her continuing interest in youth. During that busy time she also met David Inhofe and she began her second novel, *That Was Then, This Is Now* (1971). After graduation she married Inhofe and settled down in the Tulsa area, where in 1996 she and her husband resided with their son, Nicholas David.

Hinton did not become a teacher. Instead she decided to write. This may have been a loss to education, but it was a boon to millions of youths who have met her through her novels.

boon blessing

The Novels

Hinton has written five novels for adolescents: *The Outsiders; That Was Then, This Is Now; Rumble Fish* (1975); *Tex;* and *Taming the Star Runner.* Each of them has found a large and loyal readership, and all but *Taming the Star Runner* have been made into movies.

Although each of her books presents numerous themes, a few are common to several novels: loyalty, change and growth, the search for identity, and abandonment. Loyalty is demonstrated, for example, in *The Outsiders.* Its characters often fight among themselves but rally as one when gang members or even a juvenile court judge tries to harm any of them. Similarly, gang members fight as a unit to defend or avenge one of their own. In *Rumble Fish,* Rusty-James relies upon the steadfast allegiance of his buddy, Steve; and in *That Was Then, This Is Now,* Hinton portrays the intense loyalty between Bryon and Mark but then adds a fateful twist to it.

The Outsiders

Orphaned by the death of their parents, the three Curtis boys struggle to survive as a family in an impoverished neighborhood. The youngest, fourteen-year-old Ponyboy Curtis, narrates this story of fierce loyalties and equally fierce conflicts that rage within his family and challenge his gang. Ponyboy lives with his brothers Sodapop, sixteen, a carefree youth, and Darryl, the oldest, who is cast in an authoritarian parenting role. They belong to the Greasers, a group of boys—the

The **Greasers** were named for the "hair grease" they used to slick back their hair. In the 1950s and 1960s, a greaser generally came from a working-class background. The **Socs** got their name from the word "society," something a greaser could not be a part of.

About her first novel, The Outsiders, *Hinton says, "It was something I was just doing for myself and on my own. I really wasn't even thinking about getting it published or anything. I was just in there living it."*

nemesis formidable and usually victorious rival or opponent

outsiders—from the wrong side of the tracks. Their chief adversaries are the Socs, a gang of middle-class boys. When Ponyboy's best friend Johnnycake kills one of the Socs to save Ponyboy's life, events explode, tossing Ponyboy and his brothers in their wake.

Though this was her first novel, Hinton claims it was the easiest of all to write because she was so wrapped up in it. "It was something I was just doing for myself and on my own," she says. "I really wasn't even thinking about getting it published or anything. I was just in there living it."

That Was Then, This Is Now

Hinton was not to publish another novel for four years. Writer's block—every writer's nemesis—had befallen her. She attributes some of it to her success with *The Outsiders* and the pressures she felt to repeat that success, to produce another masterpiece.

That Was Then, This is Now is a story about change. Though the action in this novel takes place in the same town as that of *The Outsiders* and only a year later, gang life is less dominant. It is the late 1960s, a time of drugs, beatniks, and the Vietnam War. Sixteen-year-old Bryon Douglas tells the story, a tale of a friendship that goes bad during that turbulent time. Mark, also sixteen, has lived with Bryon and his mother since he was orphaned when his parents killed each other in a family argument seven years earlier. Though they are a study in contrasts—in looks and temperament—the boys are best friends. After a series of tragic events, however, the friends no longer connect, and ultimately Bryon must make a decision that may totally destroy their relationship. Bryon has changed. Times have changed. But there is no turning back for Bryon or for Mark.

Hinton says she was far more disciplined in the writing of this second novel, and critics generally agree that it shows more technical skill than was evident in *The Outsiders,* perhaps because of her maturation in age and writing style.

The title of the novel underscores its major theme: change. After the murder of a close friend and the destruction of another through drugs, Bryon's values, including his loyalty to Mark, alter dramatically. Similarly, other protagonists—Ponyboy (*The Outsiders*) and Travis (*Taming the Star*

Runner)—not only survive devastating events but change as a result of them.

Rumble Fish

Rumble Fish is the story of fourteen-year-old Rusty-James, who poses as a tough, cool guy yet cannot find a place for himself in a changing world. He longs for the old times when gangs were big in his neighborhood, though he was then too young to participate in them. His older brother, Motorcycle Boy, was the quintessential gang leader then, and it is Motorcycle Boy whom Rusty-James idolizes. Through a series of random and often violent events as well as through his relationship with Motorcycle Boy, Rusty-James seeks an identity for himself.

Rumble Fish is different from Hinton's other books in that its story is carried by seemingly random and impressionistic scenes instead of a linear progression of events. Though it received mixed responses from critics, Hinton believes that, while writing the book was a major challenge, it is perhaps her highest accomplishment. "*Rumble Fish* is the story I'm proudest of as far as its being a literary achievement," she has said. "It was hard to write because I ended up choosing a narrator that wasn't articulate or observant, and I still chose a pretty complicated story to tell."

impressionistic characterized by details and mental associations

Rusty-James's search for identity is an underlying theme in *Rumble Fish*. He wants to be somebody, to go somewhere in life, but he cannot figure out how to do either. Throughout the story he seeks an identity of his own. When being tough and cool does not work out for him and Motorcycle Boy is killed, Rusty-James ends up disillusioned, aimless, and adrift. Happily, other characters in Hinton's books achieve greater success in finding themselves. Though both Ponyboy and Bryon confront tragic events, each of them becomes strengthened in his sense of self.

Tex

Tex is another departure for Hinton. It is the first of her novels in which gang life is notably absent. Here she focuses instead on the development of fourteen-year-old Tex McCormick and his relationship with his older brother Mason, who must fill in for their wandering cowboy father. Tex's life is complicated by his resentment of his brother's authority, his problems at school, and his unexpected confrontations with violence and death.

Of all Hinton's characters, Tex seems to be most grounded. He seems to know who he is and what he wants out of life. Hinton describes Tex as her favorite character because, "bless his heart, he was so determined to be happy no matter what happens to him. He's the strongest one of my characters in a lot of ways."

> *Tex is Hinton's favorite character because, "bless his heart, he was so determined to be happy no matter what happens to him. He's the strongest one of my characters in a lot of ways."*

Underlying *Tex* and Hinton's other novels is the theme of abandonment. In each of her novels, parents are dead or otherwise absent, or present but uninvolved. Tex's mother died when he was a baby, and Tex's "father" is a wandering cowboy who returns home but fails to act responsibly either at home or away. Understandably, Tex constantly worries that he will be left alone if Mason goes to college or that someday his father will not come home. The parents of the Curtis boys in *The Outsiders* have died in an automobile accident. In *That Was Then, This Is Now,* Mark's parents have killed each other in a family argument. Bryon's father is gone or dead, and his mother spends much of the story in the hospital with an unexplained ailment or at home giving most of her attention to animals instead of the boys. Rusty-James's mom, in *Rumble Fish,* has abandoned her children for a chance at stardom. His father is at home, but since he is an alcoholic, he hardly seems present, much less an influence. And in *Taming the Star Runner,* Travis' father has died in Vietnam, and his stepfather, Stan, appears in the novel only long enough to kick Travis out of the home. His mother, an abused wife, interacts with him only minimally and marginally by telephone.

Taming the Star Runner

In *Taming the Star Runner,* Travis Harris is finally banished to his Uncle Ken's ranch after a brutal fight with his stepfather, resulting first in a short stay at a juvenile home. Travis' uncle is a lawyer with problems of his own—a marriage on the rocks and the challenge of raising a young son—but he welcomes Travis and provides him with a home and a stable relationship. Still, Travis must come to grips with his feelings of abandonment by his mother and hatred for his stepfather as well as his loneliness in a new town and a new school. Ultimately, it is his faith in himself and in his talent as a writer that sustains him.

Movie Adaptations

Hinton's first book to become a movie was *Tex,* with Matt Dillon playing the lead. Hinton was involved in the casting and scriptwriting. She cast her own horse, Toyota, in the role of Tex's horse, Negrito, and was herself cast as the typing teacher in the film.

The Outsiders was filmed next, with Francis Ford Coppola directing and Hinton consulting. While filming *The Outsiders,* Hinton and Coppola wrote the script for the movie *Rumble Fish,* which quickly followed. Dillon starred in both movies, as did Hinton, though Hinton appeared in contrasting roles: She played a nurse in *The Outsiders* and a prostitute in *Rumble Fish*.

That Was Then, This Is Now is the only film in which Hinton did not participate. Emilio Estevez, a star in both *Tex* and *The Outsiders,* wrote the screenplay and starred in the film.

The film adaptation of *The Outsiders* (1983) launched the careers of many of today's popular actors, including Patrick Swayze, Tom Cruise, Ralph Macchio, Emilio Estevez, Matt Dillon, and C. Thomas Howell.

The Legacy

Hinton has written five fine novels, enough to justify an important place in the history of literature for young adults. But the field may well owe her a larger debt: she broke away from the romantic novels of the 1950s and 1960s that featured teenagers going to dances or holding hands after their third date or making the winning basket in the big game, teens who, in other words, existed more in books than in real life. Hinton changed all of that, portraying teens who experience and even cause death, who live with little or no parental guidance, who are in gangs.

But her characters are not "bad" kids. They exhibit noble virtues, such as loyalty to each other and to their families. Nor are they unusual in their longings. Like most teenagers, they wonder about themselves, their identities, and their relationships. They suffer through the pains of abandonment, of change from what was to what is. In other words, they are real.

That is Hinton's legacy. She wrote novels about real people and set the literary stage for many who followed in her literary wake: Robert Cormier, Paul Zindel, and Chris Crutcher, among others, whose novels have the same hard edge as hers, the same real people. Life for these people may not always be what they would like it to be. Endings sometimes are unhappy. But few young people who read the works of Hinton and the authors who followed can ever doubt that the characters being described are indeed like people they know. And that is why they keep reading, why Hinton has earned and richly deserves the high status she enjoys. She is indeed the grande dame of adolescent fiction.

Selected Bibliography

WORKS BY S. E. HINTON

Novels for Young Adults

The Outsiders (1967)

That Was Then, This Is Now (1971)

Rumble Fish (1975)

Tex (1979)

Taming the Star Runner (1988)

WORKS ABOUT S. E. HINTON

Commire, Anne, ed. "S. E. Hinton." In *Something About the Author.* Detroit: Gale Research, 1990, vol. 58.

Daly, Jay. *Presenting S. E. Hinton.* Boston: Twayne, 1987.

Lesniak, James G., ed. "S. E. Hinton." In *Contemporary Authors New Revision Series.* Detroit: Gale Research, 1991, vol. 32.

Senick, Gerard J., ed. "S. E. Hinton." In *Children's Literature Review.* Detroit: Gale Research, 1991, vol. 23.

If you like the works of S. E. Hinton, you might also like the works of Robert Cormier, Chris Crutcher, Paul Zindel, Will Hobbs, Chris Lynch, and Ted Taylor.

How to Write to the Author

S. E. Hinton
c/o Bantam Doubleday Dell Publishing Group, Inc.
1540 Broadway
New York, NY 10036

Will Hobbs

(1947-)

by Edgar H. Thompson

I think most readers want to believe that writers of books they love are the kind of people they would be comfortable calling a friend. Will Hobbs is such a writer and such a person. His passion for the wilderness and his unswerving respect for young adults come through clearly in his novels. Both of these qualities are a direct result of his upbringing and the rich variety of his life experience.

Journey to a Writing Life

William Carl Hobbs was born 22 August 1947 in Pittsburgh, Pennsylvania, to Gregory J. and Mary (Rhodes) Hobbs. Shortly after his birth, his father, who was in the air force, was transferred to the Panama Canal Zone, and thus began a series of moves that would allow Hobbs to live in many places. When he was four, his family moved to Falls Church, Virginia, and shortly thereafter moved to Anchorage, Alaska.

Armstrong Sperry is a writer of children's books. He is best known for ***Call It Courage*** (1940). It is the story of a ten-year-old boy who overcomes his fear of the sea.

According to Hobbs, while in Alaska, "I imprinted on mountains, during my second- through fifth-grade years. That's where I fell in love with reading, too, when my fourth-grade teacher read *Call It Courage* aloud to the class" ("A Conversation with Will Hobbs," p. 244).

After four years in Alaska, Hobbs and his family moved to Marin County in the San Francisco Bay Area. He continued to interact with nature there: "I'd roam in the hills [around Terra Linda], exploring, catching lizards in a noose I'd fashion from a long oat shoot. Strictly catch-and-release" ("A Conversation," p. 244). After two subsequent moves to San Bernardino, California, and San Antonio, Texas, where Hobbs completed his first three years of high school, he and his family returned to Marin County. He then went to Stanford University and completed both a B.A. and an M.A. in English.

In 1971, Hobbs went to Mendocino County north of the Bay Area to visit some friends and study for his written comprehensive exams at Stanford. While there, Hobbs met his wife, Jean Loftus, who is originally from Minnesota. As Hobbs puts it, they took a trip to try to find a place to live:

> First we went up to look at Idaho and then came back, and I worked a semester as a long-term substitute teacher in Upper Lake, a little town in northern California. Then Jean found a job teaching in a boarding school in New Mexico, in the mountains about thirty-five miles out of Santa Fe. I'd always wanted to get back to northern New Mexico, where I had worked as a guide at Philmont Scout Ranch for four summers during late high school and early college. ("A Conversation," p. 244)

After getting his teaching certificate at New Mexico Highlands University in Las Vegas, New Mexico, he and Jean found a piece of land and moved to southwestern Colorado. He taught English for two years at Pagosa Springs High School and then taught two years at the junior high. "After that time I had another run at a Ph.D. in English, this time at the University of Oregon. . . . But we got powerfully homesick for southwestern Colorado" ("A Conversation," pp.

244–245). They returned to Colorado and have been there ever since. After twelve more years of teaching in the Durango area, Hobbs started writing full-time in 1990 to finish *Downriver.* They live in a house that he built himself over a ten-year period.

Living and scouting in Alaska were pivotal influences on Hobbs's love for things wild. One remembrance that Hobbs cites is fishing the Kenai River with his father and brothers:

pivotal   of central importance

> My Dad would take us down there fishing; we'd take off from Anchorage around four in the morning, and he would drive us down there to go fishing. I was always getting my line fouled up. It was amazing fishing, if you could only keep your line in the water. My Dad had these three sons in a row; at that time I would have been around eight and my brothers nine and ten. All three of us would have our lines kinked up. But my father never cut the line . . . he would undo all those knots and kinks. I must have learned a lot of patience from my father—a trait writers need in good supply. ("A Conversation," p. 245)

It was not just patience Hobbs was learning. He was also intimately connecting with nature. "I remember the beauty of the river and the mountains, the feeling of the place becoming a part of me. I think that feeling started there. I remember when the ship pulled out as we were leaving Alaska, I was standing at the stern and watching the mountains recede, and the tears were streaming down my face" ("A Conversation," p. 245).

Scouting took on great importance when Hobbs and his family returned to California. Hobbs and his brothers were very active in the Boy Scouts. "In the summers we'd go to camp for two weeks in the Sierras. The first week you'd do all kinds of activities around the base camp, then you'd do a week's backpacking trip into the mountains" ("A Conversation," p. 245). These backpacking trips gave him numerous images that have found their way into his books. For instance, "the mountains around Emigrant Gap were strewn with mining debris left by the forty-niners. My fascination with mining history—which showed up later in *Bearstone*

Hobbs on nature:"I remember the beauty of the river and the mountains, the feeling of the place becoming a part of me. . . . I was standing at the stern [of the ship] and watching the mountains recede, and the tears were streaming down my face."

and *Beardance,* goes back to these first hikes in the Sierras" (p. 245). His love of nature has affected the plots and settings of his other novels as well.

Journeys to Wild Places: Hobbs's Books

Hobbs's first published novel was not the first one he wrote. He first started with *Bearstone,* his second published novel, in 1980, and the book went through six drafts over an eight-year period. After receiving several rejections and some encouragement, he went to a writer's workshop in Aspen, Colorado, where he worked with the writer Russell Banks. Two important things happened. Banks, who had read some of Hobbs's letters of rejection, said that even the little encouragement the publishers had given showed they were taking him seriously. This caused Hobbs to go back home to study the craft of writing even harder. The second thing that happened at that conference was that he wrote a short story that would become his first published novel, *Changes in Latitudes* (1988).

In *Changes in Latitudes* sixteen-year-old Travis, his younger brother Teddy, and sister Jennifer accompany their mother on a vacation in Mexico. Their father stays home. As the lyrics from the Jimmy Buffet song—"Changes in Latitudes, Changes in Attitudes"—suggest, this novel is about working through problems and changing perspectives. Travis, cocky and self-absorbed, is looking for good times and imagines meeting an exotic stranger, a woman, while on vacation. His mother is trying to decide what to do about her marriage, and, as Travis discovers, has arranged a liaison with another man while she is in Mexico. Jennifer, who is fourteen, tries to keep the family together.

Shocked and angry at what he has learned about his mother, Travis avoids his problems by agreeing to help his nine-year-old brother Teddy locate the endangered sea turtles Teddy knows are nesting near their resort. Together Travis and Teddy come upon an awful secret about the turtles, and Teddy desperately tries to save them. Travis learns through a tragic accident involving Teddy just how much his family means to him.

Bearstone, Hobbs's second published novel, is about the relationship between Cloyd Atcitty, a Ute Indian boy, and

The **Ute** are an American Indian group located in Utah, Colorado, and New Mexico.

Walter Landis, a retired rancher who has recently lost his wife. They both need each other. Cloyd has been sent to a group home in Colorado, and when this does not work out, he is sent to Walter's ranch. At first Cloyd distrusts the attention Walter gives him and tests Walter's care and concern in many ways, but he eventually comes to trust the old man.

Near the ranch Cloyd finds a small carved bearstone in an ancient burial cave and gives himself a secret name, Lone Bear. Together Cloyd and Walter head for the mountains, Walter to reopen his old gold mine and Cloyd to fulfill his dream of visiting the high country where his ancestors once lived. Cloyd tries unsuccessfully to stop a hunter from killing the last grizzly bear in Colorado, but he is able to rescue Walter from a mining accident. The wilderness portions of the novel are set in one of Hobbs's favorite backpacking destinations, the Weminuche Wilderness area, close to his Colorado home.

Having rowed his whitewater raft through the Grand Canyon nine times himself, Hobbs's wrote his third novel, *Downriver* (1991), with considerable personal knowledge of the setting. An adventure story set in the mountains of the Four Corners area and in the Grand Canyon, *Downriver* is also a study in relationships among teenagers. The story is told by fifteen-year-old Jessie who grows from a troubled, egocentric teenager to a maturing young woman.

A group of seven troubled teens have been sent to an outdoor education program they call "Hoods in the Woods." They conspire to steal all the rafting equipment their leader has ready for their next trip and then ditch the leader to run the dangerous whitewater of the Colorado River on their own. Jessie, angry at her father and threatened by his new girlfriend, is drawn to the magnetic charm of Troy, the group's most powerful personality. As they travel downriver, Jessie learns just how evil Troy is, and begins to think and make decisions herself.

It is no accident that the conflicts and changes in this novel take place in a natural setting. According to Hobbs, "As I write about the crucial choices facing young people today, their struggle for identity, their relations with others, I hope also to be increasing their awareness of their relationship with the natural world" (author biography provided by Atheneum). The natural world Jessie and her friends find themselves in does not pamper them. Instead, it forces them to deal with each other in new ways. As a result, the central characters all acquire an appreciation for nature. Further, without consciously understanding why, as these characters come into a closer harmony with nature, they also get more in touch with themselves individually, with each other, and with the world around them. An adventurous trip downriver becomes a trip toward new relationships, toward hope for the future, toward maturity.

"I am glad I shall never be young without wild country to be wild in," a line from Aldo Leopold's *A Sand County Almanac,* provided an important part of the original inspiration for *The Big Wander* (1992), Hobbs's fourth novel. Set in 1962, *The Big Wander* tells the story of Clay Lancaster, who at age fourteen is the same age as Hobbs was that year. Clay and his older brother, Mike, leave Seattle in Mike's old truck and travel to the Four Corners area, where Colorado, Utah, Arizona, and New Mexico touch. They are searching for their uncle, a former rodeo cowboy. More than that, however, Clay has dreamed for years of going off on this "big wander" trip with his brother, hoping to visit the West he had known only in old John Wayne movies. Mike, lonesome for his girlfriend, goes back home and leaves Clay in Monument Valley, Arizona, working at a trading post.

The Navajo are an American Indian group located in Arizona and New Mexico.

What follows is a wonderful outdoor adventure that takes Clay, his burro named Pal, and his little dog, Curly, into the heart of the Navajo reservation, a land of red rock and canyons. Clay is helped by a Navajo family who knew his uncle and is eventually reunited with his Uncle Clay in Escalante, Utah. This book has it all—adventure, suspense, meeting new people and making friends, learning about other cultures, and romance, as Clay and his new friend Sarah help his uncle rescue wild mustangs from potential slaughter. Hobbs calls *The Big Wander* "a song of innocence, with such a whimsical tone and so many comic incidents" ("On the Beautiful Trail," p. 6).

Beardance, the sequel to *Bearstone,* finds Cloyd and Walter still together and making their way up the Pine River into the high country of southwestern Colorado in search of a lost Spanish gold mine. After they set up camp, Cloyd goes off by himself in search of a mother grizzly bear with three cubs that have been seen in the mountains. With the help of a woman named Ursa, a bear biologist, he finds the bears. When the mother and one cub are accidentally killed, Cloyd decides to stay in the mountains to help the two remaining cubs survive until winter and their hibernation. He succeeds, but only after facing many obstacles, such as starvation and being buried by an avalanche. In *Beardance,* Hobbs merges a rich texture of detail into a tightly constructed narrative. Hobbs had a hard time finding the starting point for this novel. "Usually I keep pushing all the way through a draft, but this time I kept rewriting the [first] seven chapters, knowing something was wrong but unable to put my finger on it" ("Interview with Will Hobbs: How His Novels Come into Being," p. 8). He and his wife, Jean, decided to hike back up to the real-life setting for *Beardance,* to the Window on the Continental Divide. Once there, Hobbs saw immediately what he had to do:

narrative a story told in fiction, nonfiction, poetry, or drama

> I got fired up about the writing, I'll tell you that. I went back home, and I threw away the seven original chapters, and I began with the boy and the old man riding into the mountains. In the first line of the book, Cloyd asks, "Do you think there could still be any grizzlies in the mountains?" When I started with that line, it was a magic key for this novel. The story took off at a gallop, and I had to hang onto my hat because I was writing all day long, just trying to keep up. I was in a sort of trance; I'd never experienced anything like it before. In less than a month the story was done. ("Interview with Will Hobbs," p. 9)

A companion piece to *Bearstone* and *Beardance,* Hobbs's picture book *Beardream* tells the story of the first beardance.

Hobbs's sixth novel, *Kokopelli's Flute,* is his first fantasy novel. "At first I simply wanted to write about ancient seeds. . . . Well, ancient seeds automatically brought Kokopelli to mind, the ancient humpbacked flute player" ("Interview with Will Hobbs," p. 9) whose image occurs all over the Southwest on rock formations.

fantasy novel a literary work with imaginary characters and places (such as stories involving unreal creatures and supernatural events)

> According to tradition, it was Kokopelli who brought the seeds in prehistoric times from village to village. So right away I was thinking fantasy, with this visitor from the past. He comes into the life of a boy who lives on the seed farm, after the boy has accidentally gotten involved with some ancient magic. By day Tep

is a 13-year-old boy; by night he's a bushy-tailed wood rat. (Tep is short for Tepary; his parents have named him after a hardy dryland bean.) There are a lot of animal characters in this story, and definitely a lot of adventure. ("Interview with Will Hobbs," p. 9)

Conclusion

Hobb's seventh novel, *Far North* (1996) is a winter survival story set on the South Nahanni River in Canada's Northwest Territories. *Ghost Canoe,* his eighth novel, is a mystery that takes place on the Olympic Peninsula of Washington state. In 1996, Hobbs was working on *River Thunder,* a sequel to *Downriver.* Hobbs believes that "there's a part of the human heart that longs for wild places" (*Voices from the Middle,* p. 17), and he takes joy in the knowledge that he can take his readers to these wild places in his books.

If you like Will Hobbs, you might also like Gary Paulsen, Ted Taylor, and Jean Craighead George.

Selected Bibliography

WORKS BY WILL HOBBS

Novels

Changes in Latitudes (1988; 1993)

Bearstone (1989; 1991)

Downriver (1991; 1992)

The Big Wander (1992; 1994)

Beardance (1993; 1995)

Kokopelli's Flute (1995)

Beardream, picture book (1996)

Articles

"Living and Writing *Bearstone.*" *California Reader* winter 1992, pp. 15–16.

"Developing an Authentic Young Adult Voice." *SIGNAL Journal,* spring 1994, pp. 14–18.

"On the Beautiful Trail We Go: The Story Behind *The Big Wander.*" *ALAN Review,* fall 1994, pp. 5–9.

"Denning with the Great Bear: The Story Behind the Writing of *Beardance.*" *Voices from the Middle,* April 1996, pp. 17–18.

"Survival: Micro and Macro." *Horn Book,* March/April 1996, pp. 174–177.

WORKS ABOUT WILL HOBBS

Atheneum author biography, New York: Atheneum, 1994.
Scales, Pat. "Book Strategies: *Bearstone* and *Beardance* by Will Hobbs." *Book Links,* May 1994, pp. 21–26.
Thompson, Edgar H. "How to Read a Novel Critically." *SIGNAL Journal,* winter 1993, pp. 10–11.
———. "The Revelation of Character in Will Hobbs's *Bearstone.*" *SIGNAL Journal,* winter 1993, pp. 9–12.
———. "From Egocentrism to Maturity in Will Hobbs's *Downriver:* One Girl's Journey." *Virginia English Bulletin,* fall 1994, pp. 65–69.
———. "Interview with Will Hobbs: How His Novels Come into Being." *ALAN Review,* fall 1994, pp. 7–9.
———. "A Conversation with Will Hobbs." *Journal of Youth Services in Libraries,* spring 1995, pp. 243–249.
———. Katz, Claudia. "Outsider Within a Culture." *Illinois Reading Council Journal,* summer 1995, pp. 51–56.

How to Write to the Author
Will Hobbs
c/o Simon & Schuster
Children's Publishing
Division
1230 Avenue of the
Americas
New York, NY 10020

Isabelle Holland

(1920-   )

by Lucy Rollin

Isabelle Holland says laughingly that the two questions students most often ask her when she visits schools are "How old are you?" and "How much money do you make?" She never gives the answers to those questions; she lets students figure them out for themselves. She is much more interested in answering questions about her childhood, her career, and her craft: writing.

Quotations from Isabelle Holland that are not attributed to a published source are from telephone interviews conducted by the author of this article on 27 March 1995 and 9 May 1995 and are published here by permission of Isabelle Holland.

A Child, a Foreigner

Because Holland's father was an officer in the U.S. Foreign Service, she spent much of her childhood abroad. She was born in Basel, Switzerland, but her early memories center on Guatemala, where the family moved when she was three and her brother was twelve. There they lived in a large compound that included the consulate. She spent her days visiting Cristoforo Colombo Park with her New York-born Irish

consulate residence of an official appointed by a government to help its citizens who live in a foreign country

131

American nanny, playing with friends outdoors, and watching people visiting and conducting business on the street—all the pleasures of a warm climate and friendly neighbors.

She also remembers the political unrest—there were many "minirevolutions"—and the frequent earthquakes. When the pictures on the wall began to shake, her mother would herd the family to safety. Holland once saw the roof of a house flying through the air. She also remembers a Boston bull terrier puppy named Chippy, a feisty little dog who was given to her family by a man they had sheltered during a revolution. That man later became the president of Guatemala.

When Holland was seven, her father was transferred to Liverpool, England. She remembers this period as the most **desolate** alone and   desolate of her life. Her parents were out a great deal at gov-
gloomy   ernment functions; her brother had returned to the United States; and Dolly, her beloved Irish nanny who had cared for her as long as she could remember, had left to get married. The servants in their English household offered no friendship, so she spent long spring and summer evenings alone, looking out at the cool English sky and empty English streets and remembering the warmth and bustle of Guatemala. Eventually, she attended an English boarding school, but she remembers mostly feeling awkward and foreign. She spent two years at the University of Liverpool, but as the threat of war grew, her father decided to send her to the United States with her mother. It was the first time she had lived in her own country, and once again she felt like a foreigner.

Holland attended Tulane University, first majoring in history but graduating with a degree in English literature. For a brief time, she worked for the U.S. War Department. In 1944, she moved to New York City to take a job in publishing. There she worked as a secretary and assistant in various jobs, mostly in magazines, and later as publicity director for publishers such as Crown, Lippincott, Dell, and Putnam. In her spare time, she began writing short stories and sending them to publishers, only to have them rejected. Her disappointment led her to stop writing for a while, but she found that she missed it. She then wrote two novels: *Cecily* (1967), which was published as an adult book, and *Amanda's Choice* (1970), published as a children's book. The success of these two books encouraged her to quit her publishing jobs and turn to writing full time.

Cecily and *Amanda's Choice* appeared during the time that writers for a young-adult audience were first attracting the notice of publishers and critics. S. E. Hinton, Paul Zindel, and Ann Head were producing works that appealed directly to teens. Although she did not plan it that way, with her third novel, Holland joined their ranks. *The Man Without a Face* (1972) made literary history as a young-adult novel and remains controversial today.

There is an article about S. E. Hinton in volume 2, and an article about Paul Zindel in volume 3.

Her Most Famous Novel

Holland has said that *The Man Without a Face* was the easiest book she ever wrote: it took only three months, and she had no idea that she was doing anything courageous. Told in the witty voice of her young narrator, the story concerns the friendship between Charles, a lonely fourteen-year-old boy who has had a succession of stepfathers, and Justin, a reclusive teacher and writer with a horribly scarred face who is revealed late in the novel to be homosexual. Although the novel takes place during one summer in New York, Holland says that she took an English view of this relationship, based on the hero worship she saw in the boarding schools there.

Charles has no strong male presence in his life; his real father is only a vague memory, and at home he is surrounded by women and girls. Justin is strong, intelligent, and kind, with the masculine authority that Charles has missed. Into Charles's love for Justin goes all the love he might have had for his absent father. When his cat is killed—the final blow in a series of incidents at home—Charles flees to Justin's house and spends the night in his bed. Holland poetically describes his emotions. The next day he is overcome with guilt and rejects Justin. Many months later he realizes the value of his friendship, only to learn that Justin has died.

Holland's editor required little revision of the book, asking her to remove only a few curse words before publication. When the book appeared, however, Charles's language was not at issue. Holland was both hailed and vilified as a breaker of sexual taboos in literature for young readers. Some critics thought she had handled homosexuality with taste, discretion, and psychological accuracy. Others complained about having a child seducer as a major character in a young-adult novel. Critics disagreed, and still disagree,

narrator speaker or character who tells a story

reclusive marked by a withdrawal from society

On **The Man Without a Face***: Holland does acknowledge that Justin is a flawed hero, but for her, Justin's acceptance of his own flaws is proof of his heroism.*

about whether Justin actually seduces Charles and about whether there is an act of love between them. Holland herself says she did not write a seduction or a mutual act of love, pointing to the conversation the following morning between Justin and Charles as proof. Many intelligent young-adult readers of the novel today are surprised to find that sexual seduction is a possible interpretation and see Justin as a father to Charles, as well as a fictional character worthy of respect.

Holland does acknowledge that Justin is a flawed hero, but for her, Justin's acceptance of his own flaws is proof of his heroism. In this regard, the 1993 Mel Gibson film of *The Man Without a Face* disappointed her. Although she admires Gibson's performance as Justin and the excellence of the film as a whole, she believes that the film avoided the most important theme of the novel, expressed in Charles's memory of Justin's words to him: "You can be free of everything but the consequences of what you do."

A Varied and Busy Career

The years after 1972 and *The Man Without A Face* were extremely busy ones for Holland. She published other young-adult novels, such as *Heads You Win, Tails I Lose* (1973), *Alan and the Animal Kingdom* (1977), *Hitchhike* (1977), and *Now Is Not Too Late* (1980). All were praised for their excellent writing and sensitive approach to the lives and problems of teenagers. She also began writing novels for adult audiences, in particular a series of Gothic romance and mystery tales, which generally involve a heroine in danger in a mysterious setting. Critics and readers liked these books, finding them well written and always interesting—perfect reading for relaxation. Holland says that these novels would interest young adults, as well, if they enjoy romances such as Danielle Steele's.

After *The Man Without a Face,* the novel by Holland that has most attracted the critics' attention is *Of Love and Death and Other Journeys,* which she wrote in 1975. It tells the story of Meg, who enjoys a vagabond life in Italy with her free-spirited mother. Meg has never met her father. When she discovers that her mother is dying of cancer and her father is coming to visit, she faces grief and hope at once. The book

Gothic relating to a style of fiction characterized by remote and mysterious settings

is a remarkable balance of humor and sadness, peopled with unusual and completely human characters, and touching every emotion in the reader. It was nominated for a National Book Award, a particularly high honor for a work of fiction that was written for a young-adult audience. Holland says it is being considered for a film.

During the 1980s and early 1990s, Holland published two or three and sometimes even four books a year, moving easily among young-adult fiction, novels for adults, and books for children. A series of mystery novels places a female Episcopal priest in the role of detective; one of her children's books, *Kevin's Hat* (1984), gently and humorously shows children the danger of listening to others too much; and her young-adult novel *Perdita* (1983) deals with a girl who has lost her memory. Despite the variety of their subject matter, Holland's books all have in common strong characterizations, fast-paced plots, and a concern with inner life.

Favorite Themes

Although Holland regards the story as the most important element in her books, saying she does not write about ideas, certain themes do recur. If any one unites all her work, it is the theme of being an outsider. In *The Man Without a Face,* Justin McLeod's horribly scarred face and self-imposed exile from society make him the prototype of an outsider, but most of her major characters find themselves outsiders in one way or another. From *Cecily,* her first novel, about an overweight girl in a boarding school full of slim athletic types, to *The Journey Home,* her 1990 story of two girls who go West on an orphan train, Holland's characters know what it feels like to be different. Sometimes the difference is physical, as is Jocelyn's blindness in *The Unfrightened Dark* (1990) or, more fantastically, as in her children's book about a green boy, *Green Andrew Green* (1984). More often the difference is internal, a sense that the characters just do not fit into their surroundings. Holland can create this feeling because she knows it so well, having experienced a childhood outside her own country and an adolescence as a foreigner even in her own country.

Perhaps because this loneliness is a central presence in Holland's books, another theme also appears often: taking

> *Most of Holland's major characters find themselves outsiders in one way or another. Her characters know what it feels like to be different.*

responsibility. Critics have sometimes accused Holland of being too obviously moral in the ways she reveals this theme, but its appearance is inevitable when characters must fend for themselves in a sometimes hostile world. She believes that what people do matters, whether those people are old or young. For example, Pud in *Hitchhike* comes to understand that she has caused other people a great deal of pain and trouble when she decided to hitchhike home. She discovers that responsibility is a "stone-heavy word," which breaks apart into cause and effect.

Holland often shows the growth of responsibility in her young characters through pets, a realistic way to demonstrate that caring for another living being requires dedication. Pud ends up taking on a stray dog for her hitchhike journey; Alan learns that he can not be completely independent and also care for his assortment of pets in *Alan and the Animal Kingdom.* An animal lover herself, Holland understands that the acceptance and love of a pet can comfort a lonely person, but that with the love comes responsibility.

> *Holland often shows the growth of responsibility in her young characters through pets, a realistic way to demonstrate that caring for another living being requires dedication.*

Happy to Be a Craftsperson

Holland sold her first piece of writing when she was thirteen, to an English children's magazine sponsoring a contest. She wrote a three-hundred-word story called "Naughty Betty," about a girl who, like Holland herself, hated practicing the piano, and Holland won a book as a prize. After that, she tried writing a novel about a New Orleans gambler but could not figure out how to end it. During the years of rejections for her short stories, she learned two things that still serve her well: she does not try to foresee the end of a plot, and she writes every day, even if it is only a page. Some writers outline their stories before they write; this approach, for Holland, results in complete boredom. She enjoys the unexpected characters who appear out of her imagination, the unforeseen twists of plot that appear on their own. When her writing gets blocked, she just keeps writing whatever comes to her, knowing she can always change it. She often rewrites at her editor's request, or because she prefers the short word to the long one and wants to avoid long passages of description, always aiming for economy.

Holland turned relatively late from writing on a typewriter to using a word processor, and now she enjoys not

having to pay a typist to have her work readied for her publisher. When she tried out her first laptop in the computer
store, she quickly wrote a paragraph that just appeared in
her imagination. When she took a new laptop home, she
kept thinking about that paragraph, still on the display model
in the store. She called the store and asked them to send her
the printout, and it became the opening paragraph for her
1988 suspense novel, *Bump in the Night,* which has also
been made into a television movie. Such lucky moments
make her glad she is a craftsperson in the writing trade.

At Heart Young

Holland lives in New York. As she has for years, she writes
every morning, after feeding her cats. After lunch she goes
out for necessary errands and to see friends; she finds that
the hermit life of some writers is not her style. She walks
everywhere. At home while doing chores she watches a
news channel on television, and to relax in the evening, she
often reads a novel of historical fiction or suspense. She enjoys the work of Mary Stewart and of P. D. James.

P. D. James writes
detective novels.
Mary Stewart writes
romance and adven-
ture novels.

As of 1996, Holland had written fifty books. In the 1990s,
her projects have sprung from her interest in the Irish in New
York during the late nineteenth century, an ethnic group that
suffered from discrimination well into the twentieth century.
She thinks this interest results partly from her memories of her
beloved Irish nanny and also from a course she took recently
in the history of Manhattan. She has written about the bloody
draft riots in New York City during July 1863 and is writing the
sequel to *The Journey Home,* in which an Irish uncle comes to
Kansas to fetch Mag and Annie. Once again, through this uncle, the theme of being an outsider enters Holland's work. She
also included many fragments of her own life in her 1994
novel for adults, *Family Trust,* a fast-paced story of a family
dealing with personal and political troubles.

Holland still thinks fondly of Guatemala, although she
has not returned since her childhood. As she rides the New
York buses through the crowded streets, she is reminded of
the life she enjoyed as a child in Guatemala. She sometimes
travels to Italy to visit a friend's castle there, or she visits her
brother's family in the southern United States.

Once a week Holland teaches a course, for New York
University's continuing education program, in writing for

There is an article about C. S. Lewis in volume 2.

young readers. Most of her students are adults, and she finds that those who are the most successful are still at heart young themselves. She believes, along with C. S. Lewis, that this is the secret for writing for a young audience. Although she has never married or had children herself, the vivid memories of her mother's storytelling still inspire her. Her mother told stories from legend, history, the Bible, and novels in a way that made them completely fresh and exciting to her child's ear. Holland feels that storytelling should most of all hold a reader's interest. This is the excitement she hopes to encourage in her students and that she wants to achieve in her own writing.

If you liked *The Man Without a Face* and have never read *The Catcher in the Rye* by J. D. Salinger, you might enjoy the resemblances between the main characters. You might also enjoy the work of Norma Klein and Norma Fox Mazer if you like Holland's books.

Selected Bibliography

WORKS BY ISABELLE HOLLAND

Novels for Young Adults

Cecily (1967)

Amanda's Choice (1970)

The Man Without a Face (1972)

Heads You Win, Tails I Lose (1973)

Of Love and Death and Other Journeys (1975)

Alan and the Animal Kingdom (1977)

Hitchhike (1977)

Dinah and the Green Fat Kingdom (1978)

Now Is Not Too Late (1980)

Perdita (1983)

The Island (1984)

The Unfrightened Dark (1990)

The House in the Woods (1991)

Novels for Adults

Kilgaren (1974)

Trelawney (1974)

Moncreiff (1975)

Darcourt (1976)

Grenelle (1976)

Tower Abbey (1978)

A Death at St. Anselm's (1984)

Flight of the Archangel (1985)

Bump in the Night (1988)

A Fatal Advent (1989)

Love and Inheritance (1991)

Family Trust (1994)

Books for Children

God, Mrs. Muskrat, and Aunt Dot (1983)

Kevin's Hat (1984)

Green Andrew Green (1984)

The Journey Home (1990)

Manuscript Papers

Holland's papers are housed in the Kerlan Collection at the University of Minnesota, Minneapolis, and in the De Grummond Collection at the University of Southern Mississippi, Hattiesburg.

Others

"The People Behind the Books: Isabelle Holland." In *Literature for Today's Young Adults.* Kenneth L. Donelson and Alleen Pace Nilson, editors. Chicago: Scott Foresman, 1980, p. 434.

"The Problem with Talking About My Writing." In *ALAN Review,* fall 1985, pp. 1–4. (This article is followed by a short biography and brief summaries of some of Holland's young-adult novels, compiled by Judith Bugniazet.)

"Tilting at Taboos," *Horn Book,* June 1983, pp. 299–305. Reprinted in *Crosscurrents of Criticism.* Edited by Paul Heins. Boston: The Horn Book, 1977, pp. 137–143. (This article is based on a speech Holland gave at an educator's conference in Massachusetts shortly after the publication of *The Man Without a Face.* It contains much information about her basic approach to writing novels.)

WORKS ABOUT ISABELLE HOLLAND

Finke, Kate. "The Breakdown of the Family: Fictional Case Studies in Contemporary Novels for Young People." In *The Lion and the Unicorn,* winter 1979–1980, pp. 86–95.

Gallo, Donald, ed. *Speaking for Ourselves.* Urbana, Ill.: National Council of Teachers of English, 1990, pp. 97–98.

Garrett, Agnes, and Helga P. McCue, editors. *Authors and Artists for Young Adults.* Detroit: Gale Research, 1993, vol. 11, pp. 81–90.

Gunton, Sharon R. "Isabelle Holland." In *Contemporary Literary Criticism,* 1982, vol. 21, pp. 147–154.

Hirsch, Corinne. "Isabelle Holland: Realism and Its Evasions in *The Man Without a Face.*" *Children's Literature in Education,* spring 1979, pp. 25–34.

Olendorf, Donna, and Diane Telgen, eds. *Something About the Author.* Detroit: Gale Research, 1993, vol. 70, pp. 91–95.

Rollin, Lucy. "Isabelle Holland: A 19th Century Romantic for 20th Century Realists." In *ALAN Review,* fall 1985, pp. 9–12.

How to Write to the Author
Isabelle Holland
1199 Park Avenue
New York, NY 10128

Monica Hughes

(1925-)

by Marilou Sorenson

Monica Hughes states that she primarily writes science fiction (plots logically based upon the universe that we know . . . Newton's laws and laws of thermodynamics . . .) but to classify her books as only that would miss the rich diversity of her work. For example in *Little Fingerling,* which is no watered-down re-telling of a cruel Japanese ceremonial folktale, Hughes has enhanced the language, details and sequence with exquisite horror. The legend of this diminutive victor, a dramatic take-off of Tom Thumb, is appropriate for older readers and reflects the essence of a dedicated picture book writer. Also, at least two of Hughes's popular award-winning novels harboring strong psychological undertones are surrounded with contemporary events. *Hunter in the Dark* is about an adolescent facing a terminal illness running away to the hills on an animal hunt to face his darkest fears. *The Ghost Dance Caper* considers a youth with mixed ethnic background (mother white, father American Indian) who searches for his own identity.

Tom Thumb is an old English nursery tale, of which there are many versions. In the English tale, Tom was as tall as a ploughman's thumb. His **dimunitive,** or small, size led him into many strange adventures. Henry Fielding (1707–1754) wrote the *Life and Death of Tom Thumb the Great* (1731).

141

The Author and Her Work

Hughes's science fiction, the majority of her work, is atypical of that genre for children and young adults where theme and setting traditionally dominate the story line. Well-developed characters are the hallmark of her writing. She contends that "truth of character" is evident in all good fiction, which she demonstrates through protagonists who are struggling with personal identity, survival, and transformation into maturity. Walt in *The Golden Aquarius* is warned about the impending cataclysm that will wipe out earthlings on the planet Aqua and Megan (like Lowry's Dicey) takes the responsibility of a younger sibling after her mother's death in *The Crystal Drop*. Olwen, in the Isis trilogy, achieves maturity and resistance to prejudice in a planet-world where population is exploding, environmental issues control reality and stimulated individuals are necessary for survival.

compunction moral anxiety or guilt

All Hughes's characters are faced with *real* problems, while living in an extravagant near-future, because it is in this setting that the solutions to the crises they face can and will be found. They attain a high level of compunction, that makes them into nearly epic heroes as they go about their conquests. There is always a "critical moment," that time when each surmounts the crisis (quite often caused by adults offstage) and returns with verve and success. While the accomplishments of the characters are magnanimous they never appear superhuman since the social and political crises are juxtaposed to a personal one. For example, Megan must cross the desert with her brother because they are abandoned but in their search for their uncle, they become adversaries to a threatened populace trying to protect what little resources they now have.

As in legends and epics, Hughes's characters meet obstacles that require a great deal of turns and twists in their lives. Most of them come out victorious, however, some are left behind scarred and battered. Even in those cases the final theme of hope and resilience prevails; but in an honest conclusion; never contrived or patronizing.

Gerald J. Rubio argues that Hughes's work is similar to Tomas More's, in that the "are moulded by the cultures in which they are reared but are then jolted into new perspectives on themselves and their environments through experiencing alternate ways of life" (*Twentieth-Century Children's Writers*, p. 473).

In Orwellian parameters, Hughes delves into reliance on technology such as computers to control the "imperfect." In *The Tomorrow City* those "outside" are programmed to become subliminal in their daily lives. The Isis trilogy contains a guardian robot which is a central thread throughout the series.

Even though Hughes deals with vigorous characters and issues in dramatic settings, . . . "There is a gentleness to her books that is rare in science fiction . . . the exotic flora and fauna, the humanoids, the vast intergalactic reaches, the villains and the heroes—all are enclosed in one overriding concern, subtle but every-present; the value of kindness . . . " (Ellis, p. 663).

Her drive for a story is the proverbial "what if . . . " What if a person lived underwater or in a planet other than his own. What if present-day events were dramatically transposed to another time and place. What if a computer program was threatening the outcome of the world. What if a child must live in isolation. (This, a real example from a news broadcast about a three-year-old condemned to spend his life isolated from contact with others because of his lack of immunity, was the impetus for the Isis trilogy.)

Orwellian pertaining to the style of George Orwell (1903–1950). He wrote *Animal Farm* (1945) and *Nineteen Eighty-Four* (1949), novels about the never-ending struggle against dictatorships.

proverbial well-known or expressed in a popular saying

impetus the driving force, or stimulus

The Isis Trilogy

Possibly her most noted work of science fiction is the Isis trilogy—*The Keeper of the Isis Light, The Guardian of the Isis,* and *The Isis Pedlar.* The "what if . . . " question is a thread throughout the three: What if a child is born in outer space (Isis) to research scientists from Earth who later die and leave her in the care of a robot. What if this robot understands the dilemma of the child Olwen who must adjust to her physical and mental changes to survive, helps her do that, but also realizes the atmospheric conditions are not conducive to other explorers who arrive from Earth. The Isis series follows the descendants of the colonizers from Earth as they deteriorate and finally turn to Olwen and her robot caretaker.

Olwen faces the same search of identity and ramification of prejudice that permeates other Hughes titles. In *Ring-Rise, Ring-Set* the author explores the merging of two cultures when one is more technically adept than the other. In this too, the setting of being underground during a future ice age, fits within the normal laws of nature as we know in this

> *Monica Hughes's mission in writing for children and young adults is to find answers to the world's Big Questions where a future could be an obvious extension of today's disasters on earth.*

world. But in that setting, the stirring question of "what if . . . " one technology could annihilate the other, enhances a relevant commentary on survival, moral and justice. In *Invitation to the Game* Lisse and seven of her classmates are put in a DA (Designated Area) where they experience life by computer simulation.

Monica Hughes's mission in writing for children and young adults is to find answers to the world's Big Questions where a future could be an obvious extension of today's disasters on earth. Continually she asks—as do her young readers—what is to be our future? What does life hold? How does technology and humanity interface? These questions are a natural outcome of her life which are directly influenced by her background.

Her Achievements

The following sketches outline the life of one of Canada's finest writers for children and young adults, Monica Hughes:

1. Born on 3 November 1925 in Liverpool, yet spending the first five years of her life in Egypt with her mathematician father (Edward Ince), mother and baby sister within the shadows of the pyramids.

2. Returning to England for her formal education. A fond memory of her favorite place to read and write, the top of a third-floor in Edinburgh. It was here that the science fiction bug bit her!

3. At age fourteen being sent to the Scottish country to avoid the threat of bombing attacks. Here she was encouraged to write fiction, essays and composition.

4. Being accepted in the Women's Royal Navy at the age of eighteen to work on war projects one of which was breaking the German code. Later she worked in meteorology in Scotland.

5. At twenty-one traveling to Southern Rhodesia to stay with a friend. "The excitement of travel is kin to the excitement of opening a new book. There is a hope, a sense of mystery in 'setting out' on a voyage exploration into the mind and imagination of a writer . . . " (Hughes, p. 155).

6. A year later returning to London, working in dress design but also beginning to "seriously" struggle with writing.

7. At twenty-seven sailed to Montreal, Canada, and in Ottawa worked as a laboratory technician at National Research Council. " . . . we spent many coffee breaks and lunches arguing over the possibility of life on Mars . . . " (Hughes, p. 157).

8. Marrying Glen Hughes, an engineer and writer of science fiction, whom she met in a writing class.

9. Becoming a Canadian citizen at the age of thirty-two.

10. Giving birth to her children, Elizabeth, Andrienne, Russell and Tom. "I promised myself that I would write uninterruptedly for four hours every weekday . . . in the morning . . . before the outside world could begin taking tiny bites of time . . . " (Hughes, p. 158).

11. Commissioned to write *Gold Fever Trail: A Klondike Adventure,* a historical novella for public school use.

12. Wrote *Crisis on Conshelf Ten,* a story of Kepler Masterman's adventure under the sea at the age of forty-nine. This was followed by the protagonists voyage to the far side of the moon in *Earthdark* at the age of fifty-two.

Each event in Hughes's life, like bytes in a computer program, has added to the resources, patterns and program of her writing. She had a home life of mathematics and astronomy (her father shared his love of stargazing with his daughter). She was a fastidious student and discovered the works of Jules Verne and other science fiction writers. She took opportunities to visit museums, and art galleries and was enthralled with her first experiences of film, ballet and theater. Her delight in finding and reading everything for children in a Carnegie library and delving into huge volumes on nineteenth-century literature are noted as important in her life.

Her service in the Women's Royal Navy (WRENS) opened new worlds of people, cultures and theories, as did the trip to Rhodesia. The ultimate search for a warm place to live ("I knew it couldn't be as cold as an unheated London apartment . . . ") led to her stay in Canada. Her discussions and understandings of the theories of the universe (which she passionately cares about) led naturally to becoming a writer of science fiction where the worlds are logically based upon the laws of thermodynamics.

Today, with over two dozen published books, Monica Hughes finds herself with thousands of unanswered questions, myriads of "what ifs" that could produce new stories, fascinating dramas. "It depends a great deal on persistent

Jules Verne (1828–1905) wrote *Journey to the Center of the Earth* (1864), *Twenty Thousand Leagues Under the Sea* (1870), and *Around the World in Eighty Days* (1873). All of these books were made into movies.

myriads great numbers

hard work, and on understanding how one's mind works . . . how to balance the necessary imaginative right brain and the equally necessary logical left brain which must turn the ideas into written words and sentences and paragraphs . . ." (Hughes, p. 162).

When the question is posed to Hughes about her continued writing she strongly responds in the affirmative. "[T]he world is full of thousands of unanswered questions and the possibilities of as many 'what ifs' as there are stars in the galaxy!" (Hughes, p. 162).

If you like the works of Monica Hughes, you might also like the works of Ursula K. Le Guin and Madeleine L'Engle.

Selected Bibliography

WORKS BY MONICA HUGHES

Novels for Young Adults

Gold Fever Trail: A Klondike Adventure, illustrated by Patricia Peacock and John LeBel (1974)

Crisis on Conshelf Ten (1975)

Earthdark (1977)

The Ghost Dance Caper (1978)

The Tomorrow City (1978)

Beyond the Dark River (1979)

Hunter in the Dark (1982)

Ring-Rise, Ring-Set (1982)

The Beckoning Lights, illustrated by Richard A. Conroy (1982)

The Treasure of the Long Sault, illustrated by Richard A. Conroy (1982)

Space Trip (1983, 1984)

My Name Is Paula Popwich! (1983)

Devil on My Back (1984, 1986)

Sand Writer (1985)

The Dream Catcher (1987)

Blaine's Way (1986)

Log Jam (1987), published in England as Spirit River (1988)

Litter Fingerling, illustrated by Brenda Clark (1989)

The Promise (1990, 1992)

Invitation to the Game (1990)

The Refuge (1990)

The Crystal Drop (1992, 1993)

The Golden Aquarius (1995)

THE ISIS TRILOGY

The Keeper of the Isis Light (1980)

The Guardian of Isis (1981)

The Isis Pedlar (1982)

ANTHOLOGIZED WORKS BY HUGHES

The Margook (1977)

Owl's Fun Book for Spring, Summer, and Fall (1982)

Out of Time (1984)

Dragons and Dreams (1985)

The Windows of Dreams (1986)

Canadian Children's Treasury (1988)

Take Your Knee Off My Heart (1990)

Mother's Day (1992)

WORKS ABOUT MONICA HUGHES

Ellis, Sarah. "News from the North." In *Horn Book,* September/October 1981, pp. 661–664.

Hughes, Monica. "Monica Hughes." In *Something About the Author Autobiography Series.* Edited by Adele Sarkissian. Detroit: Gale Research, 1991, vol. 11, pp. 149–162.

Mazurkiewicz, Margaret. "Monica (Ince) Hughes." In *Something About the Author.* Edited by Donna Olendorf and Diane Telgen. Detroit: Gale Research, 1993, vol. 70, pp. 95–100.

Rubio, Gerald J. "Monica (née Ince) Hughes." In *Twentieth-Century Children's Writers,* 3d ed. Edited by Tracy Chevalier. Chicago: St. James, 1989, 473–474.

AWARDS AND HONORS

Vicky Metcalf Award, Canadian Authors Association for body of work, 1981.

Hunter in the Dark received the Alberta Culture Juvenile Novel Award, 1981; Bay's Beaver Award, 1981; Canada Council prize for children's literature, 1982; Best Books List for Young Adults—American Library Association, 1983; Young Adult Canadian Book Award, 1983.

The Guardian of Isis was awarded the Canada Council prize for children's literature, 1981.

The Keeper of the Isis Light was named to the Best Book List for Young Adults—American Library Association, 1981, and the International Board on Books for Young People's Honor List, 1982.

Ring-Rise, Ring-Set was named runner-up for the Guardian Award, 1983.

Alberta R. Ross Annett Award from Writers Guild of Alberta, 1983, 1984, 1986; Hans Christian Andersen Award nomination, 1984.

How to write to the Author

Monica Hughes
c/o Orchard Books
95 Madison Avenue
New York, NY 10016

Mollie Hunter

(1922-)

by Betty Greenway

I grew up in a rural part of my native Scotland at a time when folklore was still very much alive. The deep vein of mysticism in the Celtic nature runs in me also, and being instinctively a storyteller with a great love of the poetic imagery in the language-structure of Celtic folktales, I have always found intense pleasure in attempting to recreate the effect of these in fantasies.

Celtic   relating to the people of Ireland, Wales, the Scottish Highlands, Cornwall, and Brittany

So says Mollie Hunter about the influence of her country's folklore, and its love of story, on her many books for young people. Whether she is writing fantasies, historical novels, or realistic novels set in the present day, Hunter shows herself to be, above all, a great storyteller. All of her books are set in Scotland (except one that is set in Ireland), and some take place in the far-distant past. Nevertheless, the books have been enduringly popular with young readers from widely

Quotations from Mollie Hunter that are not attributed to a published source are from an interview conducted by the author of this article by letter written on 30 January 1995 and are published here by permission from Mollie Hunter.

149

differing cultures and with little knowledge of the folklore and history on which Hunter draws because, as she herself comments, "I have yet to encounter one who can resist listening to a story!"

Fantasies

Mollie Hunter's first book for young people, *Patrick Kentigern Keenan* (1963; published in the United States as *The Smartest Man in Ireland*), grew out of stories she told to her two young sons. She had written poems, short stories, plays, and newspaper feature articles for adults, but she had not yet published a full-length work of any kind. The book is a series of adventures in which the title character, Patrick, a foolish, sometimes dishonest, but always funny braggart, tries to prove that he is the smartest man in Ireland by tangling with the fairy-people. These people can be beautiful and terrible in turn, but they are always formidable adversaries. Patrick is usually out-tricked by the fairies, but when they kidnap his young son, he finds within himself the courage and power to defeat them. He has the one thing the soulless creatures of the Otherworld lack—human love. He bravely passes a series of tests to defeat the fairy-people, who tempt him with their beautiful, sad voices. He emerges from the battle victorious, with his young son safely in tow. (See Hunter's essay "The Last Lord of Redhouse Castle," 1975, and her book *Talent Is Not Enough: Mollie Hunter on Writing for Children,* 1976, for a full account of the writing of her first books.)

motif situation or theme

With her first children's book, Mollie Hunter wrote the notes that are heard as a motif running through all her fantasies. First is the idea of the "Otherworld," the Celtic concept of the closeness of the supernatural. Patrick meets creatures from the fairy world all the time and expresses no surprise or alarm. There is nothing unusual in these encounters; they are simply part of the totality of life. The supernatural exists on a different plane from the human, but it is a plane with which humans interact on a daily basis.

Otherworld creatures are of two kinds. There are creatures and objects in themselves natural but thought to have supernatural powers, such as the seal. As we see in *A Stranger Came Ashore* (1975), the seal can become an attractive and hypnotic man on land in order to lure beautiful young girls to his underwater home. And there are creatures that do not exist in our world, whose form and substance, as Hunter says in *Talent Is Not Enough,* are only apparent "manifestations of a world that itself has no physical existence" (p. 71). Examples of this kind of creature in Hunter's books include the kelpie, a Celtic water spirit that can take the form of a black horse on land (*The Kelpie's Pearls,* 1964); the grollican, a fearsome creature invented by Hunter based on the conventions of Celtic folklore (*The Wicked One,* 1977); and the more familiar mermaid (*The Mermaid Summer,* 1988) and unicorn (*Day of the Unicorn,* 1994). In her essays "One World" and "The Otherworld" in *Talent Is Not Enough,* Hunter discusses the roots of this folklore in our persistent "longing for something you cannot name" (p. 102) and our need to project these longings, and our fears, on some imaginative situation or setting.

manifestations forms in which individuals are capable of being seen and heard

Another motif that appears throughout Hunter's work, and which is closely connected to the ever-present Otherworld, is the way creatures and objects transform themselves, shape-shift, so easily and so often. Fairy-people can change into any shape they wish, as they do in *Patrick Kentigern Keenan,* and they also can change others into any shape they wish. So fairy cattle turn into flies; a white hare turns into a fairy woman with a cold, terrible smile; and she turns Patrick into a hare. So seals change into men, and men change into crows, as in *A Stranger Came Ashore.* So priests turn into stone circles (like Stonehenge), and a boy can summon his own double to mislead dam builders, as in *The Bodach* (1970; published in the United States as *The Walking Stones*). In films such as *Terminator 2: Judgment Day,* where we *see* the shape-shifting in front of our eyes, we see computer technology finally catching up with ideas that have been current in our folklore for thousands of years.

In ***Terminator 2: Judgement Day,*** a cyborg, or bionic human, from the future is able to change his appearance to resemble things he touches, such as other people.

Hunter shows a concern with shape-shifting, doubling, interconnected worlds—in a larger sense with duplicity and deception—in all her works, not just the fantasies but the historical and realistic contemporary novels as well. For all her works are ultimately about the struggle between good and evil, "the destructiveness on one side and the creativeness on the other," which, as she says in an interview in *Top of the News,* is always at war within the human psyche (p. 144). And the challenge to humans is the difficult but necessary

theme central message about life in a literary work

inimicable antagonistic or hostile

task of distinguishing between them in our complex world. This is the theme that runs throughout all her work.

"In the fantasies," she goes on to explain in the interview, "there is always a confrontation scene, where the human characters are faced with the supernatural characters, who are inimicable to the lives and happiness of the human characters." But there is one weapon, as in *Patrick Kentigern Keenan,* and also in *The Haunted Mountain* (1972), *A Stranger Came Ashore, The Mermaid Summer,* and others, that humans have against the supernaturals—the power of love:

> **The supernaturals by definition are soulless creatures. They cannot understand what it is to love, and they cannot bring their supernatural magical forces to bear on it. If one has that power to love, to sacrifice, to give one's life for another human being—this is something the supernaturals cannot understand. (P. 144)**

The human power to love, and the confrontation scenes with those who cannot love link Mollie Hunter with an American writer, Madeleine L'Engle, whose *Wrinkle in Time* has characters playing out much the same conflict between good and evil, love and hate, in the same kind of testing moments.

Historical Novels

In Hunter's historical novels, too, courage, especially the courage to love and the moments when that courage is tested, becomes the central theme. She writes about her own process of reading in her youth in the article "If You Can Read" (1978): "I . . . began to see that a people's folklore is only one face of a coin of which the other face is that people's written history" (Part I, p. 258).

Hunter was born on 30 June 1922. Because her father died when she was young and her family had little money to spare for her education, she was forced to leave school at fourteen but determinedly began her own independent course of reading at the National Library of Scotland. It was there that her lifelong interest in the folklore and history of her own people began. After she wrote her first fantasies, based on Scottish folklore, she turned to her country's history for her next subjects and from then on began to alternate historical novels with fantasies. Scotland has a long and distinguished tradition in the historical novel, the best-known practitioner being Sir Walter Scott. Hunter says that therefore her path was a natural one.

The histories are rooted firmly in *this* world, not the Otherworld, but superstitions, witchcraft, duplicity, deception, and courage play as important a role as they do in the fantasies. Even though these books are set in the far-distant past, their themes are universal, as are the themes of the fantasies. In *The Ghosts of Glencoe* (1966), for example, the protagonist is faced with a difficult decision, as Hunter explains in her essay "The Last Lord of Redhouse Castle":

> **A sixteen year old ordered to kill stealthily and in cold blood the people who have been his friends is no different in 1692 from a youngster of similar age in our own and other centuries. The horns of his dilemma are still the same—to obey the law, or to follow his conscience. (P. 136)**

The dilemma is one not peculiar to any particular period of history, as we have seen in the Nuremberg trials after World War II and the My Lai trials during the Vietnam War.

The courage with which the boy in *The Ghost of Glencoe* faces that decision is similar to the courage of the boy in *A Pistol in Greenyards* (1965) caught up in the Highland "clearances," the euphemism for the forced evacuation of thousands of Scots from their native glens to make way for sheep farming, or the courage of the young page who must overcome his own selfish nature and help Mary Queen of Scots escape in *You Never Knew Her As I Did!* (1981); or the young boy who risks his life to help a girl caught between those who practiced witchcraft and those who hunted witches in *The Thirteenth Member* (1971). These and other historical novels by Hunter have in common young people caught in forces larger than themselves, struggling to locate the truth amid all the deception around them and to obey their consciences courageously.

Hunter's novels also have in common the totally accurate and honest, if sometimes ugly, bloody, and terrifying, depiction of historical events resulting from her meticulous

protagonist the main character of a literary work

The **Nuremburg trials** (1945–1949) tried German leaders for crimes comitted during World War II. The **My Lai** trials tried American soldiers for the 1968 massacre of civilians in My Lai, South Vietnam. Both trials emphasized the idea that people have a moral obligation to disobey inhumane orders or laws.

research, often of ancient and obscure firsthand accounts. She writes in *Talent Is Not Enough* that ultimately it is a good thing she did not have a formal education and instead spent all those hours in the National Library, because there was no one to tell her what to think as she learned the "quality of lives" of long-ago people from their own mouths.

Contemporary Realistic Novels

There came a time, however, when Mollie Hunter turned away from long-ago people and from ancient folklore to the time of her own childhood and to the quality of her own life. When asked what she most wanted to say to young adult readers to help them understand her and her works, Hunter wrote:

> For very many years of a long writing life I alternated the writing of fantasy with that of novels drawn from the history of my own country. These . . . were effectively "action" stories, the spur to which was my own love of adventure. Then came a time when I felt impelled (there is no other word for the experience) to express myself "in the round" as it were, by writing *A Sound of Chariots* [1972]—a book woven around a girl I called Bridie McShane but who is, in fact, myself between the ages of two and fourteen.

> As it happened also, it was this book which seemed to release in me the voice to write others—such as *The Third Eye* [1979] and *Cat, Herself* [1985]—all of which, similarly, have a female protagonist. All of these protagonists, too, are simply one or another version of Bridie McShane who—as I discovered by writing about her—was a much more many-sided character than even I, who live in her skin, had ever suspected.

All Hunter's novels portray strong-willed and outspoken but unschooled and lower-class young people on the road to self-discovery, especially the discovery of their own courage.

As Hunter's words here suggest, these three novels and *Hold On to Love* (1983), the sequel to *A Sound of Chariots,* are unified by the strong female voice.

All of Hunter's novels portray strong-willed and outspoken but unschooled and lower-class young people on the road to self-discovery, especially the discovery of their own courage, but her contemporary novels take such courage as their special focus. From Bridie's courage in coming to terms with the death of her father and persisting in her dreams of becoming a writer in *A Sound of Chariots,* to Cat's courage in fighting the conservative beliefs and traditions of her people and telling the man she loves that she will not be *ruled* by anyone, even a husband, in *Cat, Herself,* all these young women fill the need Mollie Hunter expresses in her essay "A Need for Heroes." Literature does not need any more Superman heroes, she says; what is needed is the ordinary person as hero. The three young women in these novels take their place with the other Mollie Hunter protagonists—"ordinary," yes, but courageous, especially in their caring and loving.

Fantasies for Young Children

With her books *The Knight of the Golden Plain* (1983), *The Three-Day Enchantment* (1985), and *Day of the Unicorn,* in which a young child dreams himself into the role of Sir Dauntless, Mollie Hunter has come full circle—as she observes in her entry in the *Something About the Author Autobiography Series*—from those first Patrick stories that she told to her children, to stories, in these books, that she has told to her grandchildren. In the best Scottish tradition, Hunter learned by listening to stories of her people as told by her great-grandmother, and she has passed on these and other stories to her children, her grandchildren, and to readers from many lands. She says that she has always been, most proudly, "just a storyteller" (p. 152). And her stories—like the ones about Sir Dauntless—are above all about young people who find the courage within themselves to do what they have to do.

> *Hunter says that she has always been, most proudly, "just a storyteller."*

Mollie Hunter on Writing for Young People

From her home in the Scottish Highlands, Mollie Hunter has written not only nearly thirty books of fiction for young people but also two full-length collections of essays, *Talent Is Not Enough* and *The Pied Piper Syndrome.* She also has written many essays on her career as a writer—information about her family and childhood experiences, about the influences on her writing and on her writing habits, about Scottish folklore and history, and about many other subjects that help a reader better understand her and her works. She has been extremely generous in granting interviews and responding to requests for essays about writing for young people. In all of these, we see her energy, enthusiasm, affection, and respect for her young readers—in short, a thinking and feeling *person* behind the books. Indeed, as she has been called many times, she is Scotland's most gifted storyteller.

If you like Mollie Hunter's historical novels, you might also like the novels of Madeleine L'Engle and Rosemary Sutcliff.

Selected Bibliography

WORKS BY MOLLIE HUNTER

Fantasies for Young Adults

Patrick Kentigern Keenan (1963), published in the United States as *The Smartest Man in Ireland*

The Kelpie's Pearls (1964)

Thomas and the Warlock (1967)

The Ferlie (1968); also published as *The Enchanted Whistle* (1985)

The Bodach (1970); published in the United States as *The Walking Stones*

The Haunted Mountain (1972)

A Stranger Came Ashore (1975)

A Furl of Fairie Wind: Four Stories (1977)

The Wicked One (1977)

The Knight of the Golden Plain (1983)

The Three-Day Enchantment (1985)

The Brownie (1986)

The Enchanted Boy (1986)

The Mermaid Summer (1988)

Day of the Unicorn (1994)

Historical Novels for Young Adults

Hi Johnny (1963)

The Spanish Letter (1964)

A Pistol in Greenyards (1965)

The Ghosts of Glencoe (1966)

The Lothian Run (1970)

The Thirteenth Member (1971)

The Stronghold (1974)

You Never Knew Her As I Did! (1981); also published as *Escape from Loch Leven*

Flora MacDonald and Bonnie Prince Charlie (1987)

Realistic, Contemporary Novels for Young Adults

A Sound of Chariots (1972)

The Third Eye (1979)

The Dragonfly Years (1983); published in the United States as *Hold on to Love*

I'll Go My Own Way (1985); published in the United States as *Cat, Herself*

Picture Book

Gilly Martin the Fox (1994)

Nonfiction

Talent Is Not Enough: Mollie Hunter on Writing for Children (1976)

The Pied Piper Syndrome: And Other Essays (1992)

Articles and Essays

"The Last Lord of Redhouse Castle." In *Thorny Paradise: Writers on Writing for Children.* Edited by Edward Blishen. Harmondsworth, England: Kestrel Books, 1975, pp. 128–139.

"One World."In *Horn Book,* December 1975, pp. 557–563.

"A Need for Heroes." In *Proceedings of the Children's Literature Association,* 1977, no. 4, pp. 20–24; reprinted in *Horn Book,* April 1983, pp. 146–154.

"Folklore: One Writer's View." In *Folk Literature of the British Isles: Readings for Librarians, Teachers, and Those Who Work with Children and Young Adults.* Edited by Eloise S. Norton. Metuchen, N. J.: Scarecrow Press, 1978, pp. 124–133.

"If You Can Read (Part I). In *Horn Book,* June 1978, pp. 257–262.

"If You Can Read (Part II). In *Horn Book,* August 1978, pp. 431–437.

"The Third Eye." In *Innocence and Experience: Essays and*

Conversations on Children's Literature. Compiled and edited by Barbara Harrison and Gregory Maguire. New York: Lothrop, Lee and Shepard, 1987.

Autobiography

"Mollie Hunter." In *Something About the Author Autobiography Series,* vol. 7. Edited by Adele Sarkissian. Detroit: Gale Research, 1989.

WORKS ABOUT MOLLIE HUNTER

Parts of Books

Aiken, Joan, et al. *Author's Choice 2.* New York: Crowell, 1974.

Cameron, Eleanor. *The Green and Burning Tree.* Boston: Little Brown, 1969.

de Montreville, Doris, and Donna Hill. *Third Book of Junior Authors.* New York: H. W. Wilson Co., 1972.

Kirkpatrick, D. L. *Twentieth Century Children's Writers.* New York: St. Martin's, 1978; 2d edition, 1983.

Kuznets, Lois R. "Henry James and the Storyteller: The Development of a Central Consciousness in Realistic Fiction for Children." In *The Voice of the Narrator in Children's Literature: Insights from Writers and Critics.* Edited by Charlotte F. Otten and Gary D. Schmidt. New York: Greenwood Press, 1989.

Riley, Carolyn, ed. *Contemporary Literary Criticism,* vol. 21. Detroit: Gale Research, 1982.

Ward, Martha E., and Dorothy A. Marquardt. *Authors of Books for Young People,* 2nd ed. Metuchen, N. J.: Scarecrow Press, 1971.

Articles

Cook, Stanley. "Children's Writers: 3. Mollie Hunter." *School Librarian,* June 1978, pp. 108–111.

Dooley, Patricia. "Profile: Mollie Hunter." *Children's Literature Association Quarterly,* autumn 1978, pp. 3–6.

Hickman, Janet. "Profile: The Person Behind the Book—Mollie Hunter." *Language Arts,* March 1979, pp. 302–306.

Hollindale, Peter. "World Enough and Time: The Work of Mollie Hunter." *Children's Literature in Education,* autumn 1977, pp. 109–119.

Hoffman, Mary. "Scottish Story Weaver." *Times Educational Supplement,* 13 January 1984.

Ryan, J. S. "The Spirit of Old Scotland: Tone in the Fiction of Mollie Hunter." *Orana,* May 1984, pp. 93–101; August 1984, pp. 138–145.

Shannon, George. "The Work of Keeping Writing Play: A View Through Children's Literature." *Children's Literature in Education,* March 1990, pp. 37–43.

Smedman, M. Sarah. "Springs of Hope: Recovery of Primordial Time in 'Mythic' Novels for Young Readers." *Children's Literature,* no. 16, 1988, pp. 91–107.

Society of Children's Book Writers, July/August 1986.

Interview with Mollie Hunter

Kaye, Marilyn. "Mollie Hunter: An Interview." In *Top of the News,* winter 1985, pp. 141–146.

How to Write to the Author
Mollie Hunter
c/o Harcourt Brace & Co.
525 "B" Street, Suite 1900
San Diego, CA 92101

Hadley Irwin

(Annabelle Irwin: 1915–   ; Lee Hadley: 1934–1995)

by Joan F. Kaywell and Heidi M. Quintana

Are two heads really better than one? In the case of Hadley Irwin, the answer is yes. Since 1979, Lee Hadley and Annabelle Irwin have been writing young adult fiction as Hadley Irwin, giving a new twist to the phrase "and two shall be as one." Together, they write honest, powerful books about current issues relevant to adolescents and adults—issues such as prejudice, alienation and identity, alcoholism, incest, divorce, and suicide.

The Writers

Hadley Irwin describes herself in the Spring 1986 *ALAN Review* as "an older young-adult or a younger old-adult, or whatever" (p. 2). Perhaps this is why her books speak to all kinds of audiences. Her style is friendly and conversational, which might explain her popularity, especially among young adults. In the *ALAN Review* article, "Dear Hadley Irwin, Are

You Living or Dead?" (Hadley and Irwin, 1986), Hadley Irwin responds to a student named Jeff, whose "assignment" was to interview an author. Hadley Irwin humorously responds to questions such as these: "Are you living or dead? If you are living, how old are you and when did you start to write?" (p. 1). "Where do your ideas come from?" (p. 2). "Why do you write for kids?" (p. 2). Jeff's last question (and the only one he did not copy from the blackboard) is: "How much money do you make?" (p. 5).

Hadley and Irwin befriended each other at Iowa State University, when they worked on the same university committee concerning the teaching of writing. The committee work turned out to be fruitless, but they produced a twenty-page report that was more of a joke than anything else. Their collaboration on that mock report served as a catalyst for something wonderful. Annabelle asked Lee to look at *Desk 15*, an unpublished manuscript she had written about the African American experience. Hadley Irwin was the result. Although *Desk 15* was never published, Hadley Irwin as a single author has written and published twelve novels.

In her speech "The Joys and Rewards of Collaborative Writing," Lee Hadley describes the process of learning to write as a team as "a painful process in many ways" (Hadley, 1991). In 1979, Hadley Irwin published her first book, *The Lilith Summer,* which Hadley describes as "sheer craziness and a surprise" to them both (Hadley, 1991). Using a sort of "let's see what happens" approach, Hadley and Irwin wrote chapters in random order based on their interests. Then they swapped and edited each other's chapters. The book developed in a piecemeal fashion, chapters written and then delivered to mailboxes or stuck under windshield wipers of cars. After a soggy manuscript experience on a rainy day, they finally realized that they had to sit down and write together in the same room. After writing and rewriting together (there were thirteen revisions to the last chapter—which was all of a page and a half), they finally completed *The Lilith Summer.* Hadley considers it a benchmark and notes that, "If that book hadn't worked, we would never have, I think, tried again" (Hadley, 1991). Fortunately for her readers, the book did work, and Hadley Irwin has gone on to prove herself as a prolific and prominent novelist.

Hadley Irwin gets ideas for stories by being perceptive to the world around her. Sometimes a particular historical event

benchmark standard by which other things are judged and measured

or experience is the inspiration. She believes in the power of daydreaming and likes to engage in the act of "reperception," which she describes as looking at things "off the wall" (Hadley and Irwin, 1991, p. 2). This ability is apparent is her writing. A simple newspaper photograph served as the inspiration for *The Lilith Summer,* and an overheard argument inspired *Moon And Me* (1981). A great example of Hadley Irwin's ability to look at something ordinary in an off the wall way was when she took a footnote in a history textbook and created *We Are Mesquakie, We Are One* (1980).

> *Hadley Irwin is not afraid to deal with sensitive issues concerning adolescents.*

Adolescent Problems

Hadley Irwin is not afraid to deal with sensitive issues concerning adolescents. For example, in *Abby, My Love* (1985), she addresses the issue of incest and its effects on the victim, her family, and friends. Sensitive and honest, this book speaks to a wide variety of audiences and makes them aware of a taboo social issue.

Similarly, *Can't Hear You Listening* (1990), *Bring to a Boil and Separate* (1980), and *So Long at the Fair* (1988) deal with the sensitive adolescent problems of alcohol and drug abuse, family dysfunction, and suicide. In *Can't Hear You Listening,* Tracy Spencer, the sixteen-year-old protagonist, has to deal with the trial separation of her parents. At the same time, Tracy must face the reality that her longtime friend, Stanley, has a drug and alcohol problem. Similarly, thirteen-year-old Katie Wagner in *Bring to a Boil and Separate* returns from camp to a surprise—her parents are separated. Joel, the main character in *So Long at the Fair,* is intelligent, handsome, and wealthy. Although he appears to have it made, his life turns upside down when his best friend unexpectedly commits suicide. Like Joel, Ashley shared in a seemingly perfect life. Her suicide forces Joel to reflect on his life and confront major issues within himself.

Culture and Identity

Finally, several of Hadley Irwin's other novels—*Jim Dandy* (1994), *I Be Somebody* (1984), *The Original Freddie Ackerman* (1992), *Kim/Kimi* (1987), and *What About Grandma?* (1982)—deal with cultural and identity issues. *Jim Dandy,* a

After the **Civil War** (1861–1865), **George Custer** became lieutenant colonel of the **Seventh Cavalry.** This regiment fought and won many battles against the American Indians.

story about a twelve-year-old boy, Caleb, and his horse, Dandy, takes place during the American Civil War. After Caleb's mean stepfather sells his beloved Dandy to Custer's Seventh Cavalry, Caleb runs away to reclaim his horse. Caleb's search, however, takes him farther than he ever expected. He sees firsthand the horrors and the senselessness of the Indian wars. In the historical novel *Be Somebody,* ten-year-old Rap goes with an aunt to a homestead in Canada in order to escape the prejudices African Americans had to face in the early 1900s in the United States.

Trevor Frederick Ackerman, the hero of *The Original Freddie Ackerman,* spends a lot of time inside the magical refuge of his own imagination. There he can be "Freddie" Ackerman, daring adventurer extraordinaire. Freddie's family is a mixed-up combination of stepparents and stepsiblings, and Freddie has trouble understanding who he is and where he fits in. When he goes to spend the summer with two eccentric great-aunts in Blue Isle, Maine, Freddie gets a chance to escape for real. Trapped as far away from "real" civilization as he thinks he can get, Freddie finds himself caught up in a number of mysteries and adventures. In the process, Freddie comes a little closer to discovering who he really is.

In 1942, when the United States was at war with Japan, 110,000 people of Japanese ethnicity—70,000 of whom were American citizens—were taken from their homes and placed in primitive **internment camps** surrounded by barbed wire because some prejudiced people were afraid that anyone who looked Asian would spy for Japan. It took many years for the government to admit that treating people this way was wrong.

Kim/Kimi focuses on a young Japanese-American girl, Kim Andrews—or is it Kimi Yogushi? Throughout this novel, the main character tries to answer this question for herself. Although her family is warm, supportive, and loving, Kim/Kimi still feels the need to find out about her Japanese half that was lost with the death of her Japanese father before her birth. In her search for information about this part of her heritage, she learns about the grim realities of internment camps where the United States imprisoned Japanese Americans during World War II. During her quest, Kim/Kimi confronts the prejudices that existed and still exist for people who are different. Another book about identity, *What About Grandma?* addresses the conflicts, concerns, and misunderstandings that occur when three generations of women—sixteen-year-old Rhys, her mother, and her mother's mother—live together in one house.

As Hadley Irwin says in *Speaking for Ourselves* (1990): "If there is one idea or theme or hope that Hadley Irwin wishes to convey to her readers it is that no matter how tragic an event may be, there is always humor alive somewhere in the world, that the human spirit can and does triumph, and that with help and love and understanding most problems of the teen years can be lived through" (p. 106).

What is the secret behind Hadley Irwin's success? Why are her books so popular with young adults? Hadley Irwin says that "maybe anyone's writing begins when that person has lived long enough to have something to say and cares enough to try to say it as well as possible" (Hadley and Irwin, 1986, p. 2). So maybe her secret is that collectively, she is over one hundred twenty-five years old. On the other hand, maybe it is just that her brain and sense of humor were "put on hold at about age twelve" (Hadley and Irwin, 1986, p. 2). Maybe it is because she has "lived through the teen years twice—once as Lee Hadley and once as Ann Irwin" (*Speaking for Ourselves,* p. 106). The critic Bonnie O. Ericson, in *Twentieth-Century Adult Writers,* came to this conclusion: "In the end, the great strength of Hadley Irwin's fiction can perhaps be reduced to a single concept: respect. In all her works, respect for others is a central theme, whether the respect is for the elderly, a parent, an adolescent, or persons different, younger, or less fortunate" (p. 326). Whatever the reason for her success, one thing is certain: The birth of Hadley Irwin, almost two decades ago, marked the emergence of a new voice in young adult literature—a perpetually youthful voice of strength, humor, wit, and power that will keep us reading her books for a long time to come.

> *Hadley Irwin on writing:"Maybe anyone's writing begins when that person has lived long enough to have something to say and cares enough to try to say it as well as possible."*

Selected Bibliography

WORKS BY HADLEY IRWIN

The Lilith Summer (1979)

Bring to a Boil and Separate (1980)

We Are Mesquakie, We Are One (1980)

Moon and Me (1981)

What About Grandma? (1982)

I Be Somebody (1984)

Abby, My Love (1985)

Kim/Kimi (1987)

So Long at the Fair (1988)

Can't Hear You Listening (1990)

If you like reading books by Hadley Irwin, you may also enjoy those written by Maya Angelou, Bruce Brooks, Robert Cormier, Chris Crutcher, Maureen Daly, Virginia Hamilton, Walter Dean Myers, Ouida Sebestyen, and Joyce Carol Thomas.

The Original Freddie Ackerman (1992)
Jim Dandy (1994)

WORKS ABOUT HADLEY IRWIN

Ericson, Bonnie O. "Hadley Irwin." In *Twentieth-Century Young Adult Writers*. Edited by Laura Standley Berger. Washington, D.C.: St. James, 1994, pp. 325–326.

Irwin, Hadley. "Hadley Irwin." In *Speaking for Ourselves: Autobiographical Sketches by Notable Authors of Books for Young Adults*. Edited by Donald R. Gallo. Urbana, Ill.: National Council of Teachers of English, 1990, pp. 105–106.

Hadley, Lee. "The Joys and Rewards of Collaborative Writing: 1 + 1 = 1 If We're Lucky." Speech given at the National Council of Teachers of English Convention, Indianapolis, Ind., Spring, 1991.

Hadley, Lee, and Irwin, Annabelle. "Dear Hadley Irwin, Are You Living or Dead? Thoughts Before Answering a Letter. In *ALAN Review,* Spring 1986, pp. 1–7.

Irby, Charles C. "Hadley Irwin: A White Writer of Colored Ethnic Fiction." In *ALAN Review,* Spring 1986, pp. 21–24, 50.

Irwin, Annabelle. "Writing for Young Adults." Speech given at the National Council of Teachers of English Convention, Indianapolis, Ind., 1991.

How to Write to the Author
Hadley Irwin
c/o Simon & Schuster
Children's Publishing
Division
1230 Avenue of the
Americas
New York, NY 10020

Norma Johnston

by Diana Mitchell

"I gloried in being an only child, but then I never considered myself a child. I was always, therefore, startled when I looked in the mirror," Norma Johnston (born Nicole St. John) says of herself. This youthful reluctance to view herself as a child was a sign of her early recognition that the outside of a person did not define her; there was always much more beneath that exterior. This understanding later contributed to her skill and success as a novelist especially in her ability to create memorable characters.

Although Johnston had no siblings, she understood what it was like to be part of an extended family because as a child she was often dragged to large family gatherings. There were no other children her age there, and she became involved in talking to the adults, often one-on-one, and in listening to their stories.

Quotations from Norma Johnston that are not attributed to a published source are from a personal interview conducted by the author of this article on 8 May 1995 and are published here by permission of Norma Johnston.

167

About Johnston's Life and Working Habits

Little Women was written by Louisa May Alcott. There is an article about her in volume 1.

Although an only child, Johnston's mother had grown up in a large extended family surrounded by relatives. Also, the books Johnston read, such as *Little Women,* had large families in them, so it seemed natural to her to write about this kind of family. She had within her family the annotated genealogy of her maternal grandmother's family dating back to the 1600s. From her mother's parents' family she used character traits that repeated themselves over the generations as part of the personality of some of her characters. One of these traits, "strength of character" or pigheadedness, worked its way into several of her main characters, such as Evie Sterling in *The Keeping Days* (1973).

Although she completed her first novel (unpublished) at the age of eleven, the only real encouragement Johnston got for her writing came from teachers because they were the ones who saw it. While her family valued her writing and thought "it was cute," they did not encourage her to view writing as a career since they felt she could not make a living by writing. When she graduated from high school at sixteen, she planned to be a costume or fashion designer. But she did not go straight from one job to the next. She said, "My life is not chronological, it's overlapping. Time does not go full circle, it moves in a spiral. We go out in one direction and come back. It looks like we're not getting anywhere, but if you look at it sideways, you're not at the same place. Everything influences everything else."

As Johnston moved from designing costumes to owning a dress shop to attending drama school to coaching drama to teaching, she was writing. Maud Hart Lovelace, author of the popular Betsy and Joe series, became her mentor. Although Johnston met her only once, she corresponded with her frequently, especially when she had problems with editors. "She was the one person 'in the know' to tell me I would get published. When I got discouraged, I relied on what she had said."

Johnston is passionate about her writing, explaining in *Something About the Author* that she writes partly "to disturb the status quo and draw people into a closer understanding of themselves, their neighbors, and their God" (p. 118). Thus, she approaches her writing with great care, outlining her books before she starts. "I'm a great believer in getting it all worked out before I write. My outline is like a map—you can take shortcuts or brilliant side-trips but to get anywhere you have to start with a map."

Characters come to Johnston from many sources. She often gets ideas for them from people she knows and from actors and actresses she sees on film or on TV. "I'm impressed by Claire Danes who appeared in the movie *Little Women* and in the TV series *My So-Called Life*. I'll probably soon find myself writing a character she could play." Instead of starting out by just creating a character, Johnston says it's "more as if I were writing roles that people I know could play." To stay true to her characters as she is writing, Johnston asks herself "if I were the character what would I do, NOT what would the character do if she was me."

In *Something About the Author,* Johnston says, "My characters are not me, but their beliefs are" (p. 118). Her beliefs and views about women come through clearly in her books as she creates intriguing and active female characters. No matter what their age, they often have such fascinating backgrounds—as the grandmother, Lady Sandiman, (in *Of Time and of Seasons* and *A Striving After Wind*) does— that we would like to read a whole book just about these characters. Johnston says, "I grew up in a matriarchy and that has made all the difference." Other females in her stories are also shown as intelligent and aware of how they can best get around limitations imposed by society. Her married female characters are shown not only as caregivers responding to the needs of others but also as women who have goals, needs, and concerns of their own.

Johnston's work in the theater and her love of the arts comes up repeatedly in her novels. Her characters act, paint, draw, write, and dance. The arts are shown as an important form of expression, not as something out of the ordinary.

Settings also have grown out of Johnston's life experiences. She writes of places she knows or has traveled to. The houses she includes in her novels are often houses she has lived in or visited frequently.

Johnston is a dedicated writer and it shows in the engrossing novels she seems to produce so easily. She is not intimidated by the act of writing. "Writing is the least of it. It's

Claire Danes played Beth in the 1994 film adaptation of ***Little Women.*** She played the lead role of Angela Chase in the television series ***My So-Called Life,*** which aired during the 1994–1995 season.

matriarchy a system of society in which mothers or other female figures control most of the power

in such things as the research, the plotting, the design of the buildings, and the characterization that takes time."

The stories of her grandmother and great uncles eventually formed the basis of the acclaimed Keeping Days series, six books that detail the events in the Sterling family from 1900 to 1917. The first four books cover the events of two years in the life of this family. The last two books, written from the point of view of the first grandchild, skip ahead fifteen years. Johnston was motivated to write these books because she believes "family does not mean a sentimentalized Currier and Ives picture."

The Keeping Days Series

To read the books of the Keeping Days series is to be enfolded into the heart of the Sterling family. The reader shares the family's moments of joy, periods of conflict, and instances of crackling tension—all the bits and pieces of interaction that define a family.

Characters spring to life in these novels. Although there are seven children, all are so well drawn that they emerge as distinct personalities. The reader becomes most involved with the three older children and with the parents because they seem like people we want to know. On the first page of *The Keeping Days,* we are introduced to Mama in this passage:

> Mama . . . just snorted. "Too sensitive," she said briskly. "Got to get over it. Time you did." Mama always talks like that, dropping half her sentences as though she's going somewhere in a hurry and hasn't time. Mama always reminds me of a little brown wren, small and compact and efficient, her brown hair skewered up every which way and not a spark of sensitivity in her soul.

By the end of the first book, through descriptions like this, the characters seem so real that readers feel they could sit down and have a conversation with any family member.

This series also illustrates Johnston's mastery in creating settings and evoking time periods. We feel part of life in 1900

evoke to call to mind

after reading passages from *The Keeping Days* like the following:

> It was an August evening, and the dishes were done, and all the kids were playing Kick the Can in the street. When it started getting dark, we drifted down to Lathams' side lawn, the way everybody did that summer. . . . When I looked up, the sky behind the maple tree was purple. Lights were going on in windows, and from houses along Vyse Avenue our mother started calling. "Celinda. . . ." "Herbert. . . ." "Mary Lou. . . ."(P. 2)

With rich, evocative language like this, Johnston sweeps us into another time. In her speeches and her writing, she has described her ability to do this by explaining her own style: "I write in a romantic, often gothic, style because I know from experience and from theatre that when you draw people into the circle of a rosy glow, they become more open to the thrust of truth."

In this family saga, themes such as the nature of love emerge that recur in Johnston's other works. She shows that love is not just a feeling or something that happens. In families, especially, it is something that has to be worked at, since it is always easier to love in the abstract. But daily contact in families is hard and gives rise to the whole spectrum of human emotions—both negative and positive—and love evolves and changes through those experiences.

theme central message about life in a literary work

The idea of family is also often linked to the theme of identity. As young people work at figuring out who they are and what is important to them, they often believe they have to free themselves from their family's expectations so they can find their own place in the world. The theme of identity also includes the idea of finding one's own gifts, the things we are really good at, the things that are our strengths.

Learning through living is a theme that surfaces in almost all of Johnston's books. Many of her stories show that we cannot hold negative or devastating experiences at bay; all we can do is reflect and grow through them. Johnston's books frequently present religious and philosophical themes and the struggle to understand our belief systems. Thus the whole Keeping Days series can be viewed as lessons on living and on growing up, because so many ideas are packed into each novel.

But because these books do include some of the philosophical doesn't mean they are not lively and fast-moving. When a house is peopled with a family as large as the Sterlings, there are bound to be frequent crises and personal and family issues that bump against each other and sometimes collide. So although these books deal with family life, they have plenty of action, adventure, and mystery.

Other Coming-of-Age Novels

Johnston also wrote pairs of books that seem to be cut from the same cloth as the Keeping Day series. Her pair of Civil War novels, *Of Time and of Seasons* (1975) and *A Striving After Wind* (1976), show a family thrust into the issues surrounding the war. In this vibrant family the ties are strong, but they are tested. Another pair, *The Swallow's Song* (1978) and *If you Love Me, Let Me Go* (1978), are set in the 1920s. These books show families that have trouble communicating with each other. One is trying to deal with a senile grandparent, while the other is immersed in cocaine and alcohol problems. Through these books that are set in the past, we are made aware that there really never has been such a time as "the good old days," since teens in these earlier eras also faced problems of prejudice, rape, hypocrisy, and addiction.

With the Carlisle Chronicles, Johnston moves into the present. Her family history again forms the basis of some of the stories. In *Carlisle's Hope* (1986), the first of the three books, research that Jess, the main character, is doing on her grandfather parallels the mystery of Johnston's father's parentage in that both men had fathers who mysteriously disappeared. The seemingly united Carlisle family has to deal with crises throughout the series that could pull apart the family. But they struggle to face these hardships by helping each other in whatever way they can. A family pulling together in times of need, another recurrent Johnston theme, is played out very realistically in these novels, since from time to time different family members are shown having a lot of trouble coping with their difficulties.

Other books set in the present include *The Potter's Wheel* (1988) and *The Time of the Cranes* (1990). Both of these books have exceptional older women as central characters as well as another of Johnston's favorite themes—the intergenerational passing of the torch. These older women want to hand down to younger women their knowledge and perceptions as the girls struggle with what life means to them.

Stories of Mystery and Intrigue

Johnston also writes compelling stories of intrigue. *Watcher in the Mist* (1986), *Shadow of a Unicorn* (1987), and *Whisper of a Cat* (1988) are such books. These riveting stories are peopled with strong female characters who are active and involved. Other page turners are *Gabriel's Girl* (1983), *Return to Morocco* (1988), and *The Delphic Choice* (1989).

These tales of international intrigue include as characters older women of substance who have carved out full, satisfying lives for themselves. The female teen protagonist often drafts a male to come along and help her in her quest to solve the mystery. This tendency seems to be more a matter of common sense and the recognition that only a fool is determined to do something dangerous by herself, not a matter of dependency on males. This teaming of a female main character with a male in these action-packed mysteries brings to mind the Nancy Drew series, in which faithful Ned is always around.

Johnston's development of setting makes the reader feel present as the characters hurry through such places as side streets and alleys in Morocco or the back streets of London. Johnston is very conscious of details as she moves the plot forward. Since there are not any annoying oversights or loose ends in these mysteries, the plots fit together tightly, producing a very satisfying read.

Mythology

Mythology was a required topic when Johnston briefly taught English to eighth graders. As part of this study students had to do a report on a book that included mythology. Johnston noticed that there were very few books appropriate for this assignment. Since she believes that anybody can benefit from reading myths, she decided to write novels that brought them to life. Three books resulted: *The Days of the*

intrigue secret plots or schemes that arouse curiosity

protagonist the main character of a literary work

The **Nancy Drew series** was created by Edward Stratemeyer. There is an article about him in volume 3.

Dragon's Seed (1982), the story of Oedipus; *Strangers Dark and Gold* (1975), the retelling of the stories of Jason and Medea; and *Pride of Lions: The Story of the House of Atreus* (1979). Written in language that involves the reader and is filled with action and detail, the shrouded, shadowy figures of mythology jump to life and become fully rounded characters that we can relate to.

Nonfiction

Norma Johnston turned to nonfiction with the publication of *Harriet* (1994), *Louisa May* (1995), and *Remember the Ladies* (1995). Louisa May Alcott and Harriet Beecher Stowe both lived during the nineteenth century, which Johnston says she got "hooked on. I was surrounded by it because I loved history, school, and biographies." Again, family is a major emphasis, especially in the well-received *Louisa May*. Johnston begins this compelling biography with the lives of Louisa's parents, so the reader can see the effects of their actions and beliefs on Louisa. The provocative opening that Johnston uses in so many of her novels is certainly present here. She begins with, "There are some people who . . . should probably never be parents. . . . Bronson Alcott was one of those people." This startling introduction forces readers into wondering why Bronson is described like this and draws them to the book in search of answers.

Johnston was asked by an editor to write a book on the first women's rights convention and her *Remember the Ladies* resulted. This book focuses on the major organizers of the Seneca Falls Convention and Johnston brings the family lives of these women to life as she describes how and why they got involved. This book is no mere recitation of the history of the events, but an immersion in the attitudes of the times and the families of women like Elizabeth Cady Stanton. Thus, the reader can see the conflict and the personal cost to these women, who took such bold steps to bring the issues of women into public debate.

Both Johnston's fiction and nonfiction are grounded in the stories of the people she writes about. Just as in her fiction, the tension in these books tempts the reader to finish the book in one sitting to know how it ends. Johnston brings her storytelling magic to these books by doing the hard re-

The **Seneca Falls Convention** in 1848 was one of the first public appeals for women's suffrage, or the right for women to vote. It took until 1919—71 more years—for women to achieve that right in the United States.

search, by reflecting, and by drawing conclusions before she puts the information in the context of family stories. Her nonfiction sparkles with vitality and leaves the engrossed reader wanting to know even more.

Norma Johnston and Other Authors for Young Adults

Norma Johnston's novels have much in common with the works of Madeleine L'Engle, Ann Rinaldi, and Lois Duncan. Her Keeping Days series and her coming-of-age books could be likened to L'Engle's Austin Family series and her Wrinkle in Time series. Both authors, besides being brilliant storytellers, touch on many spiritual issues, set the stories within strong families, show women as strong, capable people, and never become preachy as they deal with issues of the heart and the soul.

Johnston's historical novels (*Of Time and of Seasons, A Striving after Wind,* and *Ready or Not,* 1965) could be compared to the historical fiction of Ann Rinaldi. Both pay close attention to detail, both have the ability to vividly recreate the past, and both have the talent to show their characters interacting with issues of the day so we learn more about the time and the people.

Johnston's novels of mystery bring to mind the compelling nature of the works of Lois Duncan. Another master storyteller, Duncan uses the elements of mystery to move her stories forward. Both Johnston and Duncan are meticulous about detail, so their plots are believable; and they both use language to build suspense, so they succeed in creating fascinating mysteries.

Selected Bibliography

WORKS BY NORMA JOHNSTON

Novels for Young Adults
The Wishing Star (1963)
The Wider Heart (1964)
Ready or Not (1965)
The Bridge Between (1966)

If you like the works of Norma Johnston, you might also enjoy reading the work of Lois Duncan, Madeleine L'Engle, and Ann Rinaldi.

The Keeping Days (1973)

Glory in the Flower (1974)

Strangers Dark and Gold (1975)

Of Time and of Seasons (1975)

A Striving After Wind (1976)

The Sanctuary Tree (1977)

If You Love Me, Let Me Go (1978)

A Mustard Seed of Magic (1978)

The Swallow's Song (1978)

The Crucible Years (1979)

Pride of Lions: The Story of the House of Atreus (1979)

A Nice Girl Like You (1980)

Myself and I (1981)

The Days of the Dragon's Seed (1982)

Time Warp Summer (1982)

Gabriel's Girl (1983)

Carlisle's All (1986)

Carlisle's Hope (1986)

To Jess, with Love and Memories (1986)

Watcher in the Mist (1986)

Shadow of a Unicorn (1987)

The Potter's Wheel (1988)

Return to Morocco (1988)

Whisper of a Cat (1988)

The Delphic Choice (1989)

The Time of the Cranes (1990)

Image Game (1994)

Nonfiction

Harriet (1994)

Louisa May (1995)

Remember the Ladies (1995)

How to Write to the Author
Norma Johnston
c/o William Morrow & Co., Inc.
1350 Avenue of the Americas
New York, NY 10019

WORKS ABOUT NORMA JOHNSTON

Commire, Anne, ed. "Norma Johnston." *Something About the Author*. Detroit: Gale Research, vol. 29, pp. 116–118.

Gallo, Donald R., ed. *Speaking for Ourselves*. Urbana, Ill.: National Council of Teachers of English, 1990, pp. 182–185.

M. E. Kerr

(1927-)

by Alleen Pace Nilsen

M.E. Kerr, whose real name is Marijane Meaker, has created such interesting characters in her nearly twenty books for young readers that it's fun to imagine her giving something like a block party, with her main characters coming as honored guests. She could have it catered by either the Dunlinger family from *Linger* (1993) or the Schillers from *Him She Loves?* (1984), but based on what she's told readers about these family-run restaurants, it will perhaps be better to go potluck.

The not-so-dinky heroine from *Dinky Hocker Shoots Smack!* (1972) will probably be first in the food line, but thanks to P. John's support, she will not overload her plate. I hope she sits next to Alan Bennet from *If I Love You, Am I Trapped Forever?* (1973) because ever since he lost his girl-friend to Duncan Stein (formerly known as "Doomed"), he needs to meet someone original and funny like Dinky. Car-olyn Cardmaker, from *Is That You, Miss Blue?* (1975), would be another good match for Alan. Carolyn describes herself as a

potluck a commu-nal meal to which people bring differ-ent dishes to share

"category #1" student at the exclusive Charles boarding school in Virginia. Category #1 students are bright but pathetic. Cardmaker is a category #1, a P.K. (preacher's kid), who sets out to explain all the rules to Flanders Brown. In Cardmaker's system Flanders is a category #3 student—one whose parents are getting divorced or who have more exciting things to do than raise their children.

Some hosts, but certainly not Kerr, would seat all their "different," that is, minority or disabled, characters together, but Kerr's will be scattered throughout the crowd. Little Little, a dwarf from the book by the same name, will be talking to the very shy Opal Ringer, who helps her father run his Pentecostal church in *What I Really Think of You* (1982), while $uzy $lade (she's so rich her name is written with dollar signs), from *Love Is a Missing Person* (1975), will be apprehensively watching for her sister to ride in on her motorcycle with her African American boyfriend.

Some kids will steer clear of John Fell because, as his father has observed, he heads "for trouble like a paper clip toward a magnet." He's the star of the three books in Kerr's detective series: *Fell* (1987), *Fell Back* (1989), and *Fell Down* (1991). Older guests will head toward Gary Peel, from *Linger*, in hopes of finding out what happened to Gary's brother and his friend who was so horribly wounded in the Gulf War. Other serious guests will cluster around Erick Rudd, from *Night Kites* (1986), but they'll probably be too shy to express their condolences on the AIDS-related death of his older brother. Still others will want to talk to Parr and his sister Evie, from *Deliver Us from Evie* (1994). They'll be curious to meet Patsy, Evie's friend and lover, who moved with Evie from their Midwest farm country to New York City.

Librarian Miss Gwendolyn Spring (sometimes referred to as Miss G-String), from *Love Is a Missing Person* (1975), will probably sit down for some professional talk with high school teacher Ernestine Blue, who in *Is That You, Miss Blue?* was dismissed from a church-sponsored private school for being too religious. The alcoholic coach from *If I Love You, Am I Trapped Forever?* will probably avoid talking with either of them because he's still embarrassed about leaving school in midyear.

I shudder to think of all the celebrity parents sitting at the same table. Adam Blessing's politician father, from *The Son of Someone Famous* (1974), will be trying to outmaneu-

Pentecostal relating to any of the Christian religious groups that emphasize individual experiences of grace and expressive worship, and evangelism

ver Valerie Kissenwiser's comedian father, from *Him She Loves?* (1984). Rock star Vincent Haigney, from *I Stay Near You* (1985), will look bored, while Flanders' name-dropping, pop-psychologist father, from *Is That You, Miss Blue?,* will be trying to impress TV evangelist Dr. Guy Pegler, from *What I Really Think of You.*

But enough of this imaginary party! What it's meant to show is the variety of memorable characters that Kerr has created and to hint at the kinds of stories in which they are involved.

Early Aspirations

As long as Kerr can remember, she wanted to be a writer. Born Marijane Meaker in Auburn, New York, on 27 May 1927, she grew up seeking inspiration by pedaling her bicycle past the house of the town's most famous writer, Samuel Hopkins Adams. By the time she was twelve, her mother, Ida, was worrying about how much time she spent writing in her room instead of playing outside with other kids. The summer Kerr was seventeen, she adopted her first pen name and began submitting stories to magazines. She chose the name Eric Ranthram McKay for the practical reason that this name matched the initials engraved on the stationery she borrowed from her father, Ellis R. Meaker.

Kerr gives credit to both parents for making her want to write. Her father was a reader who frequently took her to the library and regularly read aloud to his only daughter, who happened to be sandwiched in age between two nonliterary brothers. Equally important is the fact that her mother was a gossip, who at dinnertime and on the phone was constantly prefacing her "true" stories with "Wait till you hear this!" These words still ring in Kerr's ears when she weighs an idea for a new book.

Unlike such fortunate writers as S. E. Hinton and Maureen Daly, whose first books were published while they were still in their teens, Marijane received so many negative responses from publishers that she once went to a college costume party wearing a black slip covered with pinned-on letters from publishers. She hoped people caught on that she was "a rejection slip."

Kerr's first major sale came when she was a twenty-four-year-old graduate of the University of Missouri (she studied

evangelist a Protestant layman who preaches the gospel with militant or crusading enthusiasm

There is an article about S. E. Hinton earlier in this volume and an article about Maureen Daly in volume I.

Marijane received so many negative responses from publishers that she once went to a college costume party wearing a black slip covered with pinned-on letters from publishers. She hoped people caught on that she was "a rejection slip."

journalism and English literature) and was living in New York City with some of her sorority sisters. She worked in various secretarial and editorial assistant jobs, but kept getting fired for spending most of her time and energy on her own career.

Kerr established herself as a literary agent representing ten different authors—really just herself under ten different names. Her big break came when she sold a short story, "Devotedly, Patrick Henry Casebolt," to *Ladies Home Journal* under the pen name of Laura Winston. She received $750 for the story, which at that time was enough to live on for two or three months. The money meant she could devote full time to her writing. An additional bonus was that the story attracted attention from a publisher who asked her to submit a few sample chapters and an outline for a book. He invited her for lunch, and in the taxi as they were going under the dark tunnel near Grand Central Station, told her he had decided to take her proposal and was advancing her $2,000. When the taxi emerged into the sunlight on Park Avenue, she was a professional writer and has been happy to remain such ever since.

Even though Kerr did not sell the stories she wrote all through high school and college, her efforts were not wasted. Her careful observations and the processing of all her experiences through the mind of a storyteller undoubtedly contributed to her treasure trove of memories, including the on-target descriptions of teenagers' emotions that fill her books today. In the early 1970s, when she decided to try writing for teenagers, the years of practice in recording her youthful experiences and the skills she had developed in twenty years of writing for adults (mostly mysteries) were a winning combination.

A Career Decision

There were two major influences on Kerr's decision to write for young people. The first was the encouragement from her friend Louise Fitzhugh, author of *Harriet the Spy*, who kept pointing out that in Kerr's mysteries and other books her best-developed characters were teenagers. The second influence was *The Pigman*, written by Pulitzer Prize–winning au-

> *Kerr established herself as a literary agent representing ten different authors—really just herself under ten different names.*

Harriet the Spy was made into a popular movie that was released in 1996.

thor Paul Zindel. When she read and then re-read this book, she was convinced first that it was a wonderful book and second that its main characters, John and Lorraine, were the kind of kids she knew and would like to write about.

Kerr obviously made a good career decision. In 1993, she won the top award given to writers of books for young people: the Margaret A. Edwards Award, presented by the American Library Association and *School Library Journal* to an author whose books "have provided young adults with a window through which they can view the world."

Four Honored Books

The four books that the library association chose to honor include Kerr's first young-adult book, *Dinky Hocker Shoots Smack!,* the story of a do-gooder mother who ignores her own daughter. While her mother is out, trying to reform drug addicts, Dinky stays home alone and eats, and eats, and eats. The title comes from the graffiti message that Dinky paints as a plea for help outside the building where her mother is being honored for outstanding community service. The story was inspired by a girl that Kerr met when she was working as a visiting writer with a group of inner-city New York kids.

The second honored book was *Gentlehands* (1978), the story of a boy who aspires to raise his social standing in the eyes of wealthy Skye Pennington by associating with his estranged German grandfather. In the end the elegant grandfather is found to have been a Nazi war criminal. Kerr modeled the boy in the book after a next-door neighbor who had a crush on one of the wealthy young women whose family spent the summer in Kerr's hometown. More important to the story than the difference in social levels between the boy and the girl is the portrayal of the grandfather's past evils. The plot came to Kerr after she read a book on the search for Nazi war criminals and also from her pondering the role her older brother played as a CIA-sponsored provocateur in Vietnam. She created Grandpa Trenker to show that in war, evil is much harder to see than it was in the stereotyped buffoonery on television's *Hogan's Heroes.* But she told interviewer Jim Roginski that when a group of students who had read the book in English class conducted a mock trial

estranged removed from customary environments or associations

provocateur an agent provocateur; one who is hired to associate with suspected persons, and by pretending sympathy with their goals, incite them to actions that will incriminate them

buffoonery foolish behavior

and let the grandfather go, under a "let bygones be bygones" philosophy, she worried that perhaps she had been too subtle.

Me Me Me Me Me: Not a Novel (1983)—a collection of autobiographical stories—was the third book honored by the library association. A postscript to each of the stories ties in the real-life individuals with their fictional counterparts who had already appeared in Kerr's previously published books. While Kerr is quick to discount any claim of total objectivity and to admit freely that she dealt loosely with names and some "facts," it is obvious that she has lived the emotions and the main events. And it is equally obvious that Kerr is her own smart-mouthed, funny-girl protagonist, who brings smiles to so many of her readers.

> *It is equally obvious that Kerr is her own smart-mouthed, funny-girl protagonist, who brings smiles to so many of her readers.*

The fourth honored book was *Night Kites,* the first novel for either adults or teenagers published in the United States about a family coping with the impending death of a beloved son from AIDS. Kerr began writing the book in 1984 when she watched what happened to a popular family in her town. When their son came home sick, word slipped out that he had a type of cancer that only homosexuals get. In previous years townspeople felt honored to get an invitation to the family's Christmas party, but this year even the caterers were too afraid to come. Kerr was touched by the poignancy of the family's sorrow, and so she wrote *Night Kites.* The story is not exactly about this family, but rather about how she imagined it would be to have to cope with such a change.

At the time Kerr began writing *Night Kites,* AIDS was not even a familiar word. She thought that whatever the illness was, a cure would soon be found, so the story would become dated. Because of this, she allowed herself the luxury of putting in references to rock music, which she loves but had avoided writing about because the music scene changes so rapidly.

If Kerr had been awarded the prize in 1995 instead of 1993, the organization would probably have listed five, instead of four, honored books because in 1994 her *Deliver Us from Evie* was chosen for so many best-book lists. The lists included those compiled by the editors of both *School Library Journal* and *Booklist,* and the "Best Books" and "Quick Picks" committees from the Young Adult Library Services Association.

Kerr's Major Themes

Kerr once took a class in advertising just to help her create appealing titles. But in going out to talk to high school kids, she learned something that the advertising class never taught. Boys were bringing her books for autographing with the covers torn off. A teacher explained that they were embarrassed to be seen carrying around books with romantic-looking covers or the word "love" in the title. Kerr wished she had known this before naming four books —*Him She Loves?; If I Love You, Am I Trapped Forever?; I'll Love You When You're More Like Me* (1977); and *Love Is a Missing Person* (1975)—especially since she includes male protagonists and tries to write stories that will appeal to both scxcs.

Kerr often explores differences among social classes, a concept she grew interested in during World War II when she left Auburn, New York, to attend an exclusive boarding school in Virginia. In Auburn she had felt privileged because her grandfather had owned the grocery stores in town, and her father owned a factory, but at the school she met girls whose fathers headed international corporations, and suddenly she felt like a small-town hick. For an article in *School Library Journal* she told interviewer Roger Sutton that ever since this experience she's paid attention to "haves and have-nots," and that her sympathies have been mainly with the "have-nots," the kids who feel like outsiders. They may be outsiders because of being physically different, belonging to a religion or an ethnic group that is looked down on or viewed as different from the majority, being a lesbian or a gay male, or being in a family with lower social status than that of their friends. The reason does not matter as much as the feeling, especially when writing for teenagers. High school is the time that kids first go out and start comparing themselves and their families with others and come away feeling that in some way they do not measure up.

hick unsophisticated person

The strength of Kerr's writing is that when she explores such differences, she alternates between being serious and funny. When things get bad, she turns the tables to make readers smile and sometimes laugh out loud. An important point is that readers do not laugh *at* her characters but *with* them. Kerr creates situations that encourage characters, as well as readers, to step back and see the kind of irony and humor that she expressed in her autobiographical stories in

Me Me Me Me Me. She thinks she would have been grateful for such an opportunity when she was living—rather than re-living—the experiences.

Readers who have enjoyed M. E. Kerr's books will probably also enjoy reading books written by Paul Zindel, Norma Klein, Judy Blume, Robert Lipsyte, and Bruce Brooks.

Selected Bibliography

WORKS BY M. E. KERR

Novels for Young Adults

Dinky Hocker Shoots Smack! (1972)

If I Love You, Am I Trapped Forever? (1973)

The Son of Someone Famous (1974)

Is That You, Miss Blue? (1975)

Love Is a Missing Person (1975)

I'll Love You When You're More Like Me (1977)

Gentlehands (1978)

Little Little (1981)

What I Really Think of You (1982)

Him She Loves? (1984)

I Stay Near You (1985)

Night Kites (1986)

Fell (1987)

Fell Back (1989)

Fell Down (1991)

Linger (1993)

Deliver Us from Evie (1994)

Short Stories

Me Me Me Me Me: Not a Novel (1983)

Autobiography

"M. E. Kerr." In *Speaking for Ourselves: Autobiographical Sketches by Notable Authors of Books for Young Adults.* Edited by Donald R. Gallo. Urbana, Ill.. National Council of Teachers of English, 1990.

Article

Meaker, Marijane. "Getting All Kids to Read My Books," *ALAN Review,* fall 1989, vol. 17, pp. 47–48.

Works About M. E. Kerr

Nilsen, Alleen Pace. *Presenting M. E. Kerr.* Boston: Twayne, 1986.

Roginski, Jim. "M. E. Kerr: An Interview," *ALAN Review,* fall 1988, vol. 16, pp. 37–41.

Sutton, Roger. "A Conversation with M. E. Kerr," *School Library Journal,* June 1993, vol. 39, pp. 24–29.

How to Write to the Author
M. E. Kerr
c/o HarperCollins Publishers
10 East 53rd Street
New York, NY 10022

Norma Klein

(1938–1989)

by Allene S. Phy-Olsen

When she gave interviews, Norma Klein was lively, articulate, and witty. She held forth on all subjects; non sequiturs and satirical thrusts were plentiful. Denouncing a rival who had just won a major award, she declared that "the kids will read her books only if we tie them to the bed posts." She was ready to indict Margaret Thatcher as a dire influence on literature in England, and suspected Ronald Reagan of ill intentions toward American writers. Clearly enjoying her frequent role as defender of artistic expression, she flew about the country speaking on behalf of embattled school officials charged with providing children with salacious books, including some of her own.

non sequitur a statement that does not follow logically from what was previously said

salacious arousing or appealing to sexual desire

Quotations from Norma Klein that are not attributed to a published source are from a personal interview conducted by the author of this article on 11 April 1986 and are published here by permission of Norma Klein.

The Life

In the spring of 1988, when the first full-length study of her writing was published, she was a strikingly attractive woman,

Phi Beta Kappa an honorary society, founded in 1776, of students with very high scholastic achievements in an American university (such as having a cumulative grade point average that is within the top ten percent of the graduating class)

Existentialism is a philosophical movement that began in the 1800s. It concerns the nature of existence or being and the struggle for freedom.

rhetoric pompous and insincere language

her beauty softened and intensified by approaching middle age. She was a feminist, and, of course, charm was supposed to be irrelevant. She did, however, bask in the recognition of her success and projected a powerful image of vitality. After all, she had fulfilled the ambition of most middle-class women who grew up in the 1950s, marriage to a high-achieving man. She spoke with pride of her molecular biologist husband, Erwin Fleissner, their marriage of over two decades, and their two talented daughters. But she also stood apart from other women of her generation, with a Phi Beta Kappa degree from Barnard College and an M.A. from Columbia University. At both institutions, she had majored in Russian literature, not ill training for a future fiction writer. As a best-selling novelist, she was earning more than her husband.

The complexities and ambiguities of Klein's personality emerged more slowly. Sensible reviewers of her work had carefully avoided the "biographical fallacy," which falsely assumes all writing to be personal confession. The increasingly strong intimations of a darker vision lurking below superficially sunny narratives had escaped close scrutiny. When pressed, Klein had indeed admitted, "I have a funny view, because I believe one has to devote one's life to changing the world, and yet I think it will never change. It is an existential thing. . . . I don't believe people should retreat and say it doesn't matter who they vote for; I believe we should fight every inch of the way. But I also believe that the world is going to go up in smoke." These dire words, uttered with some flippancy, had been dismissed largely as rhetoric, a response perhaps to a rereading of Jean-Paul Sartre, Albert Camus, or even Françoise Sagan. Yet the bleaker dimension of Klein's personality continued to find expression in her volatile temperament and her pensive reflections in letters and telephone conversations to her friends and colleagues.

Klein was immensely pleased when a literary critic described her as "a gifted writer, in mid-career, just reaching artistic maturity, whose best books are still to be written" (*Presenting Norma Klein,* pp.170–171). That prediction, however, proved tragically wrong. Only a few months after it appeared in print, Norma Klein died in a New York hospital, on 25 April 1989. The media reported that she had expired "after a brief illness." Her thousands of surviving readers were left to ponder the recurrent psychological probing in her novels, the despair that could no longer be dismissed as only a writer's flight of impassioned imagination.

More than forty books and assorted papers survived her, reflecting in many particulars the woman who wrote them and the social environment in which she moved. A lifelong New Yorker, she had been assailed in reviews for concentrating too much on the lives of upper-middle-class Jewish city dwellers. Even when a major focus of youth fiction shifted to the inner city, she had wisely declined to write about an environment she did not know. When she had occasionally introduced African Americans into her fiction, she had not been totally credible. Though she called herself an atheist and had married the son of Gentile German immigrants, both of her own parents had East European Jewish origins, and it was Jewish-American life she understood best.

Klein, born on 13 May 1938 in New York City, always acknowledged her father, Emanuel Klein, as the dominant influence in her life. Arriving in the United States from Poland at age five, he had nevertheless managed to attend the best universities and become a successful psychiatrist. Early in her own life, Norma Klein and her father had developed such an absorption in one another that the rest of the family often felt like intruders. Dr. Klein had lavished jewelry, furs, theater tickets, and money on his daughter. Because he took pride in any recognition she received, she started writing novels, and his desire for grandchildren was a main reason she decided to have children of her own. When Emanuel Klein died in 1977, she experienced what she called "a breakdown." Writer's block was one of its manifestations, a rare disability for a woman who could generally turn out books faster than reviewers could read them. Though she did resume writing, it would be ten years before she would experience her catharsis by fictionalizing that father-daughter relationship in *Older Men* (1987).

A fascination with psychiatry, an honest legacy from her father, pervades Klein's books. Yet her skepticism of therapies only increased with the years. Adolescent books are supposed to be cheerful; the genre requires a degree of optimism, and concluding chapters often recall the happy endings of old Hollywood movies. The purgatory of mental hospitals and sanatoria especially frightened Klein, yet could only be al-

Apparently many people suspect that Klein committed suicide, but they cannot be sure because they have only the indirect evidence of the themes in her fiction to support their guesses.

Gentile   here, a person of a non-Jewish nation or a non-Jewish faith (sometimes "Gentile" can also mean a Christian as distinguished from a Jew)

manifestation   the way something reveals or shows itself

catharsis   a release of emotional tensions that renews the spirit

allude to make an
indirect reference

luded to in earlier fiction. In these institutions competent professional people were reduced to cutting animal figures from construction paper, supervised by patronizing nurses. Two posthumously published books, *The World As It Is* (1989) on the adult lists, and *Learning How to Fall* (1989) for young adults, finally come clean. Patients are shown humiliated by physicians who should first heal themselves.

The Work

The Teenage Sexual Revolution

notoriety unfavorable fame

mores mental attitudes; manners

Klein's treatment of teenage sexuality has attracted both wide notoriety and large readership. More than any other writer of the 1970s, she mirrored changing youth mores of the urban middle class. Though she liked to think of herself as nonjudgmental, her critics were not entirely wrong in accusing her of advocating sexual hedonism. Contraceptive information, with abortion as a backup option, was readily available to her heroines, who suffered from no religious scruples and had parents ready to rectify the mistakes resulting from their experimentation. Plotting a seduction in a Klein book often took less time than planning a good night kiss in the emerging adolescent novel of the 1950s. On the whole, Klein's teenage characters found sexual expression normal and healthy, with some ethical considerations but few moral taboos attached. These books were never leering, though in later books the teenage characters became increasingly frenetic. They were rarely romantic; sexual initiation for them was never the quasi-religious experience that descends upon characters in true romantic fiction.

leering obscene, vulgar

Klein's narratives did not linger on the biological details of sexual encounters. Kinky sex did not interest her. In *Learning How to Fall,* when Dusty Penrose and his girlfriend, a high school clone of Marilyn Monroe, experiment with handcuffs in their lovemaking, it is only in imitation of an episode from *Something Wild,* which they have just seen. Klein was, actually, deeply offended when the editor of an influential review pounced upon her at a conference, asking, "How does it feel to be the queen of teen porn?" Another colleague came to her defense, noting that while Klein's books might be about sex, they are not titillating.

titillating erotic

While the novels do not place exploitative sex in a favorable light, neither do they reflect the somber consequences of the sexual revolution, which were becoming evident by the end of Klein's life. She seemed oblivious of the economic destitution created by inner-city single parenthood, and the AIDS epidemic was just becoming a subject for literary exploration. No doubt, the latter crisis would have inspired her, since it struck creative artists disproportionately. When she died, she was already projecting a young adult novel centered on the feelings of a gay teenager just exiting his closet.

destitution extreme poverty

exiting his closet realizing and expressing his homosexuality

Families Come in All Styles

The family story remains a staple of youth fiction. We sometimes forget that even in those cozy Victorian stories so fondly remembered, some component of the domestic scene was often lacking; either father was away fighting the Civil War or parents were too poor to afford a proper coming-out gown. Since happy families are said to be all alike, it is not surprising that fiction has thrived on the descriptions of those we now call "dysfunctional."

staple principal element

Klein's fictional families are vastly different from the "nuclear" arrangements usually regarded as the social standard. They are, however, still reassuring and supportive structures for young people. While some parents in Klein's stories are more idealistic than practical, devoting their time to editing eccentric journals or joining Save the Deer movements that harass hunters, they generally still manage to make ends meet. Fathers may express poor judgment, but they are usually present in some manner. They may even function as custodial parents.

custodial relating to guardianship

In *Taking Sides* (1974), which introduces several of Klein's most fully realized and likable characters, Nell and Hugo are being reared by their divorced father in a New York City apartment. They spend weekends with their mother, who lives outside the city with her female partner. Lesbian parenthood is further explored, still with empathy, in *Breaking Up* (1980). Though the three "Sunshine" books (1975, 1977) were fictionalizations based on television programs first created by other writers, they are among Klein's more arresting family narratives. Dedicated stepfatherhood is their dominant feature. Even a middle-aged widower becomes a loving, adoptive single parent in *The Swap* (1983), a slightly distasteful though still interesting book, when he trades a red Z-28 Camaro for the unwanted baby of a teenage couple.

Girls Can Be Anything, and So Can Boys

Klein conceded that she had never been without a male protector, first her father and later her husband. She genuinely liked men and treated them sympathetically in her fiction. But she strongly embraced the feminist movement as a liberating and energizing force for both sexes. In her picture book for young children, *Girls Can Be Anything* (1973), she preached that any trade or profession can be followed by women, though she was not happy with Roy Doty's illustrations, particularly his caricatures of Golda Meir and Indira Gandhi. Two nonathletic boys, who also exemplify Jewish-Arab friendship, decide to become cheerleaders in *The Cheerleader* (1985), despite the initial skepticism of their classmates. Many roles for men are possible: In *Give and Take* (1985) a student becomes a professional sperm donor (perhaps the only career still closed to women), while in *No More Saturday Nights* (1988) a young man, not yet fully independent, wins permanent custody of the child born of his casual affair. Feminism further encourages people of all ages to fulfill themselves. Grandmothers active with cultural and athletic interests, and busy in assignations when they do not have live-in lovers, become familiar peripheral figures in the later novels. Despite her constructive platform, Klein regularly complained that she had not been embraced by the feminist establishment and that *Ms.*, the major feminist oracle, had largely ignored her work. She suspected that the Gloria Steinems of the movement found her lacking in personal credentials, with her successful marriage and lack of experience in the male-dominated corporate world.

assignations appointed meetings with lovers

platform declaration of principles

oracle person or institution that gives wise decisions or opinions

Gloria Steinem is a well-known feminist spokesperson and the founder of *Ms.* magazine.

On the Literary Couch

Though most discussion of Klein's writing has centered on her sexual openness or her feminism, the novels prove lasting more for their psychological insights. *Hiding* (1976) is a brilliant book that Klein lamented had "fallen through the cracks, just disappeared from the shelves" all too soon after its publication. Despite its unfortunate neglect, it presents one of the most penetrating psychological portraits in teenage fiction.

With creepy precognition, it foreshadows the pained autobiography of ballerina Gelsey Kirkland, *Dancing on My Grave* (1986). Krii, the first-person narrator, is a ballet student and performer. In her precarious grip on reality, she identifies with the animal roles that usually fall to her in productions like *The Nutcracker*. Her sexual feelings are also still ill defined, and the emotions aroused by her first affair, with an older mentor, are painfully ambivalent. Though she envies the seeming forthrightness of the bisexual members of the corps de ballet, there is no idea more frightening to her than that of being sexually vulnerable to the entire human race. When misunderstandings lead to the breakup of her first relationship, and her former lover marries on the rebound, she vanishes like a wounded animal. For several days, she hides in her parents' attic, quietly watching as the hidden lives of family members unfold. Regaining her psychic strength, she is then able to venture forth, taking some control of her life. She enters college, switching to a science career, where her introversion may be an asset rather than a disability.

Angel Face (1984) is a book that demonstrates an equally powerful understanding of the adolescent male psyche. So stark is its conclusion—which finally brings the suicide epidemic in Klein's adult stories to her youth fiction—that it was almost rejected for the young adult lists. Jason, ultimately one of Klein's most sympathetic central characters, performs miserably in school, is a social loser and a "pothead." As if his coming-of-age were not difficult enough, his family is disintegrating around him. One sister is dyslexic and anorexic, while another escapes the family chaos with Harvard Law School and her own destructive romantic relationships. During a carefully staged Thanksgiving dinner, described in both funny and heartbreaking detail, Jason's parents announce their impending divorce. His mother tries to hide her desolation under a humorous facade, which quickly collapses into an hysterical rant of obscenities. No longer able to cope with family problems, much less his own, Jason accepts an invitation to spend his summer in California. Abandoned by everyone, Mom fatally crashes her automobile. While the plot alone would not make *Angel Face* memorable, several unfor-

foreshadow to suggest events yet to come

ambivalent having simultaneous and contradictory feelings toward a person or object

introversion state of turning inward

psyche soul, self; mind

gettable characterizations, the nuances of spoken dialogue, and the inevitability with which Jason's mother moves to her destruction give this novel heavy impact.

The Klein Legacy

The books are now all written, though additional publications may appear when editors have finished sifting through Klein's papers. Many ideas that gestated in her fecund mind will never see fruition. A tentative assessment of an impressive body of work is, however, now possible. Some of Klein's friends believed that the label "teen author" embarrassed her and that the lack of recognition her adult fiction received remained a constant frustration. Yet her books for adults are merely competent, with the exceptions of her truly outstanding short stories. Her young adult books are those that stand out from the work of her fellow writers. She was a prolific writer, which in her case made her work uneven and her narratives sometimes repetitive. All artists deserve to be forever judged by their best, and hers was very good indeed.

Like Judy Blume, Klein, who sometimes called herself "a brand name author," reached a defined audience, who recognized the personal stamp on all her work. But Klein was also genuinely literary. Her social commentary may be scrutinized in the future and easily challenged. It is possible that her more strident feminism and advocacy of sexual freedom will seem naive, or perhaps even tedious, in a few years. But her status as a genuine woman of letters should endure. She gave her young adult audience honest and well-crafted books. Her work has contributed to the development of the adolescent novel as a serious literary genre.

There is much genuine wit in her work, along with the more biting satire. Her family scenes are often highly visual and very lively, even when the laughter comes through tears. Complying with publishers' demands, she frequently provided abbreviated narratives and accepted from her editors book titles she always admitted were sappy. Yet her forte was the compassionate dramatization of life as it is in that vital but frightening transitional stage from childhood to adulthood. This is her legacy.

---

fecund   fertile, fruitful

strident   loud or insistent so as to call attention

satire   irony, sarcasm

Selected Bibliography

WORKS BY NORMA KLEIN

Novels for Young Adults

Mom, the Wolf Man, and Me (1972)

It's Not What You Expect (1973)

Taking Sides (1974)

Hiding (1976)

Love Is One of the Choices (1978)

Breaking Up (1980)

Domestic Arrangements (1981)

The Queen of the What Ifs (1982)

Beginner's Love (1983)

Bizou (1983)

The Swap (1983)

Angel Face (1984)

Snapshots (1984)

The Cheerleader (1985)

Family Secrets (1985)

Give and Take (1985)

Going Backwards (1986)

Older Men (1987)

No More Saturday Nights (1988)

Learning How to Fall (1989)

Just Friends (1991)

Novels for Adults

Give Me One Good Reason (1973)

Coming to Life (1974)

Girls Turn Wives (1976)

Wives and Other Women (1982)

Lovers (1984)

American Dreams (1987)

The World As It Is (1989)

Short Stories

Love and Other Euphemisms (1972)

Sextet in A Minor (1983)

If you like Norma Klein, you might also derive some pleasure from Judy Blume, Robert Cormier, Robert Lipsyte, Norma Fox Mazer, Richard Peck, and Paul Zindel.

The PEN/Norma Klein Award for Children's Fiction was established in 1990 and is awarded every two years to new authors whose books, like Klein's, demonstrate the spirit that makes up the best children's literature.

Books for Children

Confessions of an Only Child (1973)

Girls Can Be Anything (1973)

Dinosaur's Housewarming Party (1974)

If I Had My Way (1974)

Naomi in the Middle (1974)

A Train for Jane (1974)

Blue Trees, Red Sky (1975)

What It's All About (1975)

Visiting Pamela (1979)

A Honey of a Chimp (1980)

Robbie and the Leap Year Blues (1981)

Baryshnikov's Nutcracker (1983)

Sunshine (1975)

The Sunshine Years (1975)

Sunshine Christmas (1977)

French Postcards (1979)

Articles

"Growing Up Human: The Case for Sexuality in Children's Books." In *Children's Literature in Education,* summer 1977, pp. 80–84.

"My Say." In *Publishers Weekly,* 9 March 1984, p. 106. Klein's lively expression of several opinions on her writing and the literary scene.

"Norma Klein." In *Something About the Author Autobiography Series.* Edited by Adele Sarkissian. Detroit: Gale Research, 1984, vol. 1, pp. 155–168.

"The Pleasures of Midlist." In *Publishers Weekly,* 28 March 1986, p. 58. Author's discussion of her market and literary reputation.

WORKS ABOUT NORMA KLEIN

Biographical and Critical Studies

Commire, Anne, ed. *Something About the Author.* Detroit: Gale Research, 1975, vol. 7, pp. 152–154.

Phy, Allene Stuart. *Presenting Norma Klein.* Boston: G. K. Hall, 1988.

Interviews

West, Mark. Interview with Norma Klein, New York City, 11 June 1985. Portions of this interview were published in *New York Times Book Review,* 24 August 1986, p. 20.

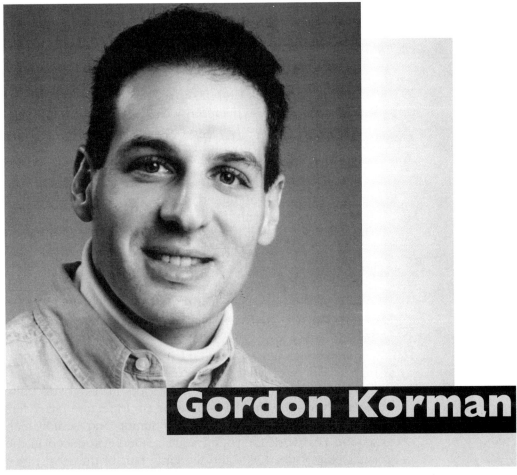

Gordon Korman

(1963-   )

by Teri S. Lesesne

For Gordon Korman, being funny has always been serious business, and business continues to boom! Korman's career began rather early. Born in Montreal, Canada, Korman grew up in and around Toronto. He admits that this early childhood was, well, less than exciting: no brothers or sisters or even pets to cause some ruckus. Little wonder, then, that Korman created his own excitement early on in life.

Off to an Early Start!

When he was in seventh grade, his teacher informed the class that the final four months of the school year would be devoted to writing; each student was expected to write a novel for his or her finished project. For that English assignment he received only a B+, but Korman was encouraged to find an outlet for publication. Because he was the class monitor for the

outlet   a medium of expression

Scholastic TAB Book Club, Korman figured he had a foot in the door. He sent the manuscript to the address on the book order, and eventually *This Can't Be Happening at Macdonald Hall!* became his first published work, in 1977. So, at the tender age of fourteen, Korman was an author.

He followed his first novel, about the antics of two boys and their friends who attend a boys' boarding school called Macdonald Hall, with other tales of their misadventures. These books, aimed at young readers, are known as the Bruno and Boots series, named after the two young rapscallions who are the focus of the books set at Macdonald Hall. Books in the Bruno and Boots series include: *Go Jump in the Pool!* (1979), *Beware the Fish!* (1980), *The War with Mr. Wizzle* (1982), *The Zucchini Warriors* (1988), and *Macdonald Hall Goes Hollywood* (1991).

As Korman grew older and moved from junior high to high school, and ultimately to New York University to study film and dramatic writing, the characters in his novels grew older along with him. His stories began to feature characters caught in ludicrous situations in junior and senior high school. His work for young adult readers, produced in the latter part of the 1980s and the early part of the 1990s, provide humorous insights into the trials and joys of being a teenager. Korman's university work in moviemaking shows up in *Macdonald Hall Goes Hollywood*; the author's life provided grist for the mill then and still does today.

It is the laughter, the humorous nature of the books that is most important to Korman. As Korman confesses in *Speaking for Ourselves,* "I know it's impolite to laugh at my own jokes, but I really crack myself up while I'm writing" (Gallo, p 113.) Perhaps that ability to amuse himself as well as his readers is one of the reasons for Korman's popularity.

ludicrous ridiculous, absurd

grist for the mill something that can be used to one's advantage

You've Got to Be Joking!

Korman believes that there is a void in the world of books available for young adults. Echoing a sentiment expressed many years ago by author Paul Fleischman, the older a reader gets, Korman asserts in *Speaking for Ourselves,* "the less fun stuff there is to read" (Gallo, p. 113). To remedy this situation, Korman uses humor to get his point across. As one adolescent observed in *Emergency Librarian,* "Mr. Korman's novels are a refreshing mix of action, humor, and true-to-life characters" (White, p. 53).

Korman manages to imbue his writing with much of his own personality and the experiences from his own life. Though his style may be breezy, Korman has some serious messages for readers. Each of his books focuses on the plight of an average adolescent who is dealing with all the normal adolescent problems, especially strict parental and even stricter school rules. Here are characters who come up against authority figures and win. More often than not, the heroes and heroines of Korman's books break the rules or, at the very least, stretch them to their limits. Though they may challenge the people in charge, they do learn to operate within the system. If a Korman character feels something within the system needs changing, she or he will do the changing from inside the system. How the characters go about claiming power is often the most humorous part of the story.

imbue to spread through thoroughly

Don't Care High

The students at Don Carey High School (*Don't Care High*, 1985) just don't care. Perhaps part of their apathy stems from the fact that their school is named in honor of a man who designed the sewer system for their town. Perhaps it is just the nature of the sophisticated high school student to remain "cool" at all times. Regardless of the reasons, Don Carey High is aptly nicknamed "Don't Care High." Enter Paul, a student new to the school. When he and Sheldon team up, Don't Care High will have to find a new nickname. They manage, within a short period of time, to create a great deal of student interest in the workings of a school that has failed to elect a student body president since 1956, only because no one has volunteered to run for the office. How Paul and Sheldon set about achieving the goal of a wildly enthusiastic student body is the setup for some of Korman's best punch lines and gags.

apathy lack of emotion; indifference

Korman skillfully avoids the easy pitfalls in this, his first novel for older readers. It would have been a much more mean-spirited book had Korman chosen to tell the story of teenage apathy from a more adult perspective. Told from the point of view of Paul, however, the humorous sting is barbed but not deadly. The use of an adolescent narrator, a sieve of sorts through which all the events and characters of the novel are filtered, is another hallmark of Korman's writing. His protagonists are occasionally objective reporters of what they observe going on; more often than not, however, they are so close to the action that objectivity is not possible for them. The fact that the main characters have a stake in the outcome of the adventure more readily allows readers to "come along for the ride," so to speak. In addition, the opening scene of the novel, set in homeroom on the first day of a new school year, is one of the most hilarious that Korman has imagined. The humor is strong, perhaps, because the scene, though exaggerated, is quite realistic. Because Korman bases his comedy firmly in reality, the humor remains good-natured.

Son of Interflux

Meet Simon Irving. His life would be perfect except for one thing: his father's involvement in a company named Interflux (*Son of Interflux,* 1986). Interflux is a source of great embarrassment for Simon. It is a company that seems to gobble up everything in sight, including Simon's father's time and attention and patience. As far as Simon is concerned, Interflux is the largest manufacturer of useless objects in the world. When the company decides to expand its holdings and buy the land next to Simon's school, the time is right for Simon to revolt. Simon "borrows" some money from the student council and reinvests it in a tiny strip of land adjacent to the school. The company that Simon founds, Antiflux, manages to thwart Interflux's plans for expansion. However, when Simon's father discovers who is at the helm of Antiflux, the craziness is just beginning.

In many ways, *Son of Interflux* is typical of Korman's work. Here is a rather average young adult who is trying to declare his independence from his father. How the character pursues his goal is partly what fashions the comic element of the novel. This same device is evident in *Don't Care High* as Paul and Sheldon attempt to change the apathetic nature of the student body. As in all of Korman's novels, moreover, there are the requisite quirky characters, such as the car mechanic/sculptor/coconspirator Phil Baldwin and

requisite necessary

the absent-minded professor of art, Mr. Querada. Korman's work is not formulaic, but certain elements do appear from one work to the next.

A Semester in the Life of a Garbage Bag

When Sean Delancey begins eleventh grade at the start of *A Semester in the Life of a Garbage Bag* (1987), he expects it to be a quiet year. No longer will he be one of the persecuted freshmen or one of the ignored sophomore class. He will join the ranks of the upperclassmen without much fanfare. Well, that *was* his plan. As the saying goes, the best laid plans and all that. What really destroys Sean's hopes for a peaceful school year is one Raymond Jardine, a fellow classmate whose middle name might just as well be "Bad Luck." Though he should know better, Sean agrees to assist Raymond in his knuckleheaded scheme to win a trip to Greece. The scheme will involve poetry and the destruction of a thirty-million-dollar piece of property.

Hapless Raymond Jardine is just one of the offbeat characters so familiar to Korman's fans. Here is someone virtually equipped with his own black cloud and a forecast of 100 percent rain! Of course, what Korman allows readers to realize is that they (the characters and the readers as well) make their own luck. Much of what Raymond chalks up to chance actually occurs because of his action, or lack thereof.

Sean and Raymond challenge the wisdom of several authority figures, including the government, in this misadventure, again with a school setting. As in much of Korman's work, the main characters are quick to spot the inconsistencies that can exist in any bureaucratic system. Once the characters begin to question the inconsistencies, they are likely to be facing a confrontation with those in charge. In this instance, the authority figure who looms large is the school principal. As in the case of many of Korman's novels with a school setting, the principal is a harried but basically well-intentioned individual who demonstrates great forbearance when dealing with the sometimes wacky characters issuing from Korman's fertile imagination. As reviewers have noted, few authors can depict the school environment as entertainingly as Korman can.

Hapless Raymond Jardine is just one of the offbeat characters so familiar to Korman's fans. Here is someone virtually equipped with his own black cloud and a forecast of 100 percent rain!

harried beset by problems

Losing Joe's Place

In this novel (published in 1990), summer vacation looks to be a dream for Jason and his two friends, Don and Ferguson (also known as "The Peach"). Each of them has acquired a job at the local plastics company for the summer. To add to the excitement, they will live on their own in the city for the entire summer—unsupervised! Joe, Jason's brother, is allowing them to use his apartment for their summer escapades. Of course, there are quite a few laws laid down by Joe, but once he is out of the picture, Jason has assured Don and The Peach that fun will begin. Ahead lies a summer full of promise. Little do the boys suspect that the summer will mean a promotion for one of them, some romance, and the probable loss of Joe's lease!

Once again, Korman employs a first-person narrative. Through Jason's eyes, we see the story unfold, and we have his immediate reaction to the ludicrous events that make up this story. This sense of immediacy places readers squarely in the story and allows them to experience the zany antics first-hand. As in the case of *Don't Care High,* the use of Jason as a narrator softens the sting as Korman pokes more than a little fun at Jason and his friends, who naively assume that their summer jobs will lead to fame and fortune.

What the boys learn is a very valuable lesson: success is not measured by the small triumphs we experience. Instead, suggests Korman, success is found in the larger picture of what we do with our lives and our talents. The theme of success, even success at a young age, is another one common to much of Korman's works. This theme seems to hearken back to Korman's early success as a writer. He is quick to demonstrate through his characters that even the young can maintain control over their lives and find success. Certainly this hopeful message is one that needs to be conveyed to adolescents who often feel like disenfranchised members of society. Korman seems to suggest that this feeling of inadequacy may be overcome.

hearken back go back to something as a source

disenfranchised deprived of privileges or legal rights

The D- Poems of Jeremy Bloom

This book (published in 1992) is a bit of a departure for Korman. It marks his first foray into poetry *and* is a collaborative venture. His coauthor is his mother. Here is the tale of Jeremy Bloom, who oversleeps on the first day of junior high, therefore missing out on an elective known fondly among the students as "Snooze Patrol." In his panic to find another easy-A elective, Jeremy stumbles across a class he thinks is pottery. He is more than a bit perturbed to discover that the class is, in reality, *poetry*. Thus begins the saga of Jeremy and his D- poems. This book is a collection of poetry held together by a narrative that recounts Jeremy's misadventures during his semester in poetry class, which include setting off a stink bomb and sending his teacher an unpleasant present.

The framework of the book serves to underscore the development of Jeremy Bloom as a writer. Attentive readers will become aware of the gradual change in the rhythm of the poems as they move from the Pterodactyl Period (early in the semester) to the Tarzan Period (the end of the semester). The school year is divided into five periods; each new division marks another milestone in the career of Jeremy Bloom, the poet. The poems Jeremy pens are frequently funny, yet they deal with important topics including how one can discern if something is indeed a poem ("Vital Question"), how to write thank-you notes for presents not particularly valued ("Honesty Is Not Always the Best Policy"), and "How to Wake a Guy for School."

This collection of poems may assist those readers who enjoyed the poetry of Shel Silverstein, Jack Prelutsky, and Judith Viorst in finding more mature, yet humorous, poems to read. For others, this would be an excellent collection to introduce a genre or to convince readers that poetry does not have to be abstract nor overly sentimental. Here are poems that demonstrate Korman's ability to use word play in a new forum.

> **Shel Silverstein** (1932–) is a cartoonist and popular poet for children. His books include *The Giving Tree* and *A Light in the Attic*. **Jack Prelutsky** (1940–) is a musician and poet for children. **Judith Viorst** (1931–) is a columnist and children's books author.

But Seriously, Folks . . .

Witty style, flippant humor, zany characters, subtle messages: these are the critical attributes of Korman's novels for adolescents. Often overlooked because he writes so-called funny books, Korman's work deserves serious examination. Korman does offer readers real insight into the world in which they live. While he takes a good-natured approach to writing about the pitfalls and the triumphs of adolescence, he never fails to provide readers with essential themes. His humorous

> **flippant** lacking proper respect or seriousness

works allow readers the opportunity to laugh at themselves and, maybe, to take responsibility for their actions and their lives. Being funny *is* serious business, and Gordon Korman really has a head for this type of funny business.

If you appreciate Gordon Korman's irreverent style and his crazy sense of humor, you might try one of the following books: *Bel-Air Bambi and the Mall Rats* by Richard Peck, *Attaboy, Sam!* by Lois Lowry, *This Place Has No Atmosphere* by Paula Danziger, and *A Fate Totally Worse than Death* by Paul Fleischman.

Selected Bibliography

WORKS BY GORDON KORMAN

This Can't Be Happening at Macdonald Hall! (1977, 1990)

Go Jump in the Pool (1979)

Beware the Fish! (1980)

The War with Mr. Wizzle (1982, 1990)

No Coins, Please (1984)

Don't Care High (1985)

Son of Interflux (1986)

A Semester in the Life of a Garbage Bag (1987)

The Zucchini Warriors (1988, 1991)

Radio Fifth Grade (1989, 1991)

Losing Joe's Place (1990)

Macdonald High Goes Hollywood (1991)

The D- Poems of Jeremy Bloom, with Bernice Korman (1992)

The Twinkie Squad (1992)

The Toilet Paper Tigers (1993)

The Three Z's (1994)

Something Fishy at Macdonald Hall (1995)

WORKS ABOUT GORDON KORMAN

Gallo, Donald R., ed. *Speaking for Ourselves.* Urbana, Ill.: National Council of Teachers of English, 1990, p. 113.

White, Valerie. "Paperbacks for Young Adults." *Emergency Librarian,* September/October 1988, p. 53.

How to Write to the Author

Gordon Korman
c/o Scholastic, Inc.
555 Broadway
New York, NY 10012

Kathryn Lasky

(1944-   )

by Barbara G. Samuels

" I like to get up every morning and recreate myself,"
Kathryn Lasky said in a May 1995 interview. "It's
easy for an author to get seduced into writing the
same kind of book again and again, but that's not the kind of
person I am." As a result, she has written in a variety of genres for all ages: stories for very young children, fiction and
nonfiction for middle-grade children and young adults, and
novels for adults. She wants her books to answer questions,
raise questions, and encourage imaginative thinking. On a
promotional flyer for Scribners she says, "For me, the most
important thing is if a story is real. Real stories can either be
fiction or nonfiction." No story is just a listing of facts about a
subject. "For me in writing I am searching for the story
among the truths, the facts, the lies, and the realities," she
says in the September/October 1985 *Horn Book* (p. 530).

Lasky is curious. Her curiosity about the past, about unusual and unique people and occupations, and about the
reasons for human actions have led her to write a number of

Quotations from Kathryn Lasky
that are not attributed to a
published source are from a
personal interview conducted by
the author of this article on 9
May 1995 and are published
here by permission of Kathryn
Lasky.

books that in various forms explore the questions on her mind. In all her writing—whether it is contemporary realistic fiction, historical fiction, mysteries, information books, or picture books—Lasky takes time to immerse herself in the subjects so that they come alive for her readers. Since 1975, when she wrote the picture book *Agatha's Alphabet,* she has written over forty books.

immerse deeply involve

Growing Up with Books

avid very eager

voracious very eager; hungry or greedy

Books were central in the Indianapolis household of readers in which Kathryn Lasky grew up. She says her parents, Marven and Hortense, were both avid readers who read to her constantly. Her sister, five years older than she, was a voracious reader. "I lived in a world of books at home," she says. Such an environment encouraged her writing, as well. On a Harcourt Brace "Author at a Glance" publicity flyer, she tells of returning home from a family outing to an A&W root beer stand in northern Indiana on a summer night. "There were no stars that night, but there were clouds, thick and wooly. Suddenly an image struck me. 'It's a sheepback sky,' I said to no one in particular. Hearing me my mother turned around and said, 'Kathy, you should be a writer.'" Her parents' support and faith in her gave her the self-confidence to overcome the grim atmosphere of an all-girls' school in Indianapolis, where, she says, "It pained them to praise you. At most a teacher might say to my mother 'She has a way with words,' but they would never tell me I could write well." It was not until she arrived at the University of Michigan that her instructors were supportive of her writing.

Trained as a teacher herself, Lasky started to write stories for children when she hated the workbooks that were part of the curriculum. She recognized that she could write appealing materials to help children learn to read. As a child, she had always invented stories. While pursuing a master's degree at Wheelock College with encouragement from her parents and her husband, she started writing for publication.

Family Ties and Jewish Roots

Lasky's novels for young adult readers reflect both her own experiences and an immersion in the subjects and issues central to the stories. For example, in Lasky's novel *The*

Night Journey (1986), Nana Sachie's story about her escape from tsarist Russia is based on the experiences of Lasky's great-aunt. After a visit to see her great-aunt in Minnesota, Lasky asked her to write about her escape. Eventually, Lasky wove her great-aunt's letter into a novel in which thirteen-year-old Rachel hears the story of her Jewish family's journey out of Russia on the night of the Jewish holiday Purim. Events in the novel shift from the contemporary United States to Russia in the late nineteenth century at the time of Tsar Nicholas II. Just as Haman had schemed to kill the Jews in ancient Persia, an adviser of Tsar Nicholas blamed Jews for the economic and social hardships of the country. The contrast between the security of Rachel's multigenerational contemporary home and the fears of a family in hiding under a pile of chicken coops in a wagon driven by a foreboding character named Wolf provides the tension for the novel. It is Sachie's story that gives the book suspense, but both stories, the contemporary one and the historical one, convey the importance of freedom and of a close and supportive family life—themes that run through many of Lasky's books.

Both *Prank* (1986) and *Pageant* (1986), novels with contemporary American settings, reflect the significance of family ties and Lasky's Jewish roots. Like *Night Journey, Pageant* clearly draws from events and remembered emotions in Lasky's life. Set in the early 1960s, Sarah Benjamin, a Jew in a Christian all-girls' school in Indianapolis, is cast each year since seventh grade as a shepherd in the Christmas pageant. When Sarah's older sister Marla (who, like Lasky's older sister, helped her with school assignments) leaves home for Wellesley College, Sarah runs up her telephone bill getting help with her homework and moral support for dealing with her problems. Her misery increases when Aunt Hattie moves in and tries to make Sarah over in her image. Sarah's John F. Kennedy button and her liberal politics make her feel like an outsider, but her parents encouragement helps her through difficult days. Growing up in this setting and time is a struggle for Sarah, as it probably was for Lasky herself.

Prank is set in blue-collar East Boston, near where Lasky lived for some of her adult life and not far from Cambridge, Massachusetts, where she lives now. In this novel, a synagogue is vandalized by a group of teens, including Tim Flynn, the brother of Birdie Flynn, the protagonist. Birdie reads some of Elie Wiesel's book *Night* to learn about the Nazi atrocities. Readers of this book learn along with Birdie

Tsarist Russia refers to the period (1547–1917) during which Russia was ruled by a tsar, or czar (an imperial title that comes from the Latin word *caesar*).

Purim celebrates the defeat of **Haman**, the right-hand man of the ancient Persian king Ahasuerus. The king's wife, Esther, was secretly a Jew, and the story is told in the Old Testament Book of Esther.

protagonist main character of a literary work

anti-Semitic hostile toward or discriminatory against Jews

The **Holocaust** was the mass murder of at least 11 million people, especially Jews, by the Nazis during World War II. The word "holocaust" means "thorough destruction by fire."

The **Amish** are Mennonite Christians who first settled in America in the seventeenth century and are known for a simple way of life that rejects modern technology.

about the horrible events of Adolf Hitler's Germany. As she realizes what her brother has done, Birdie struggles to understand the nature of her brother's anti-Semitic act in light of her growing knowledge about the Holocaust. She also struggles with her own decisions to escape the poverty-stricken and bleak environment of East Boston and become a writer. She begins to recognize the failings of her family, an angry, abusive group of individuals. Lasky uses the symbolism of a broken Madonna on the Flynns' front lawn to dramatize the dysfunctional Flynn family. Birdie's support for her brother despite his failings eventually helps him to seek training that will get him out of East Boston.

Characters and Imagery

Lasky's novels introduce strong-willed protagonists who face ethical dilemmas. One of the most memorable of those characters is Meribah, the main character in *Beyond the Divide* (1983). When her father is shunned by the Amish community in which they live, Meribah makes the decision to join him in a wagon train to the West during the Gold Rush. As we view the journey through Meribah's eyes, we feel every mile of the hardships the pioneers endured, faced with hunger, thirst, disagreements, dangers from animals, Indian attacks, rape, and suicide. Lasky introduces and develops a variety of characters, including Meribah's friend Serena, a young society woman from Philadelphia, whose interest in fancy clothing and poetry is different from anything Meribah has ever known. Just as Meribah had to decide whether to join her father or stay in Pennsylvania with her mother and the rest of her family, so too she has to decide how to respond when her best friend is raped on the trail. When she asks her father why, he responds: "There are no answers. There are only questions. 'Can one be angry with God?' Meribah whispers"(p. 132).

Asked in a phone interview about the fact that her daughter is named Meribah like the main character in *Beyond the Divide*, Lasky said that she used the name Meribah in the book because it was an old family name and one of her favorite names. "The day after I finished the book I found out that I was pregnant." At first she was disappointed that she had already used the name in the book, but her husband, Christopher Knight, convinced her that there was no reason she could not use the name again for their daughter.

The details of the journey Meribah and her father take across the country in a wagon train are evidence of the thorough research that is the trademark of Lasky's historical novels. Meribah's problems seem real because the reader can feel and smell the vastness of the prairie, the dryness of the desert, and the steepness of the rocky cliffs. Early in the trip, "the land suddenly flattened, and the sky seemed everywhere. There was an occasional tree, perhaps a single house on an otherwise unmarked horizon, but there was immensity and aloneness" (p. 44). Later, as they continue their journey, "the country began to grind on them like a giant millstone. But instead of granite, Meribah thought, this millstone is made of bad water, foul air, and leached earth that gives way under foot and wheel" (p. 84). The book is a wonderful addition to a study of this period in American history. In a review in *Language Arts,* Jean Greenlaw says, "A more important use is in the reading and rereading of an author who polishes her phrasing until it gleams with the beauty of gold that many of the people moving West sought (pp. 70–71). This richness of the descriptions was both praised and attacked by reviewers, some of whom thought too much description interrupted the flow of the story for teens.

> **leached earth** soil from which water has removed minerals

In general, reviewers commend Lasky for her well developed characters and her lyrical, vivid imagery. She created images in all her books that evoke moods, describe places, and make characters come alive. At one point in *Beyond the Divide,* Serena joins Meribah who is walking with the cow through the prairie grass.

> **lyrical** songlike or expressive

She spoke out from under the layers of gauze swathed around her straw bonnet. Around her shoulders was wrapped a thin cream-colored pelerine that fell in two points near her knees. Her hands were gloved, and she carried a white parasol.

> **pelerine** woman's short cape with long ends in front

"Serena, I thought you were an old dandelion tumbling down the road."

"How charming! An old dandelion blow! You are a funny dear, Meribah. I thought I resembled at least a meringue glacée!" (p. 46–47).

> **meringue glaceé** glazed or frosted pastry made of egg whites and sugar

Lasky's dual images of dandelions and meringue glacée quickly capture the differences in the two girls: Meribah, a simple Amish farm girl whose religion forbids decoration, and Serena, a social butterfly whose Philadelphia life has centered on debutante balls and fancy gowns.

In *The Bone Wars* (1988), another of Lasky's historical novels, she introduces a group of carefully developed fictional and historical characters. With a few carefully chosen words, for example, Lasky introduces Buffalo Bill Cody: "First came a man in buckskin britches and dirty undershirt. His blond hair flowed down to his shoulders, and his handlebar mustache dipped into a small pointed beard. He looked at Thad quickly as he swept by. 'Never get married, boy! Never!'" (pp. 56–57).

General George Custer is another historical figure who plays a role in the book. Lasky's description of him is characteristically vivid. "But there was a yellow blaze brighter than the lamps or the gleam of the scabbards. . . . It was fire unto itself. . . . A fringe of gold epaulets, stars and braid, then a thick cascade of curls. . . . The blue of the dress uniform and the figure of the man seemed to dissolve into the shadows, leaving the curls and the golden fringe to hang in a kind of mysterious suspension" (p. 92). With this description, Custer's vanity and the emptiness of his leadership are foreshadowed early in the novel.

scabbard sheath for a sword

epaulet fringed ornament on the shoulder of a military officer's uniform

Themes and Issues

Lasky explores significant themes and issues in her novels. *The Bone Wars* is about the conflict between scientific progress (in the form of paleontologists who seek fossils of ancient species) and the cultural traditions of Native American tribes. The scientists involved in seeking bones in the Great Plains of the United States in the 1870s were invading territory that was the home of Cheyenne and Sioux Indian tribes. At the same time, the region was being claimed by gold seekers, farmers and ranchers, and the U. S. Cavalry. Lasky questions the costs of progress and the values of those who promote it. In particular she questions the scientific honesty of the academics from Harvard, Yale, and Oxford who competed for the collection of bones and sought to limit public access to information. Stereotypes of cowboys, Native

stereotype preconceived idea about the characteristics of a group of people

Americans, soldiers, and scientists are for the most part avoided in this story of the West, which has the action of a lively Western movie.

Memoirs of a Bookbat (1994) also addresses a substantive issue—the censorship of books by religious fundamentalists. Harper Jessups, a voracious reader and creative thinker, is the daughter of parents who become missionaries for F.A.C.E., or Family Action for Christian Education. Growing up in the Jessup household and maintaining her love of books and reading is a challenge for Harper. With the help of her best friend Gray (a teen whose humor and love of Ann Rice novels Lasky admits is loosely based on her son Max), Harper finally recognizes the "little person, deep down in my chest, or was it in my brain, hopping around, beating its fists, and stomping its feet. . . . And she wanted her freedom" (p. 196).

Lasky believes in writing from experience. "I have always tried hard to listen, smell, and touch the place that I write about—especially if I am lucky enough to be there," she says in the September/October 1985 *Horn Book* (p. 530). The immediacy in *The Bone Wars* is the result of a trip she took to Montana. In an interview she said, "I was two-thirds through writing the book and I got stuck. I had to see the battlefield for the battle of Little Big Horn so I could get on with that chapter. At the same time I wanted the experience of actually digging for fossils." Lasky and her son Max, who was nine years old at the time, went on a digging expedition in Montana. The imagery and immediacy of the scenes describing paleontological work are the result of that trip. The next year, she went back to the site as part of a paleontological team and from that experience she wrote *Dinosaur Dig* (1990), a nonfiction book.

In her other novels, Lasky tackles serious and diverse issues with imagination and information. These books include *Home Free* (1988), which covers environmental concerns; *Beyond the Burning Time* (1994), an exploration of civic hysteria and justice during the Salem witch trials; and the Starbuck Family Adventures—*Shadows in the Water* (1992) and *Voice in the Wind* (1993)—a series of books about two sets of precocious telepathic twins who solve mysteries. Although most of her books for young adults are fiction, teens might also be interested in her information books, which reflect the same attention to story, detail, experience, and research. In addition, her books aim to convey the mystery and miracle

> *Harper finally recognizes the "little person, deep down in my chest, or was it in my brain, hopping around, beating its fists, and stomping its feet. . . . And she wanted her freedom."*

precocious unusually mature for one's age

telepathic able to communicate directly to each other's minds without speaking

aesthetic relating to ideas about art or beauty

of the subjects she explores. To write each one, she visited the person whose work she is describing or participated in the experience itself. "I try to do as little explaining as possible. . . . I seem to seek a nonfactual kind of truth that focuses on certain aesthetic and psychological realities," she says (*Horn Book,* 1985, p. 532). She looks for the special moment—the sneeze of the puppeteer (*Puppeteer* [1985]), the late night musings of the man preparing maple syrup (*Sugaring Time* [1983]), the imaginings of a fourteen year old crossing the Atlantic Ocean in a tall ship of the nineteenth century (*Tall Ships* [1978]), and the connection between a nature photographer and his subject (*Think Like an Eagle* [1992]). Each of these books is illustrated with photographs taken by Lasky's husband, Christopher Knight, a documentary photographer and filmmaker, and each grows out of the experiences they have shared. "I am still, even in my nonfiction books, more fascinated with the story within the facts, the beauty in the process, the mystery within the known, Lasky says in a Scribner's flyer. Whether she is writing fiction or nonfiction, her books challenge the imagination, stimulate questions, and promote critical thinking.

Selected Bibliography

WORKS BY KATHRYN LASKY

If you like Kathryn Lasky's books, you might also enjoy books by Avi, Paula Fox, Russell Freedman, and Ann Rinaldi.

Novels for Young Adults

Beyond the Divide (1983)

The Night Journey (1986)

Pageant (1986)

Prank (1986)

The Bone Wars (1988)

Home Free (1988)

Beyond the Burning Time (1994)

Memoirs of a Book Bat (1994)

Informational Books

Tall Ships (1978)

Sugaring Time (1983)

Puppeteer (1985)

Dinosaur Dig (1990)

Traces of Life: The Origins of Humankind (1990)

Surtsey: The Newest Place on Earth (1992)

Think Like an Eagle: At Work with a Wildlife Photographer (1992)

Monarchs (1993)

Days of the Dead (1994)

The Librarian Who Measured the Earth (1994)

Pond Scum (1995)

Adult Books

Mumbo Jumbo (under the name Kathryn L. Knight) (1992)

Dark Swan (under the name Kathryn L. Knight) (1994)

Books for Children

A Baby for Max (1987)

Sea Swan (1988)

Double-Trouble Squared: A Starbuck Family Adventure (1991)

Fourth of July Bear (1991)

I Have an Aunt on Marlborough Street (1992)

Shadows on the Water (1992)

Lunch Bunnies (1993)

My Island Grandma (1993)

The Tantrum (1993)

Voice in the Wind (1993)

The Solo (1994)

Other Works

Searching for Laura Ingalls: A Reader's Journal, with Meribah Knight (1993)

WORKS ABOUT KATHRYN LASKY

Books and Articles

Greenlaw, Jean M. Review of *Beyond the Divide. Language Arts,* January 1984, pp. 70–71.

Lasky, Kathryn. "Reflections on Nonfiction." In *Horn Book,* September/October 1985, pp. 527–532.

———. "Creativity in a Boom Industry." *Horn Book,* November/December 1991, pp. 705–711.

Metzger, Linda, ed. *Contemporary Authors: New Revision Series.* Detroit: Gale Research, 1984, vol. 11, p. 320.

**How to Write to
the Author**
Kathryn Lasky
c/o Scholastic Blue Sky
555 Broadway
New York, NY 10012

Senick, Gerald K., ed. *Children's Literature Review*. Detroit: Gale Research, 1986, vol. 11, pp. 112–122.

Promotional Materials

"Author at a Glance: Kathryn Lasky" available from Harcourt Brace Children's Books.

"Kathryn Lasky" flyer available from Charles Scribner's Sons, 1985.

Harper Lee

(1926-   )

by Claudia Durst Johnson

I n 1993, thirty-three years after the publication of *To Kill a Mockingbird* (1960), two popular American bands took their names from the book by Harper Lee. One band played under the name of "Tequila Mockingbird" and the other, "the Boo Radleys." Regardless of whether these rock groups gain or lose popularity, their names are a testament to the enduring life of the novel set in the Deep South during the 1930s.

Further evidence of the long-lived impact of *To Kill a Mockingbird* is apparent in a debate conducted in the public press in 1993 among groups of lawyers arguing about one of the novel's main characters. The lawyer who started the controversy was shocked by the public outrage over his sharp criticism of Atticus Finch, the hero of the novel, whom many lawyers regarded as their personal and professional hero. *To Kill a Mockingbird* has influenced generations who have read the novel or seen its 1962 screen adaptation, which was still shown frequently on television in the 1990s and was

Deep South the Southeastern U.S., including Alabama, Georgia, Louisiana, and Mississippi

widely available on videotape. Probably drawing on the success of the novel and film, "I'll Fly Away," a highly rated television series of the early 1990s, portrayed characters and situations similar to those in *To Kill a Mockingbird.*

None of this continuing interest in *To Kill a Mockingbird* is surprising when you realize that by 1992, more than 18 million copies of the book had been sold in paperback alone. Since its publication in 1960, the book has appeared on reading lists for high school classes as often as any book in the English language. In a survey conducted by the Library of Congress of books most often cited as "making a difference," *To Kill a Mockingbird* was at the top of the list, second only to the Bible.

Comparisons with Similar Books

There is an article about Mark Twain in volume 3.

The greatest literary influence on *To Kill a Mockingbird* is an equally enduring American masterpiece—Mark Twain's *Adventures of Huckleberry Finn* (1885). Like Twain's story, Harper Lee's is told from the relatively naive viewpoint of a young person who has not yet adopted many of the prejudices of adult society. Both books are about social outcasts, racial prejudice, and various kinds of imprisonment and slavery; both reveal the weaknesses of the society in which the characters live. Set roughly a decade later than *To Kill a Mockingbird* is J. D. Salinger's *The Catcher in the Rye* (1951). Salinger's novel is also told through the eyes of an unusually perceptive youth, a loner in society who encounters the cruel realities of the adult world in the process of growing up.

There is an article about J. D. Salinger in volume 3.

The Novel's Universality

Only a book with universal appeal to readers living in different times and places could continue to attract such a wide audience as *To Kill a Mockingbird.* It is still a profoundly moving work, long after the specific events of its day have passed. It is about children growing up and encountering the harshness of the adult world; about a time when a child realizes that adults and adult society are not always as strong, wise, or good as they pretend to be, but that many adults are far more heroic than children may assume. For example,

Scout Finch, the six-year-old narrator of the book, and her brother Jem see people in their community doing little to stop a lynching or the conviction of Tom Robinson, an innocent African American man accused of raping a white woman. They are also awed by the courage of their father, Atticus Finch, who shoots a rabid dog in the street, stands up to the lynch mob, and goes against community pressure to defend Tom Robinson in court.

To Kill a Mockingbird is also about coming to terms with people who are different from us, whether they are people of a different race, like Tom Robinson, or eccentrics like Boo Radley, the Finches' mysterious next-door neighbor. The children find that difference, particularly in the form of Boo Radley, both frightens and intrigues them. Their curiosity about Boo partly explains their love of frightening stories such as that of Dracula. In the process of getting to know the foreign and forbidding elements in the world, Scout and Jem come to sympathize with and acknowledge the same dark elements within themselves. Scout begins to realize that she also is something of an outsider in her society. One of her last actions in the novel is to look at the world from Boo's front porch, or, to use a metaphor that her father has often taught his children, "to walk around in Boo's shoes."

The Novel's Timeliness

Although the novel is timeless in its appeal, it also refers to specific events in Alabama in the 1950s. It appeared in the most turbulent time in twentieth-century southern history, when serious challenges were being made to the rigid segregation codes in the Deep South. While Lee was writing it, deep-seated racial tensions, buried for a hundred years or more, exploded on the surface of life in Alabama. The two most noteworthy events were the Montgomery bus boycott and the attempted enrollment of an African American woman, Autherine Lucy, in the all-white state university. The bus boycott, which was reported prominently in the national news and continued from December 1955 until December 1956, was begun when Rosa Parks, an African American woman, refused to move to the back of a segregated city bus.

All elements of life were segregated at that time—schools, colleges, restaurants, churches, all modes of transportation, movie theaters, recreation areas, and stores. African Americans were allowed to sit on a city bus only after all white passengers had found seats, and they usually had to go to the back of the bus. If white passengers boarded a bus that had no available seats, the African American passengers nearest the front had to give up their seats to the white people and stand in the back. When Rosa Parks, weary from her long day's work, refused to get up, she was arrested, and the African American community in Montgomery responded by boycotting the buses.

In the course of the year of the boycott, before the segregation policy was officially changed, white businesses suffered greatly, and houses and churches of African American citizens were bombed. In January of the same year, the University of Alabama admitted the first African American, but by late February, after hoodlums had rioted on the campus, her admission was rescinded. Four years later, within this social climate, *To Kill A Mockingbird* was published, addressing through its plot the racial injustice in Alabama.

plot deliberate sequence of events in a literary work

Biographical Roots of the Novel

People who admire *To Kill a Mockingbird* are always curious about its author, chiefly because the impact of her seemingly autobiographical novel is so intense. The book takes place in a small, southern Alabama town, the setting in which the young Harper Lee grew up. Atticus Finch is modeled on Lee's father, who was a newspaperman, lawyer, and legislator. The novel's conflict, arising from an African American man's being falsely accused of rape, has many elements in common with another notorious trial in northern Alabama in the 1930s. Lee is in the company of writers such as Margaret Mitchell, who wrote *Gone With the Wind,* and Ralph Ellison, who wrote *Invisible Man,* in having written a single novel, but one that is widely regarded as a masterpiece.

Yet this author is one of the most private persons with a public reputation in the United States. Since the early 1960s, just after the appearance of the award-winning novel and film, Lee has granted no interviews, has made only a handful of public appearances, and, in general, has declined to talk about herself and her life. Her insistence on privacy contrasts sharply with the publicity that many popular writers seek, appearing on talk shows and giving readings on college campuses. The public must clamor in vain for more information about Lee, an author whose book has so profoundly touched them.

If Harper Lee (known to her friends as Nelle) was able to create a convincing portrait of life in a small southern town in the 1930s, it is partly because her own childhood was so like that of Scout. Theirs was a childhood far different from that of most children today, even those who grow up in small towns. Racial segregation is no longer legal, and in few places do we find open hostility. Even less do we find violence such as lynching, which was a fact of everyday life for African Americans in places like Lee's hometown of Monroeville, Alabama. And yet, much that Lee valued in small-town life has largely been lost: the supportiveness of neighbors, the stability of extended families, the personal interest taken by town leaders in its individual residents, the relatively crime-free streets, the closeness to nature, and the carefree days before watching television became the substitute for playing imaginative games.

Like Scout's family in *To Kill a Mockingbird,* Lee's family long ago established its roots in Alabama, where she grew up. Nelle Harper Lee was born on 28 April 1926 in Monroeville to Amasa and Frances Finch Lee. The author as a child seems to have been very much like Scout—a high-spirited tomboy whose main playmates were her brother and other little boys. One of those boys, probably the one on whom she based the character in the book called Dill, was Truman Capote, another writer who drew material from his days in Monroeville. As a boy, Capote, whose parents were divorced, lived much of the time between 1928 and 1933 with relatives who lived next door to Lee.

Members of the Lee family have reported that Nelle and Truman had aspirations, even in their early preteen years, to be writers and that Amasa Lee provided them with an old typewriter with which to write stories in their tree house. Whether or not *this* story is true, there is little doubt about Lee's love of reading daily newspapers and books at an early age. Among the grandest of her childhood moments was when her father would return from the state legislature in Montgomery, his suitcases filled with books he had bought for his children.

The Scottsboro Trials

notorious widely
and unfavorably
known

Although much of Lee's childhood must have been like a lovely dream, there also were dark moments that she could not escape. For most of her young life, she must have been aware of one of the most notorious racial conflicts in the nation's history—a trial that captured the nation's headlines throughout her life in Monroeville. In 1931, in northern Alabama, nine young African American men, known as the Scottsboro Boys, were arrested on the charge of raping two white women, both of them known prostitutes. Despite all evidence to the contrary, the men were found guilty. Their appeals, going all the way to the United States Supreme Court, compelled the local courts to hold new trials as late as 1936.

By 1937, when Lee was eleven years old, she would have been reading the daily newspapers across the state of Alabama, which urged the release of the accused men. Her novel contains parallels with the Scottsboro trials of the 1930s. The charge of raping a white woman, made against Tom Robinson in the novel, is the same as the charge against the real-life Scottsboro Boys. The white women who make the accusations, both in the novel and in the real trial, have acted out of fear, in large part to conceal their secrets. In the novel, Mayella Ewell must lie to conceal her father's abuse of her, and the Scottsboro women lied to conceal their illegal acts of prostitution. The heroes of the fictional and real trials both are Alabama lawyers: Atticus Finch in the book and Judge James Horton in the real trials. Horton refused to convict the Scottsboro prisoners, because he believed that the jury had reached a guilty verdict unsupported by the evidence. Both men acted bravely in the face of formidable local opposition. And finally, a key issue in the fictional and real trials is the matter of who can serve on a jury.

formidable difficult
to defeat or deal with

Lee and Capote as Writers

By the time Lee left home to attend the University of Alabama, she had the experiences of the South and the aspiration to be a writer, both of which would contribute to the writing of her masterpiece. While she was in college, she also had the extraordinary experience of seeing herself as a character in a novel written by her childhood friend, Truman Capote. His *Other Voices, Other Rooms*—a novel drawing on life in Monroeville, Alabama—portrays a character resembling the young Harper Lee. Although both writers drew from the same background, Capote's work is markedly different in tone and style from Lee's. And although Capote was a more prolific writer, few of his works achieved the popular readership and acclaim that Lee's has enjoyed.

Lee moved to New York City in 1950 after leaving college and eventually had the manuscript of her novel accepted by J. B. Lippincott, one of the most prestigious publishing houses in the United States at the time. In 1960, literary history was made with the publication of *To Kill a Mockingbird*.

Public Reception

It was apparent even before the novel hit the bookstores that it was an immense success. Book clubs began clamoring to include it among their choice selections. And in 1961, Lee's novel was snapped up by Hollywood. She worked for two years as a chief consultant on the film, forging a lifelong friendship with the actor Gregory Peck, who played Atticus Finch. In accepting the Academy Award for his role, he paid tribute to Lee. In April of the same year she became the first woman in more than twenty years to receive the Pulitzer Prize for literature. And the prizes and awards continued to come, including the *Best-sellers* Paperback of the Year Award in 1963 and an honorary doctorate from Mount Holyoke College.

In Cold Blood

In 1959, shortly before the publication of *To Kill a Mockingbird*, Lee began collaborating with Truman Capote on a journalistic "nonfiction novel" about a murder in a small town in Kansas. Titled *In Cold Blood*, the book added a new dimension to American literature. Although Capote would receive the full credit for the project, Lee was a key figure in its creation. It was she who conducted the initial research, interviewed the townspeople, and did a great deal of the writing.

A film adaptation of *In Cold Blood* was released in 1967.

Harper Lee Today

Harper Lee, famous for keeping her life private, still spends much of her time in Monroeville, Alabama. But she also enjoys the theater in England and New York City and, still the avid reader, is an enthusiastic student of history and English literature. And even thirty years after its initial publication, managing the ongoing enterprises related to *To Kill a Mockingbird* is a full-time job. Among her tasks are the continual reissuing of the book in hardcover, paperback, and special editions; frequent television broadcasting of the film; and continual production of a play based on the novel. Lee's most recent project, begun a number of years ago, is an important and time-consuming one, eagerly anticipated by her admirers—the writing of her memoirs.

If you like *To Kill a Mockingbird*, you might also like works by Louisa May Alcott, J.D. Salinger, Robert Louis Stevenson, and Mark Twain

Selected Bibliography

WORKS BY HARPER LEE

To Kill a Mockingbird (1960)

"A Word From Harper Lee," *The Screenplay of To Kill a Mockingbird, by Horton Foote.* New York: Penguin Books, 1961.

WORKS ABOUT HARPER LEE

Barge, R. Mason. "Fictional Characters, Fictional Ethics." In *Legal Times,* 9 March 1992, p. 23.

Dave, R. A. *"To Kill a Mockingbird: Harper Lee's Tragic Vision,"* In *Indian Studies in American Fiction.* Edited by M. K. Naik. Dharwar: Karnatak University and the Macmillan Company of India, 1974.

Erisman, Fred. "The Romantic Regionalism of Harper Lee." In *Alabama Review,* 1973, pp. 122–136.

Freedman, Monroe. "Atticus Finch, Esq., R.I.P." In *Legal Times,* 24 February 1992, p. 20.

Johnson, Claudia. "The Secret Courts of Men's Hearts: Code and Law in Harper Lee's *To Kill a Mockingbird.*" In *Studies in American Fiction,* Autumn 1991, 129–139.

———. *To Kill a Mockingbird: Threatening Boundaries.* New York: Twayne, 1994.

―――. *Understanding To Kill a Mockingbird.* Westport: Greenwood, 1994.

Shaffer, Thomas L. "The Moral Theology of Atticus Finch." *University of Pittsburgh Law Review,* 1981, pp. 197–204.

Symposium: To Kill a Mockingbird. In *Alabama Law Review,* 1994.

How to Write to the Author
Harper Lee
c/o HarperCollins Publishers
10 East 53rd Street
New York, NY 10022

Ursula K. Le Guin

(1929-   )

by Suzanne Elizabeth Reid

Ursula K. Le Guin is as much a philosopher as she is a storyteller and a poet. She explores the depth and breadth of ideas as much as she experiments with different uses of language in telling her stories and in creating new worlds. A look into her childhood and young adulthood shows some of the influences that led her along her path and some of the sources she draws on, both as a writer and as a creative thinker.

Early Life

Ursula was born on 21 October 1929 in Berkeley, California, into a scholarly family. Her father, Alfred Kroeber, was an anthropologist renowned for his studies of North American Indians, and her mother, Theodora K. Kroeber, wrote *Ishi in Two Worlds* (1961), which depicts the life of the last man of the Yahi tribe. Young Ursula and her older brothers listened

Yahi a primitive American Indian tribe that lived in the foothills of Mount Lassen, California

227

> *At the age of five, Ursula had already begun writing, mostly poetry.*

Lao-tzu (around 500 B.C.) wrote **Tao-te Ching**, which poetically teaches the philosophy of Taoism. Taoist principles center around a return to a primitive, simple life in order to attain happiness.

to tall tales and Native American legends, as well as intellectual talk by the many visitors to their forty-acre summer ranch in the Napa Valley and to their home on the University of California, Berkeley, campus, where her father taught.

At the age of five, Ursula had already begun writing, mostly poetry. She read widely, and her taste ranged from comics to classics, with a special fondness for science fiction and action stories. She preferred Norse legends to Greek and Roman myths, and the Taoist *Te Ching* to the Bible. Le Guin's fiction reflects two influences: the heroic imagery of traditional Western literature that traces the adventures of an individual defending good against evil, and the Taoist tendency to unify or include opposites within the same being or adventure. One of her favorite books as a child was Lord Dunsany's *A Dreamer's Tales* (1910), which encouraged her to think deeply about the mythic elements of life.

In 1951, Ursula was graduated Phi Beta Kappa from Radcliffe College in Cambridge, Massachusetts, where she concentrated in Renaissance French and Italian literature. She then earned a master's degree in French literature from Columbia University in New York City. An exceptional student, she won a Fulbright fellowship in 1953 to study in France. Aboard the *Queen Mary*, she met a young professor of French history, Charles Le Guin, whom she married that December. Le Guin began her doctoral thesis on the French poet Jean Lemaire de Belges, but she was soon busy teaching French while her husband completed his studies. In 1957, their first daughter, Elizabeth, was born, and in 1959 their second daughter, Caroline. During this time Le Guin wrote novels and stories about an imaginary country called Orsinia, but they were rejected by publishers who thought they were too unconventional for readers of popular fiction. She was also writing much of the poetry that was later published in *Wild Angels* (1975). In 1964, Le Guin's son, Theodore, was born.

Early Publications

The sixties were breakthrough years for Le Guin's writing career. In 1961, she read "Alpha Ralpha Boulevard" by Cordwainer Smith (the pseudonym of the science fiction writer

Paul Linebarger) in *Fantasy and Science Fiction.* Intrigued by his interweaving of new ideas with charmingly clever imagery, Le Guin renewed her childhood interest in science fiction and began to write in that genre. Finally her work began to be published. A fantasy story of hers, "April in Paris," appeared in the magazine *Fantastic* in 1962, and in 1963 "The Masters," a science fiction story, was published.

In 1966, Le Guin published *Rocannon's World* and *Planet of Exile,* and in 1967, *City of Illusions.* These three novels about the Hainish universe, invented as a background for Le Guin's ideas, reflect the author's interests in anthropology, Norse mythology, technical inventions, and—most of all—human societies. The main characters travel among various cultures, each described in such detail that the reader can see and hear these beings, strange yet eerily familiar. In these novels, as in many of her other works, Le Guin's clever characterizations subtly challenge historical racial stereotypes by giving power and virtue to people who had been missing from traditional literature.

> **imagery** words or phrases that appeal to one or more of the five senses in order to create a mental picture

> **characterization** method by which a writer creates and develops the appearance and personality of a character

The Beginning of the Earthsea Books

The success of Le Guin's early novels prompted the editor Herman Schein of Parnassus Books to suggest that she write for adolescent readers. She responded with the first of her Earthsea books, *A Wizard of Earthsea* (1968). This heroic adventure follows Ged from his youth as a goat herder through his education in the art of discovering the true names of things, which enables a person to perform magic. Ged achieves mature strength when he accepts the risks of power and realizes the dangers of impetuous pride and anger. The book is widely accepted as a classic (it won a Boston Globe–Horn Book Award in 1969) because of its depth and its originality; where else can a reader of fantasy find a college for wizards? Critics have analyzed this exciting coming-of-age adventure as a moral fable about creativity, as a Jungian archetypal journey from youth to maturity, and as a Taoist lesson in balancing opposite qualities. Most agree, however, that this richly rewarding series contains literary merit as well as all these philosophical elements.

> *The magic of Earthsea is based on finding the true names of the things in the world.*

polarized divided into opposite or contrasting groups

Emphasis on Gender and Aging

Following the critical and popular success of her early books, Le Guin began to think about the effect of strictly defined gender roles in our society. In 1969, *The Left Hand of Darkness* was published. It won Le Guin critical acclaim, the 1969 Nebula Award, given by the Science Fiction Writers Association, and a Hugo Award in 1970. This novel broke new ground in the 1960s by portraying a society of androgynes, people without polarized gender roles or even distinct sexes. The book also raises questions about how anthropologists learn about other societies and examines the qualities of various kinds of friendship, especially when power differences come into play. Fast-paced and clever, this novel is as much a lively reading experience as a source of ideas.

In 1971 the second Earthsea novel, *The Tombs of Atuan*, explored the traditional female rite of passage. Oppressed by age-old assumptions about the role of women in society, Tehanu is finally rescued by Ged from her journey. The opposite of the traditional heroic adventure stretching upward toward active conquests of new worlds and ideas, her journey has been an endless retracing of dark tunnels deep in the earth. These she can feel but not see, and they are mapped by memorized rules rather than by exploration. The magic of Earthsea is based on finding the true names of things in the world. In contrast, the women of the tombs are trained to revere the nameless gods of a shadowy, vague past. This novel won a Newbery Honor Book Citation in 1972.

The Farthest Shore (1971) seems to signal the end of Ged's career and to finish the trilogy as Le Guin originally intended. Challenged by the fading of magic or that creative attentiveness to details in Earthsea, Ged takes on an apprentice. He is young prince Arren, who sails with Ged beyond the edge of the sea to find where life is slipping away and returns, not a magician, but a king with the wisdom of experience. The image of spiders and their webs permeates this novel, as does the traditional male heroic conquest to save the world from evil.

Almost twenty years later, Le Guin added to the Earthsea series *Tehanu: The Last Book of Earthsea* (1990), which takes place within a few months of Ged's return from his last adventure. This book, more mature than the others, further explores the female side of the traditional world of heroes and myths. It also describes the weakening glory of Ged as he ages and loses his youthful strength. In addition to her writing about gender and similar issues, Le Guin has supported feminism through her membership in the National Organization for Women (NOW), and the National Abortion Rights Action League. But her books are much more than simple frameworks for her views and ideas. Most of all, they are deeply thought provoking and full of action, with exquisitely detailed characterizations and striking imagery.

> *In* The Lathe of Heaven *(1971), mild-mannered George Orr is horrified to find that he can change the state of the world by dreaming.*

Emphasis on Peace

Another political concern important to Le Guin is pacifism. In the 1968 Oregon primary, she worked for Eugene McCarthy, a supporter of the peace movement, and she demonstrated against continuation of the war in Vietnam. During that time, she wrote *The Word for World Is Forest* (1972), using a science fiction setting to survey the horrid impact of modern warfare on a gentle people living in harmony with the natural world. Published as a novella in 1976, it won many honors for its memorable characters and moving scenes, including the Hugo Award for Best Novella, the American Library Association's Best Young Adult Books citation, and a place on the *Horn Book* honor list.

pacifism opposition to wars as a means of settling disputes

Another book exposing the dangers of authoritarianism, even when motivated kindly, is *The Lathe of Heaven* (1971), in which mild-mannered George Orr is horrified to find that he can change the state of the world by dreaming. One of Le Guin's funniest satirical portraits is that of the power-hungry psychiatrist from whom George seeks help. In *The Dispossessed: An Ambiguous Utopia* (1974), Le Guin fashions a society that minimizes government and personal possessions, contrasting it with the wealthy mother planet's corrupt hierarchies. The brilliant physicist Shevek, committed to anarchy, nevertheless seeks to reconcile the two worlds, a Taoist principle that informs this complex novel on many levels. *The Dispossessed* won the Hugo, the Jupiter, the Nebula, and the Jules Verne Awards in 1975. In Le Guin's short novel *The Eye of the Heron* (1978), Luz, the pampered daughter of a powerful dictator, betrays her gruff father by joining the nonviolent people he rules and by falling in love with one of them.

As in her other works, Le Guin is remarkably fair in describing different forms of government in this book.

Romantic Themes

Two other love stories feature strong young women who influence their young lovers to stretch beyond their former ambitions. In *Very Far Away from Anywhere Else* (1976), a realistic short novel, seventeen-year-old Owen blossoms as his friendship with Natalie develops into a mature love. Le Guin's spare language captures the exquisite loneliness of adolescence and the various types of communication that can bridge it. Similarly, in *The Beginning Place* (1980), Hugh escapes from his bleak life as grocery clerk to an Edenic forest, where he meets Irena. Overcoming immature fears and resentments, they learn to love each other, first as friends and then as lovers.

Le Guin's view of romantic love, explored in metaphorical settings here and in *The Tombs of Atuan,* is that each individual must become strong in his or her own right before making a lasting, loyal commitment. Most of Le Guin's characters are essentially alone, individuals who connect deeply with few other friends but who usually maintain separate goals and responsibilities. For them, romance develops slowly and infrequently. In *Malafrena* (1979), Le Guin uses her academic background in European culture to set a realistic story about rebellion and romantic love in nineteenth-century Orsinia, a land similar to its historical models.

Experimenting with Form

Since the 1970s, Le Guin has experimented with various formats of creative expression, including essays, poetry, and multimedia works that integrate several art forms. In her essay collections, *Dreams Must Explain Themselves* (1976) and *The Language of the Night: Essays on Fantasy and Science Fiction* (1979), she compares her writing process to the recording of movies inside her mind. This process reaffirms her belief in the importance of imaginative fantasies in maintaining people's awareness about values important to the survival of humanity.

Dancing at the Edge of the World: Thoughts on Words, Women, Places (1989) updates many of the basic ideas that run through Le Guin's books. Her interest in the creative process led her to collaborate in musical, dance, and dramatic productions of her work for stage, television, and radio in the early 1980s. *Always Coming Home* (1985) centers on the narrative comparing Le Guin's peaceful, family-centered culture, Kesh, with a more hierarchical, dominant one. The Kesh culture is similar to traditional Native American civilizations, integrating music, art, poetry, myth-making, and storytelling. The literary artifacts of this culture intermingle with illustrations of invented plants and animals by Margaret Chodos, a cassette of the "Music and Poetry of the Kesh" featuring music by Todd Barton, and a dictionary of the Kesh language.

In 1986, Le Guin teamed with the composer Elinor Armer in performances of *Uses of Music in Uttermost Parts* in San Francisco and Seattle. Le Guin likes collaborating with artists as an antidote to the essential solitude of writing. She also counteracts the isolation of writing by teaching workshops and participating in many science fiction conferences, appreciating the intelligence and wide range of interests of people she meets in these contexts.

Le Guin's many short stories and poems vary widely in format and subject matter. Her anthologized stories include science fiction, fantasy, retold fairy tales, realism, feminism, magic realism, and straight-out realism. Her collections of poetry reflect her affinity for natural speech and rhythms, her wry humor, and her appreciation of human individuality.

Although much of the imagery in Le Guin's work focuses on music, dance, and sailing, she claims to be more adept at appreciating these skills than at performing them. She has played the recorder for personal enjoyment since she was thirteen, but her daughter, Elizabeth, now a professional cellist, is her family's most musically talented member. Le Guin expresses her love of dance in her writing, perhaps as a compensation for her own inability to dance. Likewise, her knowledge of sailing is more intellectual than experiential. She ended a sailing lesson with a friend by capsizing in barely three feet of water while intoning "Nearer My God to Thee," and amazing the instructors with her unusual lack of ability. Like the fiction of many other talented writers, Le Guin's books contain vividly realistic descriptions of experiences that she has imagined more than lived.

> *She ended a sailing lesson with a friend by capsizing in barely three feet of water while intoning "Nearer My God to Thee," and amazing instructors with her unusual lack of ability.*

wry a tone of both amusement and displeasure or dislike

Children's Stories

The arrival of her grandchildren inspired Le Guin to write children's tales. One of her first, *Leese Webster* (1979), repeats a metaphor that is familiar to readers of the Earthsea books: spider webs. It tells the story of a spider whose creative cobwebs bring her the kind of fame that is impractical for a maker of practical patterns. In 1982, two more children's stories, *The Adventures of Cobbler's Rune* and *Adventures in Kroy* were published. Le Guin's fascination with winged cats, first evidenced as windsteeds in *Roncannon's World,* continues in *Catwings* (1988), *Catwings Returns* (1989), and *Wonderful Alexander and the Catwings* (1994). Despite many dangers, these cats find freedom and happiness away from their mother. In the last book, Alexander teaches the youngest cat to share her fears in order to find the courage to face them. *A Ride on the Mare's Back* (1992) was inspired by a souvenir wooden horse that Le Guin found on a trip to Sweden.

Traveling Further Inward

In her fiction for adults written in the 1990s, Le Guin explores more studiously how people understand themselves and others. She does so by placing herself within a variety of individual minds; these are linked by locale, as in *Searoad: Chronicle of Klatsland* (1993), or by a similar theme, as in *A Fisherman of the Inland Sea* (1994).

theme central message about life in a literary work

As we can see from this overview of her many different kinds of works, Le Guin is a philosopher who loves to follow the road of one idea—or of several. But it would be a mistake to think that she is limited to that role. She is also an artist who colors, sculpts, and gives life to those ideas with imagery, characters, and story. Her works deserve to be read, both for what they teach and for the fullness of pleasure that comes from a good book.

If you like works by Ursula K. Le Guin, you might also like works by Madeleine L'Engle, William Sleator, J. R. R. Tolkien, and Jane Yolen.

Selected Bibliography

WORKS BY URSULA K. LE GUIN

Novels and Novellas

Planet of Exile (1966; 1972)

City of Illusions (1967; 1971)

Ursula K. Le Guin • **235**

A Wizard of Earthsea (1968; 1971)

The Left Hand of Darkness (1969; 1987)

The Lathe of Heaven (1971; 1972)

The Tombs of Atuan (1971; 1972)

Rocannon's World. Bound with *The Kar-Chee Reign* by Avram Davidson (1972).

"The Word for World Is Forest." In *Again Dangerous Visions I.* Edited by Harlan Ellison (1972). Published in England as *The Word for World Is Forest* (1977).

The Farthest Shore (1972; 1973)

The Dispossessed: An Ambiguous Utopia (1974)

Very Far Away from Anywhere Else (1976). Published in England as *A Very Long Way from Anywhere Else* (1976).

The Earthsea Trilogy (1977)

"The Eye of the Heron." In *Millenial Women.* Edited by Virginia Kidd (1978; 1980).

Three Hainish Novels (1978)

Malafrena (1979; 1980)

The Beginning Place (1980). Published in England as *Threshold* (1980).

The Visionary. Bound with *Wonders Hidden* by Scott R. Sanders (1984).

Always Coming Home. Includes the audiocassette "Music and Poetry of the Kesh." Music by Todd Barton, illustrations by Margaret Chodos, and diagrams by George Hersh (1985; 1986; 1987).

Tehanu: The Last Book of Earthsea (1990)

Searoad: Chronicles of Klatsand (1991)

A Fisherman of the Inland Sea (1994)

Four Ways to Forgiveness (1995)

Unlocking the Air (1996)

Short-Story Collections

The Wind's Twelve Quarters: Short Stories (1975; 1976)

Orsinian Tales (1976)

The Compass Rose (1982)

Buffalo Gals and Other Animal Presences (1987)

WORKS ABOUT URSULA K. LE GUIN

Bucknall, Barbara J. *Ursula K. Le Guin*. New York: Frederick Ungar, 1981.

Cogell, Elizabeth Cummins. *Ursula K. Le Guin: A Primary and Secondary Bibliography*. Boston: G.K. Hall, 1983.

Cummins, Elizabeth. *Understanding Ursula Le Guin*. Columbia: University of South Carolina, 1990.

De Bolt, Joe, ed. *Ursula K. Le Guin: Voyager to Inner Lands and to Outer Space*. Writers of the Twenty-First Century Series. Port Washington: Kennikat, 1979.

Olander, Joseph D., and Martin H. Greenberg, eds. *Ursula K. Le Guin*. New York: Taplinger, 1979.

Selinger, Bernard. *Le Guin and Identity in Contemporary Fiction*. Ann Arbor: University of Michigan, 1988.

Slusser, George Edgar. *The Farthest Shores of Ursula K. Le Guin*. Popular Writers of Today: The Milford Series. San Bernardino, Calif.: Borgo, 1976.

Spivack, Charlotte. *Ursula K. Le Guin*. Boston: Twayne, 1984.

How to Write to the Author
Ursula K. Le Guin
c/o HarperCollins
10 East 53rd Street
New York, NY 10022

Madeleine L'Engle

(1918-   )

by Donald R. Hettinga

It is hard to imagine an author who has published more than forty books and won some of the most prestigious book awards being picked on by a teacher because of her writing. Yet that is exactly what happened to Madeleine L'Engle when she was about ten years old. In what sounds like a fourth-grade year from hell, her teacher would hold up Madeleine's papers and laugh at them in front of the class. Moreover, social status at the New York private school that she attended was largely determined by athletic ability, an ability that Madeleine, whose one leg was slightly shorter than the other, did not have. The other students would choose her last for teams and would groan if they had her as a teammate.

A Difficult Childhood

reserved restrained in words and actions

It is not surprising that, faced with such a school world, L'Engle became shy and reserved, comforting herself by reading stories and by writing poems and stories in her journal. Yet even this refuge of hers was violated when she entered and won an all-school writing contest only to have her teacher announce that she could not have written the winning poem. According to the teacher, Madeleine was not bright enough and must have copied the poem.

bolster to boost

Fortunately for Madeleine and for us, this was not the only teacher she had. After defending her in the fifth-grade writing contest, Madeleine's parents transferred her to another private school where she began sixth grade with a teacher who also read her papers to the class, but this time as examples of what ought to be done. This new teacher, Margaret Clapp, who later became the first female president of Wellesley College, did much to bolster Madeleine's self-confidence and love of reading and writing (Gonzales, pp. 26–27). Yet despite this positive year, it was the negative years that preceded and followed it that shaped her self-concept and that made her think of herself as unattractive, unintelligent, and unpopular. Both Meg Murry and Vicky Austin—two characters she later created—struggle with these same issues and with teachers who publicly misunderstand them. Another character—Poly O'Keefe—does not have to struggle with those issues; we can perhaps see her, with her six languages, personal confidence, and olympic-level swimming skills, as a projection of all that the young Madeleine would have wanted to be.

projection another person or object to which one has attributed one's own ideas, feelings, or attitudes

Madeleine's struggles at school were partly caused by her family situation. She was born on 29 November 1918 to Madeleine Barnett Camp and Charles Wadsworth Camp; her parents gave her the middle name L'Engle, a name she took on as her writing name when she published her first novel. Her mother was an accomplished pianist and her father a drama and music critic. Her parents, old enough to be her grandparents, had been married for nearly twenty years when she was born. Their patterns of life were firmly established, and a child was not part of those patterns. She ate on a tray in her room; they dined later by themselves. She lived in her own dreamworld and assumed that her private life would not interest her parents.

The Boarding School Novels

Those parallel yet alien worlds of parent and child appear in *Camilla*. In this novel—which was published originally in 1951 as *Camilla Dickinson* and revised with an abbreviated title in 1965—Camilla is caught between her parents, whose marriage is shaken by the discovery that Camilla's mother had an affair with another man. Although there is no reason to suspect that this aspect of the novel is autobiographical, the distance between Camilla and her parents, who love her but cannot communicate with her, matches L'Engle's experience with her parents. But at its core, Camilla is a conventional romance novel. Camilla falls in love with Frank Rowan, the brother of her somewhat worldly friend Luisa. As happens in most romance novels of the period, Frank both declares his love for her and is mysteriously violent to her, and the plot builds around the question of whether Frank will kiss Camilla or reject her in favor of an old girlfriend. At novel's end, the lovers are separated—Frank to another city and Camilla to boarding school—but it is clear that, at least in Camilla's mind, the relationship has been significant.

Boarding school figures prominently in two more of L'Engle's early novels—*The Small Rain* (1945) and *And Both Were Young* (1949)—and for good reason. When she was twelve, L'Engle, like these preteen protagonists, was sent to a boarding school in Switzerland. Though L'Engle had hoped the experience might be romantic or fun, her life in the all-girls school was dreadful. It took her a long time to become accepted by the other girls, and the teachers and house-mothers made her life miserable. She was allowed no privacy, not even in the bathroom or at prayers in the chapel, and the school rules were punishingly strict. L'Engle's experience at this school was formative; the lack of privacy taught her the skill of concentration in public settings, a skill that would later, as a busy writer, serve her well. But it was the negative experience of this school that stuck in her imagination, helping her to shape the plots and characters of these two novels. Like *Camilla, And Both Were Young* offers a conventional romance story in which the protagonist's growth comes mainly from her relationship with her boyfriend. *The Small Rain,* however, offers a plot that is more complex and interesting. As in these other novels, the protagonist struggles with issues of identity, but her struggle is complicated

autobiographical related to the author's own life

> *The distance between Camilla and her parents, who love her but cannot communicate with her, matches L'Engle's experience with her parents.*

by realistic problems—infatuations with a teacher, friendships that ebb and flow, and the hope to succeed as a pianist. Similarly, *A Live Coal in the Sea* (1996) uses the relationships between three generations—Camilla Dickinson Xanthakos, her son Artaxis, who like L'Engle's husband was the star of a popular soap opera, and Camilla's grandaughter, Raffi—to make this story of the long-term effects of romance a psychologically complex novel.

In *The Small Rain,* part of which is set in the New York drama scene, we can also see evidence of some of L'Engle's postcollege experience. After graduating from Smith College in 1941, she moved to New York, where she obtained a role as an understudy in a Broadway play. Later, while acting in a traveling production of Anton Chekhov's *The Cherry Orchard,* she met her husband, Hugh Franklin, perhaps best known for his role of Doctor Tyler on television's *All My Children.* In 1946, while on the road for another play, the couple married and eventually moved into a two hundred-year-old farm house in Connecticut. The house, which they named Crosswicks, was to figure prominently in L'Engle's fiction, inspiring the setting of the Murry's house in the time trilogy as well as the Thornhill residence of the Austins.

The Murry Novels

The Time Trilogy

L'Engle refers to the decade of the 1950s as one of child care—the couple had three children, Josephine, Bion, and Maria—and rejection slips—she had too many to count. Her situation changed dramatically, however, when *A Wrinkle in Time* was finally accepted for publication by Farrar, Straus and Giroux in 1962. The book became an immediate success and also won the Newbery Medal. Her most famous novel, translated into fifteen languages, *Wrinkle* is the first volume in the fantasy series often called the time trilogy.

"It was a dark and stormy night" is a classic way for a romantic novel to start, and the phrase is often used in jest.

On the dark and stormy night on which L'Engle playfully begins the novel, Meg Murry is disturbed because so much seems mixed up in her world. Her scientist father has been away on a secret mission and has not been heard from in almost a year, and Meg, in part because of her father's absence, is having a hard time with both peers and teachers at school. Moreover, like many young teenagers, she feels awkward and unattractive.

Meg is given reason to hope that her situation might change, however, when three rather funky guardian angels—Mrs. Whatsit, Mrs. Who, and Mrs. Which—take her, her genius younger brother Charles Wallace, and Calvin O'Keefe, another teen from the neighborhood, through space and time to rescue Mr. Murry, who is being held hostage on another planet. The questors and their guides travel via a tesseract, or wrinkle in time, which is an almost instantaneous mode of moving through dimensions. The three guardian angels reveal that the imprisonment of Mr. Murry is part of a much larger battle between good and evil, the forces of light and the Black Thing, a battle that is engaging the entire universe. In rescuing her father, a task she is forced to complete on her own, Meg discovers that love is more powerful than hate, that her flaws can also be her strengths, and that conformity is not as desirable as she thought it was.

The second novel in the time trilogy, *A Wind in the Door* (1973), similarly points to the power of love. In this book, L'Engle's fantasy takes us both into the stars and into the minute elements of a human cell. At the core of the plot again is a cosmic conflict between good and evil. The world of the novel is being attacked by ecthroi—nihilistic beings that L'Engle sometimes terms "fallen angels." One of their principal methods of operation is to get creatures to deny what they really are and shift from their created purposes, thus disrupting the order of creation and promoting chaos in its place. The ecthroi are not only responsible for the "rips" in the galaxy that disturb Mr. Murry, but also for the irrational violence that is starting to pervade the Murrys' small town. Then, too, the ecthroi are responsible for Charles Wallace's mitochondritis, enkindling a selfishness in the farandolae— hypothetical organelles that inhabit the mitochondria within a human cell—that keeps them from obeying natural law. When the mitochondria do not produce adequate energy for his cells, Charles Wallace becomes gravely ill.

With the help of Proginoskes, a cherub that looks like a dragon, Meg saves her brother in a series of battles with the ecthroi. Since one of their chief weapons is un-Naming, or making people forget who they are, Meg discovers that the ecthroi can be defeated by countering that act through "naming," which is the selfless affirmation of another creature. Such naming, however, does not come cheaply. At the climax of *A Wind in the Door,* Meg, who has traveled within a mitochondrion in her brother's body, has to risk her own de-

nihilistic believing that traditional values and beliefs are unfounded and that existence is senseless and useless

mitochondria the parts of a cell found outside the nucleus that provide energy for the cell

cherub an innocent, winged young child

affirmation positive validation

struction to try to name the ecthros-possessed principal of her school—Mr. Jenkins—a man she has had a hard time liking. In the process, she is almost annihilated, consumed by the cold emptiness of the ecthros, until Proginoskes allows himself to be annihilated in her place. At times, only such sacrificial love, akin to Christian agape, can fill the void of the ecthroi.

If in *A Wind in the Door* L'Engle suggests that risk is a significant component of love and compassion, her next novel in this series takes that theme a step further. In *A Swiftly Tilting Planet* (1978), Charles Wallace travels through time and alters historical events in order to prevent a late-twentieth-century South American dictator from initiating a nuclear war. In a complicated narrative that sometimes cinematically cuts between scenes and time periods, Charles Wallace enters into the persons of characters in earlier time periods, just as those characters were facing pivotal decisions of good and evil. Mentally supported by the newly married and pregnant Meg who kythes (uses an ESP-like form of communication) with him, Charles Wallace uses his knowledge to try to influence his hosts to make the right decisions.

Working against him in this task are the ecthroi. They tempt the time-traveling Charles Wallace to accept projections—violent parodies of past events—as truth, and his acceptance would render subsequent human history along more violent, chaotic lines. But Charles and Meg are not completely on their own in waging this battle for the safety of the world. Offering aid and transportation through time and space is Gaudior, an angelic unicorn, who is sensitive to the Wind—a positive spiritual force that encompasses the universe of the novel. At novel's end, the crisis has passed, the malevolent dictator has been replaced with a benevolent one, and the world has not even noticed. But the Murrys and the readers have; they have seen how good is stronger than evil if there are people who are willing to risk themselves in the battle of light against darkness.

malevolent productive of harm or evil

benevolent productive of good

Many Waters

Because time travel also figures in *Many Waters* (1986), some critics have called it the final book in L'Engle's time quartet. However, the novel does not follow the pattern of the novels in the trilogy. Instead of Meg and Charles Wallace as protago-

nists, *Many Waters* has Sandy and Dennys, the teenaged
Murry twins. Moreover, the twins are not on a quest, as the
protagonists were in each of the novels of the trilogy; rather,
they are on an adventure. While playing with their father's
computer, the two boys accidentally send themselves through
time and space to Palestine during the time of Noah. There the
logically minded twins find themselves in a younger, morally
troubling world. Seraphim (good angels) and Nephilim (bad
angels) compete for their loyalties, ruffians try to kidnap them,
and women try to seduce them. Moreover, the twins find
themselves in competition with each other when they both fall
in love with the same girl. Before finding their way home, the
two learn much about making decisions and taking responsibility for their actions. L'Engle also uses the contrasts between
the two times to point to the follies of nuclear weaponry and
environmental carelessness.

ruffian brutal per-
son; bully

The O'Keefe Novels

The characters in many of L'Engle's books are related. The
O'Keefes, who populate several of her novels—*The Arm of
the Starfish* (1965), *Dragons in the Waters* (1976), *A House
Like a Lotus* (1984), and *An Acceptable Time* (1989)—are the
children of Meg Murry and Calvin O'Keefe, who were among
the questors in *Wrinkle*. In these books, L'Engle explores issues of safety and risk by placing her characters in the midst
of challenging situations in which they must make hugely
significant choices. In the midst of international intrigue in
Dragons and *Starfish,* faced with unwanted lesbian advances
in *Lotus,* or confronted with human sacrifice in *Acceptable,*
Poly O'Keefe and the other protagonists must make decisions that not only have serious consequences for themselves but that also may endanger the people they care
about. They discover that, as L'Engle remarks elsewhere,
"Nothing that is worth anything is safe."

The Austin Novels

Whereas the Murrys and the O'Keefes frequently engage in
travel through time and space, the Austins, who populate
L'Engle's third series, tend to stay within the usual three dimensions. And even though the Austins are an ordinary fam-

ily—indeed, some critics think that they are a little too ordinary to be believable—they do sometimes find themselves in rather exotic circumstances. Although in *Meet the Austins* (1960), the family lives in a rural setting very similar to L'Engle's Crosswicks home and deals with the issues that arise with the adoption of a child, the other novels move them to more exciting locations. *The Young Unicorns* (1968) takes the family to New York City, where they must come to terms with gang warfare and urban violence. *The Moon by Night* (1963) takes the family all across the United States on a camping trip very similar to one L'Engle's family took around 1960, during which she first got the idea for writing *Wrinkle*. *A Ring of Endless Light* (1980) places the Austins on an island off the Atlantic coast, where the family is attempting to come to terms with the imminent death of a beloved grandfather. *Troubling A Star* (1994) transports Vicky Austin to Antarctica, where she becomes enmeshed in a plot of international intrigue. Through all of these novels, we see Vicky coming of age—trying to get along with siblings, exploring dating and love, and attempting to define her own values in a world where very troubling things happen. She, like the Murrys and the O'Keefes, discovers the power of love, the risks involved in making decisions, and the importance of choosing between right and wrong.

Such themes loom large in L'Engle's fiction, for risk-taking and moral responsibility are motifs that run through both her realistic and her fantasy novels because the shape of her fiction is closely connected to her view of the world—an essentially Christian one. "It is impossible," she claims in *A Circle of Quiet* (1972), "to talk about why anybody writes a book or paints a picture or composes a symphony without talking about the nature of the universe" (p. 63). The universe, as L'Engle explains it, is a wonderful and mysterious, yet apparently chaotic and dangerous, place that is either an enormous "cosmic accident," or the mechanical construction of an impersonal "prime mover," or the realm of a loving God. She understands reality in these latter terms—as overseen by a God who created humans with the freedom to make their own decisions—for good or for ill—by a God who is "personal and loving," a power so great that all of us really do matter to him" (pp. 63–64). Given such a view of the world it is not surprising that L'Engle has crafted novels in which the protagonists must choose between good and

---

enmeshed entangled

motif situation or theme

The universe, as L'Engle explains it, is a wonderful and mysterious, yet apparently chaotic and dangerous, place that is either an enormous "cosmic accident," or the mechanical construction of an impersonal "prime mover," or the realm of a loving God.

evil, in which good and evil are distinct, yet often entangled and never clear cut, in which heroism means taking significant risks on behalf of others, in which asking hard questions is more important than providing quick answers.

Whatever hard questions the novels raise, they also offer some possibility for hope, some indication of the mystery and the beauty that L'Engle sees behind creation. Her understanding of the difficulties and brokenness of life lends power to her portrayals of evil and of loss, but her comprehension of the possibilites of love and faith lends force to her presentation of hope. If L'Engle's fiction shows the world the way it is, it also shows the world the way she believes it ought to be.

Selected Bibliography

WORKS BY MADELEINE L'ENGLE

Novels for Young Adults

The Small Rain (1945)

And Both Were Young (1949; revised 1983)

Camilla Dickinson (1951; revised as *Camilla* 1965)

Meet the Austins (1960)

A Wrinkle in Time (1962)

The Moon by Night (1963)

The Arm of the Starfish (1965)

The Young Unicorns (1968)

A Wind in the Door (1973)

Dragons in the Waters (1976)

A Swiftly Tilting Planet (1978)

A Ring of Endless Light (1980)

A House Like a Lotus (1984)

Many Waters (1986)

An Acceptable Time (1989)

Troubling a Star (1994)

A Live Coal in the Sea (1996)

Journals and Autobiography

A Circle of Quiet (1972)

The Summer of the Great-Grandmother (1974; 1980)

The Irrational Season (1977; 1980)

If you like Madeleine L'Engle, you might also like Katherine Paterson's realistic novels or the fantasy fiction of C. S. Lewis, Lois Lowry, and Ursula K. Le Guin.

And It Was Good: Reflections on Beginnings (1983)

Sold into Egypt: Joseph's Journey into Human Being (1986)

A Stone for a Pillow: Journeys with Jacob (1986)

Two-Part Invention: The Story of a Marriage (1988)

"George McDonald: Nourishment for a Private World." in *Reality and the Vision: Eighteen Contemporary Writers Tell Who They Read and Why.* Edited by Philip Yancy. Dallas: Word, 1990.

WORKS ABOUT MADELEINE L'ENGLE

Blackburn, William. "Madeleine L'Engle's *A Wrinkle in Time: Seeking the Original Face.*" In *Touchstones: Reflections on the Best in Children's Literature.* Edited by Perry Nodelman. West Lafayette, Ind.: Children's Literature Association, 1986, vol. 1, pp. 121–131.

Esmonde, Margaret P. "Beyond the Circles of the World: Death and the Hereafter in Children's Literature." In *Webs and Wardrobes: Humanist and Religious World Views in Children's Literature.* Edited by Joseph O'Beirne Milner and Lucy Floyd Morcock Milner. New York: University Press of America, 1987, pp. 34–45.

Gonzales, Doreen. *Madeleine L'Engle: Author of "A Wrinkle in Time."* New York: Dillon Press, 1991.

Hettinga, Donald R. *Presenting Madeleine L'Engle.* Twayne's United States Authors series, no. 622. New York: Twayne, 1993.

Smedman, M. Sarah. "Out of the Depths to Joy: Spirit/Soul in Juvenile Novels." In *Triumphs of the Spirit in Children's Literature.* Edited by Francelia Butler and Richard Rotert. Hamden, Conn.: Library Professional Publications, 1986, pp. 181–197.

C. S. Lewis

(1898-1963)

by Colleen P. Gilrane

Have you ever wished for a secret place all your own? Perhaps like Leslie Burke in Katherine Paterson's *Bridge to Terabithia,* you have thought, "We need a place just for us. It would be so secret that we would never tell anyone in the whole world about it. It might be a whole secret country, and you and I would be the rulers of it" (pp. 38–39). In that case, you are just like C. S. (Clive Staples) Lewis when he was growing up in Belfast, Ireland, with his elder brother, Warren.

The Creator of Narnia

Jack (the name C. S. Lewis decided he wanted to be called when he was four years old) and Warren spent many days indoors because of bad weather. Looking out their nursery window, they could see the Castlereagh hills in the distance. Those hills seemed to be the end of the world, and Jack and

*Many of Lewis'
friends at
Oxford,
including J. R.
R. Tolkien, read
and wrote
literature.*

voracious   exces-
sively eager

Warren wondered what might be beyond them. They created their own secret land, called Boxen, and drew pictures of it in great detail. Warren drew ships and airplanes and planned imaginary battles, while Jack drew what he called "dressed animals" in his part of Boxen named Animal Land.

Jack was a voracious reader, and one of his favorite things as a young person was to have a new book. In a letter to his friend Arthur Greeves in 1915, Jack wrote,

> I quite agree with what you say about buying books, and love the planning and scheming beforehand, and if they come by post, finding the neat little parcel waiting for you on the hall table and rushing upstairs to open it in the privacy of your own room. (*Letters of C. S. Lewis,* p. 27)

All this reading filled Jack's head with countless characters, myths, legends, and stories.

This reader and dreamer grew up to create Talking Beasts and a secret land called Narnia. In 1950, the first of the Narnia books, *The Lion, the Witch, and the Wardrobe,* was published. By this time, Jack Lewis was a college tutor, university lecturer, and fellow of Magdalen College at Oxford University in England. He taught, wrote, and lectured about all sorts of literature. In fact, if you wanted to read the books that helped him create the stories and characters of Narnia, you would have to read classical, medieval, and Renaissance literature as well as Norse mythology.

There is an article on
J. R. R. Tolkien in volume 3.

Many of Lewis' friends at Oxford, including J. R. R. Tolkien, read and wrote literature. Lewis and Tolkien were members of a group called the Inklings, which met every Thursday night after dinner in Lewis' apartment to read their writing—including chapters of Tolkien's *Lord of the Rings*—to each other. In his introduction to *Letters of C. S. Lewis,* Jack's brother Warren says that the Inklings had no rules or officers or agendas, but that their meetings were always the same:

> The ritual of an Inklings [meeting] was unvarying. When half a dozen or so had arrived, tea would be produced, and then when pipes were well alight Jack would say, "Well, has nobody got anything to read

us?" Out would come a manuscript, and we would settle down to sit in judgement upon it—real unbiased judgement, too, since we were no mutual admiration society: praise for good work was unstinted, but censure for bad work—or even not-so-good work—was often brutally frank. To read to the Inklings was a formidable ordeal, and I can still remember the fear with which I offered the first chapter of my first book—and my delight, too, at its reception. (Pp. 13–14)

Jack Lewis left Oxford in 1954 to become Professor of Medieval and Renaissance English at Cambridge University. In 1956 he married Joy Davidman Gresham. Jack Lewis died at his home on 22 November 1963.

The Secret Land of Narnia

C. S. Lewis' most famous works are seven books known as the Chronicles of Narnia. Readers of all ages are fascinated by this secret land of talking beasts, dwarfs, centaurs, and dryads, where children from another world (ours) appear when there is great danger. Even fictional readers, such as Leslie Burke and Jess Aarons in *Bridge to Terabithia*, are captivated by Narnia's legends:

> Leslie named their secret land "Terabithia," and she loaned Jess all of her books about Narnia, so he would know how things went in a magic kingdom—how the animals and the trees must be protected and how a ruler must behave. That was the hard part. When Leslie spoke, the words rolling out so regally, you knew she was a proper queen. He could hardly manage English, much less the poetic language of a king. (Pp. 39–40)

The Pevensie children—Peter, Susan, Edmund, and Lucy— are transported to Narnia in *The Lion, the Witch, and the Wardrobe*. Living at the house of Professor Kirke in 1940, having been evacuated from London to avoid the air raids of World War II, they discover that an old wardrobe, in which they are hiding from grown-ups, is a doorway to a secret

centaurs mythical creatures who are half man, half horse

dryads mythical maidens who live in trees and are the trees' souls.

From 1940 to 1945 during World War II, the Germans dropped bombs on London regularly. Many people sent their children to the countryside for safety.

wardrobe large trunk in which clothes can be hung, like a closet

fauns mythical creatures with pointed ears, horns, and a goat's legs

An animated movie adapatation of *The Lion, the Witch, and the Wardrobe* was released in 1979.

land. There they meet fauns and beavers and Father Christmas, and work with Aslan the lion to help break the spell of the evil White Witch, after which they are crowned Kings and Queens of Narnia. Time behaves differently in Narnia, so that no matter how long you are there, no time at all has passed in our world. Even though King Peter and Queen Susan and King Edmund and Queen Lucy ruled long and well in Narnia and grew to be men and women, they found that when they returned to England, "it was the same day and the same hour of the day on which they had all gone into the wardrobe to hide."

A year later, waiting for the train on their way back to school, the Pevensies are whisked back into Narnia to find that more than one thousand years have passed, and their ancient castle Cair Paravel is in ruins. In *Prince Caspian: The Return to Narnia* (1951), their task is to help the young prince whose evil uncle, King Miraz, has usurped the throne and is plotting to kill Caspian. Before they return to England at the end of this adventure, Aslan tells Peter and Susan that they will not be returning to Narnia because they are getting too old.

In the third chronicle of Narnia, *The Voyage of the "Dawn Treader"* (1952), Edmund and Lucy and their cousin Eustace are drawn into Narnia through a picture on the wall of Lucy's room in Eustace's house, where Edmund and Lucy are staying for the summer. The three find themselves on a sea voyage with King Caspian, three years into his reign, searching for seven lost lords who had been sent away by evil King Miraz. Eustace returns to Narnia in the fourth chronicle, *The Silver Chair* (1953), when he and his schoolmate Jill Pole are trying to escape from bullies at their school and find themselves at Cair Paravel with a charge from Aslan to rescue Prince Rilian, the son of King Caspian.

Lewis' next two Narnia books, *The Horse and His Boy* (1954) and *The Magician's Nephew* (1955), are stories within the story, Narnian folklore, if you will. *The Horse and His Boy* is the story of Bree the horse and Shasta the boy. They are unhappy in Calormen and run away to Narnia, only to learn that Shasta is really Prince Cor of Archenland, who had been kidnapped as a baby but was protected by Aslan so that he could grow up to save Archenland from great danger. This whole story takes place during the reign of King Peter and Queen Susan and King Edmund and Queen Lucy, the time covered by *The Lion, the Witch, and the Wardrobe*.

The Magician's Nephew is the story of the creation of Narnia, and of two English children, Polly and Digory, whose adventures include being transported to Narnia on the very day it is created. Aslan gives Digory a magic apple to take back to England with him, and when Digory's dying mother eats it, she is healed. Young Jack Lewis had dreamed of being able to heal his own mother, who died when he was nine years old, and these dreams likely helped him to write this scene. After feeding his mother, Digory plants the apple seeds in the backyard, and when he grows up to be Professor Kirke and to live in the country, he has a wardrobe made of wood from the magic apple tree.

The Seven Friends of Narnia—Polly and Digory; Peter, Edmund, and Lucy Pevensie; and Eustace and Jill—return in the seventh and final book, *The Last Battle* (1956). (Susan "is no longer a friend of Narnia," according to Peter, because she has become the sort of grown-up who will not believe in fairy tales.) Eustace and Jill rescue King Tirian, fight in Narnia's last battle, and meet the others—who have been killed in a train wreck in England—in Aslan's country.

Jack's Opinion of Grown-ups

C. S. Lewis seemed to think that you had to be young enough, or old enough, to appreciate fairy tales, as he wrote in dedicating *The Lion, the Witch, and the Wardrobe* to his goddaughter Lucy Barfield:

> My dear Lucy,
>
> I wrote this story for you, but when I began it I had not realized that girls grow quicker than books. As a result you are already too old for fairy tales, and by the time it is printed and bound you will be older still. But some day you will be old enough to start reading fairy tales again. You can then take it down from some upper shelf, dust it, and tell me what you think of it. I shall probably be too deaf to hear, and too old to understand a word you say, but I shall still be
>
> your affectionate Godfather,
>
> C. S. Lewis

> *C. S. Lewis seemed to think that you had to be young enough, or old enough, to appreciate fairy tales.*

> *Those who read "books of information" that have "pictures of grain elevators or of fat foreign children doing exercises in model schools" have no idea how to handle themselves in Narnia.*

Lewis was impatient with rules and schools and parents who encouraged children to grow up in ways that discouraged their imagination. In his stories, children who read the "right" sorts of books—fairy tales, legends, and stories—know what to do and how to react, but those who read "books of information" that have "pictures of grain elevators or of fat foreign children doing exercises in model schools" (as Eustace does when we first meet him in *The Voyage of the "Dawn Treader"*) have no idea how to handle themselves in Narnia. Lewis hated the schools he attended as a young boy, and the happiest time of his education was the time he spent living at Great Bookham, the home of his father's old teacher W. T. Kirkpatrick, being tutored so that he could compete for a scholarship at Oxford. Lewis expressed his strong feelings about schooling through his scorn for Experiment House, the school that Eustace and Jill attend in the Narnia books, and in the letters that he wrote to children who asked him for advice about their own writing. In a letter to a child in America that he wrote on 26 June 1956, Lewis said:

> Don't take any notice of teachers and text-books in such matters. Nor of logic. . . . What really matters is:—
>
> (1) Always try to use the language so as to make quite clear what you mean, and make sure your sentence couldn't mean anything else.
>
> (2) Always prefer the plain direct word to the long vague one. Don't "implement" promises, but "keep" them.
>
> (3) Never use abstract nouns when concrete ones will do. If you mean "more people died," don't say "mortality rose."
>
> (4) In writing. Don't use adjectives which merely tell us how you want us to feel about the thing you are describing. I mean, instead of telling us a thing was "terrible," describe it so that we'll be terrified. Don't say it was "delightful," make *us* say "delightful" when we've read the description. You see, all those words (horrifying, wonderful, hideous, exquisite) are only saying to your readers "Please will you do my job for me."

(5) Don't use words too big for the subject. Don't say "infinitely" when you mean "very"; otherwise you'll have no word left when you want to talk about something *really* infinite. (*Letters of C. S. Lewis,* pp. 270–271)

If you want to know more about Lewis's opinion of how teachers and other adults *should* teach children, you can read about Professor Kirke in *The Lion, the Witch, and the Wardrobe* or you can read Lewis's book *The Abolition of Man, or: Reflections on Education with Special Reference to the Teaching of English in the Upper Forms of Schools* (1943).

Lewis' Writings About Christianity

Jack Lewis converted to Christianity in his early thirties, and he did a great deal of writing and speaking about his religious beliefs after that. He gave a series of talks about Christianity on the radio during World War II, and he was revising those to become the book *Mere Christianity* (1952) during the same time that he was writing the Narnia books. He insisted that the Chronicles of Narnia were written not to teach lessons but for the sake of writing a good story. Many readers find that the Narnia books stand alone as good stories at the same time that they teach about Lewis' Christian beliefs. As Madeleine L'Engle expressed in the foreword to *Companion to Narnia* (1980):

> It doesn't bother me at all that Lewis was convinced that he did not allegorize at all in the *Chronicles of Narnia*. When a writer opens up to a fantasy world, a world which has more depths of reality to it than the daily world, all kinds of things happen in his stories that he does not realize; often the fantasy writer, if he is listening well, writes far more than he knows, and I believe that when Lewis was his best he did exactly that: he listened and he looked and he set down what he heard and what he saw. If grace comes during the writing of fantasy, the writer writes beyond himself, and may not discover all that he has written until long after it is published, if at all. The Narnia stories do in-

allegory story in which the fictional figures and their actions are intended to be understood in a sense different from the surface meaning, so that the underlying meaning becomes more important

Paul Ford, the author of Companion to Narnia, *says that "the best way to appreciate a story is to step into it and enjoy it."*

In the movie *Shadowlands* (1994), Anthony Hopkins plays C. S. Lewis. The movie is about his romance with an outspoken American, played by Debra Winger.

struct, and that is all right, for they are also story, they are also real. . . . We all have an infinite amount to learn, still, as adults; the learning period should never end; and the best way for me to learn has always been in coming across a writer's shared truth in story. (Pp. xv–xvi)

Paul Ford, the author of *Companion to Narnia,* says that "the best way to appreciate a story is to step into it and enjoy it" (p. xxii). He advises that you read the books themselves first, before consulting reference books *about* them. Then, if you wish to explore the subtext that C. S. Lewis, as a scholar and a Christian, embedded in the stories, have at it.

Selected Bibliography

WORKS BY C. S. LEWIS

The Chronicles of Narnia

The Lion, the Witch, and the Wardrobe (1950)

Prince Caspian: The Return to Narnia (1951)

The Voyage of the "Dawn Treader" (1952)

The Silver Chair (1953)

The Horse and His Boy (1954)

The Magician's Nephew (1955)

The Last Battle (1956)

Letters

Letters to Children, edited by Lyle W. Dorsett and Marjorie Lamp Mead (1985)

Letters of C. S. Lewis, edited, with a memoir, by W. H. Lewis (1966)

Other Works

The Problem of Pain (1940)

The Screwtape Letters (1942)

The Abolition of Man, or: Reflections on Education with Special Reference to the Teaching of English in the Upper Forms of Schools (1943)

Mere Christianity (1952)

If you enjoy the works of C. S. Lewis, you might also enjoy the works of Madeleine L'Engle and J. R. R. Tolkien.

WORKS ABOUT C. S. LEWIS

Arnott, Anne. *The Secret Country of C. S. Lewis.* Grand Rapids, Mich.: Eerdmans, 1975.

Carpenter, Humphrey. *The Inklings: C. S. Lewis, J. R. R. Tolkien, Charles Williams, and Their Friends.* Boston: Houghton Mifflin, 1979.

Ford, Paul F. *Companion to Narnia.* San Francisco: Harper and Row, 1980.

Hooper, Walter, ed. *Through Joy and Beyond: A Pictorial Biography of C. S. Lewis.* New York: Macmillan, 1982.

Robert Lipsyte

(1938-   )

by Michael Cart

"As long as I can remember," Robert Lipsyte claims, "the only thing I ever seriously wanted to be was a writer. What was never clear," he adds, "is what *kind* of writer." This uncertainty is reflected in the diversity of Lipsyte's wide-ranging career, part of which has been devoted to award-winning and innovative fiction for young adults. Lipsyte also has been a distinguished newspaper reporter, a newspaper and magazine columnist, a screenwriter, an adult novelist, an author of nonfiction books for adults and for young adults, a radio and television essayist, a commentator and a correspondent, and an Emmy Award–winning host of his own talk show, *The Eleventh Hour,* on public television. However diverse it may be, all of Lipsyte's writing has in common a reporter's keen eye for detail, a journalist's allegiance to telling the unflinching—even if unpleasant—truth, a highly developed social conscience coupled with personal compassion, and a refreshing sense of humor.

Quotations from Robert Lipsyte that are not attributed to a published source are from personal interviews conducted by the author of this article and are published here by permission of Robert Lipsyte.

257

borough subdivision of a city

rueful regretful or sorrowful

self-deprecating playing down or discrediting oneself; belittling oneself

fledgling young or new

Growing Up

Robert Lipsyte was born on 16 January 1938 in New York City. He grew up in Queens, one of the city's five boroughs, in a neighborhood called Rego Park. As a boy he was a classic outsider for three reasons. The first was his size. "I was too fat for basketball but not fat enough to have my own zip code," he ruefully recalled in a 1992 *Horn Book* article. The second reason was his family circumstances: both of his parents were teachers, a fact that made him feel "like the preacher's kid" while growing up. The third reason was his intelligence. "I was in something called The Special Progress Class," he self-deprecatingly explains. "You know—those classes for the talented and the fat."

All these factors may have made for an uncomfortable childhood, but they were invaluable to Lipsyte's development as an author. As he points out, "I was unable to participate and so I became an observer of life and that was my training for writing."

"The Romance of Newspapering"

Thanks to a Ford Foundation program, Lipsyte went directly from his junior year at Forest Hills High School to Columbia University, where he was graduated as a nineteen-year-old English major in 1957. He initially planned to pursue an advanced degree at the prestigious Claremont Graduate School in Southern California, but a summer job as a copy boy in the sports department of the *New York Times* changed that. Quickly falling in love with what he calls "the romance of newspapering," Lipsyte remained at the *Times,* leaving long enough only to earn a master's degree in journalism at nearby Columbia University.

In 1959, after two years as a copy boy, Lipsyte was promoted to become, at age twenty-one, perhaps the youngest reporter on the *Times* staff. After a three-year apprenticeship, he was sent to Florida to cover the fledgling New York Mets baseball team. He recalls his enthusiasm for this new job: "I wanted to get out there and see what was going on and write better stories about it than anyone else."

Two years later he co-authored *Nigger,* the autobiography of the African American comedian and activist Dick Gregory. Lipsyte also began covering boxing for the *Times,* in the process meeting a young prizefighter named Cassius Clay, who as Muhammad Ali would later became world heavyweight champion. He was one of reporter Lipsyte's most important and colorful subjects.

In This Corner: *The Contender*

In 1967, at age twenty-nine, Lipsyte became one of only two internationally syndicated sports columnists for the *New York Times*. That same year he published his first young adult novel, *The Contender,* the hard-hitting story of an African American teenager named Alfred Brooks. Alfred's dreams of "being somebody" lead him to a neighborhood Harlem gym and to hopes of becoming a boxing champion. In the end he discovers that he lacks the "killer instinct" necessary to become a professional boxer, but during the training he has found something more important: the will to transform himself from an aimless drifter without a future into a contender, what his trainer Mr. Donatelli calls "a man who's willing to sweat and bleed to get up as high as his legs and his brains and his heart will take him."

The Contender, three decades after its initial publication, remains one of the most important novels in the history of young adult literature. Along with S. E. Hinton's *The Outsiders,* published the same year, Lipsyte's book ushered in a new era of realistic fiction that deals honestly with the hard-edged issues confronting and challenging young people trying to become contenders in their own lives.

In writing his first young adult novel, Lipsyte drew heavily on his personal experiences as a sportswriter covering the boxing world and befriending Ali and other fighters. Similarly, his related experiences as a sportswriter provided the raw material for his next book, *Assignment Sports,* a collection of his newspaper articles and columns.

These twenty-four short pieces vividly demonstrate how Lipsyte differed from more traditional sportswriters, who were content to focus on play-by-play accounts or statistical rehashes. What interested Lipsyte instead were the things that capture the imagination of the novelist: character, setting, unusual and offbeat moments, and the way that athletes—and fans—talk. If these stories have an overriding theme, it is how social and political contexts affect the world of profes-

Lipsyte's The Contender *ushered in a new era of realistic fiction that deals honestly with the hard-edged issues confronting and challenging young people.*

There is an article about S. E. Hinton in volume 2.

In writing his first young adult novel, Lipsyte drew heavily on his personal experiences as a sportswriter covering the boxing world and befriending Ali and other fighters.

sional sports. "Politics, race, religion, money, the law—all play roles," Lipsyte says.

This same theme illuminates Lipsyte's later, more ambitious book for adults, *SportsWorld*. In 1971, a year after *Assignment Sports* was published, Lipsyte, tired of the rigid conventions of the sports column, left the *Times* to pursue a more independent career as a novelist and screenwriter.

Enter Bobby Marks

During the next six years, Lipsyte published two adult novels (*Something Going* and *Liberty Two*), wrote a screenplay produced as *That's the Way of the World,* and became a commentator for National Public Radio. It was not until 1977, however, ten years after *The Contender,* that Lipsyte published his second young adult novel. Titled *One Fat Summer,* it introduced a bright, brash, wisecracking—and seriously overweight—teenager named Bobby Marks, who would be the hero of two other semiautobiographical novels that followed: *Summer Rules* and *The Summerboy.*

semiautobiographical loosely based on the author's own life

One Fat Summer, like *The Contender,* is a story of self-transformation. It shows how Bobby, through hard work and the exercise of will, loses weight one memorable summer and gains self-respect in the process. Told in Bobby's attractively breezy first-person voice, the book also explores another recurring theme in Lipsyte's work: the meaning of manhood. Through painful, firsthand experience, Bobby learns that being a man is not bullying those weaker than you or pretending to like baseball. Instead it means displaying the qualities of maturity that define manhood: self-confidence, a sense of self-worth, compassion, and strength of character.

alter ego a second self

Lipsyte explores this theme further in the second Bobby Marks novel, *Summer Rules,* in which his adolescent alter ego learns that when it comes to telling the truth, there are no "summer rules," no seasonal relaxing of standards. Lipsyte also dramatically demonstrates that another measure of manhood is the maturity one brings to solving moral and ethical dilemmas, a theme fully realized in *The Summerboy.* In this book Bobby takes a summer job in a laundry and finally overcomes his own fears to confront the unfeeling owner about his routine abuse of the other employees.

Because they are set in the 1950s, Lipsyte refers to the three Bobby Marks books as his "historical novels." They are filled with period flavor, but their themes are timeless, and Bobby Marks is one of the great characters in modern young adult literature. He is a stand-in for every teenager who confronts the challenge of growth and self-transformation, experiences the frustration of sexual awakening and the pain of feeling like an outsider, and discovers the need for establishing ethical and moral guidelines for the passage into adulthood.

Ali and Others

Lipsyte has always demonstrated the ability to work on a number of different, creatively demanding projects simultaneously. During the six-year period in which he was writing the Bobby Marks novels, he published two other books for young adults: a biography of Muhammad Ali (*Free To Be Muhammad Ali*) and a sports novel titled *Jock and Jill*.

Lipsyte has been highly critical of sports biographies, which he dismissively described to interviewer Betty Miles as "the junk food of publishing." Given his personal integrity, his insider's knowledge of his subject, and his interest in the social and political milieu of Ali's life, which "was touched by the civil rights movement, the anti–Vietnam War movement, the rise of the gold-plated age of sports, and the television takeover of entertainment and thought," Lipsyte's biography offers a much more substantial fare that rewards careful and thoughtful reading.

milieu environment or context

Jock and Jill is rooted in Lipsyte's concern about the win-at-any-cost mentality that leads to the abuse of talented young athletes by ambitious coaches, sports doctors, and naively overenthusiastic parents. In telling the story of Jack Ryder, a gifted high-school pitcher in suburban New Jersey, Lipsyte also reflects his fascination with the social awakening of an athlete to the problems of politics and poverty, greed and corruption that he himself had witnessed in New York City and the South Bronx during a one-year stint in 1977 as a columnist for the *New York Post*. Unfortunately, Lipsyte tries to force too much social concern onto the framework of a young adult novel. As critic John Leonard put it in the *New York Times Book Review,* "He tries too hard to teach as if our heads were drums." As a result, *Jock and Jill,* although passionate in its good intentions, is Lipsyte's least successful novel.

Much more successful are *The Brave* and *The Chief,* two novels about Sonny Bear, a seventeen-year-old boxer whose mother is a Native American and whose father was a white soldier killed in Vietnam. "*That* was something I felt I could deal with," Lipsyte states, "the two aspects of his life: the Indian part and the white part and the struggle between the two."

The Brave has been billed as a sequel to *The Contender* because it brings back the character of Alfred Brooks, now a middle-aged police officer in New York City. Brooks befriends Sonny, who has fled his upstate New York reservation, and through the discipline of boxing, he helps the younger man find himself and his own unique identity as a latter-day contender.

In *The Chief,* Sonny continues his progress toward becoming a professional boxer. At the same time he finally embraces his Native American identity as a "Running Brave," a spokesperson for his tribe and also a fighter for his people's rights and welfare. This time we see Sonny's compelling quest through the eyes of an African American college student named Martin Witherspoon, who has signed on as one of Sonny's trainers and who wants to be his biographer.

In purely literary terms *The Chief* is one of Lipsyte's most interesting novels, because in it he experiments with a form known as "metafiction"; that is, fiction that blurs the line between imagination and reality by being playfully aware of itself as a work of art. Part of the novel, for example, is presented as Martin's own book-in-progress, which is then discussed by him and his college professor—a grown-up Bobby Marks—who is, of course, Lipsyte's own alter ego

Battling the Beast

Lipsyte's other recent young adult novel, *The Chemo Kid,* is also experimental in form and departs from the author's established practice of writing grittily realistic fiction. When Lipsyte was diagnosed with cancer in 1991 (he had survived an earlier bout in the late 1970s), he vowed in his April *American Health* column, "This time I would do what I hadn't done the first time—I would write about it. I would be the first man to write an honest book about cancer the second time around, a cancer whose treatment would cause me to reevaluate the meaning of manhood."

Lipsyte's account of teenage Fred Bauer's battle with "the beast" (as he refers to cancer) borrows the narrative style of cyberpunk science fiction and infuses it with the kind of gallows wit that Lipsyte calls "tumor humor." When Fred is put on a course of experimental hormone treatments, he develops superpowers, becoming "The Chemo Kid," a superhero powerful enough to defeat not only his cancer but also the book's drug-dealing and environment-polluting villains.

cyberpunk having a style or attitude combining the brash anarchy of 1970s punk rock culture with an interest in futuristic technology

Ultimately, Lipsyte believes, *The Chemo Kid* is about "surviving cancer on your own terms. In most books about kids with cancer, they die at the end. But the point is not to find gallant ways to die with cancer; the point is to live."

The Television Years

The publication of *The Chemo Kid* and the two Sonny Bear novels heralded Lipsyte's recommitment to young adult fiction after another ten-year silence. He had devoted the preceding decade of his career, the 1980s, to television. In the spring of 1982, Lipsyte became on-air sports essayist for the critically acclaimed CBS television news program *Sunday Morning*. In 1986 he left CBS to assume a similar role for the NBC network, filing stories for *NBC Nightly News* about offbeat subjects such as the impact of political turmoil on baseball in Nicaragua.

Lipsyte left NBC in 1989 to undertake, for two seasons, the hosting of his own public affairs program, *The Eleventh Hour,* which aired on PBS in New York. Looking back at his eight-year television career, Lipsyte admits with his usual candor that he "didn't really enjoy most television. The work is easy," he explains, "very easy. But the life is very hard—so much traveling, so much standing around, so much unnecessary stress."

The Contender Is a Champion

Lipsyte was ready to return to the world of fiction and also to his first professional home, the *New York Times,* where he resumed writing a sports column in 1991. That same year he added to his writing repertoire a monthly column for *Ameri-*

repertoire list of works or capabilities

can *Health* magazine and, in 1993, a second *Times* column called "Coping," which appears in the Sunday newspaper.

Additionally he has undertaken writing, for younger readers, a series of sports biographies called "Superstar Lineup." His subjects have included Arnold Schwarzenegger, Jim Thorpe, Michael Jordan, and Joe Louis. In these biographies Lipsyte continues to demonstrate that he is more interested in the sociopolitical impact of athletes' careers than in the games they play.

Although other writers may be more prolific and more focused on devoting their careers exclusively to young adult fiction, few have had a greater influence on the development of the form than Robert Lipsyte. He has played a major role in introducing authentic realism into a field that, before his appearance, had tended to sugarcoat reality. Moreover, he almost single-handedly transformed the sports novel from predictable, formula fiction into thematically rich and socially relevant literature. Robert Lipsyte has firmly established himself as a champion in the arena of young adult novels.

If you like Robert Lipsyte, you might also like Bruce Brooks and Chris Crutcher.

Selected Bibliography

WORKS BY ROBERT LIPSYTE

Novels for Young Adults
The Contender (1967; 1987)
One Fat Summer (1977; 1991)
Summer Rules (1981; 1992)
Jock and Jill (1982; 1983)
The Summerboy (1982; 1984; 1992)
The Brave (1991; 1993)
The Chemo Kid (1992; 1993)
The Chief (1993)

Nonfiction
Assignment: Sports (1970; 1984)
Free To Be Muhammad Ali (1978)
Arnold Schwarzenegger: Hercules in America (1993)
Jim Thorpe: Twentieth-Century Jock (1993)
Joe Louis: A Champ for All America (1994)
Michael Jordan: A Life Above the Rim (1994)

Short Story

"Future's File." In *Within Reach* Edited by Donald R. Gallo (1993).

Books for Adult Readers

Liberty Two (1974)

The Masculine Mystique (1966)

Nigger, with Dick Gregory (1964)

Something Going, with Steve Cady (1973)

SportsWorld: An American Dreamland (1975; 1978)

Screenplay

That's the Way of the World, also known as *Shining Star* (1975)

Newspaper and Magazine Columns

New York Times column (1967–1971, 1991–   )

New York Post column (1977)

American Health column (1991–   )

Articles/Reportage

New York Times (1959–1967)

[Lipsyte also has been a regular contributor to the *New York Times Magazine* since 1961 and an occasional contributor to *The Atlantic, Coronet, English Journal, Esquire, Harper's, Horn Book, The Nation, New York Times Book Review, Newsweek, People Weekly, Reader's Digest, Sport, Sports Illustrated,* and *TV Guide.*]

Articles and Essays

"For Teen-Agers, Mediocrity?" *New York Times Book Review,* 18 May 1986, p. 30.

"Facets," *English Journal,* March 1987, p. 16.

"Listening for the Footsteps," *The Horn Book Magazine,* May/June 1992, pp. 290–296.

INTERVIEWS WITH ROBERT LIPSYTE

Kenny, Kevin. "An Interview with Robert Lipsyte." In *The VOYA Reader* Edited by Dorothy M. Broderick. Metuchen, N.J.: The Scarecrow Press, Inc., 1990, pp. 284–299.

Miles, Betty. "Robert Lipsyte on Kids/Sports/Books." *Children's Literature in Education ,* Spring 1980, pp. 43–47).

WORKS ABOUT ROBERT LIPSYTE

Books and Parts of Books

Cart, Michael. *Presenting Robert Lipsyte.* New York: Twayne, 1995.

Chevalier, Tracy, ed. *Twentieth-Century Children's Writers,* 3d edition. Chicago: St. James Press, 1989, p. 597.

Collier, Laurie, ed. *Authors and Artists for Young Adults.* Detroit: Gale Research, 1991, vol. 7, p. 139.

Evory, Anne and Linda Metzger, eds. *Contemporary Authors, New Revision Series.* Detroit: Gale Research, 1983, vol. 8, p. 329.

Gallo, Donald R., ed. *Speaking for Ourselves.* Urbana, Ill.: National Council of Teachers of English, 1990, p. 122.

Gunton, Sharon R., ed. *Contemporary Literary Criticism.* Detroit: Gale Research, 1982, vol. 21, p. 207.

Holtze, Sally Holmes, ed. *Fifth Book of Junior Authors and Illustrators.* New York: The H.W. Wilson Company, 1983, p. 196.

Nilsen, Alleen Pace and Kenneth L. Donelson. *Literature for Today's Young Adults,* 2nd edition. Glenview, Ill.: Scott, Foresman and Company, 1985.

Olendorf, Donna, ed. *Something About the Author.* Detroit: Gale Research, 1992, vol. 68, p. 135.

Senick, Gerard J., ed. *Children's Literature Review.* Detroit: Gale Research, 1991, vol. 23, p. 199.

Articles

Feldman, Sari. "Up the Stairs Alone: Robert Lipsyte on Writing for Young Adults." In *Top of the News,* Winter 1983, p. 198.

Plimpton, George. "Sports: How Dirty a Game?" *Harper's Magazine,* September 1985, p. 45.

Robinson, George. "The Twenty-Four-Year Comeback." *Publishers Weekly,* 26 July 1991, p. 11.

Scales, Pat. "*The Contender* and *The Brave* by Robert Lipsyte." *Book Links,* November 1992, p. 38.

Simmons, John S. "Lipsyte's *Contender:* Another Look at the Junior Novel." *Elementary English,* January 1972, p. 116.

Spencer, Pam. "Winners in Their Own Right." *School Library Journal,* July 1990, p. 23.

How to Write to the Author
Robert Lipsyte
c/o HarperCollins Children's Books
HarperCollins Publishers
10 East 53rd Street
New York, NY 10022

Jack London

(1876-1916)

by Daniel Dyer

Jack London was a jailbird. A hobo. A sailor, seal-hunter, pirate, gold-miner, launderer, yachtsman, and coal-shoveler. He was a drinker, a brawler, a heavy smoker. He was a husband (twice) and a father (twice). He was a socialist candidate for mayor of Oakland, California. He was a rancher. A world-traveler. A voracious reader. A loyal correspondent whose collected letters fill three large volumes. A lecturer whose fiery speeches ignited controversy wherever he went. A journalist who covered wars and sporting events and natural catastrophes. He was an author of fifty books dealing with subjects as varied as sailing, boxing, out-of-body experiences, dogs, ranching, and Hawaii. He wrote about gold mining and animal rights, architecture and war, earthquake and fire, alcoholism and leprosy, surfing and socialism. He wrote one novel set in a prehistoric civilization, another set many centuries in the future. He wrote a murder mystery; he wrote a short novel about a devastating disease that wipes out nearly all human life. He wrote what may be

voracious excessively eager, avid

> *London wrote about survival and love and loneliness, about fairness and unfairness, about right and wrong. He exhumed (brought back from neglect) our past, examined our present, and predicted our future.*

the first "novelization" of a movie. He wrote about survival and love and loneliness, about fairness and unfairness, about right and wrong. He exhumed our past, examined our present, and predicted our future. And at the age of forty, he was dead.

Hobo and Prisoner

In 1894, 'Frisco Kid, age eighteen, was on the road, illegally sneaking aboard eastbound trains. He had left his home in Oakland, California, to join General Coxey's Industrial Army, a rag-tag collection of people marching to Washington, D.C., to protest unemployment. "'Frisco Kid" was the youth's "monica" (moniker)—the nickname by which he was known to his fellow outlaw riders of the rails.

In Missouri, 'Frisco Kid and some companions—suffering from hunger and discouraged by the entire enterprise—deserted the army and returned to the trains, heading east. On 29 June, he was arrested in Niagara Falls, New York, by police who were rounding up the hundreds of homeless who had been, according to local newspapers, "flocking to this vicinity."

Unable to pay the twenty-five-dollar fine, 'Frisco Kid was sentenced to thirty days of hard labor in the Erie County Penitentiary, a dark, forbidding structure that housed about 800 inmates. They were serving sentences for crimes ranging from murder to rape to robbery to throwing snowballs. 'Frisco Kid's name appears on the roll of prisoners as John Lunden, occupation: sailor.

Released from the penitentiary, 'Frisco Kid eventually turned toward home, where he planned, at age nineteen, to enroll in high school. He had seen enough of the rough and unforgiving world he would later call "the abyss"—the pit of life.

A dozen years later (1907), 'Frisco Kid—now known to an admiring readership around the world as Jack London—published *The Road,* a collection of stories about his experiences as a hobo and prisoner. He accomplished in this volume, his nineteenth book, what he did in approximately fifty other works of fiction, nonfiction, and drama. By sheer effort, self-discipline, and talent he transformed what he called "raw life" into an enduring work of literary art.

London was part of a group of writers known as "realists" and "naturalists," the best known of whom were Mark Twain, Edith Wharton, Henry James, Frank Norris, Stephen Crane, and Theodore Dreiser. These writers sought to create a popular literature that closely reflected real life, that involved characters struggling against the forces of nature and society. They wanted readers to recognize places and situations and problems similar to their own.

Many of London's tales take place in locations he knew intimately. In fact, the geography is often so precise that the movements of characters can be traced on a map. Some of his stories contain the names of actual historical figures—and of friends and family. Many of his characters face problems that he himself had faced.

Boyhood on the Bay

John Griffith London was born in San Francisco on 12 January 1876, to Flora Wellman. She always insisted that her son's father was William Chaney, an astrologer to whom she briefly had been married. Chaney, however, denied being the father and promptly abandoned Flora. Because she had difficulty nursing her little boy (called John Chaney at this time), Flora employed a wet nurse (a woman to breast-feed her child). She was Jennie Prentiss, an African American who maintained a lifelong friendship with Jack London.

In September 1876, Flora married a man fifteen years older than she, John London, forty-five, who by a previous marriage had eleven children, most of whom he had been forced by poverty to place in orphanages.

Throughout Jack London's boyhood, his stepfather—a friendly, gentle man—failed at a variety of occupations, forcing the little family to move frequently. By the time Jack was five years old, he had lived in nine different houses.

Jack London later wrote that he developed his lifelong reading habit when he was nine years old and first discovered Washington Irving's *The Alhambra* and other books about the long ago and far away. He discovered, to his delight, that at the Oakland Public Library he could sign out all the books he wanted—and he wanted them all.

On the waterfront young Jack discovered other delights. He taught himself how to sail and spent many exciting hours

Many of London's tales take place in locations he knew intimately.

There is an article about Mark Twain in volume 3 and an article about Stephen Crane in volume 1.

Edith Wharton wrote *The Age of Innocence* (1920), which was made into two movies—one released in 1934, and the other in 1993. Henry James wrote *The Portrait of a Lady* (1881), which was also made into a movie and released in 1997.

on the San Francisco Bay. For a time, he was an "oyster pirate," robbing the commercial oyster beds by night and selling his illegal catch by day. Later, he joined the Fish Patrol to round up and drive out of business other pirates with whom he had once competed. These experiences London brought to life in a number of tales collected in two books, *The Cruise of the Dazzler* (1902) and *Tales of the Fish Patrol* (1905).

At the age of seventeen he sailed to the Sea of Japan aboard the *Sophia Sutherland,* a seal-hunting vessel, and when he returned home, his mother urged him to enter a writing competition sponsored by the *San Francisco Examiner.* He submitted "Story of a Typhoon off the Coast of Japan," and this, his first published story, won the first prize: twenty-five dollars. Later, these experiences would help London write one of his best-known novels, *The Sea-Wolf* (1904), much of which takes place aboard a seal-hunter named *The Ghost,* whose captain is the brutal Wolf Larsen.

Student and Writer

When London returned to Oakland from his tramping trip, he enrolled in Oakland High School. Although he stayed only one year, he published a number of stories in the school's literary magazine, *The Aegis.* In the spring of 1896, bored and impatient with high school, he holed up in his tiny room and prepared for the college entrance examinations by studying nineteen hours a day. In a few months he learned—with the aid of some devoted friends—the entire high school curriculum, and in August he took the tests. And passed them.

In September, he enrolled in the University of California at nearby Berkeley, but because of financial difficulties he stayed only a single semester. He never returned to school.

Throughout the winter of 1896 London again holed up in his room, this time trying to make a living as a writer. He wrote a little bit of everything—stories, poems, plays, essays, and jokes. He mailed his efforts away to magazines, and one by one, every single item came back to him—rejected. He did not publish a word of his enormous daily output.

Finally, absolutely impoverished, he took a job in a laundry and became once again what he would later call a "work

> *In the spring of 1896, bored and impatient with high school, he holed up in his tiny room and prepared for the college entrance examinations by studying nineteen hours a day. In a few months he learned the entire high school curriculum.*

beast." He saw no end to the drudgery of physical labor. Later, London fictionalized many of these rough, frustrating experiences in his autobiographical novel *Martin Eden* (1909). Readers who wish to know about London's desperate struggle to become a writer have no better resource than this, his most personal book.

Gold! Gold! Gold!

On 14 July 1897, the steamship *Excelsior* arrived in San Francisco bearing a load of gold and miners with exciting tales to tell about an enormous gold strike in the Klondike River region of the Canadian Yukon. Tens of thousands of people quit their jobs, left their farms and shops and families, and headed northward.

Among the first to leave was Jack London. Racing against time because the Yukon River freezes in October, London and his companions landed at Dyea, Alaska, and packed their ton of supplies over the mountains to British Columbia, where they built two boats and began their five-hundred-mile float down the Yukon River to Dawson City, Yukon, center of the gold rush activity. But the North temporarily defeated them. About sixty miles short of Dawson, realizing that the river would soon be impassable, London and his companions decided to occupy some abandoned cabins. During the long winter London did a little prospecting, filed a claim, studied the theory of evolution in Charles Darwin's *On the Origin of Species,* and greeted a wide variety of travelers—American Indians, Northwest Mounted Police, gold-seekers, and government mail couriers.

On the Origin of Species presented Darwin's theory of evolution—that all species of plants and animals had evolved from a few common ancestors. The book, published in 1859, shocked most people.

On one visit to Dawson, London camped near the cabin of Louis and Marshall Bond, two brothers whose father, Judge Hiram G. Bond, owned a large ranch in Santa Clara, California. London was very impressed by one of the Bonds' dogs. It was a large animal, part Saint Bernard and part collie, named, oddly, Jack.

When he returned to California, London visited the Bonds, and he was so taken with their place that two years later, while writing what many consider his masterpiece, *The Call of the Wild* (1903), he placed the Bonds' dog Jack (now named Buck) on the ranch of Judge Bond (now called Judge Miller). Thus began the great adventure of the Southland dog

> *Jack London's pen would produce far more gold than any miner's pick or shovel.*

that is stolen from the ranch and taken to the Northland, where he eventually leaves civilization to run with a pack of wolves.

London himself found little gold, but his year in the Klondike provided a resource even more precious: experience. Fashioned into powerful stories and novels and articles by his enormous imagination, this experience soon propelled him into worldwide celebrity. Jack London's pen would produce far more gold than any miner's pick or shovel.

His first book, *The Son of the Wolf: Tales of the Far North* (1900), is a collection of his earliest Klondike stories. *A Daughter of the Snows* (1902), his first novel, is about a woman named Frona Welse who seeks her fortune in the Klondike. *Scorn of Women* (1906), his first play, is a Klondike love story. And throughout his career London continued to revisit the region in his writing, the final effort being *Smoke Bellew* (1912), published a few years before he died.

In addition to those already mentioned, the best-known of these Northland tales are *White Fang* (1906), a novel, and "To Build a Fire" (1910), a short story. London wrote *White Fang* as a companion to the hugely successful *The Call of the Wild*. He wished, he said, to reverse his earlier story of the civilized dog that returns to the wild. So White Fang, the wolf-dog from the Yukon, returns at the end of the novel to the same California valley from which Buck had been stolen in *The Call of the Wild*.

There are four film adaptations of **White Fang**. They were released in 1925, 1936, 1974, and 1991. There are eight film adaptations of **The Call of the Wild**.

"To Build a Fire," the tale of a foolish, unnamed man who meets his death on a bitterly cold day, is probably London's most frequently published short story. London set the tale in a region he knew well (it was on Henderson Creek that he had filed his own gold claim), and in no other story did he so clearly portray the fatal consequences of ignoring nature's laws and humanity's accumulated wisdom.

London's Northland tales range widely in subject: from portrayals of people and animals struggling to survive in a bleak world governed by the harsh natural laws that Darwin had described, to examinations of the effects of the gold rush upon the native peoples in the region, to explorations of timeless human concerns like love and loyalty, dignity and self-respect, good and evil, crime and punishment, betrayal and revenge.

Marriage ... and Love ... and Marriage

On 17 April 1900, on the heels of his first literary successes, Jack London married Bessie May Maddern, a friend who had helped him pass his college entrance examinations. His other friends were surprised, for he had never really expressed any romantic interest in Bessie. On 15 January 1901, his first daughter, Joan, was born; on 20 October 1902, a second daughter, Becky, arrived.

In July 1903, the same month *The Call of the Wild* was published, London shocked his friends by leaving his wife and pursuing in public a relationship with another woman, Charmian Kittredge. On 17 November 1905, his divorce was finalized, and two days later he married Charmian. His daughters remained with their mother, and London was never again very close to either one of them.

Jack and Charmian were happy together, although they had no children and twice they suffered the heartbreak of miscarriage. Like her famous husband, Charmian loved the rugged outdoor life, and they spent many hours together swimming, sailing, horseback riding—and even boxing. Together they traveled to distant parts of the world, and Charmian helped Jack by typing his work (he wrote everything longhand) and by organizing and preserving his correspondence and manuscripts. Before he married Charmian, he had routinely discarded all his manuscripts once they were published.

A Snark

In 1905 London decided to build his own yacht and sail it with Charmian around the world on a seven-year cruise. They called the vessel the *Snark,* after a poem by Lewis Carroll. London had by this time developed the habits of writing that he maintained throughout his career: he rose early each morning and wrote between 1,000 and 1,500 words. In the afternoon Charmian typed his morning's output, and in the evening—and late into the night—he read books and magazines and edited what Charmian had typed for him. He continued this routine even while at sea; he performed it the day before he died.

On 22 April 1907, the *Snark*—after many delays and troubles—set sail for Hawaii and for what the Londons

> *London rose early each morning and wrote between 1,000 and 1,500 words (about six double-spaced typed pages). In the evening and late at night, he read books and magazines and edited what Charmian had typed for him. He continued this routine until the day before he died.*

hoped would be seven years of continual adventure. When they arrived in Hawaii on 20 May, they learned from newspapers that they had been declared dead—all hands lost at sea!

After a rest in Hawaii—a spot they loved so well that they returned for an extended visit from 1915 to 1916—they sailed on, visiting Tahiti, Samoa, the Solomon Islands, and Australia. But by December both Jack and Charmian were so weakened by various ailments that they were forced to end their voyage, sell the *Snark,* and return to California.

London's travels in the South Seas figure in many of his stories, including his nonfiction account of his voyage, *The Cruise of the "Snark"* (1911). In 1915, Charmian also published a book about their journeys called *The Log of the "Snark"*. The principal stories appear in *South Sea Tales* (1911), *The House of Pride and Other Tales of Hawaii* (1912), *A Son of the Sun* (1912), and *The Red One* (1918).

A Wolf

In 1905 the Londons began buying ranch land in the Valley of the Moon region near Glen Ellen, California, about forty miles north of San Francisco. Jack had become greatly interested in agriculture and wanted to make his ranch a self-supporting community.

Although there was an old ranch house already on the property, the Londons planned to build a large stone home to be called Wolf House. On 22 August 1913, just as they were preparing to move in, a fire destroyed the building For many years the origin of the fire was a mystery. But forensic scientists have recently determined that workers applying a finish to a fireplace mantel forgot to take with them their rags soaked in linseed oil. These rags ignited by spontaneous combustion. Wolf House had been insured for only a fraction of its original cost, and London did not have the money to rebuild. Today, the Jack London State Historical Park comprises much of the original ranch, and the ruins of Wolf House can still be seen. London wrote a number of stories set in his beloved Glen Ellen, including *The Valley of the Moon* (1913), *The Scarlet Plague* (1915), and *The Little Lady of the Big House* (1916).

The Jack London State Historical Park is located at:
2400 London Ranch Road
Glen Ellen, CA 95442

"A World So New, So Terrible, So Wonderful"

Even while he was suffering personal tragedy (Charmian's miscarriages), personal loss (the disruption of the *Snark* voyage, the fire at Wolf House), and poor health, London maintained his daily writing routine. In the final months of his life, he began reading the works of the psychologist C. G. Jung, who wrote about the unconscious mind and the power of myth. London told his wife that Jung's ideas were leading him to a "new" and "terrible" and "wonderful" world. He set to work using Jung's ideas in "The Red One" and "The Water Baby," two of his last stories.

But Jack London would not live long enough to explore this new psychological world. In November 1916, he was suffering from a variety of illnesses, some acquired on the *Snark* voyage. On 22 November he could not be awakened, and he died later that day on the porch of his ranch house. The attending physicians declared that the causes were uremia and kidney failure. Physicians today who have examined his symptoms and medical records have concluded that he probably suffered a stroke and heart failure as well.

Stories that Jack London died a suicide—stories that began in the late 1930s, probably instigated by a novel based on his life—have persisted even until today. They are false.

A Lasting Legacy

Today, some of London's ideas seem out of fashion—and occasionally offensive. In some of his writings, for example, he expresses an excessive pride in his Anglo-Saxon heritage that makes modern readers feel uncomfortable. Jack London, however, grew up in a country in which slavery had only recently been abolished, a country in which the predominantly white population was at war with the Plains Indians. He lived in a time when the magazines and newspapers of the day were openly racist.

Despite these unpleasant elements of some of his minor writings, London's literary reputation today remains secure. His major works continue to be popular all over the world. Readers enjoy Jack London, not simply because his books are compelling to read but because they do what all enduring works of literature do: instruct our minds and touch our hearts.

Readers enjoy Jack London, not simply because his books are compelling to read but because they do what all enduring works of literature do: instruct our minds and touch our hearts.

If you like the works of Jack London, you might also enjoy the works of Mark Twain and Ernest Hemingway.

Selected Bibliography

WORKS BY JACK LONDON

The Son of the Wolf: Tales of the Far North (1900)

The God of His Fathers (1901)

Children of the Frost (1902)

The Cruise of the Dazzler (1902)

A Daughter of the Snows (1902)

The Kempton-Wace Letters, with Anna Strunsky (1903)

The Call of the Wild (1903)

People of the Abyss (1903)

The Faith of Men (1904)

The Sea-Wolf (1904)

War of the Classes (1905)

The Game (1905)

Tales of the Fish Patrol (1905)

Moon-Face and Other Stories (1906)

White Fang (1906)

Scorn of Women, play (1906)

Before Adam (1907)

Love of Life and Other Stories (1907)

The Road (1907)

The Iron Heel (1907)

Martin Eden (1909)

Lost Face (1910)

Revolution and Other Essays (1910)

Burning Daylight (1910)

Theft: A Play in Four Acts (1910)

Adventure (1911)

The Cruise of the "Snark" (1911)

South Sea Tales (1911)

When God Laughs and Other Stories (1911)

The House of Pride and Other Tales of Hawaii (1912)

Smoke Bellew (1912)

The Son of the Sun (1912)

The Abysmal Brute (1913)

John Barleycorn (1913)

The Night-Born (1913)

The Valley of the Moon (1913)

The Mutiny of the Elsinore (1914)

The Strength of the Strong (1914)

The Scarlet Plague (1915)

The Star Rover (1915)

The Acorn-Planter: A California Forest Play (1916)

The Little Lady of the Big House (1916)

The Turtles of Tasman (1916)

The Human Drift (1917)

Jerry of the Islands (1917)

Michael, Brother of Jerry (1917)

The Red One (1918)

On the Makaloa Mat (1919)

Hearts of Three (1920)

Dutch Courage and Other Stories (1922)

The Assassination Bureau, Ltd., completed by Robert L. Fish (1963)

MODERN EDITIONS AND COLLECTIONS

The Complete Short Stories of Jack London. Edited by Earle Labor, Robert C. Leitz III, and I. Milo Shepard. 3 vols. Stanford, Calif.: Stanford University Press, 1993.

Letters from Jack London. Edited by King Hendricks and Irving Shepard. New York: Odyssey, 1965.

Novels and Social Writings. Edited by Donald Pizer. New York: Library of America, 1982.

Novels and Stories. Edited by Donald Pizer. New York: Library of America, 1982.

WORKS ABOUT JACK LONDON

Calder-Marshall, Arthur. *Lone Wolf: The Story of Jack London*. New York: Duell, Sloan and Pearce, 1961.

Day, A. Grove. *Jack London in the South Seas*. New York: Four Winds Press, 1971.

Franchere, Ruth. *Jack London: The Pursuit of a Dream*. New York: Thomas Y. Crowell, 1962.

Garst, Shannon. *Jack London: Magnet for Adventure.* New York: Julian Messner, 1944.

Labor, Earle, and Jeanne Campbell Reesman. *Jack London.* Rev. ed. New York: Twayne, 1994.

London, Charmian Kittredge. *The Book of Jack London.* 2 vols. New York: Century, 1921.

Schroeder, Alan. *Jack London.* New York: Chelsea House, 1992.

Walker, Dale L. *The Alien World of Jack London.* Grand Rapids, Mich.: Wolf House Books, 1973.

Lois Lowry

(1937-   )

by Melinda L. Franklin

What is a sure way to travel as a child? That is right, have a parent in the military. Lois Lowry was born in Honolulu, Hawaii, on 20 March 1937 to Robert E. Hammersberg, an army dentist, and Katharine Landis Hammersberg. She was the second of three children.

Lois Lowry Yesterday and Today

During World War II, Lowry lived in her mother's hometown in Pennsylvania and, after the war, in Tokyo, Japan. She attended high school in New York City. Just after Lowry's nineteenth birthday, she married Donald Grey Lowry. Her marriage and her husband's military career cut short her college days at Brown University in Rhode Island. In 1972, after having had four children and helping her husband through Harvard Law School, Lowry received a B.A. in writing from the University of Southern Maine. She went on to publish two textbooks, *Black American Literature* and *Literature of the American Revolution,* numerous magazine and newspaper articles, and a book of photographs, *Here in Kennebunkport* (vacation home of former President George Bush).

How did she move from this type of work to writing for young adults? After reading one of her published stories about her childhood, a Houghton Mifflin editor asked Lowry if she would be interested in writing books for younger audiences. She was, and she published her first book for young adults, *A Summer to Die,* in 1977.

More than twenty books later, Lois Lowry is still evolving as a writer. She splits her work and play time between an old section of Boston called Beacon Hill and a farmhouse in New Hampshire. Her children are grown, and she is a grandmother.

Autobiographical Elements

leukemia cancerous disease in which there is an abnormal increase in the number of white blood cells

Like many writers, Lowry uses events from her own life as inspiration for her stories. *A Summer to Die,* Lowry's first novel, features the relationship between two sisters. The older sister, Molly, is dying of leukemia. Lowry's own sister, Helen, died at an early age of cancer. Although the specific circumstances of the book are fictional, Lowry is able to effectively express the emotions surrounding the premature death of a family member.

turbulent unstable or disturbed

Autumn Street (1979) reflects Lowry's experiences as a young girl in the time of World War II. Like the narrator, Elizabeth, Lowry lived with her mother's family. During these turbulent times, Lowry depended on her grandfather for support and affection. This influence resulted in many strong, older male characters in Lowry's works. Some examples include: Will Banks from *A Summer to Die,* Gregor Keretsky,

paleontologist scientist who studies fossils

the museum paleontologist in *The One Hundredth Thing About Caroline* (1985), and the elder Receiver of Memory in *The Giver* (1993). Each of these men provides support and encouragement for central characters in Lowry's works.

Themes in Lowry's Work

Common themes pervade Lois Lowry's books for young adult readers. Although the tone, setting, and cast of characters vary, Lowry's purposes are constant.

First, Lowry emphasizes the vital part that memories play in individual lives. Memories offer a glimpse of people, places, and events of the past. While memories hold pleasurable recollections, they also serve as reminders of lessons learned. Anastasia, Lowry's most popular character, begins to understand the importance of memories in *Anastasia Krupnik* (1979). She is frustrated by her aging grandmother who cannot keep names and facts straight. After visiting her father's poetry class on William Wordsworth, Anastasia questions, "Memory is the happiness of being alone?" (p. 72). From a line of poetry, she realizes that memories of the past provide her grandmother with comfort and happiness.

Many of Lowry's other works emphasize the importance of having, keeping, and using memories. For older characters, Lowry demonstrates how memories are comforting; she portrays Anastasia's grandmother as she recalls her husband, Sam; the Krupniks' suburban neighbor, Gertrude Stein, as she thinks of her life as a young girl; and Will Banks from *A Summer to Die* as he remembers the legacy left by the homes his family built. There are also young people, like Rabble Starkey thinking of life with her mother and Meg Chalmers remembering good times with her sister, who use their memories for support and encouragement.

Second, Lowry draws attention to the cyclical aspect of life by emphasizing themes of birth, life, and death. The best example of this is found in her first novel, *A Summer to Die*. In this story, Meg Chalmers loses her sister, Molly, to leukemia, and later witnesses the birth of her neighbors' first child. Through these experiences, Meg is able to see the end and the beginning of life as part of the same cycle. By witnessing the cycle of life, Lowry's characters learn more about their own lives.

Perhaps the most dominant theme in Lowry's work is the interdependence among all people. She believes, as is evident from her stories, that all people are connected with a strong and binding responsibility to, and need for, each other. The families and the extended relationships are beautifully drawn examples of this sustaining link. Lowry creates universal characters who are not able to function without the help, influence, or wisdom of others.

William Wordsworth (1770–1850) was an English poet who helped to found the literary movement of Romanticism in England. The Romantics typically found inspiration in the relation between nature and their own feelings and memories.

legacy heritage passed on to later generations

cyclical circular or recurring

Voices in Lowry's work

Lois Lowry uses both the first- and third-person points of view in her writing. Regardless of which voice she chooses, each work has a dominant character who speaks directly to the reader. Perhaps Anastasia Krupnik is Lowry's strongest voice. Anastasia is witty and frank. She solves problems by talking with people: her parents, friends, other adults, and herself. Her confidence is evident in her direct approach to people and situations.

In *Autumn Street,* Elizabeth speaks in a different voice from Anastasia. The story is told by an adult Elizabeth reflecting on her family life during World War II. Elizabeth is timid and unsure. During the time of the story, her world is shadowed by war, death, and the mysteries of adults. Her voice, like the setting, contains a certain darkness and sadness.

Rabble Starkey's (1987) narrator, Parable Ann, speaks not only with a different tone, but with a different dialect from any of Lowry's other characters. In *The Voice of the Narrator in Children's Literature* (1989), Lowry asks of Rabble's voice, "Why did that voice, that diction, that tone, emerge for that particular book? Why not the wry and outspoken voice of Anastasia Krupnik, or the more lyrical, innocent, and introspective voice of Elizabeth of *Autumn Street*? I can only guess" (p. 182). Rabble's voice is simple, straightforward, and serious. She was born when her mother, Sweet-Ho, was fourteen, and together Rabble and Sweet-Ho tackle the challenges of small-town life.

lyrical songlike or expressive

Anastasia and the Krupniks

Anastasia and her family, the Krupniks, are the central element in ten of Lowry's books for young adults. The Anastasia series, which includes many of Lowry's most popular works, combines wit and wisdom. Although some critics of the novels say that the stories are too perfect, the Krupnik family is a delightful depiction of parents and children working through day-to-day choices and challenges.

Anastasia Krupnik is the first book in the series. Here the reader meets Myron, a college professor who writes poetry and loves baseball; Katherine, a freelance artist and determined housewife; Anastasia, a frank and curious ten year old; and Sam, a precocious newborn.

precocious skilled or mature at an early age

apprehensive anxious or fearful

In this story, Anastasia is apprehensive about the arrival of the new baby because she thinks her parents are a bit strange. And with good reason—her father conducts imaginary operas in his study and her mother always has an embarrassing dab of paint on her face. Besides that, they insist that they are having a love affair, with each other. "Parents," marvels Anastasia, who is given the task of naming the new baby. At first she chooses a horrible name, but eventually names the baby Sam after their grandfather.

In *Anastasia Again!* (1981), the second installment in the Krupnik series, the family is moving into the suburbs. In a plan to stop the move (Anastasia fears that moving to the suburbs will turn her family into boring, typical people), Anastasia requests that her room have a tower. The plan is foiled when Anastasia gets her tower room. She later decides that she likes her new situation after all.

The Krupnik stories continue as Anastasia works as a housekeeper for her soon-to-be best friend's grandmother, has adventures raising gerbils, prepares a romantic dinner, struggles up and falls off the physical education rope while reciting poetry, and responds to a classified advertisement. With each charming venture, Anastasia becomes a bit wiser and a bit more endearing.

All About Sam (1988) and *Attaboy, Sam!* (1992) are two of Lowry's tales that focus on Sam rather than Anastasia. Sam, who has an impressive vocabulary but refuses to be potty-trained, is as enjoyable as Anastasia as a central character.

Number the Stars

Number the Stars (1989) won Lowry her first Newbery Medal. This story looks at the Holocaust and World War II through the relationship between two young girls in Copenhagen, Denmark. In 1943, life has changed a great deal for Annemarie Johansen and her best friend Ellen Rosen. The Nazis have occupied Copenhagen, soldiers are marching about town, and food is rationed. The worst, however, is still to come for Ellen and her family because they are Jewish. When the Nazis begin to relocate Jewish people (often to concentration camps or foreign prisons), the Johansens become part of the resistance by helping families, including the Rosens, escape from Denmark. By completing a dangerous errand, it is Annemarie who ensures the safety of the fleeing people.

After Ellen and her family escape into Sweden, Annemarie is afraid she will never see her friend again. Her Uncle Henrik comforts her, "You will, little one. You saved her life,

The **Holocaust** was the mass murder of at least 11 million people, especially Jews, by the Nazis during World War II. The word "holocaust" means "thorough destruction by fire."

after all. Someday you will find her again. Someday the war will end. . . . All wars do" (p. 127). In this work, Lowry emphasizes the power individuals have to help, even save, others. At the same time, she reminds the reader of a period in history that cannot be forgotten or repeated.

This piece of historical fiction was inspired by and dedicated to Lowry's Danish friend, Annelise Platt, who was a child in Copenhagen during World War II. Lowry concludes in the afterword of *Number the Stars,* "Surely that gift—the gift of a world of human decency—is the one that all countries hunger for still. I hope that this story of Denmark, and its people, will remind us all that such a world is possible" (p. 137).

Diary of a Young Girl is a suitable companion to *Number the Stars.* It is a nonfiction account of the war written by Anne Frank while in hiding. Anne Frank was a Jewish girl who hid in the top story of an Amsterdam building with her family and four other people to avoid relocation by the Nazis. Like Lowry, Louisa May Alcott, James L. and Christopher Collier, and Ann Rinaldi also write historical fiction. Try one of their books if you like *Number the Stars.*

There are articles about Anne Frank, Louisa May Alcott, and James L. and Christopher Collier in volume 1. There is an article about Ann Rinaldi in volume 3.

The Giver

Lois Lowry inscribed her 1994 Newbery Medal winner, *The Giver* (1993), "For all the children to whom we entrust the future." The book serves as a warning and a hope for times to come. Although the setting of this novel is strikingly different from Lowry's other works, the themes are the same: the importance of memories, the interdependence of families and greater communities, and the cycle of life.

The Giver is set in a perfect world of the future. This utopian community is free of disease, prejudice, and crime, but it is also missing diversity, memories, and love. Each family is structured exactly the same and participates in identical daily rituals.

utopia ideal of a perfect society

In this world, each child progresses through regulated stages of maturity in a yearly meeting, the Ceremony of Age. Jonas, the protagonist of *The Giver,* prepares for the Ceremony of Twelve. This is an important ceremony for Jonas and the other children his age at which each individual is assigned his or her lifelong role in the community. In Jonas' protected world, individuals do not hold memories of pain or pleasure. All the memories are given to one person, an esteemed member of the society. Jonas is chosen to be the next Receiver of Memory for the community. His training is both joyful (for the first time he knows love, colors, snow, and the sun) and painful (he learns of sadness, hunger, physical pain, and war).

Besides enduring the pain of his training, Jonas is further incensed when he discovers that his "perfect" community is built on a series of lies. The lack of memory prevents members of the community from seeing or understanding truth in their world. The Giver, Jonas' trainer, says, "Without the memories [the knowledge of the community] is meaningless. They gave that burden to me." (p. 105). Rather than the whole community having independent memories, the society depends on the Receiver of Memory to hold all of the pain and joy of the past and to serve as wise council when memories are required to make decisions. The entire burden rests on the Receiver.

The type of interdependence that Lowry describes in *The Giver* is very different from the connections that are central to many of her works. The utopian world is structured with a series of rituals and rules for families and the community. In the family they have Telling of Feelings, Telling of Dreams, and set statements that are made by a person who has been rude or vain. The community takes part in such rituals as strict daily schedules, the Ceremony of Age, and Releases (sanctioned euthanasia for the elderly or undesirable members of the community). This community relies on rules and structure to hold it together, instead of connections among people. The relationships among the people of *The Giver* look especially shallow when contrasted with familial and communal relationships in Lowry's other works such as *Rabble Starkey, Autumn Street,* and the Anastasia books.

Finally, Lowry uses several examples of the cyclical aspect of life in *The Giver.* Jonas is being trained to replace the old Receiver of Memory, an elder in the community. Jonas is young and inexperienced. He is challenged emotionally, mentally, and physically by the memories he receives. The Giver, as Jonas comes to call the present Receiver of Memory, has been exhausted by his responsibilities. Jonas is his relief. The Elder must pass his burdensome task to Jonas, a progression that represents the natural patterns of life.

sanctioned allowed

euthanasia killing of a person to spare him or her from suffering

The "newchild," Gabriel, is another component in the life cycle. Gabriel is a weak baby, so Jonas' father, a Nurturer of newchildren in the community, gets special permission to bring the baby home. The troubled Gabriel cries and frets during the night. Jonas finds that he can calm the baby by giving him some of the pleasant memories he has inherited in his training. In this way, Jonas passes the wisdom of The Giver onto the newchild.

In the end, Jonas decides to leave the community and release the memories he has been given into the community. While The Giver stays to help the community handle the released memories, Jonas and Gabriel escape in the night for the unknown land beyond the community boundaries. In freedom, the two young characters are allowed possible rebirth. In this way the cycle continues.

In Closing

Although it is impossible to highlight all of Lowry's works, each is consistently witty and insightful. She is a talented storyteller with a gift for creating dynamic characters and engaging dialogue. She continues to push herself and her craft to new horizons.

If you like Lois Lowry, then you will also like Jerry Spinelli and Cynthia Voigt. If you enjoyed *The Giver*, you might also like the works of Madeleine L'Engle, Ursula K. Le Guin, C. S. Lewis, and J. R. R. Tolkien. Like Lowry, these writers create other worlds to help their readers see this world with a clearer perspective.

Selected Bibliography

WORKS BY LOIS LOWRY

Novels for Young Adults

A Summer to Die (1977)

Find a Stranger, Say Goodbye (1978)

Anastasia Krupnik (1979)

Autumn Street (1979)

Anastasia Again! (1981)

Anastasia at Your Service (1982)

Taking Care of Terrific (1983)

Anastasia, Ask Your Analyst (1984)

Us and Uncle Fraud (1984)

Anastasia on Her Own (1985)

The One Hundredth Thing About Caroline (1985)

Switcharound (1985)

Anastasia Has the Answers (1986)

Anastasia's Chosen Career (1987)

Rabble Starkey (1987)

All About Sam (1988)

Number the Stars (1989)

Your Move, J. P.! (1990)

Anastasia At This Address (1991)

Attaboy, Sam! (1992)

The Giver (1993)

Short Story

"Holding." In *Am I Blue? Coming Out from the Silence.* Edited by Marion Dane Bauer (1994).

Essay

"*Rabble Starkey*: A Voice from a Surprising Place." In *The Voice of the Narrator in Children's Literature: Insights from Writers and Critics.* Edited by Chalotte F. Otten and Gary D. Schmidt (1989).

Autobiography

"Lois Lowry." In *Something About the Author Autobiography Series.* Edited by Adele Sarkissian (1987).

WORKS ABOUT LOIS LOWRY

Commire, Anne, ed. "Lois Lowry." In *Something About the Author.* Detroit: Gale Research, 1981, vol. 23, pp. 121–122.

Johnson, David P. "Lois Lowry." In *Something About the Author.* Edited by Donna Olendorf and Diane Telgen. Detroit: Gale Research, 1993, vol. 70, pp. 134–137.

Zaidman, Laura M. "Lois Lowry." In *Dictionary of Literary Biography.* Vol. 52: *American Writers for Children Since 1960: Fiction.* Edited by Glenn E. Ester. Detroit: Gale Research, 1986, pp. 249–261.

How to Write to the Author:
Lois Lowry
c/o Houghton Mifflin Co.
222 Berkeley Street
Boston, MA 02116

Chris Lynch

(1962-   )

by James M. Brewbaker

Chris Lynch has strong feelings about adolescence, which he calls "the great lurch between childhood and adulthood." In describing his reading audience in 1995, Lynch pointed out that most adults, especially parents and teachers, think of teenagers in these terms: "God, I wish they'd just grow up. Or stay small." Teenagers, of course, would not follow this plan even if they could, because adolescence, being the great lurch that it is, is rarely quick, neat, or painless. Lynch's novels, the first published in 1993, appeal to readers—especially boys—who relate to characters that are neck deep in a difficult, sometimes unsuccessful, search for their identity. This search frequently leads to antisocial behavior of one kind or another, even violence. More often than not, Lynch's teenage characters rebel against the fact that others—members of family, school, or the greater community—attempt to define them in ways they cannot accept. Lynch's teenage characters work simultaneously toward self-definition and getting others to accept who they are.

lurch abrupt or unsteady movement

School Years

autobiographical related to the author's own life

Lynch's own teenage years in Boston were, indeed, much of a lurch themselves. He was the fifth of seven children; his father died when he was five. At school, Lynch was a misfit, a loner, in many ways very much like Eric, the brooding fifteen-year-old hockey player in *Iceman* (1994). Lynch points out that this novel is, in psychological terms, his most autobiographical. This means that the events of the plot are fictional, but Eric's moods, feelings, and worries are very close to what the writer experienced at the same age.

Sister Elizabeth Brennan, a seventh-grade teacher, turned Lynch on to writing, but he lost his interest soon after that. The arts were not cool—were not accepted—in the Boston parochial school that he attended. Boys who painted or wrote stories or even read much ran the risk of being defined as nerds, dweebs, or worse. Lynch has likened the values of his high school to those of the Christian Brothers Academy, the fictional high school that is the setting for *Slot Machine* (1995). Everyone at Christian Brothers Academy is supposed to fit in, to find a slot; desirable slots for boys are defined strictly in terms of sports such as football, wrestling, and basketball. In *Slot Machine,* boys attending a retreat prior to the beginning of ninth grade believe that failing to fit into this scheme—failing to find one's slot—equals failure in general. Overweight, free-thinking Elvin Bishop experiences one rejection after another at the camp, and he witnesses his friend Frankie undergo an extreme hazing ritual to gain popularity. At the story's conclusion, Elvin accepts his own uniqueness while realizing that the slots filled by others might not be worth what is lost along the way. "I'm still whatever I am," Elvin writes to his mother. "They can't touch that."

hazing harassment and ridicule sometimes used to initiate younger members of a group

Not at all sure of who or what *he* was, Lynch was sure of one thing: he hated high school. Aware that Boston University accepted qualified students without a diploma, he dropped out after his junior year. Enrolling at BU, he drifted at first, majoring in government and discovering along the way that he had little talent for music, a lifelong interest. Then Lynch enrolled in a newswriting course, which marked the beginning of his journey toward becoming a writer. He transferred to Suffolk University, also in Boston, where he majored in journalism. He graduated in 1983.

Writing for Young Readers— and Nonreaders

Ten years later, *Shadow Boxer* was published. With four novels sold and in print between 1993 and 1995, and three more (the Blue Eyed Son series: *Mick, Blood Relations,* and *Dog Eat Dog*) slated for 1996, Lynch decided late in 1995 that he could be a full-time writer and teacher. Previously, he had supported himself and his family as a house painter, truck driver, and proofreader. IIe and his wife have two children, Sophia and Walker, born in 1990 and 1993, respectively. Lynch taught writing on a part-time basis at Emerson College, where he earned a master's degree in writing and publishing in 1991. In 1997, he joined the faculty at Vermont College's new graduate program in writing for children and teenagers; as a working novelist and teacher, he will bring to this job the expertise of a writer whose fiction is selling well in the 1990s.

The gritty novels of Lynch have quickly become popular among young adults, particularly those who are turned off by reading. Because he tells realistic stories about nonconventional teenage characters—especially tough boys who cut class, stay home, spend a lot of time in detention, and think hard about dropping out—he has been compared with S. E. Hinton, who wrote *The Outsiders.*

Lynch's novels are praised by teachers, librarians, and critics. Each of his first three novels was selected by the American Library Association as a Best Book for Young Adults as well as a Recommended Book for the Reluctant Young Adult Reader.

There is an article about S. E. Hinton earlier in this volume.

Shadow Boxer (1993) focuses on George and Monty, brothers who find life increasingly tough in the years following the death of their father, an over-the-hill prizefighter. Before his death he taught George how to fight, but he died too soon for the boy to learn another lesson: "how *not* to be a fighter, how to walk away." George has to learn this on his own as well as figure out what to do with the talent and passion that Monty, his younger brother, develops for boxing. Reviewers were quick to praise the novel's fight sequences, strong characterizations, and tense episodes; they found its tough-talking characters both believable and appealing.

Sports in the Novels of Chris Lynch

Lynch writes convincingly and powerfully of athletes and the games they play. Team sports serve an important function in his novels, but they are not, he points out, sports books. As they do not deal with becoming an athlete, training, or winning the big game, he has a point. Instead, sports—hockey in *Iceman,* boxing in *Shadow Boxer,* and the full gamut of high school team sports in *Slot Machine*—provide situations in which characters learn about themselves and the world. For example, Eric is the unhappy, violent hockey player in *Iceman,* wondering why he continues to play the game when, ultimately, he hates it. In *Slot Machine,* Elvin Bishop fails miserably at finding his slot, first in football, then in baseball and wrestling. He is finally exiled to the "Arts Sector," where everyone is ridiculed by those who have already found their slot.

gamut variety or range

As a teenager, Lynch was more a spectator than a player. Boston is a hockey town, especially among so-called blue-collar Irish Americans like Lynch's family and friends. When he was in grade school, the Boston Bruins, the hockey team led by the legendary player Bobby Orr, won the Stanley Cup. That event, Lynch explains, dominated his childhood and that of his friends, and he knows hockey with the passion of a true fan.

Lynch also knows boxing. "Nobody ever watched boxing more closely than I did," he has said. "Nobody." Heavyweight champion Muhammad Ali was one of his heroes as an adolescent, not only because Ali was a wonderful fighter but also because, as a convert to Islam, he held strong pacifist beliefs about the evils of war and was willing to go to jail rather than deny his principles.

Clearly, it is Lynch's writer's eye as well as his passion for sports that equips him to tell of them so effectively. Although play-by-play (or, in the case of boxing, blow-by-blow) descriptions fill only a minor portion of his novels, the passages are gritty, realistic, and memorable. The opening passage of *Shadow Boxer,* for example, almost makes readers wince:

> **I was nine years old . . . the first time I hit my father and made him bleed. He was proud.**

"Atta' baby, atta' baby!" he screamed without looking at me. He was staring at the little puddle of blood that was gathering in the palm of his hand. It wasn't that cutting his lip was such a hard thing to do—he opened old cuts every morning just brushing his teeth—it was that I finally landed the big punch. (P. 1)

Memorable Fathers

Unlike some writers for young readers, Lynch often includes important, thoroughly developed adult characters in his novels. Three fathers in particular are memorable. George's prize-fighter father is recalled only in flashbacks, but his dogged efforts to teach his son not only how to fight but how *not* to determine all major events in the plot. In *Iceman,* Eric's loudmouth father lives for his son's hockey games and little else. The thought that Eric would give up the sport never enters his mind. Instead, he comes alive on weekend road trips into New York State and Canada, encouraging Eric's violence, brashly offending other parents, those of teammates and opponents both. Sneaky Pete, the father in *Gypsy Davey* (1994), is rootless, a chronic gambler who spends his time in Florida. He is inclined to shower his children, Davey and Joanne, and his ex-wife with gifts one year, then disappear for the next two.

"When I Don't Have My Fastball, I Still Take the Mound"

In an *ALAN* address in 1995, Lynch told English teachers, "I stumbled my way into writing." In an autobiographical sketch included in the *Seventh Book of Junior Authors and Illustrators* (1996) he writes, "Like many other authors . . . I knew early on what I wanted to do. I wanted to do nothing."

While it may be true that Lynch disliked school and discovered his interest in writing in his mid-twenties, it is equally clear that he takes seriously the working life, the routine of a writer. In graduate school at Emerson College, an instructor told Lynch's class that only one in a hundred would-be professional writers actually makes a living at writ-

> *"Like many other authors . . . I knew early on what I wanted to do. I wanted to do nothing."*

ing. Lynch reasoned that, in fact, ninety-five percent of those who say they want to write, even when they have talent, drop out. "Only five percent really compete," he concluded.

Because Lynch believes that writing is serious work, he follows a set routine for his working day. Responsible in part for taking care of his young children, he completes the typical morning tasks that most parents face, then spends the remainder of the day writing, whether he feels like it or not. Only rarely, however, does he continue writing into the evening hours.

Themes: From Family Relations to Social Issues

Lynch's first three novels deal with themes tied to family relations. These works emphasize the responsibility of brothers and sisters toward one another, the need to find one's way with minimal or sometimes negative guidance from parents, the hope of remaining true to real or apparent family ideals. Almost every scene occurs at home or in the neighborhood where the main character lives. *Gypsy Davey,* which Lynch believes is his best novel, illustrates the family-relations theme at its bleakest. Davey, the main character, has been all but abandoned by his affectionate but incompetent and distracted mother. He is cared for, truly loved, by his sister Joanne, who at the age of seven makes him macaroni and cheese each day after school. By the time Joanne turns seventeen, though, she has her own baby, is no longer willing to be a surrogate parent to Davey, and, worst of all, drifts into a life that threatens Dennis, her baby. Davey resolves to take Dennis somewhere safe, to love him, to care for him as he himself had once been cared for by Joanne.

Slot Machine, a departure from Lynch's first three novels, signals the author's movement from a focus on family toward larger issues. The later books of the Blue Eyed Son series continue to address family issues, but they move beyond the family to examine society's most troublesome problems, including racism, homophobia, youth violence, drugs, and alcohol abuse. The main character of these three closely related titles is Mick, a fifteen-year-old Irish Catholic youth who begins to question the life laid out for him. His family and friends are bigots and heavy drinkers. They settle their dis-

surrogate substitute

homophobia hostility toward or discrimination against gay, lesbian, or bisexual people

bigot one who is prejudiced against others

putes violently. Their houses smell of sweat, beer, urine, and worse.

Mick's traditionally Irish American neighborhood and world are changing: blacks, Asians, and Latinos live only a few blocks away. Contingents of Cambodians and gay Irish Americans attempt to march in the annual St. Patrick's Day parade, providing an excuse for vandalism and street violence by Mick's older brother, Terry, and his roughneck friends toward "different" Bostonians: those whom these boys think do not know and respect their place.

Terry, whose traits Lynch may have exaggerated to make his point, embodies the worst in working-class Irish Catholic Boston. He is an alcoholic, and his May Day binges are so filled with violence as a form of entertainment (he arranges to have a neighborhood dog kill a young goat in his parents' home) that his parents leave town for the weekend. Worst of all, Terry works hard to make sure that Mick turns out the way he has. Terry's efforts land Mick in the hospital.

Mick, though, has ideas of his own. Influenced by Hispanic friends at school—Toy and the intelligent, beautiful, and straight-talking Evelyn—Mick wants to break out of the mold that others have shoved him into. But doing that turns out to be far easier said than done, as he explains in *Blood Relations*. "Getting out of my neighborhood, my *family,* was a lot like getting out of the priesthood," Mick senses. "You couldn't just wake up one day and say, 'Okay, I'm not what I was anymore,' and that would be it. There was a lot of explaining to do, maybe some vows to be broken."

In the Blue Eyed Son series, Mick wants to break out of the mold that others have shoved him into. But doing that turns out to be far easier said than done.

An Impressive Newcomer, a Bright Future

Because Chris Lynch is much younger than many authors of young adult fiction, it may be that his best writing lies ahead of him. He points out that he has worked consciously to improve his craft. He wants to avoid being labeled strictly as either a sports author or a boys' writer. Clearly, *Gypsy Davey* is a step away from his first two novels. For one thing, it is more complex in structure. In alternating chapters, Lynch moves from Davey's here-and-now narration to a series of flashbacks covering a decade or more. In *Slot Machine,* Lynch's next novel, Elvin Bishop's letters home display the author's considerable sense of humor for the first time. In the Blue Eyed Son series, he writes powerfully of young people caught up in dangerous and difficult social issues.

Much to Lynch's credit, he avoids pat or easy answers. As a result, he avoids patronizing his readers. Mick, in *Dog Eat Dog,* the third and final Blue Eyed Son story, must leave town in order to have a chance at getting out of his neighborhood. He may be his own worst enemy.

Lynch believes that he writes convincingly of what "older" adolescents face—especially fifteen- to twenty-year-old youth. Although he would not want to have carved out a niche at this stage in his career, this is an accurate assessment of his strengths. On the other hand, he has yet to create fully drawn female characters, especially sympathetic adolescent girls. Evelyn in *Mick, Blood Relations,* and *Dog Eat Dog* is a promising exception to this, although she is not a primary character. If, as Lynch says, he wants to develop his ability to write of adolescent girls and their lives, he is likely to turn his attention in that direction soon.

If you enjoy reading books by Chris Lynch, you might also enjoy reading those by Chris Crutcher and Harry Mazer.

Selected Bibliography

WORKS BY CHRIS LYNCH

Novels

    Shadow Boxer (1993)

    Gypsy Davey (1994)

    Iceman (1994)

    Slot Machine (1995)

Blue Eyed Sons series

    Mick (1996)

    Blood Relations (1996)

    Dog Eat Dog (1996)

Short Fiction

    "The Hobbyist." In *Ultimate Sports: Short Stories by Outstanding Writers for Young Adults.* Edited by Donald R. Gallo (1995)

    "Bearing Paul." In *Night Terrors.* Edited by Lois Duncan (1996)

WORKS ABOUT CHRIS LYNCH

Chance, Rosemary. "Families." *Emergency Librarian,* January 1996, pp. 57–58.

Comeford, Lynda Brill. "Flying Starts." *Publishers Weekly,* 20 December 1993, p. 34.

Hearn, Michael Patrick. "Children's Books." Reviews of *Shadow Boxer, Iceman,* and *Gypsy Davey. Washington Post,* 1 January 1995, p. WBK 11.

IIoffman, Marvin. "Powerful Trilogy Wrestles with Disaffected Youths." *Houston Chronicle,* 10 March 1996, p. Z23.

Anne McCaffrey

(1926-)

by Karen S. Kutiper

Imagine yourself living on a planet called Pern in a fictional world of telepathic dragons, singing fire lizards, and life-consuming spores that descend periodically to devastate the people and their lands. Just what in Anne McCaffrey's life led her to create this compelling futuristic world and ultimately become one of the most recognized names in the world of science fiction for adults and younger readers alike?

About the Author

Born on April Fool's Day 1926, McCaffrey describes herself in *Speaking for Ourselves* (Gallo, 1990) as "a totally uncompromising egregious domineering opinionated brat" of a child who used her imagination to entertain herself. In the same essay she recalls that her parents, individualists in their own right, read widely to their children, thus creating in her

egregious outstandingly bad

impetus the driving force, or stimulus

a love of books and writing that, combined with a healthy imagination, probably became the impetus for her career as a writer.

McCaffrey graduated from Radcliffe College in 1947 and worked as an advertising copywriter from 1947 until 1952. Her first publication was the 1959 novella *The Lady in the Tower* and her first published book was *Restoree,* which appeared in 1967. An interest in music prompted her to study voice, and she worked in the production of operas and operettas. In 1970, she moved to Ireland with two of her three children and her mother. She still lives at Dragonhold, the family home in the hills of County Wicklow, where she continues to write and raise horses for shows and jumping competitions.

One of her young competition riders was a model for Menolly, the gifted young musician in her Harper Hall trilogy of Pern-based novels written especially for adolescent readers. The trilogy that features Menolly as the central character was written at the request of McCaffrey's publisher, who hoped that a strong female character would interest more young female readers in science fiction.

Life on the Planet Pern

The Harper Hall trilogy, McCaffrey's most widely read works for young adults, is made up of the companion novels *Dragonsong* (1976), *Dragonsinger* (1977), and *Dragondrums* (1979). The story in each novel takes place on the planet Pern, one of the five planets of the star Rukbat. She first introduced this world in her three novels *Dragonflight* (1968), *Dragonquest* (1971), and *The White Dragon* (1978). The Red Star, a wandering planet close to Pern, complicates life for the people of Pern (the Pernese). The Red Star had gone unnoticed for several generations until its native life-form, parasitic spores that devour organic matter, began dropping to Pern's surface, causing massive destruction of people, crops, and vegetation. The major thrust of life on Pern becomes one of surviving recurrent and unpredictable attacks by these life-consuming spores, which the Pernese call Thread.

genetic engineering the alteration of genetic material, especially by gene-splicing

The Pernese survival plan calls for the genetic engineering of a highly specialized dragonlike life-form that can instantaneously transport itself from one place or time to another.

These fire-breathing, telepathic giants also can devour Thread in midair. The social, cultural, and political world of the planet grows in response to the people's need to protect themselves from Thread with these dragons. Extinct volcano cones are the only places large enough to house the dragons, and the Pernese community assigns groups of people to live among the dragons and support them. Six of these dragon communities, called Weyrs, are strategically located on Pern. The rest of the Pernese seek refuge and shelter in natural caves. Eventually these settlements, called Holds and governed by Lord Holders, develop their own community structure. Children from one Hold are commonly reared in another Hold to keep inbreeding at a minimum—a practice called fostering.

McCaffrey's own musical background surely influenced the creation of a culture whose most respected leaders and teachers are the musically talented Pernese. Called Harpers, these teachers and entertainers of Pern hold the major responsibilities of educating the young children of Pern and guiding the elders in the traditions and duties of the planet. As McCaffrey explains in *Dragonsong,* "Harpers were not simply tellers of tales and singers of songs, they were arbiters of justice, confidants of Holders and Craftmasters, and molders of the young" (p. 45).

Dragonsong

McCaffrey has created a compelling female protagonist in Menolly, a gifted musician and the main character in *Dragonsong*. Menolly is the daughter of Janis, Seaholder of the rather primitive Half Circle Sea Hold. After the death of her mentor and teacher, Harper Petiron, Menolly's life at Half Circle becomes unbearable. She has many musical talents: she sings, plays several musical instruments, and even writes music. But a young woman's role in Half Circle Sea Hold is merely to serve the men of the Hold, and Menolly's musical gifts are an embarrassment to her parents.

Menolly is just fourteen *turns* (the Pernese term for "years") when she must face her parents' abuse following the death of Petiron, the Harper who has recognized and fostered her musical gifts. McCaffrey explains, "Cheated of the one thing that had made her life bearable, she makes a life-changing decision when she runs away to the desolate sea-coast" (p. 41). After her escape from Half Circle Sea Hold, Menolly must focus on her own survival. She saves a nest of fire lizard eggs from the rising tides by moving them to a seaside cliff cave. (Fire lizards are tiny, highly prized relatives of the fire-breathing dragons.) Later, when she must save herself from Thread, she seeks shelter in a cave just as the baby fire lizards are about to hatch.

Menolly feeds and cares for the nine young hatchlings from the moment of their birth, and they bond with her for life. Never far away from their protector, these tiny telepathic creatures know when Menolly is in danger or need. The story focuses on Menolly's ability to find the resources to survive Thread and to keep herself and her fire lizards alive. Finally, after being discovered by dragonriders during a Thread fall, Menolly and her fire lizards are taken to Harper Hall, where Masterharper Robinton welcomes Petiron's gifted protégée.

protégée a female protégé—someone who is trained by an experienced or prominent person

Dragonsinger

In the second Harper Hall book, *Dragonsinger,* readers follow Menolly's life after her arrival at the Harpercraft Hall and Hold. Here she matures into a respected Harper journeyman whose talents receive appropriate recognition. At the Harpercraft Hall, Menolly meets the rascally Piemur, a young boy with a brilliant soprano voice who befriends her and her fire lizards. Menolly's eventual acceptance at Harper Hall does not come easily. She faces hurdles similar to those that teenagers face today: finding a place among her peers; adjusting to the bustling, energetic atmosphere at Harper Hall (a place very different from her home, where the entire focus of the community was fishing and preserving fish for Pernese survival); making friends; dealing with conflicts with peers; and coming to accept herself and her talents as the gifts they are. Through her experiences Menolly becomes resourceful and self-sufficient, confident that life at Harper Hall is her destiny.

In Dragonsinger, Menolly faces hurdles similar to those that teenagers face today: finding a place among her peers; making friends; dealing with conflicts with peers; and coming to accept herself and her talents as the gifts they are.

Dragondrums

With his friend Menolly as a supporting character, Piemur ultimately takes center stage in the last book of the trilogy, *Dragondrums.* With the onset of adolescence, he must adjust to his changing voice and the loss of his childlike soprano voice. He becomes a messenger-drum apprentice and finds himself involved in the politics of the planet. When he undertakes mysterious errands for the Harper, the story becomes almost like a spy thriller. Piemur's newfound skills and his intriguing tasks help him mature into a responsible young man with a real place at Harper Hall and in the Pernese society.

What the Critics Say

McCaffrey's three Harper Hall books have been praised for their strong characters and their detailed and compelling settings. As the *Horn Book* critic Mary M. Burns wrote in her 1977 review of *Dragonsinger*: "Details of the apprentices' lives—rigorous curriculum and teaching methods, food, clothing, and societal relationships—give verisimilitude to a superbly crafted fantasy in the heroic tradition." Yet, as Ruth Stein has noted in her 1980 *Language Arts* review of *Dragondrums,* "references to characters, places, and events from McCaffrey's earlier Pern novels can make it difficult for new readers to follow all the intricate details of plot and setting. McCaffrey seems to assume that readers are as familiar with Pern as are the author and readers of her earlier books. For the details of setting and character to be as meaningful as possible, first-time readers will want to approach the Harper Hall trilogy in the correct sequence, beginning with *Dragonsong*" (p. 189).

Of the three volumes, *Dragonsong* contains the most action and suspense. Its well-structured plot focuses on Menolly's difficulties at Half Circle Sea Hold, her life as a runaway, and her eventual arrival at Harper Hall. In the words of a reviewer in the 1976 *Booklist*: "Menolly comes through as a resourceful young girl searching for a way to give vent to her talents" (p. 1267).

Dragonsinger and *Dragondrums,* which focus more on daily life at Harper Hall and the relationships among the characters, provide less dramatic action and excitement. Ruth M. Stein, in her 1977 *Language Arts* review, has called *Dragonsinger* an "inferior sequel that depends on the first book for its meaning" (p. 807). Neither does *Dragondrums* live up

verisimilitude the quality of being true to life

plot the deliberate sequence of events in a literary work

Readers will likely become thoroughly entranced by the Pernese world and by the intriguing characters that McCaffrey has skillfully created, no matter which volume they choose to read.

to the action-filled first book in the series. But as the *School Library Journal* critic Sara Miller says in her 1979 review: "Though the plot lacks form at times, placing little emphasis on the major incidents, leaving readers with a loose, episodic adventure, young people will be entranced—again by Pern's ways—and in Piemur find an impulsive, thoroughly sympathetic hero" (p. 64).

These minor reservations aside, readers will likely become thoroughly entranced by the Pernese world and by the intriguing characters that McCaffrey has skillfully created, no matter which volume they choose to read. Perhaps the creation of that world, developed with realistic detail, reflects the author's most outstanding literary achievement.

Science Fiction or Science Fantasy?

Readers and critics alike have difficulty labeling McCaffrey's work as either science fiction or fantasy. As R. J. Lukens explains in *A Critical Handbook of Children's Literature,* "The writer of fantasy creates another world for characters and readers, asking that readers believe this other world could and does exist within the framework of the book." In McCaffrey's writing we find many elements of fantasy. The dragons, although scientifically created, recall mystical tales of dragon-slaying knights. The wild fire lizards, so revered by the Pernese and so integral to Menolly's story, are another element of fantasy. Hatched in clutches on barren seashores, these tiny, whimsical creatures must be "impressed" (joined to the mind of the first person who feeds or cares for them) just as the telepathic dragons are to their riders.

On the other hand, Pern is a world with scientific laws and technological inventions that seem both plausible and possible. The dragons, a creation of DNA (genetic) manipulation, are able to go instantly to the areas of nothingness that exist between one place and another. Although readers will find nothing about space travel in these books, the Pernese are descendants of space colonists from another solar system. Once they realize the simplicity of their new world, they rid themselves of technological advances. And Thread, with all its devastating, almost mystical, powers, is certainly a creation of science fiction.

Perhaps science fantasy might a be more appropriate label because McCaffrey's books merge the elements of science fiction and fantasy both. Science fantasy is described in *Essentials of Children's Literature* (Lynch-Brown and Tomlinson, 1993) as "a popularized type of science fiction in which a scientific explanation, though not necessarily plausible, is offered for imaginative leaps into the unknown," a fitting description of McCaffrey's work.

Sometimes overriding the question of whether her work is science fiction or science fantasy is the flavor of medieval life and historical fiction that pervades the pages of the Pern novels. Craft Halls, in which skilled artisans such as the Harpers dwell, are castlelike structures with large halls for meals and smaller compartments for living and working. Living conditions are somewhat primitive in the Holds that are built into the rocky walls of mountainsides. For example, people sleep on straw mats. Harpers write music in sandboxes and cover their written notations with glass until they can be transcribed onto priceless pieces of paper. Periodically, Harpers have "gathers," times of celebration. Stalls are set up where crafts, art, and food are sold. Dancing, eating, and drinking merriment entertain the people of the Hold in much the way that a medieval festival would.

Regardless of how her work is classified, McCaffrey has created an inventive world peopled with realistic characters and intriguing adventures that continue to capture readers' imaginations.

Selected Bibliography

WORKS BY ANNE MCCAFFREY

The Lady in the Tower (1959)

Dragonrider (1968)

Decision at Doona (1969)

Dragonsong (1976)

Dragonsinger (1977)

Get Off the Unicorn (1977)

Dinosaur Planet (1978)

Dragondrums (1979)

The Girl Who Heard Dragons (1991)

If you like Anne McCaffrey's books, then you might also enjoy the works of Ursula K. Le Guin and Madeleine L'Engle.

WORKS ABOUT ANNE MCCAFFREY

Burns, Mary M. Review of *Dragonsinger* in "Summer Booklist." *Horn Book,* vol. 53, no. 3, 1977, p. 320.

Elleman, Barbara. "Children's Books: *Dragonsong.*" *Booklist,* vol. 72, 1976, p. 1266.

Gallo, Donald R., ed. "Anne McCaffrey." In *Speaking for Ourselves: Autobiographical Sketches by Notable Authors of Books for Young Adults.* Urbana, Ill.: National Council of Teachers of English, 1990, p. 128–130.

Lukens, Rebecca J. *A Critical Handbook of Children's Literature.* New York: Harper Collins, 1995.

Lynch-Brown, Carol, and Carl M. Tomlinson, *Essentials of Children's Literature.* Boston: Allyn & Bacon, 1993.

Miller, Sara R. "Dragondrums." *School Library Journal,* vol. 25, 1979, p. 64.

Stein, Ruth M. "Book reMarks." *Language Arts,* vol. 54, 1977, p. 807.

———"Book reMarks" review of *Dragondrums.* In *Language Arts,* vol. 57, no. 2, 1980, p. 189.

AWARDS

McCaffrey has received several awards, including the Nebula and the Hugo, for her science fiction novels. She was the first female science fiction writer to win the prestigious Hugo, which she received in 1967 for *Dragonflight*. The Science Fiction Writers of America honored her with the Nebula Award in 1968 for the novella "Dragonrider." *Dragonsong,* the first in the Harper Hall trilogy for young adults, earned her an American Library Association Notable Book citation in 1976, and she received that same recognition, as well as the Horn Book Fanfare Citation, for *Dragonsinger* in 1977.

How to write to the Author
Anne McCaffrey
c/o Tor Books
175 Fifth Avenue,
14th Floor
New York, NY 10010

Margaret (May) Mahy

(1936-)

by Patricia P. Kelly

Talking about her work in an interview, Margaret Mahy said about *The Haunting* (1982), her first novel for young adults,

> After I'd written the book, I was intrigued to detect pieces which you think you're inventing but, of course, you're often inventing them out of some sort of experience. . . . Tabitha is very similar in most ways to what I was like as a child. I was talkative; I wrote in little notebooks; I talked more than people wanted to hear. But at the same time while that was going on, I imagined myself as being rather like Troy, who is dark, gypsyish, and mysterious. I can think of one or two occasions of my life where I very consciously imagined myself like that and looked at myself in the mirror with surprise when I saw I wasn't

Quotations from Margaret Mahy that are not attributed to a published source are from a personal interview conducted by the author of this article on 21 April 1995 and are published here by permission of Margaret Mahy.

307

banal commonplace

really at all like Troy. I was much more ordinary, a banal sort of person.

A former librarian and well-known writer of children's books, short stories, and poems before turning to writing for young adults, Mahy had started *The Haunting* as a short story, but found the form restrictive for the story she wanted to tell. All her novels take place in New Zealand, her homeland, but there are few place-specific references regarding setting. Other than celebrating Christmas during summer, occasional differences in word choice and references to the Maori or to particular land features, her stories have a universal quality of setting. But within these settings arise memorable characters and events.

Family Relationships as a Theme

One of Mahy's major contributions to literature for young adults is the variety of family relationships she has created, but for her there are no typical families. She draws two family portraits, both responsible but different, in *The Catalogue of the Universe* (1985), the novel that Mahy says is her favorite. Dido May is an unmarried mother, who has worked hard to provide a loving home for her daughter Angela. But the old house is a source of irritation to Angela because of its outside bathroom and perilous mountain road. Dido is a strong woman who allows her daughter the freedom to become equally strong. On the other hand, Tycho's mother, Mrs. Potter, has been dashed by life, is a little fearful, and allows her two older children to use her. Two other families, however, serve as counterpoints. Angela's grandmother, who has coldly managed her son's life, is the antithesis of Dido; and Africa, who refuses to accept the responsibilities of being a wife and mother, is the opposite of her own mother, Mrs. Potter.

antithesis opposite

In *Underrunners* (1992), Tris's father also is alone since his wife left, rejecting the isolated home he had built at the shore. His father's lifestyle isolates Tris even further: "His father's ponytail, the outside lavatory, the bath in the marigolds, and the usual after-school lack of cake" (p. 38) keeps Tris from inviting school friends to play. But Winola, his friend from the children's home, comes from a family so dysfunctional that she says, "I only have to hang on a bit longer and I'll be grown up" (p. 167). Neither of their mothers is a source of stability for them, but when Tris's father decides to take a regular job, buy a car, and perhaps marry his girlfriend, life for Tris, at least, begins to take on a more ordinary flavor, something he has longed for. One can only hope that Winola has not been irrevocably damaged by her family.

irrevocable unable to be changed

Another single-parent family appears in *The Changeover* (1984). Kate Chant, left by her husband for a young woman soon after her son Jacko was born, works as a bookseller and struggles to maintain a household alone. When she begins dating seriously, her daughter Laura is upset, but ultimately remarrying will make life easier for Kate and the children. A completely different family in the same book is that of the Carlisles, a family of good witches made up of grandmother Winter, mother Miryam, and Miryam's son Sorenson. The everyday problems of the Chant family contrast sharply with the dark, mysterious Carlisle household as Laura moves between both worlds.

Jack and Naomi Hamilton in *The Tricksters* (1987) seem to be the ideal family to everyone, including Emma, their daughter's friend. She compares the Hamiltons with her own family of separated parents: ". . . . the Hamiltons just seemed to me like one of those great, big, wonderful storybook families—dashing father, loving mother, brothers, sisters, garden, pets, holidays, stories by the fire, birthday parties—the whole bit. I longed to be part of it all" (p. 75). However, their relationship has been tested by Jack's extramarital affair with Emma, which has produced a child. Naomi accepts both mother and child into the family circle, thus preserving the strength of the family for all concerned.

Family is at the center of *The Haunting,* with the story unfolding primarily through family conversations. The Palmer and the Scholar families are real people despite having magician traits. Claire, a loving stepmother, has brought to the Palmer children a warmth and unity that Barney, the young child, feels is threatened by her pregnancy. Because his own mother died at his birth, he fears that Claire will die. The Scholar family, on the other hand, has exuded little warmth in rearing its children as generations of tyrannical mothers have tried to stamp out the magic.

exuded abundantly displayed

A different sort of family unit evolves in *Memory* (1988) when Jonny Dart begins caring for Sophie West, who lives

Alzheimer's disease
a disease of the central nervous system, often involving loss of memory

alone although she suffers from Alzheimer's disease. Jonny, in flight from his own family, originally has no intention of doing more than crashing for a few days at Sophie's apartment, but he progressively takes on more responsibility for her welfare. He cleans and cooks for her, tries to understand what is happening to her, and protects her from thieves. Creating order out of Sophie's disorderly life and mind gives Jonny the opportunity to move outside of himself, to consider the needs of others rather than just his own.

Teen Problems as a Theme

Although Mahy does not write problem novels as readers have come to identify such books, her characters are engaged in real-life problems typically associated with growing up. They struggle with defining their identities; they suffer from feeling different; and they are angered by parents who act with disregard for their families.

Angela's search for her father in *The Catalogue of the Universe* is embedded in her desire to define her identity and thus to know herself. She needs him to recognize her, to claim her as his daughter, and to that end she plans an elaborate series of encounters. Angela eventually comes to understand that it is her mother who has already helped her become a fine young woman, and ultimately she does not need her father's affirmation.

Jonny Dart in *Memory* has a different sort of struggle to define himself. As a child performer in commercials, with hair bleached to match his sister's, he tap danced as the Chickenbits boy and fell victim to Nev, who enjoyed beating him up. Jonny is further frustrated by his own memory, for he cannot remember the details of his sister's death. He spends five years searching for answers and for himself.

Perhaps the character with the most fragmented identity is Winola in *Underrunners,* who has three names associated with different periods of her life. Controlling her own identity, she names herself Winola, which she says is Teutonic for fairy princess, a role uncharacteristic of the real Winola, whose actual name is Cecily Tyrone. However, in Tris's childlike talk, she became Selsey Firebone, his fearless protector. Ultimately, Winola needs the characteristics from all

Teutonic characteristic of the Teutons (members of an ancient Germanic or Celtic people)

three identities to help her as she faces growing up on her own.

The pain of being different haunts many of Mahy's teen characters, but especially Tycho in *The Catalogue of the Universe* and Jake in *Aliens in the Family* (1986). Named after a star and a crater on the moon, Tycho, the youngest, quietest child with two flamboyant siblings, has managed his life by staying on the fringe of happenings and spending his time thinking. He poignantly tells Angela, "when I was a little kid people used to think I was subnormal" (p. 43), a view grounded in others' perceptions of him. In the end, his love for Angela has opened him to many possibilities; he has become "the catalogue of the universe, never finished, always being added to" (p. 185).

poignant touching or moving

Appearance first reflects Jake's difference in *Aliens in the Family*. Dressed in cowboy clothes and closely cropped hair, she is as different as any alien landing in her father's new family, contrasting sharply with Dora, her stepsister, who is concerned with clothes and hair. Even though she cannot ride a horse, Jake believes she is "entitled to dress as if she did, because they were the clothes of adventure, and once you gave difficult or even sad things the name of adventure their meaning changed" (p. 102). Unfortunately, the reality of Jake's life has not been changed by adopting different clothes. Bond, who is truly an alien, recognizes Jake's anguish. He tells her, "I know you have to be the man of the family when you're at home with your mother, but here you can let yourself be a daughter" (p. 103).

The lives of several teenage characters in Mahy's novels are marked by anger at parents over deep, hurtful issues, although all come to some degree of understanding and growth as a result of their experiences. In *The Changeover,* Laura Chant is angry that her father has left his family for a younger woman, making life difficult for them financially and emotionally. Laura resents the time and money he has for his new wife but not for them. Anger fills Angela May in *The Catalogue of the Universe* from two sources. She is not only hurt deeply by her father's rejection but also angry that her mother has created a fiction about him and the circumstances of her birth. A father's infidelity is the source of Harry's anger in *The Tricksters*. Perhaps the only character that has a right to be angry is Winola, whose parents have

The lives of several teenage characters in Mahy's novels are marked by anger at parents over deep, hurtful issues, although all come to some degree of understanding and growth as a result of their experiences.

failed at being parents in *Underrunners*. Neither all good nor all bad, the parents in Mahy's fiction seem convincing with their faults and mistakes. They are engaged in believable family conflicts with realistic resolutions.

Realism Combined with the Supernatural

Although *The Catalogue of the Universe, Memory,* and *Underrunners* are realistic fiction, Mahy's artful blending of the supernatural into everyday situations is a characteristic of her other novels. Lines between the real and the imagined become blurred, making the action believable, even rationally explainable. Mahy maintains that the supernatural events she devises for her novels are "just exaggerations of things that happen in real life anyway. . . . I exaggerate reality."

> *Mahy maintains that the supernatural events she devises for her novels are "just exaggerations of things that happen in real life anyway. . . . I exaggerate reality."*

Even in one of the most surreal scenes in *The Changeover,* where Laura Chant becomes a witch to gain the power to save her brother, the events are tied to family members and people and places she knows, making her transformation believable though dreamlike. The ritual takes place in the bathroom with Laura "looking at the bathmat under her feet" (p.136). Next she imagines she's standing in sand and reads "TAM HTAB . . . between her feet" (p. 136). Later "huge in the sky, in faint letters hundreds of miles high the words TAM HTAB appeared" (p. 147). When "she opened her eyes to see her hand lying like a pale shell, not on sand but on fabric, small and clear and insignificant, the words TAM HTAB" (p. 151). Such clues tie her specifically to the bathroom throughout her imaginative journey.

The unreal and the real weave together throughout *The Haunting,* but many of the fanciful events can be rationally explained. For example, Great-Uncle Guy offers Tabitha several arguments for Barney's fears of death and visions of ghosts. The imaginative Tabitha concedes, seeing "the ghost vanishing away into the world of grown-up explanation and theory" (p. 61). In another scene Claire and Barney watch Troy conjure up a "tiny sun no larger than a mustard seed" (p. 132), the center of a solar system with a planet that she pushed with one finger. When Claire cautions her about using such powers, Troy replies that it's a game everyone plays: "Tabitha plays it in a way—with her novel writing. Everyone does it—dreams of spinning the world" (p. 133). In other words, through our imaginations we all produce magical events.

Bond is the most evident alien in *Aliens in the Family.* However, all of us in some measure are aliens and alienated because we can never be completely like anyone else or be fully understood by others. The scene when Bond escapes earth to return to his own time and place involves a time warp, the earth seeming to return to a primordial time and the appearance of "historical men" (p. 155), is the major supernatural event in the novel. Even the children later question whether the occurrence is an earthquake or perhaps a volcano. The appearance of Maori and other people they do not recognize would not be unusual in a public park area. Whatever the reason, natural or supernatural, the event alters the family's life.

> *All of us in some measure are aliens and alienated because we can never be completely like anyone else or be fully understood by others.*

The Writer's Craft

In addition to being masterful at interweaving the real and the unreal into her stories and her strong character development, Mahy's use of language to paint images is one of her strengths as a writer. Every page of every novel can yield examples of just the right comparison, the sharply turned phrase, the fresh image. From the humorous image of a greedy pony, "looking yearningly from side to side at the grass rather as if he was shopping in a supermarket" (*Aliens,* p. 91) to Tabitha's harsh criticism of Great-Granny Scholar, whose "wrinkles are so angry. She's like a wall with furious swear words scribbled all over it" (*Haunting,* p. 11), Mahy's words conjure vivid images in the reader's mind. Consider this description of Tycho's thinking:

> Thought after thought crowded in on him, some only half-finished. They jostled to find a place of power in his consciousness as if every mind in the world but his was dying and he was the sole, safe repository of understanding. Once in him, they bred like miraculous but threatening viruses, turning their faces towards him, as the foxgloves had done. It would take a long

time to understand what he was producing, or absorbing, in such ferociously, concentrated bursts. (*Catalogue,* p. 159)

The passage is filled with tension and contrasts— miraculous but threatening, viruses and foxgloves, power and dying—that give a quick urgency to it.

But how does Mahy go about writing such passages? She believes that most writers, including herself, are both driven to begin a novel and hesitant about it. Once she begins, however, the writing flows well until the middle of the novel. At that point for her, the beginning is planned and the ending is fairly clear in her mind, but "exactly how to get from one to the other is a little bit more obscure." She does not plan, or outline, a book's plot before beginning. Instead, "it's the actual act of writing that pushes me on into the state of actually being able to perceive possible ways for the story to go."

impetus the driving force, or stimulus

Experiences in her life are often impetuses for a book. For example, she got the idea for *Memory,* not from caring for an aunt with Alzheimer's disease, but from driving through the city one night at two o'clock in the morning and seeing an old man pushing an empty supermarket cart in the store's parking lot. She says that she has "a bit in common" with Dido in *The Catalogue of the Universe* because she used to drive over the hill to work with her two daughters, having meaningful discussions on the way. These bits and experiences of Mahy's life end up woven into the fabric of her work.

If you like the supernatural elements in Mahy's novels, you will like Madeleine L'Engle's novels, *The Night the White Deer Died* by Gary Paulsen, and *Water Girl* by Joyce Carol Thomas.

Selected Bibliography

WORKS BY MARGARET MAHY

Novels for Young Adults

The Haunting (1982)

The Changeover (1984)

The Catalogue of the Universe (1985)

Aliens in the Family (1986)

The Tricksters (1987)

Memory (1988)

Dangerous Spaces (1991)

Underrunners (1992)

WORKS ABOUT MARGARET MAHY

Berkin, Adam. "'I Woke Myself': *The Changeover* as a Modern Adaptation of 'Sleeping Beauty,'" *Children's Literature in Education,* December 1990, vol. 21, pp. 245–251.

Major Authors and Illustrators for Children and Young Adults. Detroit: Gale Research, 1993, vol. 4, pp. 1561–1566.

Raburn, Josephine. "*The Changeover,* A Fantasy of Opposites," *Children's Literature in Education,* March 1992, vol. 23, pp. 27–38.

How to write to the Author
Margaret Mahy
No. 1 Road
Lyttelton, New Zealand

Kevin Major

(1949-   )

by Wendy K. Sutton

Kevin Major prides himself on being the only Canadian Newfoundlander in his family because he was born the youngest of seven children in 1949, the year the island of Newfoundland, fondly called The Rock, became Canada's newest and most easterly province. Because of its harsh Atlantic environment and economic reliance on fishing, Newfoundland has few cities, and many people continue to live in outports, small coastal towns completely isolated by and dependent on the sea. Major grew up in such an outport with its local dialect and way of life. As was quite common among rural Newfoundlanders, neither of his parents received more than an elementary school education; however, they valued and supported the education of their children. Major and most of his brothers and sisters went on to complete university degrees.

Although initially his studies took him away from courses in English, Major has always enjoyed reading and listening to stories. Newfoundland has a strong oral tradition, and he de-

Quotations from Kevin Major that are not attributed to a published source are from an electronic mail interview conducted by the author of this article between 23 April and 7 May 1995 and are published here by permission of Kevin Major.

scribes his father as "a great storyteller who relished the opportunity to relate incidents, often humorous, that had occurred throughout his life." Many of Major's feelings and experiences as a young boy growing up in this isolated island province are woven into his stories and the lives of his fictional characters as they struggle to cope with the personal concerns and situations challenging them.

The Early Years

Although he came from a large family, being the youngest meant that for many years Major was the only child at home. He recalls his childhood as a comfortable but rather lonely time because his parents, although supportive and loving, were overly protective and as old as his friends' grandparents. Throughout his school-age years, he read a great deal. His interests ran from *David Copperfield* and *Pilgrim's Progress* to James Bond novels and the Hardy Boys. Mark Twain and Ernest Hemingway are two authors whom Major cites as having a significant influence upon him later as a writer. He was not merely a bookworm, however, for he enjoyed hockey, fishing, and other outdoor activities associated with rural life.

Major describes himself as being timid and somewhat self-conscious in his early teenage years, which he does not remember with much fondness. "I especially disliked being in classes with some idiot troublemakers. By grade eleven they had quit school, leaving the rest of us to have a much more pleasant time of it. The next year I was gone and the world opened up for me." Whether Major's young adult readers are from cities or small towns, concerns such as feeling awkward or not fitting in are familiar to teenagers and make it easy for them to relate to many of the characters and situations in his novels.

Major vividly recalls the music that was popular when he was a teenager. When he was in grade nine the Beatles appeared on television's *Ed Sullivan Show*. Recalling those school years, Major says:

> My hair gradually drifted down to my forehead. I was
> the first one to buy a Beatles record in my hometown.
> And a classmate who had relatives in Scotland had the

Charles Dickens (1812–1870) wrote *David Copperfield*. There is an article about him in volume 1. John Bunyan (1628–1688) wrote *Pilgrim's Progress*. There is an article about Ernest Hemingway earlier in this volume and an article about Mark Twain in volume 3. The **Hardy Boys** mystery series was created by Edward Stratemeyer; there is an article about him in volume 3.

record album *Sergeant Pepper* sent to him before it was released in North America. Wow! I made my mother alter the legs of the suit I had for high school graduation—tapered, of course—until they were near skin-tight. We all did 'the twist' and 'the shake.' My soon-to-be partner in pre-med, Don, and I hung out at the Bayview Restaurant, with Sandra and Anne. That last year of high school was great.

Other music favorites turn up as details in some of Major's books. In *Eating Between the Lines* (1991), the parents of the main character, Jackson, listen to José Feliciano. In *Dear Bruce Springsteen* (1987), Major's personal fondness for the music of Springsteen triggered the book's fictitious letters to "The Boss." It is the intense feelings of the teenage years, however, rather than specific references, that have found their expression in his novels and given them universal appeal. In addition to being widely read in Canada and the United States, his books have been translated into French, Spanish, German, and Danish.

School Days

Although an interest in writing was not something Major saw in his family or classmates, his desire to write was fostered in school, especially by an encouraging tenth-grade teacher who predicted that someday Major would write a book. Yet although he enjoyed writing, Major says he was a university student before he discovered that there was such a phenomenon as a "living author." Consequently, as a teenager, he had not regarded writing as a career option.

Partly because his best friend decided to go to the university to study medicine, and partly because his own marks in science were often higher than those in English, Major also entered pre-medicine. After three years of study that earned him admission to medical school, he left Newfoundland and traveled extensively in the West Indies and Europe. His travels cemented his interest in writing and his attachment to Newfoundland. They also confirmed that he should not venture into the world of medicine for fear that he might never "surface to try my hand at being an author." He became certified as a teacher and, although he wanted to teach

English, his science background came back to haunt him and he became a high school biology teacher.

The Starting Point

idiom manner of speaking

Teaching and being among teenagers daily helped Major capture their speech patterns and idiom in his writing and made him increasingly sensitive to their interests and concerns. Acutely aware of how little information about Newfoundland was available in the schools, he researched and compiled *Doryloads* (1974), an anthology of stories and tall tales that captures the old way of life in the Newfoundland outports. As he followed teaching opportunities from one small community to another, his first novel, *Hold Fast* (1978), began taking shape in his mind. The novel dramatizes an inevitable chain of events that occur when a quick-tempered fourteen-year-old newcomer to the school finds himself being taunted by some of his classmates. Michael, who has recently lost both his parents in an accident, is already having difficulty in his uncle's excessively restrictive home. When he is expelled from school for fighting, he runs away and hides out with his cousin in a national park. At the time of my interview with Major, his own two boys had not reached the age of most of his fictional characters, but he wondered whether, when they were deep into their teenage years, they would complain that they were not allowed to do some of the things he lets his characters get away with. He also wondered: "Will they resent it if they and their friends have to study a Kevin Major novel and answer exam questions on it? I hope not."

Another reason that Major began writing for teenagers was his own memories of how confusing, perplexing a time the teenage years were for him and for many of his friends. As a teacher he also became increasingly aware of how little contemporary fiction there was for teenagers, particularly Newfoundland young people, and of how seldom the characters in the books that were available resembled the young people in his classes. Ironically, some years later his success at capturing the teenage "voice" caused a secondary school principal to refuse to allow Major's books in the school because the characters sounded too much like the students.

Other concerns that have been cited as preventing Major's first three novels from being read in Newfoundland

Major's success at capturing the teenage "voice" caused a secondary school principle to refuse to allow Major's books in the school because the characters sounded too much like the students.

schools are the "foul" language, references to sexual interest or activity, the "macho" references to girls by certain teenage boys, and, more specifically, the fact that Michael in *Hold Fast* steals a car (he considered it as "borrowing") and gets away with it. *Blood Red Ochre* (1989) was on the ninth-grade novel list in Newfoundland in 1996, but his earlier novels were on none of the Department of Education lists, despite the fact that they had been used for years in other parts of Canada. Although Major's books were not officially banned, individual teachers who wanted to use them had to get special permission. Unfortunately, according to Major, few bothered. "I am now much better known by students within Newfoundland than I used to be," he says. "Yet I am still distressed by the fact that my first books have never really reached the audience of young people who would most appreciate them: the young Newfoundlanders like Michael and Chris, the central outport characters of the novels."

Perhaps adults who are overly sensitive and cautious about what teenagers read would benefit from hearing Major share some of the reactions of his readers:

> **There's surprise that there is someone their age in a book who swears or thinks about sex. There's joy at sharing similar interests with a character, at seeing someone like themselves take control of a situation. There's a girl who wrote to say she had fallen desperately in love with Chris in *Far from Shore* [1980]. There's a boy who had just lost a parent who wrote to say that he felt a lot like Michael in *Hold Fast.***

On the strength of responses such as these, Major turned down publishers' requests that he write sanitized, "school editions" of his novels.

Influences on Major's Work

Major usually finds that his writing is strongly influenced and shaped by situations that concern or upset him. For example, for years he had seen people from the outports being looked down upon by the city dwellers of St. John's, where he now lives, because of their accents and way of life. His first novel, *Hold Fast,* in which an outport boy fights for the way of life

Major usually finds that his writing is strongly influenced and shaped by situations that concern or upset him.

protagonist the
main character of a
literary work

William Faulkner
(1897–1962) was an
American novelist
and short-story
writer. His stories re-
flect the traditions
and history of the
South.

he has had to leave behind because of his parents' death, is very much a response to such prejudice.

That contemporary economic and political changes have threatened the traditional life of Newfoundlanders and caused mass unemployment is another of the author's concerns and the backdrop for his second novel, *Far From Shore*. Here the teenage protagonist, Chris, whose father has left home to find a job, gets deeper and deeper into trouble at school and with the law as his family seems to be splitting apart. Extending the single perspective of *Hold Fast,* Major uses five narrative voices to provide the reader with multiple perspectives on the situations with which the main character tries to cope. (Major says that the inspiration to try this literary structure came from reading a story by William Faulkner.) *Far From Shore* dramatically reveals the destructive consequences that the breakdown of an economy can have on people living in a specific area.

The impact on young people of losing traditional and anticipated sources of employment is also a major theme in Major's third novel, *Thirty-Six Exposures* (1984). Revealed through scenes he calls "snapshots," the uncertainty facing a group of high school graduates plays itself out in powerful, often irreversible, ways as each of them faces the challenge of the future. Drawing upon his interest in photography, Major employs the thirty-six frames of thirty-five-millimeter film as the literary structure for this novel.

Disturbing historical events have also been the driving force behind Major's writing of a novel. In *Blood Red Ochre* he uses a time-slip device to take the reader back into the lives of the Beothuk native people, who were annihilated by white settlers through starvation, disease, and murder. By alternating the chapters between fifteen-year-old David and Dauoodaset, a young Beothuk in the early 1800s who is struggling to find food for his starving family, Major makes you experience and reexamine a tragic historical event. To heighten the reader's empathy and understanding of what Dauoodaset and his people endured, he writes about them in first-person perspective, in contrast to David's present-day circumstance, which is presented in third-person narrative.

Another tragic historical event and the focus of Major's powerful 1995 book, *No Man's Land,* is the Battle of the Somme in France during World War I. Describing it as a battle that should never have taken place, the author reconstructs in detail the events and human emotions that climaxed in the unjustifiable slaughter of the Newfoundland regiment. This is his first book to be marketed as an adult novel, but its topic and insights into the realities of war also make it an important novel for young adult readers.

A Humorous Side

Tackling a concern of his in a more humorous way—this time the incidents of censorship involving his first three novels—led Major to write his first comic fantasy, *Eating Between the Lines*. Through the magic properties of a solid gold pizza medal, Jackson finds himself physically projected into any book he is currently reading. For example, he prepares a winning argument against censorship for a school debate by propelling himself into Mark Twain's *Huckleberry Finn* and, as the black slave Jim, experiencing the hardships of a slave's life. In his foray into Homer's *Odyssey,* Jackson cunningly escapes the one-eyed Cyclops, and by becoming Romeo in Shakespeare's *Romeo and Juliet,* he wins the love of his beautiful girlfriend Sara. Some readers would say that this novel has all the components to make a great Spielberg-type movie.

Humor also characterizes Major's book *Diana: My Autobiography* (1993). In this parody of some people's obsession with royalty, he introduces his first female protagonist and fictional daughter, Diana. Named after Britain's "Princess Di" and convinced that she is going to marry a prince, Diana expounds in her italicized autobiography, "a work in progress," on her imagined royal connections. She also describes the shortcomings of her family members and friends, and her infatuation with an English boy visiting Newfoundland for the summer, whom she assumes to be related to royalty. Her autobiographical entries are interrupted by the daily feelings and events of the summer, which readers recognize as her true autobiography.

Through the fictional father of Diana, Major reveals much of himself as a person. For example, Diana is always complaining that her father makes a political issue out of everything. For example, when the Coca Cola plant in Newfoundland is shut down because it is cheaper to make Coke somewhere else and ship it in, many jobs are lost. As a con-

There is an article about William Shakespeare in volume 3.

Steven Spielberg (1947–) is an American director known for such popular movies as as *Jaws, Close Encounters of the Third Kind, Poltergeist, E. T.: The Extra Terrestrial,* The Indiana Jones trilogy, and *Schindler's List.*

parody an exaggerated or satirical imitation (especially for purposes of ridicule)

sequence, Diana and her brother are forbidden to buy or drink another Coke, "when the whole world is drinking the stuff like crazy. Can you believe it?" (To this day, the "real" Major will not drink Coca Cola.)

Major's Views on Writing

When asked about his approach to writing, Major offers some valuable insights:

> My stories often start with character—someone I can see at the centre of a story whose life is interesting enough that I will want to spend the months and years with him or her that it will take to complete the story. Hand in hand with that, I need to figure out the purpose of the book: what am I trying to do with it? What point am I trying to make?

Major goes on to describe how he works through a general plot and tries to get to know the characters. If it has historical dimensions, as in *Blood Red Ochre* and *No Man's Land,* he does the research required to make his story accurate. "Then it is on to the first draft. That has taken anywhere from ten weeks to two years. A second, third, and fourth polishing and then to the publisher, where work with an editor begins."

As Major's bibliography will confirm, he completes a book every two to three years. Recalling your own feelings when others react to what you have written, you can imagine that working with an editor can be a very emotional, often traumatic experience. Sometimes a writer comes to a crossroads where he and the editor do not see eye to eye. When this happens, as it did with *Eating Between the Lines,* the author either has to agree to the editor's changes or, as Major did, withdraw the book and hope to find another publisher and editor.

When asked at what point in his writing he chooses the narrative form, Major replies: "That is decided before I start to write. What will best bring out what I am trying to do with the book? Will it be interesting without being intrusive? It is a challenge. Am I up to the challenge? These are the questions I ask myself." Major is considered by many critics to be one

traumatic damaging, shocking

of the most innovative and successful authors writing for teenagers today. His mastery of many narrative forms is one of the reasons.

While visiting schools or public libraries, Major is often asked which of his books is his favorite. His reply offers an amusing summary of his writing to date:

> Favorite book? Well, *Hold Fast* is my favorite because it was the first I was able to get published, and I like the way the main character stands up for himself. *Far from Shore* is my favorite because Chris reminds me a lot of some fellows I knew at the time I was writing it and because I still get a charge out of his sense of humor. And *Thirty-Six Exposures* is a favorite because it was a risky book that never plays it safe. And, well, *Dear Bruce Springsteen* (1987) has to be a favorite because every morning I would get up and write a letter to Springsteen and listen to his music while I was doing it. *Blood Red Ochre* was a tough book to write and it's a favorite because I think it works pretty well. Of course, *Eating Between the Lines* is a favorite because nobody believed in it as much as I did, until it started winning awards. And *Diana*, she's a favorite because I always wanted a daughter and she is it. And now *No Man's Land*. It's a favorite because it's the best writing I've done.

Perhaps this introduction to an outstanding Canadian author will encourage you to discover some Kevin Major favorites of your own.

Selected Bibliography

WORKS BY KEVIN MAJOR

Novels for Young Adults
Hold Fast (1978; 1980)
Far from Shore (1980; 1981)
Thirty-Six Exposures (1984)
Dear Bruce Springsteen (1987; 1988; 1989)
Blood Red Ochre (1989)

Readers who enjoy Keven Major's works might also enjoy books by J.D. Salinger.

Eating Between the Lines (1991)

Diana: My Autobiography (1993)

Novels for Adult Readers

No Man's Land (1995)

Nonfiction

Doryloads: Newfoundland Writings and Art, edited by Kevin Major (1974)

Terra Nova National Park: Human History Study, with James A. Tuck (1983)

WORKS ABOUT KEVIN MAJOR

Chevalier, Tracy, ed. *Twentieth-Century Children's Writers.* Detroit: St. James, 1989, pp. 629–631.

Kealy, J. Kieran. *Dictionary of Literary Biography: Canadian Writers Since 1960.* Detroit: Gale Research, 1987, vol. 60, pp. 206–209.

Lesniak, Jim, and Susan Trosky, eds. *Contemporary Authors New Revision Series.* Detroit: Gale Research, 1993, vol. 38, pp. 249–250.

Stine, Jean C., ed. *Contemporary Literary Criticism.* Detroit: Gale Research, 1983, vol. 26, pp. 284–288.

How to Write to the Author
Kevin Major
c/o Bantam Books
1540 Broadway
New York, NY 10036

Harry Mazer

(1925-   )

by Arthea Reed

Harry Mazer writes about relationships. Ironically, he freely admits that as a teenager he had difficulty with both writing and relationships.

An Aspiring Writer

For many years Mazer did not write at all, unless you count writing required for schoolwork, which he does not. However, he always dreamed of being a writer, and as a teenager at Bronx High School of Science he posed as a writer. He remembers, too, that his high school friend Leo was a writer and had proof—he carried a notebook in his pocket. Mazer told a group of Illinois librarians in 1986,

> It was only recently that it occurred to me that I never saw [Leo] write anything. I had notebooks, too, I was always buying notebooks. That's the first thing you do

Quotations from Harry Mazer that are not attributed to any source are from a personal interview conducted by the author of this article on 3 March 1995 and are published here by permission of Harry Mazer.

327

when you become a writer. You buy notebooks of different sizes, the kind that fits in your pocket. I had all kinds of names—I called them journals, diaries, workbooks, and I liked all those names. I liked them a lot. That gave me the feeling I was really doing something, but of course what I really had, finally, was a fine collection of empty notebooks.

Mazer loved the idea of writing, of self-discipline, order, and routine—all the things he did not have. He says that he wanted to write but did not know how. He gives this sense of frustration to his seventeen-year-old protagonist, Marcus, in *I Love You, Stupid!* (1981). Marcus, like Mazer, wanted to be a writer. Unlike Mazer, Marcus did some writing and even had limited success publishing it. However, Marcus spent most of his time posing as a writer rather than being a writer—setting up his room so he could write, making lists, sharpening his pencil, telling everyone he was a writer, and then having to face their criticism when he had only lists to show for his time.

> *As a teenager, Mazer, too, had lots of plans for becoming a writer, but most of these plans were merely posing.*

As a teenager, Mazer, too, had lots of plans for becoming a writer, but most of these plans were merely posing. He lived in a Bronx apartment like the one he describes in *Cave Under the City* (1986), which is the story of two brothers who try to survive on their own during the Great Depression. The fourth-floor walk-up apartment was small for a family of four—only two rooms—making it difficult to write when everyone was home. So Mazer planned to write when he came home from school and his mother and father were still at work and his brother was not yet home. As he told the same group of Illinois librarians,

The **Great Depression** was a severe recession that began when the stock market crashed in 1929 and lasted almost ten years. By the winter of 1932–1933, 14 to 16 million Americans were unemployed. Many died from a lack of food and inadequate living conditions.

> My plan was . . . I'd write till everyone came home. Another plan was—skip food, I was too fat anyway, and I'd just write. I'm thinking of this as I'm going up the stairs, and as I'm going up the stairs I get more and more rigorous. "This is what I'm going to do. This is the first day of my new regime. Let's go Marcus, I mean Harry. And you're going to lose weight. You're going to get slim. Right? You're going to be famous. Dotty isn't going to be able to keep her hands off you." I unlocked the door and I go straight to the re-

frigerator (only it's an icebox). And all that planning has exhausted me. I felt weak. I said, "I'll eat first, and then I'll write."

Mazer and His Father

Mazer claims that Marcus of *The Dollar Man* (1974) and *I Love You, Stupid!* is more like him than any of his characters, with the exception of Jack Raab in *The Last Mission* (1979), a Jewish teenager who enlists in the Army Corp during World War II with hopes of fighting Hitler's army and becoming a hero. Not only did both Mazer and Marcus pose as writers, not only were they both overweight and unsure of themselves, but each of them was also in search of the father he never knew. Unlike Marcus' father, Mazer's father lived with him. Mazer says: "My father was there in my life. He was there every night. He didn't go other places. He worked. He was steady as rock." Mazer also admits that he never knew his father—never even knew if his father loved him. "He was so tight. He was so ungiving of himself and, so, I never knew."

Mazer suggests that perhaps because of his difficult relationship with his father he created the ideal father in his first book, *Guy Lenny* (1971). "At the beginning, when he was on the river with his father, I was remembering when I was fishing with my uncle on the Hudson River." Mazer admits that initially he was surprised by the ending of *Guy Lenny,* in which Lenny's father betrays him. But, today he recognizes that he was simply writing from his own experiences.

Mazer's father was never pleased with his son; the last thing he wanted was for Mazer to become a writer. Sam Mazer was a Polish Jewish immigrant, who, like Willis' father in *The War on Villa Street* (1978) and *The Girl of His Dreams* (1987), walked across the bridge from Canada to Michigan with only a lunch pail and the clothes on his back. "My father," says Mazer, "wasn't American; he was a Polish Jew. He spoke with an accent. He spoke Yiddish. He was always dressed formally. There was no such thing as going around like this [Mazer points to his blue jeans and plaid flannel shirt]. He always had his suit on; his shoes were polished; he wore a tie. It was the way to dress. I never in my life, to the day he died, dressed to please or satisfy him. I never looked right. He didn't play ball; he didn't know anything about ball games. It was not his life."

> *Not only did both Mazer and Marcus (the protagonist in* The Dollar Man*) pose as writers, not only were they both overweight and unsure of themselves, but each of them was also in search of the father he never knew.*

Sam Mazer's life was his work and his community. Both Sam and Roz Mazer, Harry's mother, worked in the New York City garment district. They each belonged to several unions and were union stewards in the factories. The Mazers lived in an apartment complex known as "the coops." The coops were developed by Jewish immigrants who shared common values, traditions, work, and religion. Mazer describes the community as "Europe over here—right here in New York. You had the Jewish theater; you had the Jewish newspapers, Jewish choruses and orchestra."

Maintaining their identity as hard-working European Jews was critical to Mazer's parents. Although Sam Mazer always loved to read books, the idea of his son becoming a writer was foreign to his work ethic and way of life. Mazer remembers his father's voice telling him to not read so much, not dream of becoming a writer. "Don't be a fool," Mazer remembers his father saying, "Learn a trade. With a trade in your hands you're a free man. A writer is a fool" (unpublished speech, 1986). His father's practical belief in the value of hard work and the importance of earning a living did not mesh with Mazer's adolescent dreams for himself, and this conflict became the path of frustration he followed during much of young adulthood.

As a teenager, Mazer attempted to live his dreams by posing as a writer or a musician or even a character in a novel. While Harry posed, carrying notebooks that remained empty, he heard a disembodied voice—perhaps the voice of his father, perhaps his own. "You have nothing worth saving," the voice would tell him. "You are nothing but a dreamer; don't waste your time." His dreams and posings were thwarted by the practical side of him —the side that said, "Learn a trade; get a job; support yourself and your family." Mazer listened to the voice and for many years ignored his dreams.

> *"Don't be a fool," Mazer remembers his father saying, "Learn a trade. With a trade in your hands you're a free man. A writer is a fool."*

Dreaming of Girls

Mazer's frustrations came not only from an unrealized dream, but also from wanting a girl. He was a romantic who dreamed of girls. He wrote to an adult reader about one of his novels:

> **As an adolescent, I made the mistake of going to an all boy's high school. . . . I didn't know how to talk to**

girls. Near girls I kept my head high—(remember the opening image of *I Love You, Stupid!*)—or I kept my nose in a book. I was given to carrying big books with impressive titles like Karl Marx's *Das Kapital.*

When girls weren't looking (were they looking?) I looked. I didn't date in high school, and I lacked every social skill. I didn't dance. I didn't know how to make small-talk. I got red and embarrassed just standing near a girl. What would I do alone with a girl? What would we talk about? What did you say to a girl?

According to Mazer, his shyness around girls in high school is the reason he writes romances for boys. It is his own adolescent frustration, posturing, and longing that can be found on the pages of *The Dollar Man, The War on Villa Street, I Love You, Stupid!,* and *The Girl of His Dreams.* Even in the romances Mazer has written with his wife, Norma Fox Mazer— *Heartbeat* (1989) and *Bright Days, Stupid Nights* (1992)— a boy's feelings of ineptness and frustration are evident. Harry wants young men to read these books and say, "Yes, this is the way I feel. It's a relief to know I'm not alone." He also wants girls to read them and say, "Oh, that's the reason he acts that way."

posturing assuming an artificial character

Some of the girls Mazer painfully remembers from his adolescence appear on the pages of his books. He describes one such girl in *Something About the Author*:

Isabel was a girl in my sixth-grade class in PS 96 in the Bronx, a tall, skinny girl with long hair. I followed her slavishly around for weeks. My sixth-grade picture shows me a big, fat kid, in need of a haircut, the only one wearing a dark shirt in a field of white shirts and blouses. . . . Here it is forty years later and that puppy-love incident I call Isabel still works itself into my books. . . . In *The Dollar Man* . . . Marcus stands on the street looking longingly up at Vivian's windows, alternately dreaming of rescuing her, and creating fantasies about a father he has never known.

Isabel and a girlfriend also appear in *The War on Villa Street.* This time they are Willis' tormentors. Mazer remembers the only time Isabel noticed him: "She noticed me only once. I was across the street one day. She was with a girl friend. When they saw me they threw their arms around each other and started laughing and jeering at me" (*Something About the Author,* p. 129).

Now Mazer admits that, although he dreamed of girls, he was as unsuccessful with them as he was with writing. In fact, he learned about girls and about writing in the same way—by reading. His teenage relationships with girls came from stories. "I loved the girls in *War and Peace,* and I identified with these characters. I put myself into these stories, so my relationships were really literary. My relationships with girls were more literary than real," he says.

> *He learned about girls and about writing in the same way—by reading.*

Books and Life

Mazer also recognizes that books taught him to write.

> When I was young, I gobbled up books. I wanted to read every book by every author: American, English, Russian, French, Irish. I didn't read books so much as *authors.* I read all of Dostoyevsky, most of Tolstoy, Maxim Gorki. I liked the Russians. I also read every American novel I could lay my hands on—above all, those of Thomas Wolfe. I loved his enormous, verbose novels. I identified with his artistic hero— admired the man's sensitivity, his appetite for life, his exuberance and rages. I was going to be that artist. I was going to dazzle the world. ("A Huge Appetite for Books," p. 15)

According to Mazer, "the size of the book never daunted me. I plunged into Tolstoy's *War and Peace.* I read only for story. My eyes skidded over lengthy descriptions and philosophical ruminations. It's only as I grew older that I became interested in meaning and symbolism and the realistic treatment of character" (*Books I Read When I Was Young: The Favorite Books of Famous People,* p. 113).

Are all Mazer's books autobiographical? In a way they are. "Every book I write is as true as I can make it, but it's true to me not to things outside," he says.

How about his survival stories—*Snow Bound* (1973), *The Island Keeper* (1981), and *The Last Mission*—are they autobiographical? More or less. "What I'm very much concerned with is survival, in one form or another," Mazer says in *Something About the Author* (p. 130). "All my life there's been a war going on—war between life and death, and there's been someone trying to kill me." Mazer is not referring to a mad killer stalking him like Derek is stalked in *The Solid Gold Kid* (1977); instead he is referring to an inner struggle—the struggle against negativity and denial.

In each of Mazer's survival novels, the inner struggle is the most important. Tony and Cindy in *Snow Bound* are alone on the forbidding great windswept plateau called Tug Hill during a blizzard, but their major struggles are against their internal weaknesses rather than against the environment and physical hardships. The overweight Cleo in *The Island Keeper,* one of Mazer's few female protagonists, is alone on a deserted island in Canada, but to escape she must first escape her feeling of negativity and defeat.

> *In each of Mazer's survival novels, the inner struggle is most important.*

protagonist the main character of a literary work

The Last Mission

Mazer's most autobiographical novel is *The Last Mission*. The story parallels Mazer's own experiences as a waist gunner in a bomber that was shot down over Czechoslovakia in the final days of World War II. Although there are significant differences in Mazer's real-life story and Jack Raab's fictional story, the feelings of fear and horror are very real in the novel.

This is how Mazer describes those feelings in *The Last Mission:* "When the briefing officer pulled the curtain aside, Jack focused on the long thread that ran across the map of Europe. That was their mission. A shiver went through Jack" (pp. 62–64). Harry, like Jack, learned that becoming a hero did not protect him from the horrifying knowledge of what he had done.

This is how he describes those feelings:

It wasn't the war he'd dreamed it would be back home in The Bronx. Then he'd thought he was going to be one of those flying aces zipping around the sky in a fighter plane, shooting down Germans left and

right. It hadn't happened that way. He hardly thought about Hitler anymore. It was just the war, day after day, like a foot jammed in his belly. (p. 83)

Ironically, it was not until 1994 that Harry learned what happened to the crew of his plane. He returned to the village in the Czech Republic to speak at a ceremony marking the fiftieth anniversary of the end of the war in Europe. There Harry met some young men researching the crash, and they took him to where the plane had gone down. The young Czech men had been born in the village long after the end of the war and now worked in a factory that Mazer and his crew had bombed. The leader of the group took Harry to his home, introduced him to his mother, and presented him with a piston from the engine of Harry's plane. He showed Harry a picture taken shortly after the war had ended of a boy in shorts standing on the wing of the plane. The boy had gone to the plane immediately after it was shot down, found the co-pilot in the plane, and identified the dead man by his dog tag. For the first time, Mazer, who had bailed out of the plane, knew it had actually been shot down. He had previously thought that the co-pilot had bailed out with him.

Harry reports that even when he was faced with the realization that he was about to be captured by the Germans, he relied on his literary experience. He remembers that he had just been burying his chute, his hands were shaking badly, and he had just released his chest pack when two German soldiers appeared over the hill. Unlike Jack Raab in *The Last Mission*, Harry did not spend several days running from his eventual captors. Harry remembers that he had no idea what to do when he saw the Germans. So he put his hands way up over his head and yelled the German word for comrade. According to Harry he had read it in *All Quiet on the Western Front*. Today he realizes that his literary experiences and his knowledge of Yiddish may have saved him.

The young Czech whom Mazer met in 1994 told him that Mike Brennan, Mazer's best friend and crewmate, had bailed out with Harry but he was not so fortunate. Up to that time, Mazer had believed that Mike went down with the plane, as Jack's friend Chuckie had in the novel. The young researcher took Mazer to the wheat field where Mike had landed. He showed Mazer where the crew had been buried against a

chest pack pack worn across the chest containing a reserve parachute

All Quiet on the Western Front by Erich Maria Remarque is a novel about World War I.

Yiddish a language similar to German that is written in Hebrew characters and spoken by Jews of central and Eastern European origin

stone wall in a beautiful Catholic cemetery. He told Mazer a witness had seen Mike shot by a German officer. Mazer speculates that Mike may have done something to alarm the German or that this was simply the officer's day to kill an American. "I don't know what it was," Harry says. But he does know what he learned from a book helped keep him alive to tell his story.

Harry Mazer is still telling stories. Today he is a successful author of seventeen young adult novels, three written with his wife, Norma Fox Mazer; the father of four grown children; and a frequent speaker about writing and literature.

Selected Bibliography

WORKS BY HARRY MAZER

Guy Lenny (1971)

Snow Bound (1973)

The Dollar Man (1974)

The Solid Gold Kid, with Norma Fox Mazer (1977)

The War on Villa Street (1978)

The Last Mission (1979)

I Love You, Stupid! (1981)

The Island Keeper (1981)

Hey Kid! Does She Love Me? (1984)

When the Phone Rang (1985)

Cave Under the City (1986)

The Girl of His Dreams (1987)

City Light (1988)

Heartbeat, with Norma Fox Mazer (1989)

Someone's Mother Is Missing (1990)

Bright Days, Stupid Nights, with Norma Fox Mazer (1992)

Who Is Eddie Leonard? (1993)

Articles and Speeches

Mazer, Harry. "A Huge Appetite for Books." *Scholastic Voice*, 18 October 1979, p. 15.

———. Unpublished speech to the Illinois School Librarians, Young Adult Services, Champaign, Ill., 16 October 1986.

If you like the works of Harry Mazer, you might also enjoy the works of Richard Peck, Norma Fox Mazer, Chris Crutcher, and Robert Lipsyte.

————. Unpublished letter about *I Love You, Stupid!*

————. "Two Boys from the Bronx." Unpublished essay, 1995.

WORKS ABOUT HARRY MAZER

Commire, Anne, ed. "Harry Mazer." In *Something About the Author*. Detroit: Gale Research, 1993, vol. 3, pp. 126–131).

Cullinan, Beatrice, and M. Jerry Weiss, eds. *Books I Read When I Was Young: The Favorite Books of Famous People*. New York: Avon, 1980, p. 113.

Norma Fox Mazer

(1931-   )

by Joni Bodart

Norma Fox Mazer remembers herself at thirteen, watching the world as if through a window, silently recording everything she saw, ignored by those around her. One day she realized that while adults were older, louder, and pushier than children, they were all playacting in some way, and inside, they were not any older or more grown-up than she was. This discovery allowed her to write about adults, as well as about herself, her sisters and her friends, because now she understood them. In some ways, she is still that thirteen-year-old girl, looking, remembering, recording, and writing. Pieces of her life and the lives of those she meets drop into the characters and plots she creates in her novels.

A Writer's Beginnings

Mazer grew up as the middle sister in her family, the filling in the sandwich, but she never felt as if she fitted in. When she was a teenager, her family called her the "cold one" because

At thirteen, Mazer joined the school newspaper staff, but that was not enough.

It was a friend's comment that made her realize she wanted to be a writer: "Norma Fox! What an imagination!"

they thought she was selfish. But she was not thinking about herself as much as she was watching the world and the people around her, trying to make sense of what she saw. Although she spent much of her childhood scribbling—diary entries, thoughts, ideas, and the beginnings of stories—none of her teachers encouraged her to write. In fact, it was a friend's comment that made her realize she wanted to be a writer: "Norma Fox! What an imagination!" Suddenly, that imagination was good for more than seeing witches in doorknobs or making up games. It was a way to control the world with the words and ideas and people she created.

At thirteen, Mazer joined the school newspaper staff, but that was not enough. She wanted to write her own stories, stories that would allow her to step into the most intimate of mysteries—someone else's life. But that chance did not come until after she was married and became a mother. One day she looked around her and discovered that the day she had been putting off and waiting for, the day when she would be all grown-up, had arrived without her noticing. And she still had not become a writer.

That discovery led to a conversation with her husband, Harry Mazer, who also had always wanted to write, and they decided to write every day, something Mazer says is "an essential habit" for anyone who wants to be a writer. For several years, they both got up at 3:30 in the morning to write. When an insurance settlement allowed them to write full-time, they wrote stories for women's romance and confession magazines, each of them producing a short story every week. It left little time for writing novels, so seven years passed before Mazer's first book, *I, Trissy,* was published in 1971. In 1976, with the publication of *Dear Bill, Remember Me? and Other Stories,* her fourth book, Mazer finally decided she was a real writer, that she would write for the rest of her life, and she stopped being afraid that the stories in her head would run out.

Today, Mazer says she loves to write and goes to her computer eagerly, dividing her days among writing, reading, and doing something active and fun. She writes every day she is at home, and when she is away, she makes notes. Her goal in writing is not just to tell an entertaining story. Because she does not start with a fully developed plot, she also writes to get to the end of her story, to find out what happens and why, because she cares about the people she has created. An author who writes only to entertain, she says, tells stories that have no hearts at their center, nothing to keep the reader involved with and thinking about them. Mazer's stories have hearts, so they live in the minds of her readers long after the last pages are read.

Mazer's characters encounter the same problems her readers have to confront in their own lives. They begin to separate from their parents and their families and learn to find their own answers to their questions, problems, and secrets, whether or not those answers reflect their philosophies or their parents. And those answers do not always involve happy endings with complete resolutions; more frequently, Mazer's readers must figure out for themselves what the ultimate result or outcome will be. Her novels reflect life, which seldom provides us with pat or absolute answers.

> *Mazer's stories do not always involve happy endings with complete resolutions; more frequently, Mazer's readers must figure out for themselves what the ultimate result or outcome will be.*

Dealing with Ambiguity

Even when at least some of the questions Mazer poses in her books are answered, and some of the problems resolved, there still remains a kernel of something unanswered and unresolved for readers to continue to think about. This characteristic is most strongly seen in four of her novels, two written early in her career and two written more recently. In the latter two, Mazer seems more able to trust her characters to find their own way and trust her readers to keep thinking about the story. *Out of Control,* written and published in 1993, and *Missing Pieces,* published in 1995, have ambiguous endings. Each story simply stops, and the reader is left to decide what the final resolution might be. *Taking Terri Mueller* (1981) and *Downtown* (1984), in contrast, have far more completed story lines, although the problems in them are not altogether resolved.

Terri Mueller's father kidnapped her when she was four years old, and they have both been on the run ever since, never staying in one place more than a few months. Terri believes her mother is dead and enjoys their gypsy lifestyle. But when she is fourteen, she begins to see how far from normal it is to have no past and no family. She begins asking questions that eventually reunite her with her mother, although the question of who she will live with and what kind of relationship she will have with either of her parents is left unanswered.

In *Downtown,* Pax Connors finally learns the truth about his parents, who have been in hiding for eight years, when his mother, now divorced from his father, comes back. She begins serving a prison sentence for killing two people as part of a nuclear war protest, and Pax decides to visit her. But we are left to wonder what will happen when they meet, whether or not Pax will ever be reunited with his father, who is still in hiding, and whether he will decide to live near his mother or with the uncle who has been his entire family while his parents were gone.

Missing Pieces also deals with an absent parent, and it has an even more ambiguous ending. Jessie has grown up with the story of her father, "The Disappearing Dude," who walked out one day when she was a toddler and never came back. It is not until Jessie is fourteen that she begins to want to know more about him and decides to find out who and where he is, despite her mother's objections. But when she does find him, she cannot bring herself to talk to him, and even though she promises herself that she will the next time, the reader is left to wonder about that meeting, especially since Jessie's mother has characterized him as cold and emotionless.

Out of Control is about harassment and its aftermath. Valerie decides that she no longer wants to live with the secret of what three of the most popular boys in school did to her when they attacked her in a deserted school hallway and how different her life has been ever since. She writes a letter to the editor of the newspaper, but the novel ends before the letter is published. The reader must decide what happens when the story is made public, and how Valerie's life and the lives of the three boys, all from prominent families, will change.

Individuation from Parents

The teenagers in Mazer's books learn from their parents and then learn to think for themselves and reject the ideas, beliefs, and philosophies that conflict with their own. Growing up is a process of separation, individuation, and growing independence, as teenagers begin to become true individuals, with their own understanding of themselves and their world.

The parents in Mazer's books are real people and not all of them are good at the job of parenting. Her characters show a wide range of relationships with their parents, from very close to very distant and from cordial to hostile. Some parents are overinvolved in their children's lives, and others are not present at all.

Vicki's and Chris's parents in *Bright Days, Stupid Nights* (1992), which Mazer wrote with her husband, Harry, seem to be trying to live their lives through their children's, pushing them to succeed in ways they themselves were not able to. Vicki is fourteen, two years too young for the summer internship program at a Pulitzer Prize–winning newspaper, but her mother convinces her to lie and apply anyway. When she makes it, she must continue to lie to everyone. Chris's father rejects his son's ambition to be a writer, and when Chris accepts the internship, rejects his son as well. Faith, the daughter of fabulously wealthy and dysfunctional parents, is interested only in escaping her past and the limelight she has always lived in, so she can live her own life. Elizabeth's parents are divorced and also distant. It is her boyfriend who controls her life almost completely, and from whom she needs to separate.

Mazer shows how, during the summer, each of these characters begins to think more independently, moving away from parental mores and expectations. Secrets, and whether or not they should be kept, are also an important part of the plot. Vicki struggles not only to hide her own age, but also to decide whether or not to reveal Faith's background in a feature story. Her decision not to make herself look good at Faith's expense shows her increasing ability to put herself in someone else's shoes, an important developmental task of adolescence.

Jenny and Finn keep their boyfriends' identities from their parents in *When We First Met* (1982), the sequel to *A Figure of Speech* (1972) and *Up in Seth's Room* (1979). Jenny is dating the son of the woman who was driving the car that killed her sister, and Finn is dating the younger brother of her sister's boyfriend, who is four years older than she is. Both girls try to meet their parents' expectations but ultimately discover that their own definitions of what is right and what is wrong work better for them. The scenes of confrontation in both books show teenagers who have spent time considering their actions carefully and who are able to explain to their parents in a calm

dysfunctional impaired, functioning abnormally

mores moral attitudes

In When We First Met, *both girls try to meet their parents' expectations but ultimately discover that their own definitions of what is right and what is wrong work better for them.*

and appropriate way why they must do what they believe is right. The resulting confusion that both sets of parents feel at the reversal of roles and demand for independence is clearly and sympathetically drawn. These parents are forced to learn to cope with their daughters' decisions and to trust them to do what is best for themselves.

Finn does not reject her parents' views, and although she is determined to date Seth, she decides not to have sex with him in spite of his pressure to do so. "Too young, too soon, too important," she asserts, even ready to give up the relationship to do what she believes is right.

Another parent-teenager confrontation highlighting the teen's process of individuation occurs in *After the Rain* (1987). Rachel's grandfather is dying, and she realizes that she is the only person in her family who has genuinely connected with him since he got lung cancer. They have become friends; he trusts her and is closer to her than anyone else. Because of this friendship, Rachel knows she has to defy her parents and stay with her grandfather when he is forced into the hospital, even when they order her to go to school. Her grandfather is the most important person in her life, and his needs take precedence over everything else. Later, when she feels compelled to spend the night at the hospital and sends her parents home, Rachel seems more of a parent than a child. Early that morning, she is with her grandfather when he dies, able to connect one final time because she had the courage to do what she knows is right.

precedence priority of importance

Secrets

Part of separating from parents has to do with keeping secrets about one's thoughts or life. Mazer's characters keep a wide variety of secrets from their parents, who, in turn, hide things from their children.

Sarabeth, in *Silver* (1988), has only one parent, and she and her mother have always been very close. Because they have never had enough money, when she meets rich and lonely Patty, Sarabeth is sure that Patty's life must be perfect—that she has everything that money can buy. But money cannot but safety or a mother's trust and faith—all of which Sarabeth has taken for granted because she has always had them. When Patty reveals that her uncle is sexually abusing her, it is Sarabeth and her mother who are able to convince Patty's mother of the reality of the situation and the need to escape from it.

Martine and Toni, nicknamed *Babyface* (1990), are sisters, yet they grew up in very different families. Martine remembers parents who fight constantly and are about to get a divorce when her mother gets pregnant with Toni. Everything changes because of the new baby. They move into a new house and stop fighting—everything has to be prefect for Toni, even if it was not for Martine. Toni grows up in a picture-postcard family, knowing nothing about the past until she has to spend two weeks alone with Martine after their father has a heart attack. Martine tells her the truth about their family, which explains why she is a cold, untrusting, and unloving person—she has lived with lies too long. Later Toni confronts her parents, and eventually she is able to understand their actions, learning that their years of pretense have finally brought about their reconciliation.

In *Out of Control,* Valerie is forced to tell her father about her attack, but shields him from how she feels about it, or how it has affected the rest of her life. But even while she believes he is too fragile and too out of touch with reality to handle the truth, she is still angry that he cannot protect her, and that in some ways, she has to be his parent. Making her story public is one way of forcing him, as well as others, to confront reality.

Short Stories

Mazer's short stories, in *Dear Bill, Remember Me? and Other Stories* and *Summer Girls, Love Boys, and Other Stories* (1982), also show teenagers learning to take control of their own destiny. Like Elizabeth in *Bright Days,* Jessie in "Up on Fong Mountain" refuses to let her boyfriend control her or their relationship, and she discovers that her independence has made her more attractive to him. "Chocolate Pudding" shows Chrissy's realization that she is not trapped by her life of poverty unless she believes that she is. Louise must also transcend her situation, and to confront the reality of her imminent death, she must show her family and friends how to do so, as well, in "Guess Whose Friendly Hands." Sara is also struggling to deal with a death, her sister's, and she asks, "Do

transcend rise above

> *Through their experiences, the results of their and others' actions, the teenagers in Mazer's books learn to believe in themselves and trust their own instincts and beliefs.*

You Really Think It's Fair?" We listen to her half of her therapy sessions as she begins to make sense of what has happened. "Something Expensive," "Peter in the Park," and "Mimi the Fish" deal with mothers' expectations of their daughters, as their daughters realize that they are changing and moving away from their families before their mothers are willing or able to acknowledge it. Life for Bibi, in "De Angel and De Bow-Wow," may not be either easy or what she expected it would be, but she says, "It's all we've got," so she is determined to enjoy it. Zelzah, from "Zelzah: A Tale of Long Ago," would agree with her.

Through their experiences, the results of their and others' actions, the teenagers in Mazer's books learn to believe in themselves and trust their own instincts and beliefs. It is a process of discovery, of making decisions and evaluating them, and of change and growth. They learn from their parents and their families; they also learn through their relationships with their friends, girlfriends, and boyfriends. Friendship is important in Mazer's books, because through their friends, her characters see glimpses of the ways that others live, new perspectives on themselves, their parents, and other adults in their world. Friends are also sounding boards for new opinions, ideas, and questions that are too risky to share with adults, just as Mazer's books are sounding boards for the teens who read them.

Finally, in confronting the hard situations and problems that real teens deal with, Mazer's characters discover that although life is not always easy, it is ultimately what you yourself can make of it—free to decide who you are now and who you are going to be—even when you change your mind about it. As Mazer herself says, "Life is tough, but go for it!"

If you enjoy the works of Norma Fox Mazer, you might also enjoy the works of Robert Cormier, Norma Klein, Harry Mazer, and Marilyn Sachs.

Selected Bibliography

WORKS BY NORMA FOX MAZER

I, Trissy (1971)

Saturday, the Twelfth of October (1971)

A Figure of Speech (1973)

Dear Bill, Remember Me? and Other Stories (1976)

The Solid Gold Kid, with Harry Mazer (1977)

Up in Seth's Room (1979)

Mrs. Fish, Ape, and Me, the Dump Queen (1980)

Taking Terri Mueller (1981)

Summer Girls, Love Boys, and Other Stories (1982)

When We First Met (1982)

Someone to Love (1983)

Supergirl (1984)

When We First Met, co-author of film script based on her novel (1984)

Downtown (1984)

Three Sisters (1986)

A, My Name Is Ami (1986)

After the Rain (1987)

B, My Name Is Bunny (1987)

Heartbeat, with Harry Mazer (1988)

Silver (1988)

Waltzing on Waters, Poems by Women, edited with Marjorie Lewis (1989)

Babyface (1990)

C, My Name Is Cal (1990)

D, My Name Is Danita (1991)

E, My Name Is Emily (1991)

Bright Days, Stupid Nights, with Harry Mazer (1992)

Out of Control (1993)

Missing Pieces (1995)

Articles

"The Ice-Cream Syndrome (aka Promoting Good Reading Habits)." In *Authors' Insights: Turning Teenagers into Readers and Writers.* Edited by Donald R. Gallo. Portsmouth, N.H., Boynton/Cook, 1992.

"Norma Fox Mazer." In *Speaking for Ourselves: Autobiographical Sketches by Notable Authors of Books for Young Adults.* Edited by Donald R. Gallo. Urbana, Ill.: National Council of Teachers of English, 1990, pp. 139–141.

"Norma Fox Mazer." In *Something About the Author Autobiography Series.* Edited by Adele Sarkissian. Detroit: Gale Research, 1986, vol.1.

"Growing Up with Stories." *Top of the News,* winter 1985.

WORKS ABOUT NORMA FOX MAZER

Garrett, Agnes, and Helga P. McCuen, eds. "Norma Fox Mazer." In *Authors and Artists for Young Adults.* Detroit: Gale Research, 1990, vol. 5, pp. 161–175.

Stine, Jean C., ed. "Norma Fox Mazer." In *Contemporary Literary Criticism.* Detroit: Gale Research, 1983, vol. 26, pp. 289–297.

Holtze, Sally Holmes. *Presenting Norma Fox Mazer.* New York: Twayne, 1987; New York: Dell, 1989.

Olendorf, Donna, ed. "Norma Fox Mazer." *Something About the Author.* Detroit: Gale Research, 1992, vol. 67, pp. 131–135.

How to write to the Author
Norma Fox Mazer
c/o Avon Books
1350 Avenue of the Americas
New York, NY 10019

Milton Meltzer

(1915-   )

by Catherine Mairs and E. Wendy Saul

Milton Meltzer came of age during the 1930s, a period in American history when millions of people found themselves unemployed, homeless, and hungry. It was a time when people who had once been rich joined those who were poor in bread lines, when racism flourished, when a college education did not guarantee a job, and when the people fought to maintain their dignity. Meltzer, who was a student at Columbia University in New York, dropped out during the height of the Great Depression and quickly discovered firsthand the suffering of unemployed Americans. After he got a writing job with the WPA (Works Progress Administration) Federal Theater Project—the government's newly instituted program to create jobs in the arts—Meltzer picketed for higher wages and traveled to Washington, D.C., to demand help for his fellow citizens. Such a time of massive economic and social change could not help but shape Meltzer as a person and an author. As he writes in his award-winning *Brother, Can You Spare a Dime? The Great Depres-*

> *This desire to inquire into the past, to search for connections between history and the present, inspires each of Meltzer's books.*

sion, 1929–1933 (1969), "No one can understand the America of today without knowing something about the Great Depression of the 1930s" (p. 4). This desire to inquire into the past, to search for connections between history and the present, inspires each of Meltzer's books.

Milton Meltzer was born on 8 May 1915, during World War I. His parents had come to the United States as teenagers and found jobs working long hours at low wages in New York's factories. Shortly after they met and married, Meltzer's mother and father moved to Worcester, Massachusetts, hoping to discover a better life than that offered on the crowded city streets. They soon realized, however, that few opportunities were open to Eastern European Jewish immigrants who possessed little formal education. Meltzer's father took a job as a window washer and his mother worked part-time while raising Milton and his two brothers.

Meltzer grew up in a neighborhood of families from many different countries. But neither his parents nor the books he read in school discussed his own culture or the diverse backgrounds of his neighbors. Everyone seemed to want to forget their pasts and fully adopt the ways of their new home. Meltzer talked about this aspect of his young life in a speech he gave at Northern Illinois University on 15 March 1991: "Born in this land, I was gifted to be what my parents sensed they would never become—a 100 percent American. They did whatever they could to bury their own past in the tiny villages of Austro-Hungary."

Visits to the library and the influence of a high school teacher helped Meltzer better understand himself and the world around him and also launched him on his future career as a writer. The library he discovered by accident, and he returned there again and again. He read every book from one wall to the other, often finding himself transported into the lives of fictional characters. Eventually, he became more selective in his choice of books, going back to those authors who captured his imagination, writers who made him feel as well as think. Anna Shaughnessy, his favorite high school teacher, guided Meltzer to such authors. Much later, Meltzer would write a biography of Henry David Thoreau, one of the authors to whom Miss Shaughnessy introduced him.

Meltzer did not write his first book until he was forty years old. Before then, he worked as an editor; an air traffic controller during World War II; and a writer of magazine

Henry David Thoreau (1817–1862) wrote *Walden*, which records his simple life in harmony with nature. He also wrote the essay "Civil Disobedience," which advocated peaceful resistance to the government and was adopted by several twentieth-century reformers.

articles, radio show documentaries, news releases, and speeches. In 1956, he collaborated with Langston Hughes on *A Pictorial History of the Negro in America*. Writing a book appealed to Meltzer because, unlike the shorter works he had been composing, a book could be read more than once and by many different people and still have meaning. Since he was writing books in his spare time, he needed the support of his family. In *Something About the Author Autobiography Series*, Meltzer states: "My wife was very understanding. 'I'll let you out of the dishes,' she said, 'if you write a book.' Later she turned around and told everybody the only reason I wrote books was to get out of doing dishes" (p. 216).

Biographies of Individuals

In 1968, after being nominated for the National Book Award for *Langston Hughes: A Biography,* Meltzer decided to devote himself full-time to writing books. Meltzer's admiration for his subject was profound. Friend, artist, and social critic, Hughes tried, through his poems and books, to improve the condition of African Americans. This attempt to change the world for the better characterizes most of the men and women about whom Meltzer writes. Referring to these individuals in *Nonfiction for the Classroom: Milton Meltzer on Writing, History, and Social Responsibility* (1994), he notes: "In times of trouble they never said there was nothing they could do about it" (p. 66). Neither Hughes nor the others whose lives Meltzer has documented—abolitionists Lydia Maria Child and Samuel Gridley Howe, birth control pioneer Margaret Sanger, photographer Dorothea Lange, women's rights advocate Betty Friedan, and educator Mary McLeod Bethune—stood helpless in the face of injustice. They acted.

In all his biographies, Meltzer describes his subjects' personal insecurities and failures as well as their successes. This decision stems from the belief that readers can learn as much from peoples' mistakes as from their accomplishments. "In writing biography, whether of the famous or the obscure," Meltzer states in *Nonfiction for the Classroom,* "I want to give young readers vision, hope, energy. And to do it honestly, without concealing the weaknesses, the false starts, or the wrong turns of my heroes or heroines" (p. 20). For example,

Langston Hughes (1902–1967) was an African American poet and writer.

in *Columbus and the World Around Him* (1990), Meltzer contrasts the well-known fact of Columbus' discovery of the New World with evidence that he enslaved Native Americans. His biography of Dorothea Lange portrays her as a photographer with the ability to awaken a nation to the suffering of the Depression, but he shows her also as a mother who abused her own children. Meltzer respects his readers' ability to reason, ask questions, and make judgments. He also admits that biography can only go so far toward illuminating the life of a another person. "I realized that the best I could do was to explain *how* things happened, to show my subject in action, but not pretend to know the *why* of it" (unpublished interview). Although he accepts that he will never unearth every detail of his subjects' lives, Meltzer nevertheless is thorough in researching not only their personality and careers, but also the historical events and people who surround them. His biographies emphasize the role the societal context plays in hindering or motivating an individual's actions.

Biographies of Underrepresented Groups

Just as it was important to the young Meltzer that someone talk to him about the diversity of his neighborhood, as a mature writer he is committed to helping young people learn about the optimism, suffering, and perseverance of African Americans, Chinese Americans, Jewish Americans, and Hispanic Americans. He warns in *Nonfiction for the Classroom,* "If we don't have the capacity to think ourselves into another's skin, then we are in deep trouble in this polyglot nation" (p. 96). He also reminds the reader, "If there's one thing in American history that every one of us shares, it is the immigrant experience. All Americans, the Indians too, have come here from other parts of the world" (p. 76).

Meltzer helps his readers bridge the gulf between their reality and that of others by allowing the people he writes about to speak in their own words. Meltzer realizes how easy it is for a reader to remain distant from a history of dry facts. His books, diary entries, narrative accounts, interviews, and letters bring readers into closer connection with other people's thoughts, opinions, values, and feelings. Through these techniques, he asks, What does it mean to have people de-

Meltzer helps his readers bridge the gulf between their reality and that of others by allowing the people he writes about to speak in their own words.

spise you because of the color of your skin, your religious beliefs, or your culture? In *The Chinese Americans* (1980), for example, a young girl whose father sewed clothes for a living in San Francisco's Chinatown tells her story in her own voice: "There was no thought that dim and airless quarters were terrible conditions for living and working, or that child labor was unhealthful. The only goal was for all the family to work, to save, and to become educated. It was possible, so it would be done." (p. 88).

Meltzer's concern for those who lack power in society is reflected not only in the people he chooses to write about, but also in the way he chooses to depict history. Again, in *Nonfiction for the Classroom,* Meltzer recalls the questions that undergird the award-winning *The Black Americans: A History in Their Own Words: 1619–1983* (1984), a three-volume documentary history: "But what about people on the bottom? How did the strange new land look to kidnapped Africans carried in chains across the Atlantic? What was life like for the slave picking cotton or cutting cane?" (p. 39). Meltzer strives to convey the importance of investigating all sides of a situation instead of blindly accepting the perspective of those who hold power and traditionally write history—in this case slaveowners, government authorities, and other white people.

undergird to provide the basis or foundation of

Meltzer also believes that an ability to look at the world from another person's perspective helps break down the stereotypes and ignorance that feed racism. In *The Chinese Americans,* he begins by filling in some of the gaps left by many history books. In this case, he presents an engraving of a photograph that depicts the celebration marking the completion of the first transcontinental railroad.

stereotype a character that is not original or individual because it conforms to a preconceived category

> But something is wrong with this picture.
> Look closely at the faces in it.
> Nowhere can you see a Chinese person.
> Yet no group of workers did more to build that railroad than the Chinese. Their bone, their muscle, their nerve, their sweat, their skill made an impossible dream come true. (P. 2)

While giving his readers cause to respect Chinese Americans, long buried voices, facts, songs, and photographs allow

> *"The collective memory of a people is a treasure-house we cannot do without. In delving into that store of historical and personal memory I think I discovered myself—who I am and what I might be."*

Meltzer to present a fuller and more accurate picture of American history, a people's history. He attributes great importance to a society's ability to remember all aspects of its past, both the evil and the good. "The collective memory of a people is a treasure-house we cannot do without. In delving into that store of historical and personal memory I think I discovered myself—who I am and what I might be" (unpublished interview). Meltzer hopes his books will leave readers with a greater understanding of history and more insight into what links them to the past.

Books on Historical Periods and Events

Milton Meltzer anticipates that his readers will perceive much of what he writes about—the Holocaust, early twentieth-century labor uprisings, the period of Reconstruction, and the Depression—as distant pieces of history that have minimal influence on how society operates today and even less applicability to their personal lives. To combat these misconceptions, he tries to engage adolescents with their own questions or with a revelation. In the opening to *Never to Forget: The Jews of the Holocaust* (1976), named a *Boston Globe–Horn Book* Nonfiction Honor Book and a finalist for the National Book Award, he writes: "That it happened once, unbelievable as it seems, means it could happen again. Hitler made it a possibility for anyone. Neither the Jews nor any other group on earth can feel safe from that crime in the future" (p. xvi). When Meltzer connects the past with the present and future, the Holocaust suddenly takes on a new light.

As he begins his research, Meltzer says he does not always know what facts he will uncover. "Sometimes I think I will know the answers before I start work on a book. The act of writing often teaches me better. If I am lucky, I may find out what the true questions are" (*Nonfiction for the Classroom,* p. 38). Meltzer models for the reader the thinking process required for a historian and a moral citizen. "The Councils, their staffs, and their police forces became agents of the Nazi killing machine and instruments of their own execution," he writes in *Never to Forget*. He then asks: "Can they be condemned outright and wholesale? Could they have done anything else but carry out the functions dictated by the Nazis?" (p. 83). Meltzer seeds his books with questions, intending that additional ones will sprout. In a speech he gave at Simmons College on 24 March 1990, Meltzer said: "If questions are not raised, if the spirit of inquiry is missing, why bother to teach history?" History as a search for answers, Meltzer believes, becomes both an opportunity to learn and an inspiration for action.

Books That Analyze Contemporary Issues

Although Milton Meltzer is best known for his biographies and history books, he has also written a number of books that analyze such issues as crime, terrorism, American politics, Constitutional rights, poverty, pacifism, and child labor. As in his other books, Meltzer makes a point of including the perspectives of both the underdog and of those who hold power. For example, in his study of crime, he discusses street crime, perpetuated largely by people who are poor and addicted to drugs, and then explains the phenomenon of white-collar crime. He is honest, citing myths used against rape victims as well as problems with the American judicial system. Nevertheless, Meltzer does not intend to depress his readers. Instead, he encourages them to evaluate their own morality and values and search for ways to bring about social change. In the last chapter of *Crime in America* (1990), entitled "What Can Be Done About It?" he challenges the reader:

> *Meltzer makes a point of including the perspectives of both the underdog and of those who hold power.*

> We need to examine what we do to each other. When we see someone go wrong, someone doing harm, we need to think about such behavior and make a judgment. Is this the way we want to live? Is that what we want to be? Are profit and power all there is in this world? Can we stand by and watch the slow erosion of our humanity? Have we forgotten that we are supposed to care about one another? (P. 158)

At other times, Meltzer provides models for his readers to emulate. In *American Politics: How It Really Works* (1989), he describes real people who have sought to improve the status quo, whether by advocating for the homeless or running a food bank.

genre a particular style or form of writing

> *Meltzer strives to do more than disseminate (circulate) facts; he wants to engage his readers in thoughtful dialogue.*

This genre of Meltzer's writing deals with contemporary issues, an ideal context for talking one-on-one with readers. Within the foreword to *The Bill of Rights: How We Got It and What It Means* (1990), Meltzer strikes up a conversation: "Let's suppose you say, I'm the kind of person who never gets into trouble. I mind my own business, I never complain or criticize, and of course I would never commit a crime. Perhaps true, but what if you are falsely accused of committing one? what would help protect you from a miscarriage of justice?" (p. xi). Meltzer strives to do more than disseminate facts; he wants to engage his readers in thoughtful dialogue. Most of these books spend time examining the past—asking such questions as where and when was terrorism launched? what were the underpinnings of the Bill of Rights?—and then come full circle, as Meltzer reveals how insight about the past helps us understand our own times.

New Ventures

Meltzer's talent and desire to help young people connect their own lives to the lives of those who came before them have found yet another outlet. Two titles, one on gold and one on potatoes, examine how such objects shaped history and how cultures past and present give meaning to artifacts. He continues to write about biographical subjects of interest: two beautifully illustrated volumes, *Lincoln: In His Own Words* (1993) and *Frederick Douglass: In His Own Words* (1995), consist of speeches, letters, and writings. He has also recently completed a new book on an issue of great contemporary import, *Who Cares? Millions Do: A Book About Altruism* (1994).

Each of the turning points in Meltzer's life has been marked by an era of social change in American society. He witnessed firsthand how war, discrimination, and unemployment inspire courage and incite action. This optimism and perseverance, this belief that the individual can and will make a difference, characterizes Meltzer's books and his view of history. "Yet history as the story of human society is explosive with energy and genius," he writes in *Nonfiction for the Classroom.* "It is the story of evil as well as good, of failure as well as success, of frustration as well as achievement, of hate as well as love" (p. 46). By modeling his own sense of wonder and allowing the people he writes about to narrate their own stories, Meltzer helps his readers to feel this energy and understand how their lives connect to both the past and the present.

Selected Bibliography

WORKS BY MILTON MELTZER

A Pictorial History of The Negro in America, with Langston Hughes (1956)

Mark Twain Himself (1960)

Milestones to American Liberty (1961)

A Thoreau Profile, with Walter Harding (1962)

Thoreau: People, Principles, and Politics (1963)

A Light in the Dark: The Life of Samuel Gridley Howe (1964)

In Their Own Words: A History of the American Negro, 3 vols. (1964)

Tongue of Flame: The Life of Lydia Maria Child (1965)

Time of Trial, Time of Hope: The Negro in America, 1919–1941, with August Meier (1966)

Black Magic: A Pictorial History of the Negro in American Entertainment, with Langston Hughes (1967)

Bread—and Roses: The Struggle of American Labor, 1865–1915 (1967)

Thaddeus Stevens and the Fight for Negro Rights (1967)

Langston Hughes: A Biography (1968)

Brother, Can You Spare a Dime? The Great Depression, 1929–1933 (1969)

Margaret Sanger: Pioneer of Birth Control, with Lawrence Lader (1969)

Freedom Comes to Mississippi: The Story of Reconstruction (1970)

Slavery: A World History, 2 vols. (1971)

To Change the World: A Picture History of Reconstruction (1971)

Hunted Like a Wolf: The Story of the Seminole War (1972)

If you like the works of Milton Meltzer, you might also like books by John Steinbeck and Laurence Yep.

The Right to Remain Silent (1972)

Underground Man (1972)

A Pictorial History of Black Americans, with Langston Hughes and C. Eric Lincoln (1973), 4th rev. ed. of *A Pictorial History of The Negro in America* (1956)

Bound for the Rio Grande: The Mexican Struggle (1974)

The Eye of Conscience: Photographers and Social Change, with Bernard Cole (1974)

Remember the Days: A Short History of the Jewish American (1974)

World of Our Fathers: The Jews of Eastern Europe (1974)

Never to Forget: The Jews of the Holocaust (1976)

Taking Root: Jewish Immigrants in America (1976)

Violins and Shovels: The WPA Arts Projects (1976)

Dorothea Lange: A Photographer's Life (1978)

The Human Rights Book (1979)

All Times, All Peoples: A World History of Slavery, illustrated by Leonard Everett Fisher (1980)

The Chinese Americans (1980)

The Collected Correspondence of Lydia Maria Child, with Patricia G. Holland (1980; text-fiche)

The Hispanic Americans (1982)

The Jewish Americans: A History in Their Own Words: 1650–1950 (1982)

Lydia Maria Child: Selected Letters, 1817–1880, with Patricia G. Holland (1982)

The Truth About the Ku Klux Klan (1982)

The Terrorists (1983)

A Book About Names (1984)

The Black Americans: A History in Their Own Words: 1619–1983 (1984)

Ain't Gonna Study War No More: The Story of America's Peace-Seekers (1985)

Betty Friedan: A Voice for Women's Rights (1985)

Dorothea Lange: Life Through the Camera (1985)

Mark Twain: A Writer's Life (1985)

The Jews in America: A Picture Album (1985)

Benjamin Franklin: The New American (1986)

George Washington and the Birth of Our Nation (1986)

Poverty in America (1986)

Winnie Mandela: The Soul of South Africa (1986)

The American Revolutionaries: A History in Their Own Words (1987)

Mary McLeod Bethune: Voice of Black Hope (1987)

The Landscape of Memory (1987)

Rescue: The Story of How Gentiles Saved Jews in the Holocaust (1988)

Starting from Home: A Writer's Beginnings (1988)

American Politics: How It Really Works (1989)

Voices from the Civil War: A Documentary of the Great American Conflict (1989)

African-American History: Four Centuries of Black Life, with Langston Hughes (1990), 5th rev. ed. of *A Pictorial History of The Negro in America* (1956)

The American Promise: Voice from a Changing Nation (1990)

The Bill of Rights: How We Got It and What It Means (1990)

Columbus and the World Around Him (1990)

Crime in America (1990)

Thomas Jefferson: Revolutionary Aristocrat (1991)

The Amazing Potato: A Story in Which the Incas, Conquistadors, Marie-Antoinette, Thomas Jefferson, Wars, Famines, Immigrants, and French Fries All Play a Part (1992)

Andrew Jackson and His America (1993)

Gold: The True Story of Why People Search for It, Mine It, Trade It, Fight for It, Mint It, Display It, Steal It, and Kill for It (1993)

Lincoln: In His Own Words, illustrated by Stephen Alcorn (1993)

Cheap Raw Material: How Our Youngest Workers Are Exploited and Abused (1994)

Nonfiction for the Classroom: Milton Meltzer on Writing, History, and Social Responsibility (1994)

Theodore Roosevelt and His America (1994)

Who Cares? Millions Do: A Book About Altruism (1994)

Frederick Douglass: In His Own Words (1995)

WORKS ABOUT MILTON MELTZER

Brown, Joshua. "Telling the History of All Americans: Milton Meltzer, Minorities, and the Restoration of the Past." *The Lion and the Unicorn,* April 1987, pp. 7–25.

Commire, Anne, ed. *Something About the Author.* Detroit: Gale Research, 1983, vol. 50, pp. 297–309.

De Luca, G., and R. Natov. "An Interview with Milton Meltzer." *The Lion and the Unicorn,* vol. 4, no. 1, pp. 95–107.

Donelson, K. L., and A. P. Nilsen. "The Evaluation of Nonfiction." *Literature for Today's Young Adults,* 3rd ed. Glenview, Ill.: Scott, Foresman, 1989, pp. 258–260.

Heffernan, Mary Ann. "Milton Meltzer." In *Dictionary of Literary Biography: American Writers for Children Since 1960: Poets, Illustrators, and Nonfiction Authors.* Detroit: Gale Research, 1987, vol. 61, pp. 214–223.

Sarkissian, Adele, ed. *Something About the Author Autobiography Series.* Detroit: Gale Research, 1988, vol. 1, pp. 203–221.

Saul, E. W. "Milton Meltzer's *Brother Can You Spare a Dime: A Study of Passionate Fact."* In *The Phoenix Award of the Children's Literature Association, 1985–1989.* Edited by A. Helbig and A. Perkins. Metuchen: Scarecrow, 1993.

Senick, Gerard, ed. *Children's Literature Review.* Detroit: Gale Research, 1987, vol. 13, pp. 114–152.

Stine, Jean C., ed. *Contemporary Literary Criticism.* Detroit: Gale Research, 1983, vol. 26, pp. 297–309.

Weedmon, J. "A Step Aside from Self: The Work of Milton Meltzer." *Children's Literature Association Quarterly,* spring 1985, pp. 41–42.

How to Write to the Author
Milton Meltzer
c/o HarperCollins
10 East 53rd Street
New York, NY 10022

Gloria D. Miklowitz

(1927-   )

by Charles R. Duke

If you want to read books in which young people face such serious contemporary problems as rape, suicide, AIDS, nuclear war, obsessive behavior, and religious cults, then you will want to become familiar with the writing of Gloria D. Miklowitz. She has written over forty books for young people on a wide variety of topics. Some of these are picture books for young children; others are based on interviews with successful young people or are biographies of public figures like Dr. Martin Luther King, Jr. Most of her work, however, is fiction. Some of her novels have been turned into television movies as After-School or Schoolbreak Specials.

Starting as a Writer

Miklowitz (pronounced MICK-lo-witz) admits that she did not start off with a strong liking for reading. But in the third grade, she wrote a story called "My Brother Goo Goo," for which she received an A. Her family was so impressed that they told her she was going to be a writer. But her career writing books did not really begin until she went to work for the U.S. Navy in the 1950s. Before then, she says in *Something About the Author Autobiography Series* (1994), she worked as a writer for the *Socorro Chieftain,* a small-town newspaper in New Mexico, where she was responsible for a column called "Shopping Around with Gloria Miklowitz." She also worked briefly as a secretary for a lawyer and in a bank and also as a substitute high school teacher. Then she was hired as a secretary in a navy office. Eventually she was able to convince her bosses that she should be given the opportunity to write scripts for films the navy was going to produce. As a result, she learned how to research subjects, develop scripts, and even assist with the shooting of the film. Her books show the influence of these early experiences. Her research skills are reflected in both her fiction and non-fiction works because they are filled with details taken from real life. Her novels, in particular, show an influence from scriptwriting because they have well-developed plots, strong characters, and convincing dialogue.

> *Eventually she was able to convince her bosses that she should be given the opportunity to write scripts for films the navy was going to produce.*

This early training in scriptwriting also probably contributed to the success several of her novels had as television specials. *Did You Hear What Happened to Andrea?* (1979) became the After-School Special "Andrea's Story: a Hitchhiking Tragedy" and won five Emmys; *The Day the Senior Class Got Married* (1983) was turned into a Schoolbreak Special and won the Humanitas Prize for its humanitarian values. *The War Between the Classes* (1985) also became a Schoolbreak Special.

Her experiences at the navy taught her to write, but it was her experiences with her children that prompted her to write for young people. When her children were young, Miklowitz frequently read them picture books, often as many as ten a week. After taking a writing course, she wrote her first story for young children, called *Barefoot Boy* (1964). This story was followed by a number of others, including *The Zoo that Moved* (1968), *The Parade Starts at Noon* (1969), *The Marshmallow Caper* (1971), and *Save that Raccoon!* (1978).

As her children grew and became involved in many of the things teenagers experience, Miklowitz moved along with them, finding topics that were of interest first to middle graders and then to young adults. The stimulus for Miklowitz's first novel for young adults came from her talks with a cleaning lady who worked for her. As Miklowitz tells it in an interview reported in *Something About the Author* (1992), "We'd have lunch together and she would tell me about all the problems she had with one of her sons involved in drugs. That, combined with talks I'd had with the director of the Los Angeles Zoo about young people involved in animal rescue operations, made me realize that when you reach your hand out to others, you usually don't get into trouble" (p. 172). From that experience came her first novel, *Turning Off* (1973).

The Writer's Technique

Miklowitz tackles some serious problems in her writing. She has written about the effects of nuclear war (*After the Bomb, 1985,* and *After the Bomb: Week One, 1987*); sexual abuse (*Secrets Not Meant to Be Kept, 1987*); rape (*Did You Hear What Happened to Andrea?*); racism (*War Between the Classes*); steroid abuse (*Anything to Win, 1989*); and obsessive relationships between girls and boys (*Desperate Pursuit, 1993*). Naturally curious about the problems people face, Miklowitz asks many questions. As she says in her 1991 interview in *Authors and Artists for Young Adults,* "This curiosity, I think, is almost childlike, and maybe that's why I know what children might find interesting. If it interests me, it should interest them" (p. 158).

Like many writers, Miklowitz gets her ideas for writing from a variety of places. Sometimes she draws on two or three ideas that she has been keeping in her mind as possible items that could provide a story. For example, *Turning Off* tells the story of an African American boy who was on drugs and was afraid he would never get off them. Eventually he gets a job at an animal reserve, and through his work with the animals and staff he starts to take pride in his work and learns that doing a job well and earning the respect of those with whom you work is far better than returning to a life of drugs. The story is inspired by an actual flood at an animal reserve; the main character is based on a boy that Miklowitz knew; and the theme is drawn from her belief, practiced in her life, that having something interesting to do with your time usually results in your being productive and responsible. She also finds news stories and headlines useful in alerting her to possible stories. *The Day the Senior Class Got*

> *The theme (central message) of Turning Off, is drawn from her belief, practiced in her daily life, that having something interesting to do with your time usually results in being productive and responsible.*

Married, an account of what happens when teenagers get to role-play what it would be like to be married, and *The War Between the Classes,* a school experiment in race relations, were among the books sparked by such sources.

Research is an important part of any writer's work, whether it is for fiction or nonfiction purposes, because factual details make a story convincing. For instance, when working on a story about rape, Miklowitz participated in a rape hotline service and talked with doctors, victims, and the police. When she was working on *The Love Bombers,* a story about religious cults, she spent time with a Moonie group to gain a better understanding of what life in a cult is like. For the novel *Standing Tall, Looking Good,* a story about three Los Angeles teenagers and their experiences in the U. S. Army's basic training program, Miklowitz spent considerable time talking to army veterans to be sure she correctly described the technical details and dialogue of military training correct. *Earthquake (1977),* a nonfiction book, also shows Miklowitz's attention to detail, providing a great deal of information about how earthquakes form and how we predict and measure them.

In the article titled "Writing the Juvenile Short Story," which appeared in *Writer* (March 1994), Miklowitz discusses what it takes to write an effective short story for young people. Much of what she suggests applies to the writing of novels as well.

plot the deliberate sequence of events in a literary work

Miklowitz says that writers have to decide on the kind of plot they want. For example, there is the *"purpose achieved"* story, in which the story sets a goal and then shows how it is achieved. An example of this plot is in *After the Bomb,* when Philip, the main character, has to overcome a number of obstacles to save his mother who has been badly burned during the explosion of a nuclear device near Los Angeles. Another type of plot is one that hinges on a "misunderstanding, discovery, and reversal." In *The War Between the Classes,* for example, the main character, Emiko Sumoto, finally realizes that how she and her classmates act is really a form of discrimination, and she sets out to correct the situation. The same kind of plot appears in *The Emerson High Vigilantes*, in which Paul Ross, the editor of the student newspaper and the main character, joins a group of classmates who he thinks want to make the school safe for everyone only to discover that control and power can lead to abuses of personal freedom. He must choose between standing up for the rights of everyone or going along with the crowd. *Anything to Win* has the same type of plot. It tells the story of Cam, a star athlete who believes that steroids will not hurt him and that even if there are side effects, he only needs to take steroids long enough to build up his body weight so he will be recruited by colleges. Only after he discovers that his trainer has developed liver cancer as a result of heavy steroid use does Cam realize the short-term gains caused by steroids are not worth the long-term effects on his life.

In addition to plot, Miklowitz stresses the importance of characters because readers need to care about the people in a story. The writer has to present a likable hero or heroine with whom we can identify. We need to know enough about the characters—what they do, how they look, what they like and dislike, and how they feel about themselves—to want to stay with them throughout the story. Here is a sample of Miklowitz's skill in creating characters. It is an excerpt from *Secrets Not Meant to Be Kept*, a story about the sexual abuse of young children:

> Creating characters is called "characterization."

> Ryan's mother is playing, a look on her face of peace, love, and joy. Behind her stands Mr. O'Connor, one hand on her shoulder, his deep voice booming out the lyrics. Guests, some with drinks in their hands, or with arms around loved ones, join in. I lean my head back against Ryan and close my eyes. It feels so good to sing, to be here. I feel so much trust, and hope, goodness and love here in this group that I almost cry. (P. 15)

Besides heroes and heroines, stories also need an antagonist, or villain, or opponent to create tension. Antagonists are not always people; steroids, for example, could be considered the villain in *Anything to Win*. In this excerpt, Cam's brother Pete tries to help him realize what might happen with steroid use:

> "What's *it*? You seem to be having trouble saying the word. *Steroid.* That's what *IT* is". Peter cradled the ashtray and rose to his feet. "And if you think you won't be taking it forever, think again." Think what? I threw my jacket over one shoulder and stared him

down. "Figure it out," he said. "Once you start, the temptation's always there. There's always someone stronger or bigger than you. When—*if* you get to play college football, the pressures will be even greater. You think you'll quit then?" He stubbed his cigarette into the ashtray and went to the door. "Not to mention the whole big issue of *ethics*. But who am I to talk, right? You're old enough to make up your own mind. Just don't say I didn't warn you." (P. 45)

Another important part of Miklowitz's work is setting. The details she provides make readers believe that the setting is real. Her books are effective in giving a sharp sense of where a story takes place. For example, in *Secrets Not Meant to be Kept*, Gail, the main character, goes to the doctor because she is having difficulty relating to boys, but she is afraid of what the doctor might tell her. We see the examining room through her eyes in this vivid description: "The room is cold. Not just physically. It's so undecorated. Except for a calendar on the beige and white checked wallpaper there is nothing that isn't white or chrome. I pace back and forth the length of the little cell, eyeing the examination table with distrust, wishing I'd never come" (p. 76).

The person who tells the story is called the "narrator."

Another part of the writer's craft is choosing the best viewpoint from which the story is told. The writer has several choices, all focusing on the main character. Will the viewpoint be from the first person—the main character telling his or her story? Miklowitz uses this technique in *Anything To Win*: "Two weeks before the Senior Switch Dance four girls—four!—all popular and good looking, asked me to be their dates. I should have felt great" (p. 1). Miklowitz uses some version of the first person in most of her novels, but she sometimes varies the viewpoint. For example, in *Good-bye Tomorrow* (1987), the telling of the story moves between Alex, the main character, who discovers he has HIV; his girlfriend Shannon; and his sister Christy. She uses the technique again in *The Love Bombers*, in which the story is told from the viewpoint of Jeremy, who has come under the influence of a religious cult, and his sister Jenna, who tries to help him escape. Miklowitz saves the third person personal, in which the author narrates the story, for her nonfiction books, such as *The Young Tycoons* (1981), in which she interviews ten young people who have achieved financial success, or in such biographies as *Dr. Martin Luther King, Jr.* (1977) and informational books like *Movie Stunts and the People Who Do Them* (1980).

Finally, Miklowitz suggests that all stories need a theme. This is usually a kind of moral statement that sums up the story. The theme is conveyed not in a simple sentence but in the way the author leaves you with a sense of what is important. For example, in *After the Bomb,* the theme is "never give up." *Runaway* (1977), a story of a rebellious teenage girl who runs away from home, shows us how important it is to be true to yourself. *Suddenly Super Rich* (1989), a story about what happens to a family when the mother wins a lottery, reminds us of the importance of family and social responsibilities. *The War Between the Classes* explores the effect of racism and bigotry.

racism hatred for or intolerance of another race

A writer must be aware of his or her audience, and Miklowitz is no exception. For her, she says, the teenage years were the most emotional and with family life no longer as close as it once was, teenagers need all the help they can get. She knows about teenage life from having been a teenager herself and from having raised teenagers. She continues to hear from her readers on a regular basis who write to tell her how accurate she has been in capturing their feelings and problems.

Miklowitz says that the teenage years were the most emotional and with family life no longer as close as it once was, teenagers need all the help they can get.

Much of her success as a writer can also be traced to her doing the research necessary to make sure she represents accurately the situations in which she places her characters. Readers of *Past Forgiving,* a forthcoming novel, will recognize the careful attention to detail as she tells the story of date abuse, a situation that an increasing number of girls between twelve and twenty are experiencing. She carefully researches her books not only by talking to people and reading documents, but also by traveling widely. In addition to traveling within the United States, she has also visited South Africa, Europe, and Peru. Two current projects include a historical novel dealing with the fall of Masada, an ancient Jewish fortress near the Dead Sea, and a novel about survival in the Amazon Rain Forest, based on a recent trip to Peru.

In describing her writing process, Miklowitz says that once she has a strong sense of the beginning and the ending she is eager to get started. She likes to write a chapter a week if possible. If she finishes the chapter on a Thursday, then she rewards herself by visiting with friends, but if she has to go until Saturday to complete the task, she does. She dislikes working on the middle of a project; she compares it to encountering a dark hole or being lost and not knowing what lies behind a blank wall. But she finds that when she gets stuck in the middle, she can get started again by sharing her work with a group of friends. This group has been meeting every week for thirty years. They take turns reading their writing to each other and offering honest criticism about what works and what does not. And if she goes to meetings for one or two weeks without anything to share, she says that the guilt drives her back to work.

As Miklowitz says in an article in *Something About the Author Autobiography Series* (1994), "I found that what gives me purpose and structure to my life, and most importantly, *meaning,* is what I've done for most of it—writing. Each new book stretches me in a new direction, treats me to new adventures. How fortunate I am to have this small talent" (p. 240). And how fortunate are we as readers that she chose to share her talent not only with her own children but with all of us.

If you like the works of Gloria Miklowitz, you might also enjoy the works of Norma Klain or M. E. Kerr.

Selected Bibliography

WORKS BY GLORIA D. MIKLOWITZ

Nonfiction for Young Adults
The Zoo Was My World, with Wesley A. Young (1969)
Harry Truman, illustrated by Janet Scabrini (1975)
Earthquake!, illustrated by Jaber William (1977)
Dr. Martin Luther King, Jr. (1977)
Nadia Comaneci (1977)
Save That Raccoon! (1978)
Steve Cauthen (1978)
Tracy Austin (1978)
Natalie Dunn, Roller Skating Champion (1979)
Roller Skating (1979)
Movie Stunts and the People Who Do Them (1980)
The Young Tycoons (1981)

Fiction for Young Adults

The Zoo That Moved, illustrated by Don Madden (1968)

The Parade Starts at Noon (1969)

The Marshmellow Caper (1971)

Turning Off (1973)

A Time to Hurt, A Time to Heal (1974)

Paramedic Emergency (1977)

Runaway (1977)

Unwed Mother (1977)

Did You Hear What Happened to Andrea? (1979)

The Love Bombers (1980)

Before Love (1982)

Carrie Loves Superman (1983)

Close to the Edge (1983)

The Day the Senior Class Got Married (1983)

After the Bomb (1985)

The War Between the Classes (1985)

Love Story, Take Three (1986)

After the Bomb: Week One (1987)

Goodbye Tomorrow (1987)

Secrets Not Meant to Be Kept (1987)

The Emerson High Vigilantes (1988)

Anything to Win (1989)

Suddenly Super Rich (1989)

Standing Tall, Looking Good (1991)

Desperate Pursuit (1993)

The Killing Boy (1993)

Boiling Point (1994)

Articles and Short Stories

Miklowitz, Gloria D. "Writing the Juvenile Short Story." *Writer,* March 1994, pp. 13–16.

Miklowitz has contributed anthologies of short stories and periodicals, including *American Girl, Hadassah, Seventeen, Sports Illustrated, Publishers Weekly, Wildlife Conservation,* and *Writer.*

Manuscripts

Miklowitz' writings are housed in the DeGrummond Collection at the University of Southern Mississippi.

Autobiography

"Gloria D. Miklowitz." In *Something About the Author Autobiography Series.* Detroit: Gale Research, 1994, vol. 17, pp. 225–241.

WORKS ABOUT GLORIA D. MIKLOWITZ

Commire, Anne. "Gloria D. Miklowitz." In *Something About the Author.* Detroit: Gale Research, 1973, vol. 4, pp. 154–156.

Garrett, Agnes, and Helga P. McCue, eds. Interview with Mark Caplan. In *Authors and Artists for Young Adults.* Detroit: Gale Research, 1991, vol. 6, pp. 155–162.

Olendorf, Donna, ed. "Gloria D. Miklowitz," In *Something About the Author.* Detroit: Gale Research, 1992, vol. 68, pp. 170–172.

How to Write to the Author
Gloria D. Miklowitz
c/o Simon and Schuster Children's Publishing Division
1230 Avenue of the Americas
New York, NY 10020

Nicholasa Mohr

(1935-)

by Lois Buckman

Nicholasa Mohr is a talented writer as well as a gifted artist whose paintings have been exhibited in New York and Puerto Rico. When she wrote her first novel, *Nilda* (1973), she also illustrated the book and designed its dust jacket. This book was followed by *El Bronx Remembered: A Novella and Stories* (1975), *In Nueva New York* (1977), *Felita* (1979), and *Going Home* (1986). Mohr writes in *Speaking for Ourselves* (Gallo, 1990), "Growing up I never had seen or read any book that included Puerto Ricans (or Hispanics for that matter) as citizens who worked hard and contributed to this nation. . . . Writing has given me the opportunity to establish my own sense of history and existence as a Puerto Rican woman in the literature of these United States." With her award-winning, critically acclaimed books for young adults, Nicholasa Mohr has succeeded in showing what life was really like for people growing up Puerto Rican in New York's Lower East Side.

> *Mohr has succeeded in showing what life was really like for people growing up Puerto Rican in New York's Lower East Side.*

Beginnings

Nicholasa Mohr was born on 1 November 1935 in New York City to Pedro and Nicholasa (Rivera) Golpe, into a family with six sons. She grew up surrounded by Puerto Rican migrants who had moved to America after all Puerto Ricans had been granted American citizenship in 1917. In her introduction to *El Bronx Remembered,* she describes their plight as "strangers in their own country, [who] brought with them a different language, culture, and racial mixture. Like so many before them they hoped for a better life, a new future for their children, and a piece of that good life known as the 'American Dream.'"

In 1935, when Mohr was born, America was in the middle of the Great Depression, and many families were struggling everywhere, especially in the Barrio (Spanish-speaking neighborhood). In addition, it was a time when her cultural tradition dictated that women should stay home, marry, and have children. Nicholasa was lucky. Her artistic abilities were noticed, and she was able to study at the Art Students League of New York (1953–1956), the Brooklyn Museum Art School (1959–1966), and the Pratt Center for Contemporary Printmaking (1966–1969). She supported herself by working as a waitress, a clerical factory worker, and a translator. On 5 October 1957, she married Irwin Mohr, a child psychologist; they had two sons, David and Jason.

The Nuyorican Experience

The children of the Puerto Rican immigrants living in the Barrio of New York were called Nuyoricans. The Nuyoricans considered themselves New Yorkers, but not everyone agreed. The typical family unit was large, in many cases including children with different fathers. Parents, children, grandparents, and aunts and uncles all lived together in one small tenement apartment. Barrio life receives an excellent portrayal in Mohr's work; she captures not only the physical world, but the emotional one as well. Her characters' family lives and their struggles to survive are flavored with humor, just as they are in reality. Although day-to-day life in the Barrio may be grim, Mohr shows that there is always hope to be found for the future.

Nilda

Mohr's first novel, *Nilda,* winner of the 1974 Jane Addams Children's Book Award and chosen as the Outstanding Children's Book of the Year 1973 by the editors of the *New York Times Book Review* and the Best Children's Book of the Year by *School Library Journal,* is her most autobiographical book, although it takes place during World War II. Mohr's description of the Barrio makes it come alive. Her descriptions of the people and their struggles are so vivid and real that the Barrio is almost like a character in the evolving plot structure. There is such strong characterization that, as Nilda bravely faces life, a sense of who Mohr was as a child and who she is as an adult clearly emerges.

Nilda is a young Nuyorican girl growing up in the Barrio of New York during World War II. It is hard being a Nuyorican in an environment of fear, prejudice, and hatred; it is hard being called "spicks," "animals," and "you people" by the police, teachers, social workers, and others on whom the Nuyoricans depend. When her father becomes ill and is hospitalized, Nilda must miss school to accompany her mother to the welfare agency because her mother is insecure about her English. At the end of a grueling interview, the case worker looks at Nilda's dirty fingernails and, in a nasty and patronizing manner, asks, "How often do you bathe?" The case worker continues to berate Nilda while her mother sits by quietly. When they leave, Nilda verbally attacks her mother for not defending her, but her mother stops her by saying, "I have to do what I do. How do you think we're going to eat? We have no money, Nilda. If I make that woman angry, God knows what she'll put down on the application. We have to have that money in order to live" (*Nilda,* p. 70).

Nilda manages to put aside her hurt feelings and let her drawings comfort her. Mohr's illustrations, intermingled with the text, make Nilda's feelings come alive. Nilda loves to draw and has an active imagination. In one poignant scene when she is upset, she goes into her parents' room and lies down on her cot:

> Very carefully, she started to search in between and around the cracks, discolorations, and peeling paint, that took on different shapes and dimensions, for her favorite scenes. This was a game she loved to play. By

Mohr's descriptions of the people and their struggles are so vivid and real that the Barrio is almost like a character in the evolving plot structure.

poignant touching or moving

using her eyes she discovered that, if she concentrated carefully, she actually began to see all kind of different shapes and forms and exciting events taking place on her ceiling. (P. 76)

Nilda does not need money to entertain herself.

Yet Nilda's imagination cannot hide her from all the pain and prejudice in her neighborhood, particularly not from that inflicted by the police. When Nilda is returning from walking a friend home, two of her friend's brothers, knowing it is dangerous for her to be out alone at night, agree to escort her home. They are not mindful of a neighborhood gang fight taking place nearby until approached by the police. They try to explain what they are doing in the area, "but the first policeman held Chucho by the collar and up against the side of the building. 'Look!' he shouted into Chucho's face. 'Don't give me any shit, spic. I'm tired of this trouble. Now, either you tell me where you punks are, and quit lying, or I'm gonna smash your face.'" Manuel, Chucho's brother, tries to explain that because they are Pentecostal, they do not believe in fighting. The policeman then releases his grip on Chucho and starts beating Manuel so severely that he is blinded. Nilda can do nothing but stand by helplessly. Although *Nilda* is a realistic portrayal of the hardships of the times, there is laughter to be found in the daily lives of the characters, especially that of Nilda's eccentric aunt who lives with her family. When Nilda's mother dies after a lengthy illness and Nilda is forced to live with an aunt she doesn't like, she has only her drawings to give her hope for the future. Mohr's illustrations add greatly to the richness of *Nilda*.

El Bronx Remembered

El Bronx Remembered, a *New York Times* Outstanding Book of the Year and a National Book Award finalist, is a collection of short stories depicting the postwar decade from 1946 to 1956. By this time many Nuyoricans, as the characters in these stories aptly depict, have forgotten what Puerto Rico was really like; instead, they recall their homeland in an idealized, dreamlike way. Mohr's descriptions of the lush gardens and beauty of Puerto Rico make it easy to see why these immigrants have forgotten the poverty of their country.

They still have not found the American dream, and they still struggle with their day-to-day existence, but they do not let life beat them down, and they endure. Without using any heavy-handed devices, Mohr shows the sorrows and trials of these Puerto Ricans by making them real people with real fears, loves, hopes and desires, but always with a sense of humor.

One of the stories, "A Very Special Pet," describes a pet chicken bought to provide eggs for the children. When it does not lay any eggs, the mother decides to kill it and cook it for dinner. While chasing the chicken through the kitchen, the mother notices her children watching. She explains that the chicken is sick, and that she is just trying to catch it to give it medicine. The mother's struggle with the chicken is analogous to her struggle with life. Mohr, as in all of her writings, ends this story with a feeling of hope: the children are reassured that their beloved chicken is fine, and the mother knows she has not given in to her environment by killing the chicken. There can be other solutions.

"Shoes for Hector," another story in *El Bronx Remembered,* offers a protagonist who suffers the same trial that is universal to all teenagers—having nothing to wear. It is Hector's graduation, and his uncle lends him his suit to wear, but what is Hector to do for shoes? Unfortunately, his Uncle Luis has a pair of orange shoes that fit Hector perfectly. But Hector is to give a speech at graduation; how can he wear the orange shoes with the pointy toes? He can just hear the kids calling them "roach killers."

The shoes are symbolic of the struggle between the two generations. The parents, recent migrants, view the shoes quite differently. They see them as new, shiny, well-fitting, and suitable to be worn with a suit. They feel that Hector should be grateful for such an opportunity. Hector views the shoes as another stumbling block in his assimilation into the social structure of his American school. What teenager, for whatever reason, has not been forced to wear, at a parent's insistence, something he or she knows all the other kids will make fun of? Mohr's story is an example of a universal truth. Parents and teenagers often have conflicting values, regardless of their culture.

Other stories in the book also cross social and ethnic lines, showing the versatility of Mohr's talent. In "The Wrong Lunch Line," Yvette (Puerto Rican) and Mildred (Jewish) de-

heavy-handed clumsy or unskillful

device something, such as a figure of speech, in a literary work to achieve a desired effect

symbolic representative of an abstract concept

What teenager, for whatever reason, has not been forced to wear, at a parent's insistence, something he or she knows all the other kids will make fun of?

cide to share the Passover lunch line so that they can sit together. The principal intervenes, telling Yvette she cannot go where she does not belong. In "Mr. Mendleson," an aging Jewish man spends every Sunday with the Nuyorican Suarez family. They disguise a pork dish as "Puerto Rican Chicken" so that Mendleson does not miss a Sunday meal. Later, Mendleson's sisters relocate his home, and when the Suarez family go to visit him there, a nurse tells them that "deliveries are made in the rear of the building." This story was based on something that happened to Mohr's family.

Herman and Alice

Mohr is not afraid to take risks with her writing. The publication of her novella *Herman and Alice* was delayed because of its subject matter. The book's absence would have been a great loss. It is a sensitively told story about Alice, pregnant and unwed, who is befriended by Herman, an older homosexual man in her apartment building. She is flattered by his attention, and her mother is pleased that such a distinguished gentleman is interested in Alice. They enter into a marriage of convenience, neither of them mindful of the possible consequences. Alice becomes bored and starts seeing her friends. She falls in love with a boy closer to her own age, and Herman finds that he is left with Kique, Alice's son, every night. Their marriage deteriorates, and Herman leaves to return to Puerto Rico because the stigma that followed him to the United States has been erased by his marriage.

Although in *Nilda,* the Barrio is almost a character in itself, this is not the case in *El Bronx Remembered.* Here, it is the characters and their problems that are prominent. *In Nueva New York,* winner of several awards including *School Library Journal*'s Best Books for Young Adults, 1977, also focuses on characterization more than on location.

In Nueva New York

In Nueva New York is another semiautobiographical collection of short stories, but is written in a completely different style from *El Bronx Remembered,* again showing the versatility of Mohr's writing. This is a series of stories interconnected by the characters living in one part of the Barrio. Survival is the theme, immediately apparent when the opening scene focuses on a tattered orange cat rummaging through a garbage can on the sidewalk in front of a tenement building where Old Mary sits. Both of them, on the surface, appear to be beaten down by life, but they are survivors. The cat reappears in subsequent chapters, always searching for food in order to exist. The last paragraph again zooms in on the cat as it finds a dry space in an alleyway to fall into a contented sleep. This recurring vision of the battered cat is very effective at adding a touch of realism to the stories of ongoing life in the Barrio.

realism fidelity to real life

In the story "Old Mary," Old Mary sits on a stoop, sipping her first beer of the day, when she sees the cat. "She shook her head and laughed, pointing a finger at the cat. 'You bastard you. You're still lusting around and fighting. You know what you are? A survivor, that's what you are—like me. . . . You don't know enough to die either, do you?'" Yes, they are both survivors. Old Mary does not have an easy life either, every day being a struggle, but the letter she receives just might change things. It is from her son, William, whom she gave away at birth. Now at the age of forty, he has found his mother and longs to come to New York and take care of her. Old Mary is sure that her life will change. But when William arrives later in another story, he isn't exactly what Mary had hoped for; he is a dwarf.

All of the stories in *In Nueva New York* center around Rudi's restaurant (lunchroom). Rudi consistently appears throughout the book and is one thread holding the stories together. Many of the characters reminisce about life in Puerto Rico, but Rudi does not because, he says, "I been here once. I got my discharge in 1946 from the army. I married my first wife here. I love Nueva York . . . it's my home. I go to Puerto Rico and I can't take the slow pace there no more. Nuyoriguino that's me now."

The strength of characterization is shown in "The Robbery," a story in which Rudi shoots and kills a fifteen-year-old boy during a holdup. The mother of the boy harasses Rudi, standing outside his lunchroom and demanding money to pay for a headstone for her son's grave. Rudi insists that he will never change his mind. With "Coming to Terms," he once again encounters the orange cat, his nemesis, which he has threatened to kill if ever their paths cross. Yet he comes to terms with his life in the Barrio and everyone's struggle to

characterization creation of characters through descriptions of their appearance, actions, and thoughts.

survive, a message clearly shown when he gives the battered cat a saucer of milk and slowly goes back to the lunchroom.

Felita

Felita, which was named a Notable Trade Book by the National Conference of Social Studies because it shed a new light on a historical event, tells about twelve months in the life of a girl named Felita. But it is in *Going Home,* a sequel, that Mohr most strongly shows the harm of prejudice and the young person's search for identity. This novel is meant for a younger audience than her other books. Its plot structure, not the locale, is its driving force. As immigrants go to a new country and generations pass, they assimilate more into their new culture, and in the process their own cultural heritage may be lost. Felita grows up in the Barrio, but this summer she is going to Puerto Rico to spend her entire vacation with her grandfather in his small village. Felita does not speak much Spanish, but she has always thought of herself as Puerto Rican.

assimilate absorb (a minority group) into the culture of a population or dominant group

Some of the children in the village make fun of Felita, jeering at her and calling her names. They say she does not belong; she should go home. Felita is crushed, and in a poignant scene she thinks:

> All my life I've been Puerto Rican, now I'm told I'm not, that I'm a gringa. Two years ago I got beaten up by a bunch of mean girls when we had moved into an all-white neighborhood. I hadn't done anything to them, nothing. They just hated me because I was Puerto Rican. My whole family had fought back in the neighborhood until we finally moved out. . . . Even today, back home when anybody tries to make us ashamed of being Puerto Rican, we all stand up to them. What was Anita talking about? It made no sense. At home I get called a "spick": and here I'm a "Nuyorican."

Mohr aptly describes the problems of the children of immigrants. In *Felita,* the Puerto Rican population has remained in the Barrio for generations, and the sense of who they are has been passed from generation to generation. In only one summer, Felita discovers that she does not know who she is supposed to be.

The Message

Mohr clearly, and with wonderful characterization, admits young adult readers into the personal world of her youth, which allows them to gain an understanding of life in New York's Lower East Side—El Barrio—during the time in which she was growing up. Generations of readers will benefit from having been exposed to these books, not only for their historical and cultural interest but also for their vivid portrayals of young adults' lives as they search for identity in a complex world of family and cultural struggles.

Selected Bibliography

WORKS BY NICHOLASA MOHR

Novels for Young Adults

Nilda, illustrated by the author (1973; 1974; 1986)

El Bronx Remembered: A Novella and Stories, illustrated by the author (1975; 1986)

In Nueva New York (1977; 1988)

Felita (1979; 1981)

Going Home (1986; 1989)

BOOKS FOR CHILDREN

The Magic Shell, children's novel (1995)

"Taking a Dare," short story. In *When I Was Your Age: Original Stories About Growing Up,* 1995

Old Letivia and the Mountain of Sorrows, an original fairy tale, 1996

WORKS ABOUT NICHOLASA MOHR

Flores, Juan. "Back Down These Mean Streets: Introducing Nicholasa Mohr and Louis Reyes Rivera." In *Revista Chicano-Riqueña,* Spring 1980, vol. 8, pp. 51–56.

If you like the works of Nicholasa Mohr, you also may enjoy stories by other Hispanic writers such as T. Ernesto Bethancourt and Gary Soto.

Gallo, Donald, ed. In *Speaking for Ourselves.* Urbana, Ill.: National Council of Teachers of English, 1990, pp. 145–146.

Miller, John. "The Emigrant and New York City: A Consideration of Four Puerto Rican Writers." *Melus,* fall 1978, vol. 5, pp. 94–99.

———. "Nicholasa Mohr: Neworican Writings in Progress 'A View of the Other Culture.'" In *Revista Interamericana,* 1979–1980, vol. 9, pp. 543–549.

Nilson, Alleen Pace. "Keeping Score on Some Recent Winners." In *English Journal,* February 1978, vol. 67, pp. 98–101.

"Puerto Ricans in New York: Cultural Evolution and Identity." In *Images and Identities: The Puerto Rican in Literature.* Edited by Asela Rodriguez de Laguna. New Brunswick, N.J.: Transaction Books, 1987.

Sachs, Marilyn. "Nilda." In *The New York Times,* 4 November 1973.

Turner, Faythe. *Something About the Author.* Detroit: Gale Research, 1976, p. 138.

How to Write to the Author
Nicholasa Mohr
c/o Arte Publico Press
University of Houston
4800 Calhoun
Houston, Texas 77204-2090

L. M. Montgomery

(1874-1942)

by Melissa Comer

Imagine a world where an ordinary road lined with apple trees becomes the White Way of Delight and a regular pond the Lake of Shining Waters. This world also has a Snow Queen and a Haunted Wood that frightens even the bravest of souls. It is a world where brooks babble and Dryad, a grown-up fairy, lends her name to a water spring. While imagining, picture a girl with red hair who wants more than anything to have puffed sleeves and a real home. If you can leave your everyday world behind and think about why it is important to have a "kindred spirit," you can enter into Anne Shirley's romantic, imaginative, and loving world of Green Gables.

> kindred spirit   a person with a similar nature or character; a special friend

Lucy Maud Montgomery, better known as L. M. Montgomery, gives breath to Anne. Anne experiences life much the same way children everywhere do, with results that are sometimes humorous and sometimes tragic. She does not look for trouble yet it always seems to find her. While reading about Anne Shirley, you have to remind yourself that she is a character in a book and not someone you know. You laugh with her and sometimes at her (after all, when she accidently dyes her hair green, it is a funny sight!). We follow Anne through romantic fancies of men who have alabaster brows and the sadness of losing a loved one. She grows up before our eyes, the ugly duckling transforming into the graceful swan. Montgomery weaves the tale of Anne so well that she and her wondrous adventures seem real.

Montgomery's Life

Montgomery sets *Anne of Green Gables* (1908) in her native Prince Edward Island, Canada, where she spent her whole life. The countryside she describes is one of lush green, rolling hills, and sparkling water. To say that it is beautiful is an extreme understatement. Based on her descriptions, you can visualize what it must look like. You can smell the apple blossoms that line the White Way of Delight and hear Mrs. Rachel Lynde's brook as it trails by her house. You know that the shadows from the Haunted Wood will, at any moment, sprout arms and legs and devour you.

Montgomery began writing when she was nine. She published her first piece at sixteen. Short stories, poetry, and essays made up her early career. In 1908 *Anne of Green Gables,* her first novel, captured the hearts and minds of the world. Montgomery, at last, knew success. Readers were left wanting to know more about Anne Shirley. In the five sequels that follow *Anne of Green Gables,* Anne matures from an eleven-year-old orphan to a wife and mother. The situations she encounters mirror Montgomery's own life—a life that was often bittersweet due in part to being orphaned as a young child and placing her own life on hold to care for her elderly grandmother. For example, Anne, for a while, is a school teacher, and Montgomery taught school for three years. Montgomery said that she could not remember the time when she was not writing or when she did not intend to be an author. Anne Shirley shares the same view of writing, and eventually her work is published. Anne learns, as Montgomery did, that when faced with rejection "the first, last, and middle lesson—Never give up!"

If you had a time machine and traveled back to the early 1900s when Montgomery was creating her novels, you

Anne learns, as Montgomery did, that when faced with rejection "the first, last, and middle lesson—Never give up!"

would find her writing every day. When she did not physically have pen in hand, "she wrote in her head." Harry Bruce, author of *Maud: The Life of L. M. Montgomery,* believes that it was more than just a strong will that drove her and that she wrote as a retreat from boredom and fear. According to Bruce's biography of her, Montgomery once said that writing was a method of soul cultivation and that you should "write something every day, even if you burn it up after writing it" (p. 130). In a *Contemporary Authors* article Montgomery is quoted as saying, "To write has always been my central purpose around which every effort and hope and ambition of my life has grouped itself" (p. 312).

> *Montgomery once said that writing was a method of soul cultivation and that you should "write something every day, even if you burn it up after writing it."*

The Anne Series

Imagination is a key to Anne Shirley's whimsical personality. It is an active theme throughout the sequels. The eleven-year-old Anne in *Anne of Green Gables* possesses the power to make ordinary things special, such as finding friends in glass reflections. She is often alone, but because of her ability to create her world through imagery, she is never lonely. *Anne of Windy Poplars* (1936) allows Anne the freedom to share her gift of imagination with Little Elizabeth, a lonely next-door neighbor. The two of them invent a fairy-tale land called Tomorrow, where everything is perfect. Little Elizabeth's life is controlled by a tyrannical grandmother and aided by someone referred to only as the Woman. Imagination is her key to survival. Anne helps her to unlock the dreariness in the world of Today, where Elizabeth is miserable, and see that life can be happy in reality as well as in dreams. Anne's children in *Anne of Ingleside* (1939) have the same power of imagination. Nan, one of her daughters, concocts lives for the Glen St. Mary folks, lives that they would never dream of living. The Glen people, thanks to Nan, have imaginary lives in which they have secret love affairs and perform sinister acts of evil. Nan's life is never dull, thanks to her ability to pretend.

The power of friendship is important in the *Anne* series. Names such as "kindred spirits" and "the race that knows Joseph" are used to represent true and lasting friendships. Anne has many kindred spirits and learns in *Anne's House of Dreams* (1917) how to belong to the race that knows Joseph.

imagery words or phrases that appeal to one or more of the five senses in order to create a mental picture

The circle of friends that surround Anne Shirley sustain her. They allow her the freedom to be romantic, to dream, to be herself. Anne's hunger for a true friend in her early days at Green Gables is found in Diana Barry. The bond that the two young girls form in childhood lasts throughout their lives. They share heartache and joy and name their children after one another. The first true adult friendship Anne forms is with Leslie, in *Anne's House of Dreams*. They become soul mates and confidants.

theme central message about life in a literary work

Grief is another theme found in Montgomery's novels. The world that Anne Shirley lives in is, for the most part, one of happiness. But as in any life, sadness enters in. In *Anne of Green Gables,* Matthew, Anne's adoptive parent, dies. It is the first time the young orphan is able to remember the death of a loved one. Ruby Gillis, a childhood friend, faces the Grim Reaper in *Anne of the Island* (1915). Anne realizes that sometimes young people, who have their life in front of them, die. Captain Jim, a man that Anne respects enough to name her son after him, dies, or "passes the bar", as he calls it in *Anne's House of Dreams*. The greatest grief that Anne suffers, however, is caused by losing her firstborn child in *Anne's House of Dreams*. The loss changes Anne. She matures and, to a degree, the death produces a bitterness that never fully goes away. She no longer has the carefree, sunny personality she has always shown the world.

Anne of Green Gables (1985) and *Anne of Avonlea* (1987), the sequel, are wonderful film adaptations of the novels about Anne Shirley. Megan Follows plays the role of Anne.

Emily, Pat, and Other Characters

Although Montgomery is most noted for her novels about Anne Shirley, she wrote many other books with characters that are just as memorable. The plots of Montgomery's stories center on young girls who grow into maturity. There are common threads throughout her writings. Anne loves Green Gables more than anything or anyplace. She never feels at home anywhere else, except Ingleside, her home after she is married. Pat in *Pat of Silverbush* (1933) is no different. She believes Silverbush to be the most beautiful place on earth and hates to leave it even for a night. In the trilogy about Emily, her home, New Moon, earns a lasting commitment from the young girl. Anne, Pat, and Emily feel that their homes are more than houses. Inanimate objects come to life, and the girls often view the things in their homes as friends.

trilogy a series of three literary works that are closely related and share a single theme

They believe the rooms they occupy are able to love them and welcome them home after an absence.

Similarities among the books do not end with the love the characters feel for their homes. Prince Edward Island is always the setting, and nature plays a major part. Jane in *Jane of Lantern Hill* (1937), like Anne, enjoys being outside. The open sky and rolling hills offer peace and give her an opportunity "to get back into herself" (p. 99). Emily, in *Emily Climbs* (1925), swears that the trees and hills love her. She feels a kinship with them as much as she does with her family. Anne, from the *Green Gables* series, cannot wait to walk down Lover's Lane or under the White Way of Delight. The beauty of nature astounds her. If Jane, Anne, or Emily leave, they long to return. The countryside beckons them home like a loving parent or friend.

By naming the things that surround them, the characters are able to give the objects life. Nothing escapes being called something special. Marilla's geranium in *Anne of Green Gables* becomes Bonnie, and an ordinary pond is called the Lake of Shining Waters. Tipsy is the name that Jane, from *Jane of Lantern Hill,* gives her teakettle; Mr. Muffet is the frying pan, and Polly is the dishpan. The Emily books are full of things Emily has named. She has a Land of Uprightness which, for all intents and purposes, is a simple valley with a steep wooded hill. The sound of the wind becomes a person when Emily names it the Wind Woman, and dreams are dreamt on the Tomorrow Road.

The characters that populate Montgomery's novels are loyal to their families. They cherish and respect them and are willing to make personal sacrifices to help their loved ones. When Matthew dies in *Anne of Green Gables,* Anne refuses to attend Queens, a college designed to train students for the teaching profession. She decides instead to stay home and help Marilla with the farm. Pat, in *Pat of Silverbush,* gives up her plans to teach after her mother becomes ill. Both girls have a sense of obligation and love for their families that outweighs anything else in their lives. They learn from their relatives, and Emily in *Emily Climbs* realizes "that you may fight with your kin—disapprove of them—even hate them, but that there is a bond between you for all that," and that "blood is always thicker than water" (p. 282).

Orphans play an important role in Montgomery's books, perhaps because Montgomery herself was orphaned. Anne

Shirley is adopted by Matthew and Marilla at age eleven. Emily, in *Emily of New Moon* (1923), is taken in by an aunt when her parents die. Jingle, or Hillary, as he wants to be called when he accepts the fact that his mother does not want him, is being raised by an uncle in *Pat of Silverbush*. Little Elizabeth in *Anne of Windy Poplars* is abandoned by her father after her mother's death. Even Jane, in *Jane of Lantern Hill,* for a while is ignored by her mother and father, and her upbringing is left in the hands of an unkind grandmother. Despite their sad beginnings, happy endings for the orphaned children are common. They all find love, either by being reunited with their parents or learning to care for the adoptive family with whom they live.

Religion and prayer are vital to the plots of Montgomery's novels. When Anne is scolded by Marilla for not saying her prayers in *Anne of Green Gables,* she responds by saying that she was told that God had made her hair red on purpose and that she had not had any use for him since. Once she realizes, however, that God can be kind, she learns to depend on and love him. She teaches her children in *Anne of Ingleside* to draw strength from God and to never think of him as vengeful or hateful. For all her spiritual growth, she reverts back to her early feelings about God when her firstborn child dies in *Anne's House of Dreams*. Anne does not understand how God could take a baby's life and believes him to be selfish. She eventually overcomes her feelings of anger and blame and learns to love God again.

Romance is a hard subject for the protagonists in Montgomery's books to understand. They fantasize about who their Prince Charming should be and how he should look and behave. The boys they know are unable to come close. Pat, in *Pat of Silverbush,* recognizes that Jingle is a wonderful friend but has a difficult time seeing him as anything else. He vows at the end of the book that he will have her. Even though Montgomery does not continue the story by writing a sequel, you have a feeling that if she had, Jingle would have won Pat's heart. Gilbert, throughout the *Anne* series, declares his love for Anne, but she thinks of him only as a chum. He is determined to win her love and, through persistence, does. By the second book of the *Emily* trilogy, Emily is beginning to believe that Teddy, a childhood pal, may possibly be someone she can care for and love. Montgomery seems to be saying that friendship often results in love.

All Montgomery's characters hate change. Pat loves everything about Silverbush and hates to see it altered in any way. The trees that surround the house are her friends, and she weeps when one has to be cut. The paper on the walls is frayed and needs to be removed, but Pat cannot stand to think of the change that would come from taking it off. She learns that time passes, and that change must occur. The girls and young women of Montgomery's novels grow physically, mentally, and emotionally and become different from what they were. Montgomery, however, remains true to her descriptions of the beautiful landscapes of Prince Edward Island, her characters' strong and vivacious personalities, and what life is like for girls growing up in the early 1900s. You will laugh with them, for them, and sometimes at them and cry about their sorrow. Montgomery weaves tales of sadness and joy, success and failure. She makes you love the people that live between the pages of her books and leaves you wanting to know more about them.

> *The girls and young women of Montgomery's novels grow physically, mentally, and emotionally and become different from what they were.*

Selected Bibliography

WORKS BY L. M. MONTGOMERY

Anne of Green Gables (1908)

Anne of Avonlea (1909)

The Story Girl (1911)

Chronicles of Avonlea (1912)

Anne of the Island (1915)

Anne's House of Dreams (1917)

The Watchman, and Other Poems (1917)

Rainbow Valley (1919)

Rilla of Ingleside (1921)

Emily of New Moon (1923)

Emily Climbs (1925)

Emily's Quest (1927)

Pat of Silverbush (1933)

Courageous Women (1934)

Anne of Windy Poplars, also published as *Anne of Windy Willows* (1936)

Jane of Lantern Hill (1937)

If you like L. M. Montgomery, you might also like Louisa May Alcott or Mark Twain.

Anne of Ingleside (1939)

The Alpine Path (1974)

The Doctor's Sweetheart, and Other Stories (1979)

The Selected Journals of L. M. Montgomery (1985–1987)

The Poetry of Lucy Maud Montgomery (1987)

Akin to Anne: Tales of Other Orphans (1988)

A house that many people think of as the Green Gables farmhouse, where Anne grows up in *Anne of Green Gables,* is located in Prince Edward Island National Park. For more information, you can write to:
The Department of Canadian Heritage
2 Palmers Lane
Charlottetown,
Prince Edward Island
Canada C1A5V6

WORKS ABOUT L. M. MONTGOMERY

Bruce, Harry. *Maud: The Life of L. M. Montgomery.* New York: Bantam Books, 1992.

"L. M. Montgomery." *Twentieth-Century Literary Criticism,* 1994, vol. 51, pp. 174–175.

"L(ucy) M(aud) Montgomery." *Contemporary Authors,* 1992, vol. 137, pp. 310–313.

Montgomery, L. M. "The Alpine Path: The Story of My Career." *Everywoman's World* (1917). Reprinted in *Twentieth-Century Literary Criticism,* 1994, vol. 51, p. 175+.

Rubio, Mary. "Satire, Realism, and Imagination in *Anne of Green Gables.*" *Canadian Children's Literature,* 1988. Reprinted in *Twentieth-Century Criticism,* 1994, vol. 51, pp. 182–185.

Ryan-Fisher, Bonnie. "The Magic of Believing." *Canadian Children's Literature,* 1988. Reprinted in *Twentieth-Century Literary Criticism,* 1994, vol. 51, p. 212.

Walter Dean Myers

(1937-)

by Rudine Sims Bishop

S ometime in 1940, two-year-old Walter Milton Myers arrived in Harlem on a bus, his nose running, wearing a pair of his sister's socks and a note pinned to his clothes. When he was born in Martinsburg, West Virginia, on 12 August 1937, the nation was still recovering from the Great Depression, and for many underprivileged Americans, jobs and money were still hard to come by. Before Walter's third birthday, his father, George Myers, had become a widower, and was trying to care for a large family with virtually no money. So, when Herbert Dean and his wife Florence, who had been a friend of Walter's mother, offered to take one of the little Myers boys to live with them in New York City, George Myers accepted their proposal. The adoption was informal, but Walter grew up, along with two sisters, as the Deans' child. He retained the Myers name, but when he published his second book, he paid tribute to the Deans by changing his pen name to Walter Dean Myers.

The **Great Depression** was a severe recession that began when the stock market crashed in 1929 and that lasted almost ten years. By the winter of 1932–1933, 14 to 16 million American were unemployed. Many died from a lack of food and inadequate living conditions.

387

The Deans had no way of knowing that the little boy they chose to raise would some day be one of the premier writers of books for young adults. Between 1968—when he won a writing contest for the text of his first picture book—and 1997, he published more than four dozen books, including two Newbery Honor books and four Coretta Scott King Award winners. His work includes not only picture books and novels for young adults, but poetry, history, and biography as well. The Margaret A. Edwards Award honored four of his novels: *Hoops, Fallen Angels, Motown and Didi,* and *Scorpions.*

Growing Up in Harlem

Harlem during Myers' childhood was an exciting place to live, the cultural capital of Black America. The Church of the Master, near his home, was important both as a religious center and as a community center. It had a gym for basketball games and dances, a summer Bible school, and a Sunday school all year. There were parks and playgrounds nearby and outdoor city games to play. There was enough of a sense of community in the neighborhood that adults felt responsible for all the children. On Sunday mornings, the Sunday school teacher would collect the young children and march them to the church two by two, holding hands and singing "Jesus Loves Me" to mark the time and set the proper mood.

Although his childhood at home and in the neighborhood was generally happy, Myers had his share of problems. From the time he was very young, he had difficulty enunciating certain speech sounds. He does not, to this day, have a label for the difficulty, nor has it completely disappeared. It was not until he started school that his speech became a problem. Children made fun of him, and in frustration and anger he lashed out. By the time he was in fourth grade, his behavior was such a problem that the teachers tried to have him suspended from school indefinitely. An appendectomy precluded the need for suspension, and the next year he went to fifth grade in a new school.

His foster parents were the first ones to introduce him to books, and he had already learned to read before he went to school. His foster father had told him stories, and his foster

enunciate to pronounce clearly

appendectomy the surgery in which the appendix is removed

mother, who had very little formal education herself, had taught him at home and listened as he read *True Romance* magazines to her while she did household chores. Nevertheless, Myers credits his fifth grade teacher, Mrs. Conway, with teaching him to love books. One day, when she caught him reading a comic book, she tore it up. But the next day she brought him what she considered some good books. With those books and the library, Myers found a refuge.

Mrs. Conway also was responsible for getting Myers started as a writer. She required that her students read aloud to the class, a minor torture for Myers. Recognizing the difficulty, she permitted him to write his own material. He created poems that avoided the speech sounds that he could not pronounce. His interest in poetry continued, and his first published work as an adult was a poem in honor of his daughter, Karen. In some of his later work he has returned to writing poetry.

It was not until high school, however, that Myers even considered the possibility of becoming a writer. Ms. Liebow, his English teacher, gave each of her students an individualized reading list. Myers devoured his, often skipping school and spending the day in the park up in a tree reading or writing. Ms. Liebow also recognized Myers' writing talents and encouraged him to pursue his writing. School in general, however, was mostly an unsatisfying experience. He finally dropped out at age seventeen and joined the army.

When Myers came home from the army, a veteran at twenty, he worked at a series of unfulfilling jobs, married, and started raising a family. He also continued to write. At first he thought he wanted to write like the European writers whose works he had read in high school, but when he discovered the work of Langston Hughes and James Baldwin, both of whom wrote about Harlem, he realized that he could write about his own neighborhood and about life experiences similar to his own.

Langston Hughes (1902–1967) was an African American poet. His poetry expressed pride in African Americans and used the rhythms of black music. **James Baldwin** (1924–1987) was an African American novelist, essayist, and playwright. His works focused on interracial conflict and struggle.

Remembering the Good Times

The Harlem where Myers grew up, the one he remembers and portrays affectionately in his early novels, was a gentler, happier place than the Harlem generally portrayed in contemporary media. Four of those early novels—*Fast Sam,*

Cool Clyde, and Stuff (1975), *Mojo and the Russians* (1977), *The Young Landlords* (1979), and *Won't Know Till I Get There* (1982)—are humorous accounts of the escapades of groups of young people who get themselves in and out of trouble, support each other when the going is rough, and generally try to do the right thing.

Myers' talent was recognized early in his career. *Fast Sam,* his first novel, was cited as an American Library Association Best Books for Young Adults, as was *The Young Landlords.* Critical response to his early novels pointed to what would become accepted as among Myers' greatest strengths as a writer: his ear for dialogue, his ability to create likable and sympathetic characters, and his ability to write humorously. Many of the themes that recur in his work are evident in these early works as well: African Americans helping each other, the relationships of fathers and sons, the importance of friendship, and the peer group as a small supportive community.

These characteristics are notable in *The Mouse Rap* (1990). The Mouse is fourteen-year-old Frederick Douglas, who lives in Harlem and loves basketball. He and several of his friends become involved in the search for the loot from a 1930s bank heist, rumored to have been left in an abandoned building. Meanwhile, his father, who is separated from his mother, is doing his best to work his way back into the family.

Each chapter begins with a rap, such as this one, which opens the book:

> *Ka-phoomp! Ka-phoomp! Da Doom Da Doom!*
>
> . . .
>
> You can call me Mouse, 'cause that's my tag
> I'm into it all, everything's my bag
> You know I can run, you know I can hoop
> I can do it alone, or in a group. (P. 3)

discourse conversation

style a distinctive manner of expression

One of Myers' most notable skills is his knack for capturing the way urban African American teenagers, especially boys, often talk to each other. Even if the specific expressions threaten to become outdated, the flavor of their talking—the bragging, exaggerating, and image making—does not. These kinds of oral expressions come out of traditional African American discourse styles. Myers often uses this style in the voices of both his narrators and his other characters. This is particularly true when the narrator is the main character, as in *The Mouse Rap*. Here is Mouse introducing himself to the reader:

> Me, I can hoop. I can definitely hoop. I ain't jamming but I'm scamming. You may look great but you will look late. You got the ball against me and you blink and all you got left is the stink because I got the ball and gone. I played one on one with my shadow and my shadow couldn't keep up. (P. 7)

It is easy to undervalue this kind of language, partly because what is current changes so quickly. But this language is the reflection of an important aspect of African American culture, and for young urban African American men, one of the ways they establish themselves among their peers.

Typical of Myers' early humorous novels, *The Mouse Rap* includes a cast of characters that represents a mix of ages (teenagers, their parents, and their grandparents) and of sociocultural groups (African American, white, and Mexican American). Equally typical, Myers treats his characters with sympathy and affection.

It is possible to criticize *The Mouse Rap* and Myers' other humorous novels as lacking credibility, but Myers has a good sense of drama, knows how to keep a story moving, and in spite of some serious underlying themes, is playing strictly for laughs. These books are farcical, full of exaggerated comedy, and meant to be enjoyed.

> *Myers has a good sense of drama, knows how to keep a story moving, and in spite of some serious underlying themes, is playing strictly for laughs.*

Urban Realities: On the Darker Side

With his third novel, *It Ain't All for Nothin'* (1978), Myers began to portray some of the darker realities that some city dwellers face. Cited as an American Library Association Notable Book, it is the story of Tippy, who, when his grandmother becomes ill, is forced to live with his father, a weak minor criminal with no parenting skills. Later came *Hoops* (1981) and its sequel, *The Outside Shot* (1984), both concerned with a young man trying to use basketball as a way to a good life. *Motown and Didi* (1984), an urban love story, won the Coretta Scott King Award. *Crystal* (1987) is the story of a teenage model who experiences both the glamour and corruption of modeling and must ultimately decide who and what she wants to be. One of the important features of these books is that they are hopeful. Even when his characters are unsympathetic, as is the father in *It Ain't All for Nothin'*, Myers treats them with compassion. In the end it is clear that, even under the worst of circumstances, the characters do have choices, and they must take responsibility for the decisions they make. The reader is also left with the impression that the characters will survive, partly because of their own strength and partly because they have the support of at least one other individual.

Scorpions (1988), a Newbery Honor Book, seems somewhat less hopeful; there is no sense of certainty about the fate of its characters. It reflects the kind of change that time has brought to Myers' old neighborhood. The two boys at its center, Jamal and his best friend Tito, are twelve, but the days of Fast Sam are long gone; whatever innocence these boys have at the beginning of the book, they lose as the story unfolds. Jamal's older brother Randy is in jail, having been involved in a robbery with some members of his gang, the Scorpions. Over Tito's protests, Jamal is persuaded by one of Randy's friends to accept a gun and try to lead the Scorpions as they attempt to acquire money to pay for Randy's appeal. Inevitably, the gun leads to tragedy, and although the boys both survive, their childhood is gone, and their relationship has suffered irreparable damage.

Although there are touches of humor in *Scorpions*, it is mostly a serious statement about what can happen when poor and powerless young people turn to drugs and guns as the means to money and power. The honing of Myers' craft is apparent in this novel. His characters are not only likable, they are memorable. His own compassion for them is strong enough to make his readers care deeply about these two boys. His ear for dialogue remains unerring, even though he has moved away from a first-person narrator and the hip talk of the older teenagers found in his humorous novels. His portrait of the city and the environment in which the boys are trying to survive is vivid. The city is no longer a backdrop; it is almost a character itself. And, in spite of its somewhat open ending, *Scorpions* makes clear that survival is at least possible, a theme prevalent in African American literature.

first-person narrator a speaker or character in the story who tells the story using the pronoun "I"

Somewhere in the Darkness

Even in his humorous novels, Myers often explores father-son relationships. In *Somewhere in the Darkness* (1992), the relationship between a son and his father is the central theme. Crab, Jimmy's father, shows up at the home Jimmy shares with his foster mother, lying that he has been paroled from prison, where he has spent time for armed robbery and homicide. He and Jimmy set out together on an odyssey, Crab in search of vindication, Jimmy in search of a father and, ultimately, himself.

Somewhere in the Darkness, the second of Myers' Newbery Honor Books, was highly acclaimed. Hazel Rochman says in the 1 February 1992 *Booklist* that "Myers has never written better. . . . The scenes are cinematic, taut. . . . The main characters are drawn with quiet intensity. . . . As in *Scorpions,* Myers allows no sentimentality, no quick fix of self-esteem. Jimmy's hope is that he has a loving foster mother to return to and a chance to break from his own prison dreams" (p. 1028).

Fallen Angels

If *Somewhere in the Darkness* is cinematic, *Fallen Angels* (1988) is almost a script for a movie. In fact, Myers uses movies as an extended metaphor that recurs several times in this riveting story that contrasts the actual horror of war with the romanticized visions of old Hollywood movies. Myers did not fight in the Vietnam War. He did, however, lose a brother to that war, and his experiences in the military along with his strong feelings about war made it possible for him to create a novel that transports the reader into the "hours of boredom and seconds of terror" that define war for Richard Perry. Perry is a teenager from Harlem who shares nearly exact life experiences and characteristics with Myers, although the book is not autobiographical. *Fallen Angels* also recalls, in some respects, his early novels; the humorous discourse of Perry's friend Peewee and the camaraderie of the squad members are finely tuned echoes of similar elements in those books. *Fallen Angels* is, however, a singular achievement, comparable to several novels of war and coming-of-age that have become classics.

metaphor a figure of speech in which one thing is referred to as something else, for example, "My love is a rose"

camaraderie a spirit of friendliness

> Fallen Angels *is a singular achievement, comparable to several novels of war and coming-of-age that have become classics.*

African American Culture and History

Myers has a strong interest in African American history and culture, and he has produced a number of books, fiction and nonfiction, reflecting that interest. *Now Is Your Time! The African American Struggle for Freedom* (1991) is a nonfiction work that combines history, biography, and a bit of Myers' own genealogy to tell the story of African Americans from Africa to the present. *The Glory Field* (1994) is a novel that follows one African American family for 250 years, from the Middle Passage (the forced voyage of enslaved Africans to America) to the present. *Brown Angels: An Album of Pictures and Verse* (1993) features old photographs of African American children, accompanied by original verses. It marks Myers' return to publishing poetry.

Myers' interests and writings continue to deepen and expand. The father of three grown children, Myers is also a grandfather. He lives in Jersey City, New Jersey, where he writes full-time. He considers that if he can produce ten pages a day, he has done a good day's work. His major contribution to literature for young adults has been to illuminate the lives and history of African Americans and to do so with humor and affection as well as with seriousness and great skill. In the process, he offers to readers of any social group insight into the human experiences and emotions that connect us all.

If you like the works of Walter Dean Myers, you might also enjoy the works of Maya Angelou, Larry Bograd, and Brenda Wilkinson.

Selected Bibliography

WORKS BY WALTER DEAN MYERS

Novels

Fast Sam, Cool Clyde, and Stuff (1975)

Brainstorm, photographs by Chuck Freedman (1977)

Mojo and the Russians (1977)

It Ain't All for Nothin' (1978)

The Young Landlords (1979)

Hoops (1981)

The Legend of Tarik (1981)

Won't Know Till I Get There (1982)

The Nicholas Factor (1983)

Tales of a Dead King (1983)

Motown and Didi (1984)

The Outside Shot (1984)

Adventure in Granada (1985)

The Hidden Shrine (1985)

Ambush in the Amazon (1986)

Duel in the Desert (1986)

Sweet Illusions (1986)

Crystal (1987)

Fallen Angels (1988)

Me, Mop, and the Moondance Kid (1988)

Scorpions (1988)

The Mouse Rap (1990)

The Righteous Revenge of Artemis Bonner (1992)

Somewhere in the Darkness (1992)

The Glory Field (1994)

Picture Books

The Dragon Takes a Wife, illustrated by Ann Grifalconi (1972). Reissued/revised with illustrations by Fiona French (1995).

The Golden Serpent, illustrated by Alice and Martin Provensen (1980).

Nonfiction

Now Is Your Time! The African American Struggle for Freedom (1991)

Malcolm X: By Any Means Necessary (1993)

Poetry

"Migration." In *The Great Migration: An American Story.* Paintings by Jacob Lawrence (1992).

Brown Angels: An Album of Pictures and Verse (1993)

"History of My People." In *Soul Looks Back in Wonder* by Tom Feelings (1993).

"Glorious Angels" (1995)

WORKS ABOUT WALTER DEAN MYERS

Bishop, Rudine Sims. *Presenting Walter Dean Myers.* Boston: Twayne, 1990.

How to Write to the Author
Walter Dean Myers
c/o Scholastic, Inc.
555 Broadway
New York, NY 10012

Commire, Anne, ed. *Something About the Author.* Detroit: Gale Research, 1985, vol. 41, pp. 152–155.

Rochman, Hazel. Review of *Somewhere in the Darkness. Booklist,* 1 February 1992, p. 1028.

Sarkissian, Adele, ed., *Something about the Author Autobiography Series,* Detroit: Gale Research, 1986, vol. 2, pp. 143–156.

Phyllis Reynolds Naylor

(1933-   )

by Lois Thomas Stover

Since 1965, Phyllis Reynolds Naylor has published eighty-five books, eighty of which are for children and young adults, and she lists at least ten works as "in progress." That is quite a publication record, one indicating the tremendous contribution that she has made to literature for children and young adults. In addition, she wrote regular columns for twenty-five years for various church publications, contributed numerous essays and short stories to magazines such as *Highlights* and *Jack and Jill,* and worked as an editorial assistant writing columns for the National Education Association. Unlike many authors who have taught school, worked as counselors, or made their living through avenues other than writing, Naylor has supported herself as a professional writer since 1960.

Not only is Naylor more than unusually prolific, her work has consistently received critical acclaim. She was awarded the John Newbery Medal for *Shiloh* (1991) in 1992. Many of her titles have been selected as American Library Association

prolific   marked by producing many works

"Notable Books for Young Adults," several have received recognition as "Notable Children's Book in the Field of Social Studies." Others have been selected as Junior Literary Guild selections, and *Night Cry* (1984) won the Edgar Allan Poe Award from the Mystery Writers of America in 1985.

Family Background

Naylor, born on 4 January 1933 in Anderson, Indiana, the daughter of Eugene, who worked in sales and moved often, and Lura, a teacher, had little sense of "home" as a place when she was growing up. Her family moved frequently throughout the Midwest, but no matter where her family lived, they remained deeply religious, and reading was always an important part of their lives. She describes, in *How I Came to Be a Writer* (1978), how delicious it was to shiver when her mother read James Whitcomb Riley's "Little Orphan Annie," and how she and her siblings read favorite titles such as Egermeier's *Bible Story Book, Grimms' Fairy Tales,* the complete Mark Twain, and a collection of Sherlock Holmes stories, as well as *Collier's Encyclopedia* over and over again. This early delight in reading has continued throughout her life, and references to the literary classics permeate her work; her characters frequently quote authors from Shakespeare to Plutarch to Chief Joseph.

From her experiences as a reader grew Naylor's desire to write. As early as first grade Naylor was dictating her own stories to her mother, and by fifth grade she was "on call" as the school's writer, being asked, on the spur of the moment, to carry out such duties as generating a poem to celebrate the principal's birthday. At age ten, she wrote little books of her own—a whole series of mysteries with titles like *Penny and the Mystery of the Secret Relics* on the back of any available scrap paper. When she was sixteen, she sold "Mike's Hero" to *Boys and Girls Comrade* for $4.67, and that was the start of her career.

Another constant in Naylor's young life was vacationing during the summers on farms in Iowa and rural Maryland. In Iowa, Naylor stayed with one set of grandparents she characterizes as rather staid and conservative; in Maryland, Naylor visited with her other grandparents, a pastor and a midwife. These two locales feature prominently in her books.

James Whitcomb Riley (1849–1916) was an Indiana poet. There are articles about Mark Twain and William Shakespeare in volume 3.

Plutarch (around A.D. 46–120) was a Greek biographer. **Chief Joseph** (1840?–1904) was a noble American Indian chief who fought many battles against the U.S. Army. He was known for his skillful retreat in 1877, which saved the lives of many Nez Perce Indians.

The Role of Religion

The religious environment she experienced in both these rural households permeates her work. She originally wrote primarily for the Sunday school market, learning how to craft a plot while dealing explicitly with religious issues. Before she attempted her first novel, she wrote several collections of short stories for the Christian press portraying young people learning moral lessons about how to live with diabetes, for example, or about how to feel better about themselves by helping others in need. In her novels, Naylor describes faith healers and itinerant preachers, scripture races, "Bible bees," and revival meetings in great detail, pointing out a few of the contradictions and difficulties that some of her characters come to perceive as inherent in the belief structure of Christian fundamentalism and exploring the kinds of questions young people have about the nature of organized religion.

itinerant traveling from place to place

In some of Naylor's books, a pastor is a significant positive force in the main character's life, helping him or her to accept the cards life has dealt and to search honestly for answers to genuine questions of faith, as Evie's father does in *A String of Chances* (1982). In *Maudie in the Middle* (1988) the power of religion to bind a family together is lovingly portrayed in a tender scene in which Maudie's mother washes Maudie's feet. Some of the concepts associated with Christianity—a positive work ethic, tolerance, and having faith in something larger than oneself—can all be found throughout her writing.

Some of the concepts associated with Christianity—a positive work ethic, tolerance, and having faith in something larger than oneself—can all be found throughout her writing.

Use of Autobiography

Naylor now makes her home in suburban Bethesda, Maryland, where she lives with Rex, her husband of thirty-five years, who is a speech pathologist, and two cats. She and Rex have two grown sons.

There are many incidents in Naylor's books that reflect her experiences as a wife and mother. *In Small Doses* (1979), for instance, is a collection of humorous essays about family life, and the 1993 novel *The Grand Escape* features her feline family members. However, much of her writing derives from the difficult eight years she spent as caretaker for her first husband, a brilliant man who began to exhibit signs of serious mental illness shortly after their marriage, when she was eighteen.

Crazy Love: An Autobiographical Account of Marriage and Madness (1977) chronicles Naylor's relationship with her first husband and shows the tremendous pressure Naylor felt to write both as a way to support herself and her husband while paying for his medical treatments and as a way to maintain a sense of self while her husband was losing his. In *How I Came to Be a Writer,* Naylor describes the effect of his illness on her way of life. Her husband had been accepted into a doctoral program in mathematics, but one day, while they were living in Chicago, he announced that his professors were trying to kill him. Thus began several years of agony. She writes: "For the next three years, as we moved from state to state, hospital to hospital, I wrote in earnest and in panic to support us. Sometimes I would take a whole afternoon and go off to a remote spot just to brainstorm—writing down ideas however they occurred to me until I finally had a list of plots to see me through the next few months" (*How I Came to Be a Writer,* p. 54).

Finally Naylor lost all hope that her husband could ever recover from his paranoid schizophrenia and decided to file for divorce. Although it was a difficult process, because at that time the divorce laws of most states demanded that he be declared incurable by several doctors, she did succeed. While she was waiting for her divorce, she finished her undergraduate degree in psychology at American University, committed herself to a career as a writer, and fell in love with Rex Naylor, whom she married in 1960.

paranoid schizophrenia a mental disorder characterized by unpredictable disturbances in thinking. This behavior may be caused by the supposed hostility of others.

Naylor's experiences with her first husband provided the insights and emotions she later explored in *The Keeper* (1987). In this novel, Nick, an adolescent, watches helplessly at first as his father becomes distrustful, then paranoid, and finally buys a gun and threatens others with it. *The Keeper* received a great deal of critical acclaim for Naylor's ability to capture the complexity of Nick's thoughts and feelings during this very difficult time in his life. It was even adapted for television as the 1989 Afterschool Special "My Dad Can't Be Crazy . . . Can He?" starring Loretta Swit as Nick's mom.

A Wide Variety of Books

Naylor writes in many genres. *The Keeper* is one of her many realistic, slice-of-life "problem" novels written for young adults. She offers advice to children in books such as *Getting*

Along with Your Teachers (1981) or *Getting Along in Your Family* (1976), and she gives insight to young adults on *How to Find Your Wonderful Someone, How to Keep Him/Her If You Do, and How to Survive If You Don't* (1972). She also writes mysteries, such as *Night Cry,* and the humorous "Bessledorf Hotel" books. Her two "Witch" trilogies demonstrate Naylor's ability to write suspenseful books about the supernatural.

Naylor's "York Trilogy" books, *Shadows on the Wall* (1980), *Faces in the Water* (1981), and *Footprints at the Window* (1981), involve time travel. Dan moves back and forward in time, from the days of the Roman dominance at York to the age of the Black Plague to today, learning through his encounters with a gypsy family in various eras how to cope with the uncertainties of his present-day situation. His life is complicated by the inability of medical science to determine whether his father will begin to deteriorate as a result of Huntington's disease—a genetic illness that mimics chronic alcoholism and that does not manifest itself until adulthood. The York novels clearly illustrate Naylor's desire to use art "to emulate life with all its risks" and to face "problems on paper where they're not so threatening, looking for my own strengths, deciding how, or even whether, I could cope" (*How I Came to Be a Writer,* pp. 105–106).

Enormous Difficulties and Minor Crises

In general, Naylor is praised for her ability to create believable characters and dialogue; to write convincingly from a young adult's point of view; and to demonstrate empathy for the needs, interests, and feelings of her characters. In particular, Naylor's books for young adults show her sensitivity to the problems with which adolescents continually wrestle as they strive to achieve a sense of identity and self-esteem and to take responsibility for their futures.

In many of Naylor's books, the characters have to face enormous difficulties. For example, Evie is spending the summer with her cousin and her husband, helping Donna Jean to care for their newborn son, who dies of crib death (sudden infant death syndrome) in *A String of Chances.* In *Send No Blessings* (1990), Beth's younger sister becomes pregnant, and Beth learns that her father is illiterate. Doug, in *The Fear Place* (1994), has to overcome his fear of heights if he and his brother are to survive in the wilderness. In *The Dark of the Tunnel* (1985), Craig's mother is dying of cancer and his uncle is under fire as the leader of a civil defense practice drill that increasingly illustrates the lack of government planning for the advent of nuclear war. Naylor's books also frequently show her concern about significant social issues. She has written about race relations, nuclear war, the destructive and unsafe practices of coal mining companies, abusive parents, and homelessness.

In addition to her skill in reflecting the realities of contemporary society, Naylor is also adept at portraying the equally real but rather minor crises that fill our daily lives. For example, Patrick asks Alice to dinner at his parents' country club in *Alice in Rapture, Sort of* (1989), and Alice has no idea what to wear, how to order, or which fork to use when; and George from *The Year of the Gopher* (1987) has to deal with an older female boss who would like to be more friendly with him than he likes.

> *Naylor has provided comfort to many readers who know, through Alice, that they are not alone in their panic over how their breath smells before an impending first kiss or in their need to hide from a new boyfriend the new perm that has made their hair smell weird and look worse.*

Humor

Perhaps Naylor is most widely known and valued by readers of all ages for the sense of humor with which she describes everyday problems. She has provided comfort to many readers who know, through Alice, that they are not alone in their panic over how their breath smells before an impending first kiss or in their need to hide from a new boyfriend the new perm that has made their hair smell weird and look worse. Often her humor is derived from an exaggeration of an awkward situation. For example, Jed, from *Wrestle the Mountain* (1971), challenges a neighbor girl to hide in the trunk of his sister's boyfriend's car so they can spy on the two lovebirds during a date. But it turns out that on this particular night, the couple is eloping, and Jed and company are in over their heads.

Naylor often combines humor with poignancy. Readers share the painful but funny embarrassment of George, in *The Year of the Gopher,* who realizes that the girl of his high school fantasies has been able to hear him singing at the top of his lungs in an elevator; or the acute discomfort Alice feels when she learns that the boys are calling the girls by the names of states based on the way in which their developing bust lines compare to the topography of that locale. Readers of *Alice in April* (1993) wonder, along with Alice and her friends, who will be Colorado and who, to their horror, will be Iowa?

Dialogue

Another of Naylor's skills is her ear for dialogue and dialect, which contribute to her development of characters. She is as much at ease with the giggling phone conversations of seventh-grade girls featured in the "Alice" books as she is with the after-prom dissection of sexual encounters among high school senior boys in *The Year of the Gopher*.

In *Unexpected Pleasures* (1986), which she describes as a novel for young adults but which is marketed for adults, Naylor alternates points of view. In *The Craft of Writing the Novel* (1989), Naylor describes why she uses this strategy. In the chapters narrated by April Ruth, a scrappy sixteen year old living on her own, the use of the first person allows her to show readers that April Ruth has a good heart but is impulsive, saying the first thing that pops into her mind. Naylor switches to third person when Foster Williams, a thirty-two-year-old bridge worker, takes the stage because that strategy helps the reader feel some distance from Foster, which is appropriate because Foster is shy and reserved.

Themes

Several themes permeate Naylor's work, whether she is writing for young children, students in the elementary grades, teenagers, or adults. The importance of work, of being constructive and useful, is a key theme in many of Naylor's books even when it is not central to the plot development. In *Wrestle the Mountain, Send No Blessings, A String of Chances,* and *The Year of the Gopher* the main characters are focused on finding a way to make a living in the future, and in so doing, to craft an identity for themselves independent of their family's vision of them.

The importance of community is also a common theme expressed in Naylor's work. She has been active in various projects and groups, such as the Council for a Liveable World, NAACP, and Zero Population Growth, responding to urgent social issues, and this commitment to the community is one many of her characters share. In *Wrestle the Mountain* the community finally feels hope for the future when it bands together to establish a mail order business for the local handicrafts they produce. In the "Witch" series, Mrs. Tuggle is finally defeated when the young adults, rather than continue to operate independently, join forces with their parents and with a psychologist to create a "circle of goodwill" that renders her evil harmless.

In Naylor's world, the mature individual is one who recognizes the value of family and community, accepts help when it is needed, works to make the world a better place, and accepts responsibility for his or her own future. This responsibility is exemplified in Beth, from *Send No Blessings,* who figures out that if she wants a better future for herself then she will have to study spelling and vocabulary, resist pressures from her older boyfriend to consummate their relationship, and face up to her father, who wants her to quit school and work as a waitress to help support the family.

As she says in the "The Writing of *Shiloh,*" Naylor is most interested in exploring the ways in which characters who do not have many material or educational resources deal with the problems that face them. How does Alice, a young girl without a mother, make it through the ins and outs of puberty and first boyfriends, first dates, first kisses? How can a young man like Craig from *The Dark of the Tunnel* use his talent for photography to help his community and make a better life for himself in the future? In *Shiloh* (1991), how can Marty care for his dog Shiloh when his family barely has enough food for their table and when Shiloh does, in fact, belong legally to the abusive Judd?

Writing Methods

Naylor says she still writes her first drafts in longhand on legal pads, revises at least twice, gives the manuscript to her husband for review, and then edits to make sure every word is the best possible choice. She works on many projects at once, keeping a row of three-ring binders (one for each future book), lined up in her living room, in which she jots ideas and records details and bits of conversation or plot as they come to her.

Sometimes a newspaper article will start Naylor thinking about a topic. *No Easy Circle* (1972) was born as a result of reading a piece on runaway teenagers and their lives on the streets. Sometimes she has an experience that will not let her go until she processes it through writing, as was the case with *Shiloh*. Naylor and her husband were walking in the West Virginia countryside while visiting friends when the dog that would become Shiloh latched onto them. Naylor was so concerned about the possible fate of the dog that she decided, on her husband's advice, to "do something about it," meaning write a book. Through the young boy named Marty Preston, Naylor resolved to rescue that dog.

When Naylor is not writing, she enjoys walking, singing in a madrigal group, and beachcombing. She is a member of the Author's Guild, the Society of Children's Book Writers, and the Children's Book Guild of Washington. She describes herself politically as an Independent, and she attends a Unitarian church. But she is, primarily, a writer. Unlike other authors who constantly fear their ability to break through writer's block or to find a new book inside themselves, Naylor says, in *Something about the Author,* that her biggest problem is

madrigal a song from the 1500s performed by several singers without instruments

> that there are always four or five books waiting in the wings. Scarcely am I halfway through one book than another begins to intrude. I'm happy, of course, that ideas come so easily, but it is like having a monkey on my back. I am never quite free of it. Almost everything that happens to me or to the people I know ends up in a book at some time, all mixed up, of course, with imaginings. I can't think of anything else in the world I would rather do than write. (P. 176)

She is convinced that, even on her deathbed, she will have at least five more books she wants to write!

Selected Bibliography

WORKS BY PHYLLIS REYNOLDS NAYLOR

Novels for Young Adults

To Shake a Shadow (1967)
When Rivers Meet (1968)
Making It Happen (1970)

If you enjoy books by Phyllis Reynolds Naylor, you might also enjoy the work of Judy Blume, Hadley Irwin, Zibby Oneal, and Katherine Paterson.

No Easy Circle (1972)

Walking Through the Dark (1976)

Shadows on the Wall (York Trilogy, Part I; 1980)

Faces in the Water (York Trilogy, Part II; 1981)

Footprints at the Window (York Trilogy, Part III; 1982)

A String of Chances (1982)

The Solomon System (1983)

Night Cry (1984)

The Dark of the Tunnel (1985)

The Keeper (1987)

The Year of the Gopher (1987)

Send No Blessings (1990)

Ice (1995)

THE "ALICE" SERIES

The Agony of Alice (1985)

Alice in Rapture, Sort Of (1989)

Reluctantly Alice (1991)

All But Alice (1992)

Alice in April (1993)

Alice in Between (1994)

Alice the Brave (1995)

Alice in Lace (1996)

Short-Story Collections for Young Adults

Grasshoppers in the Soup (1965)

Knee Deep in Ice Cream (1967)

Dark Side of the Moon (1969)

The Private I (1969)

Ships in the Night (1970)

A Change in the Wind (1979)

Never Born a Hero (1982)

A Triangle Has Four Sides (1984)

Children's Novels

What the Gulls Were Singing (1967)

To Make a Wee Moon (1969)

Wrestle the Mountain (1971)

To Walk the Sky Path (1973)

How Lazy Can You Get? (1979)

Eddie, Incorporated (1980)
All Because I'm Older (1981)
Beetles, Lightly Toasted (1987)
Maudie in the Middle (1988)
One of the Third Grade Thonkers (1988)
Shiloh (1991)
Josie's Troubles (1992)
The Boys Start the War (1993)
The Girls Get Even (1993)
The Grand Escape (1993)
Boys Against Girls (1994)
The Fear Place (1994)
Being Danny's Dog (1995)
Shiloh Season (1996)

THE "WITCH" SERIES
Witch's Sister (1975)
Witch Water (1977)
The Witch Herself (1978)
The Witch's Eye (1990)
Witch Weed (1991)
The Witch Returns (1992)

THE "BESSLEDORF HOTEL" SERIES
The Mad Gasser of Bessledorf Street (1983)
The Bodies in the Bessledorf Hotel (1986)
Bernie and the Bessledorf Ghost (1990)
The Face in the Bessledorf Funeral Parlor (1993)
The Bomb in the Bessledorf Bus Depot (1977)

Children's Picture Books
The New Schoolmaster (1967)
A New Year's Surprise (1967)
Meet Murdock (1969)
Jennifer Jean, Cross-Eyed Queen (1978)
The Boy With the Helium Head (1982)
Old Sadie and the Christmas Bear (1984)
The Baby, the Bed, and the Rose (1987)
Keeping a Christmas Secret (1989)
King of the Playground (1991)

Duck's Disappearing (1996)

I Can't Take You Anywhere (1997)

Short-Story Collection for Children

The Galloping Goat and Other Stories (1965)

Nonfiction for Children and Young Adults

How to Find Your Wonderful Someone, How to Keep Him/ Her If You Do, How to Survive If You Don't (1972; Young Adults)

An Amish Family (1974; Young Adults)

Getting Along in Your Family (1976; Children)

How I Came to Be a Writer (1978; Children)

Getting Along With Your Friends (1979; Children)

Getting Along With Your Teachers (1981; Children)

Fiction and Nonfiction for Adults

Crazy Love: An Autobiographical Account of Marriage and Madness (1977)

How I Came to Be a Writer (1978; 1987)

In Small Doses, humorous essays that appeared in *McCall's* and *Woman's Day* (1979)

Revelations (1979; Novel)

Unexpected Pleasures (1986; Novel)

The Craft of Writing the Novel (1989)

"The Writing of *Shiloh.*" In *Reading Teacher,* September 1992, pp. 10–12.

Audiotape

"A Talk with Phyllis Reynolds Naylor." Scarborough, N.Y.: Tim Podell Productions, 1994.

Manuscripts

Copies of all Naylor's books are in the Kerlan Collection of Walter Library at the University of Minnesota.

Works About Phyllis Reynolds Naylor

Bonetti, Kay. "Interview with Phyllis Reynolds Naylor." In *American Prose Library,* no. 7036, February 1987.

Commire, Anne, ed. *Something about the Author: Facts and Pictures about Contemporary Authors and Illustrators of Books for Young People.* Detroit: Gale Research, 1977, vol. 12, pp. 156–157.

Graham, Joyce. "An Interview with Phyllis Reynolds Naylor." In *Journal of Youth Services in Libraries,* summer 1993, pp. 392–398.

Olendorf, Donna, ed. *Something about the Author: Facts and Pictures about Authors and Illustrators of Books for Young People.* Detroit: Gale Research, 1991, vol. 66, pp. 170–176.

How to Write to the Author
Phyllis Reynolds Naylor
c/o Simon and Schuster
Children's Publishing
Division
1230 Avenue of the
Americas
New York, NY 10020

Joan Lowery Nixon

(1927-   )

by Patricia P. Kelly

J oan Lowery Nixon began writing for children, and later
for young adults, when she had two preschoolers at
home and two in school. Upon telling her children about
attending a writers' conference, the two oldest girls decided
their mother should "write a book, and it had to be a mystery, and she had to put them in it." Nixon says she had such
a good time doing it that she just kept on. She has won numerous awards from state and national associations, but her
major distinction is being the first author to win the Edgar Allan Poe Award three times: in 1980, 1981, and 1987 for, respectively, *The Kidnapping of Christina Lattimore, The
Seance,* and *The Other Side of Dark.* In addition to writing
mysteries—many of them set in Texas, where she lives—
Nixon writes historical fiction.

Quotations from Joan Lowery
Nixon that are not attributed
to a published source are from
a personal interview conducted
by the author of this article on
11 April 1995 and are
published here by permission of
Joan Lowery Nixon.

Mysteries

The Kidnapping of Christina Lattimore

The **Nancy Drew** and Hardy Boys mystery series were created by Edward Stratemeyer. There is an article about him in volume 3.

protagonist main character of a literary work

Well known for writing "light," Nancy Drew–type mysteries, Nixon began writing psychological thrillers with her first young adult novel, *The Kidnapping of Christina Lattimore* (1979). This novel, like the thrillers that followed, has strong female protagonists who, Nixon says, "think things out and take action and who are not dependent upon somebody else to do it." These female characters grow personally, while at the same time they solve a crime through a thoughtful consideration of the details. Nixon's mysteries are well crafted: the clues are openly presented along with credible misleaders. In addition to being suspenseful, she frequently deals with important concerns for young people, such as suicide or environmental issues.

The Kidnapping of Christina Lattimore, like many of Nixon's mysteries, is drawn on incidents from real life, incidents that she accumulates—clippings and ideas that she keeps in a "one-inch, legal-size pocket file" that she fills with "scraps of paper." She says, "If I get an idea about something, I'll write down as much as I can think of about it and drop it in there, cut clippings out of magazines, newspapers. There have been some instances of children of wealthy families being accused of staging their own kidnappings." In Nixon's usual "what-if" approach to developing a plot, she asked herself in this case, "What if I were the teenage daughter in a family in which we love each other very much, but we didn't communicate. It's a wealthy family, and when all of this happens to me and the kidnappers are caught and they claimed I did it, nobody believes me. What would I do? And so in answering the question I came up with a plot and how the story would work."

Christina's grandmother Cristabel controls the family with money. Her mother, who has married into money, fears losing it; her father knows that the family money helps him pursue his religious interests. The kidnapping has been cleverly planned so that if they are caught, it will appear that Christina has masterminded the whole thing. Her family is willing to forgive her, but they do not believe her. Although Kelly, an aspiring television journalist, wants to solve the case to get a big story to win a scholarship, it is Christina's thinking that solves the case. In the end Christina demonstrates her thinking and how it all adds up. Interestingly, the clue that becomes the final piece that Christina connects occurs early in the story.

In the end she rejects her family's money, claiming, "I can make it on my own" (p. 178). She plans on getting a part-time job and working her way through college in much the way that Kelly has been doing. Christina is an intelligent, independent young woman, who refuses to choose an easy path for her life.

The Other Side of Dark

In 1995 *The Other Side of Dark* (1986), another of Nixon's award-winning mysteries, was made into a successful television movie called *Awake to Danger.* In the novel, seventeen-year-old Stacy McAdams awakes from a four-year coma brought on by a gunshot suffered at the time of her mother's murder. She cannot remember the killer's face, but the killer is afraid that Stacy's memory will return. A subplot involves Stacy's coming to terms with her adult-looking body and learning all the things she has missed: how to put on makeup, trendy clothes and music, how to date, and how to drive.

Again characteristic of Nixon's independent, intelligent female characters, Stacy reacts when Jarrod corners her with a gun, saying that he always gets his own way. Stacy thinks, "I'm a woman who's able to think rationally, to want *my* own way. And I have a plan" (p. 180).

The Seance

In *The Seance* (1980) Nixon combines murder, foster care, and folklore in creating a compelling mystery. Lauren, orphaned at four and cared for by her Aunt Melvamay, becomes jealous when Sara comes to live with them, for Sara is not only beautiful, but she and Lauren also have nothing in common. A seance, initially set up to make Sara disappear in a dramatic way, results in her murder. Nixon carefully places clues to the murderer's identity while at the same time she skillfully makes other characters suspect. Lauren is determined not to be a victim, and as a result, discovers her own strength and the love of her aunt.

seance group ritual performed to communicate with the spirits of the dead

Other Thrillers

Nixon says that some of her novels contain messages relevant to young adults. For example, *Secret, Silent Screams* (1988) is about teenage suicide. She began *Shadowmaker* (1994) because she was "disturbed about the pollution in Brownsville, Texas." Throughout the novel she includes as an integral part of the story details about toxic-waste dumping and its effects. Kate Gillian's mother is an investigative reporter of environmental issues, but it is Kate who solves the murder of her friend while the sheriff persists in believing that outsiders, not boys in the town, are to blame.

integral necessary and essential

In addition to her well-crafted plots, Nixon's use of language helps generate suspense in her mysteries. In *The Other Side of Dark,* the recurrence of the killer's yellow eyes triggers Stacy's memory and her search. She recalls, "Four years ago those awful yellow cat eyes stared into mine. . . . I'll never forget those eyes!" (p. 140). With each mention of the yellow eyes, the tension builds.

Nixon's stark realism can sometimes make a reader wince. Throughout *The Specter* (1982), Julie cannot recall the face of the man who killed her father, but she insists his name is Sikes and he "is mean. . . . I told my mother the things he did to me when she wasn't there, and she said I was lying. And Sikes found out I told her, and he whipped me until my back was bleeding" (p. 95). Julie's uncertainty about the name and lack of physical description causes doubt, but her fear is real; and each mysterious encounter or mention of his name intensifies her fear.

From the first paragraph of each novel, Nixon's language creates fear and suspense, which are characteristics of psychological thrillers. For example, in chapter one of *The Dark and Deadly Pool* (1987), Mary Elizabeth's fear builds as she closes the health club for the night. Stepping to the edge of the pool, she sees:

> A shadow at the bottom of the pool, blacker than the dark water above it . . . quivered in my direction like a shimmer of lightning. I watched it come, too terrified to move, too frightened to scream, as the shadow loomed upward, ripping the water. Hands clutched at the edge of the pool, one of them grabbing the toe of my sneaker . . . and a face—eyes and mouth gaping and gasping—met my own. (P. 5)

Such use of action-filled and emotionally charged verbs creates the suspense that keeps readers turning the pages to find out what happens next.

The Orphan Train Adventures

Originally envisioned as a quartet of books describing the lives of the six Kelly children taken from New York City in the 1850s to be adopted by midwestern families, the stories of the Orphan Train Adventures have grown as the children have. A fifth novel became part of the series, with more planned. The exodus of almost a quarter million children became known as the Orphan Train, although many were not really orphans. Like the Kelly children, they were given up because a parent believed they would have a better life outside the poverty and squalor that existed at that time in New York City.

squalor filth

A Family Apart (1987) is devoted to the children's sense of abandonment, their train trip to Saint Joseph, Missouri, where families come to adopt, and the story of Frances Mary. After masquerading as a boy and then becoming involved with the Underground Railroad, Frances becomes equally loved by her family as a daughter. Dorothy M. Broderick, writing in *Children's Literature Review,* called *A Family Apart* "close to a perfect book. . . . The plot is rational and well paced; the characters are real and believable; the time setting important to U.S. history, and the values all that anyone could ask for" (p. 150).

Nixon ties the novels in the Orphan Train series together by having two children read the journal of their great-great-great-grandmother Frances Mary. She also connects the stories through references to previous occurrences, so the stories can be read in any sequence with understanding. In the second novel, *Caught in the Act* (1988), Mike is mistreated and called a thief by the family that takes him in. His life is hard before he is rescued and goes to live with an army officer. Believing a gypsy has cursed her with bad luck, Megan, the heroine of *In the Face of Danger* (1988), worries that the misfortunes of the young couple who take her in are all her fault. In *A Place to Belong* (1989), Danny plans a reunion of the family; the children see the directions their lives have taken; and their mother remarries. Mike's story, begun in *Caught in the Act,* continues in *A Dangerous Promise* (1994),

The **Battle of Wilson's Creek** took place in Missouri in 1861 during the Civil War. Missouri militiamen led by the state's pro-South governor joined with a Confederate force to defeat Union troops in a bloody battle.

when he becomes a Union drummer and is injured in the Battle of Wilson's Creek. In trying to fulfill a promise to a friend who dies, he sees both sides of the war and its ravaging of people's lives.

Nixon has carefully researched the historical period for these novels. She says, "I read and read and read, and I also go to the place that I am going to be writing about. . . . I wanted to know what it feels like to stand in the tall grass in Kansas . . . what the river looked like . . . and about St. Joseph. . . . I walked the Wilson's Creek Battlefield. . . . I'm researching even while I'm writing."

Ellis Island Series

The three Ellis Island novels are accurate fictional accounts of the American immigrant experience in the early 1890s. During the passage across the Atlantic Ocean in *Land of Hope* (1992), the three protagonists of the series meet: Rebekah Levinsky, a Jewish girl and her family who are fleeing Russia to settle in New York City; Rose Carney, an Irish girl who is joining her father and brothers in Chicago (*Land of Promise,* 1993); and Kristin Swensen, a Swedish girl whose family has bought a farm in Minnesota (*Land of Dreams,* 1994). Nixon has developed three strong female characters who succeed in different ways in their new lives and in ways that would have been impossible to do in their native countries. Throughout, Nixon makes the historical period come alive by weaving into the stories political and economic issues. The concerns are sometimes specific to particular immigrant groups, although all share the hope, expressed in *Land of Dreams,* that the United States "was a land in which more than one dream was possible" (p. 151).

Rebekah in *Land of Hope* longs to go to Columbia University. For her, America represents the opportunity to be educated, to succeed even though she is female. However, she and her family find themselves doing what's called "piecework"—each sewing clothes at home, fifteen hours a day, seven days a week. The portrait of the garment industry during this period, though bleak, is accurate. As Rebekah learns, even though conditions at home are exhausting and the work is poorly paid, "factory workers keep almost the same hours and earn much less . . . [and] factories are like death traps—no ventilation, no air or space" (p. 142).

Rebekah sees the importance of education and cannot understand why her brother Nessin refuses to attend night school. She tells him "the only way to escape the sweatshop is with an education" (p. 163). Her father eventually understands that America is different: "My daughter will make me proud with her education" (p. 169). A symbol of Rebekah's need to assimilate into the American culture is the clothing she receives at the Settlement House: a black skirt, white blouse, and straw hat that she envisions herself wearing to Columbia College.

Nixon says she chose the Irish immigrant experience for *Land of Promise* because two of her grandparents came from Ireland, and she was able to use some of her family stories indirectly in writing about Rose. Like Rebekah and other immigrants, Rose also must adapt her clothing in order to become a salesperson to earn money to bring her mother and sisters to the United States from Ireland. But more central to the story are the politics surrounding the graft in Chicago's City Hall, the social work of Jane Addams at Hull House, and the Irish Americans' support of Ireland's independence. Rose's brother Johnny and Tim, the man she loves, are both involved with raising money for the Irish cause. However, the British catch Johnny trying to smuggle money to Ireland. Against this backdrop, Jane Addams is calling for world peace and trying to show that people of all countries can live together in harmony.

Jane Addams (1860–1935), an American social activist, founded the **Hull House** neighborhood center in Chicago in 1889. She worked for rights and reforms on behalf of women, children, and the poor.

The lack of hospitalization and the early endeavors to unionize labor are authentic to the period, as well as the glimpses we get of women's roles in the family. Although Rose works long hours, she is expected to do everything to maintain the house for her father and brothers. She observes: "Cooking was ever and always a woman's lot in life . . . the whole routine . . . over and over and over again" (p. 139).

Like Kristin in *Land of Dreams*, Rose questions why women cannot vote. Both are told by men that women do not understand politics: "That's why they'll never have the vote" (*Promise*, p. 116); "Politics, government, laws . . . those are a man's concern, not a woman's" (*Dreams*, p. 75). But Kristin longs to work for women's suffrage; she hears stories of Susan B. Anthony and other university women who speak out. Her father and mother do not understand her independence and her belief that she can speak her mind as well as a man and that men should also learn to bake and clean. Her resistance to an arranged marriage causes a great

Susan B. Anthony (1820–1906) was a vigorous reformer who fought for women's **suffrage** (the right to vote). In 1872 she was arrested for attempting to vote.

deal of conflict. She has not rejected the young man, however; she has only rejected the notion that she has no choice in the matter.

Nixon's use of details makes all three novels authentic. She does a great deal of research when writing a historical novel; she says, however, that as little as "one percent" finds its way into the story. But it is that research that provides the cultural and historical details that place characters in a realistic setting. For instance, Nixon visited and read histories of Ellis Island; she studied the Jewish religion and immigration history. In that way she was able to depict the anguish that Rebekah's family feels when they must work instead of sitting shivah for seven days (shivah is the traditional Jewish mourning period); the political corruption of boodling, a process of paying off city aldermen, that Rose observes; and the belief of Kristin's mother in spöken, ghosts that do mischief throughout the house.

Conclusion

Nixon, born on 3 February 1927, is a prolific writer as well as a master of two very different forms: the psychological thriller and the historical novel. She likes developing independent, intelligent female characters, and she also takes pride in the extensive research she does that allows her to use just the right details to make a setting or situation authentic. She frequently includes social, political, or environmental issues in her plots, though these are secondary to her emphasis on telling a good story, a characteristic that keeps her readers turning the pages.

If you like the historical novels of Joan Lowery Nixon, you may want to read some of Ann Rinaldi's novels. Richard Peck's *Are You in the House Alone?* is a psychological thriller much like those of Nixon.

Selected Bibliography

WORKS BY JOAN LOWERY NIXON

Mysteries: Psychological Thrillers
The Kidnapping of Christina Lattimore (1979)
The Seance (1980)
The Specter (1982)
Days of Fear (1983)
A Deadly Game of Magic (1983)

The Ghosts of Now (1984)
The Stalker (1985)
The Other Side of Dark (1986)
The Dark and Deadly Pool (1987)
Secret, Silent Screams (1988)
Whispers from the Dead (1989)
A Deadly Promise (1992)
The Weekend Was Murder (1992)
A Candidate for Murder (1993)
The Name of the Game Was Murder (1993)
Shadowmaker (1994)

Orphan Train Adventures
A Family Apart (1987)
Caught in the Act (1988)
In the Face of Danger (1988)
A Place to Belong (1989)
A Dangerous Promise (1994)

Hollywood Daughters Trilogy
Star Baby (1989)
Encore (1990)
Overnight Sensation (1990)

Ellis Island Series
Land of Hope (1992)
Land of Promise (1993)
Land of Dreams (1994)

WORKS ABOUT JOAN LOWERY NIXON

Broderick, Dorothy M. "Joan Lowery Nixon." In *Children's Literature Review*. Edited by Gerard J. Senick. Detroit: Gale Research, 1991, vol. 24, pp. 131–154.

Contemporary Authors, New Revision Series. Detroit: Gale Research, 1993, vol. 38, 301–305.

Lystad, Mary. *Twentieth-Century Children's Writers*, 3d ed. London and Chicago: St. James Press, 1989, pp. 723–724.

Nixon, Joan Lowery. *Something About the Author Autobiography Series*. Detroit: Gale Research, 1990, vol. 9, pp. 267–284.

> **How to Write to the Author**
> Joan Lowery Nixon
> 10215 Cedar Creek Drive
> Houston, TX 77042

Scott O'Dell

(1903-1989)

by Suellen Alfred

Anyone interested in stories about young people from the past will enjoy the books of Scott O'Dell. In historical settings, O'Dell writes about strong, resourceful young people who use intelligence and creativity to survive extremely difficult circumstances.

For example, in his most famous book, *Island of the Blue Dolphins* (1960), which is based on a true story, Karana, an adolescent girl, lives alone on an island near the California coast during the middle of the nineteenth century. With very few resources, she lives by her courage and her knowledge of survival. We find out about what happens to her in the sequel, *Zia* (1976), in which the title character many years later encourages a group of sailors to search for Karana.

> *O'Dell was not satisfied merely to win awards. He also wanted to give them.*

Sacagawea was an American Indian woman who served as an interpreter and guide on the Lewis and Clark expedition (1804–1806). The expedition sought to find a land route to the Pacific Ocean.

Awards

Literary critics were so impressed with *Island of the Blue Dolphins* that in 1961 they awarded it the John Newbery Medal, the most prestigious award for outstanding books for young people and children. Three other O'Dell books have been designated Newbery Honor books, the second highest Newbery Award: *The Black Pearl* (1967) in 1968, *The King's Fifth* (1966) in 1967, and *Sing Down the Moon* (1970) in 1971.

In addition to winning awards for individual books, Scott O'Dell won several awards for lifetime work. In 1972 he became the second American to win the coveted Hans Christian Andersen Award for Lifetime Achievement. His other awards include the Regina Medal in 1978, the *Focal* Award in 1981, and the School Library Media Specialist of Southeastern New York Award in 1989.

O'Dell was not satisfied merely to win awards. He also wanted to give them. In 1981 he established the Scott O'Dell Award for Historical Fiction, a five-thousand-dollar award that is presented annually to a U.S. citizen for a book of historical fiction set in the New World. After establishing the award, O'Dell won it himself in 1986 for *Streams to the River, River to the Sea: a Novel of Sacagawea* (1986).

How Life Influenced Art

Many of O'Dell's books, such as *The Black Pearl, Zia,* and *Island of the Blue Dolphins,* are set near the California coast where O'Dell spent much of his life. As a boy, he lived in San Pedro, California, near San Nicolas Island, where the events that inspired *Island of the Blue Dolphins* actually took place. He was born in Los Angeles in 1903, and he died in New York in 1989.

O'Dell's family often moved around the southern California area, following his father's job as a railroad man. They lived for a while in a house on stilts on Rattlesnake Island, where the ocean waves washed under the house every day. "*Island of the Blue Dolphins* . . . came directly from my memory of the years I lived at Rattlesnake Island [now called Terminal Island] and San Pedro," O'Dell said (*Something About the Author,* p. 162).

An early indication of O'Dell's interest in action and adventure became evident in his work as a technical director for Paramount Studios. He also worked for Metro-Goldwyn-Mayer, a movie company that sent him to Rome as a cameraman for the movie *Ben Hur*. O'Dell used the first Technicolor camera, handmade by engineers at the Massachusetts Institute of Technology. He also taught a course in and wrote a textbook on the subject of "photoplay" or script writing. Two of O'Dell's books have been made into films: *Island of the Blue Dolphins* (Universal, 1964) and *The Black Pearl* (Diamond Films, 1976).

Research and Writing Habits

Like most effective writers, O'Dell wrote about what he knew, what he liked, and where he lived or traveled. In the process, he did a great deal of research. "Writing is hard work," he said. "The only part I really enjoy is the research, which usually takes about three or four months. The story itself as a rule takes about six months" (Commire, p. 163).

When asked to name "the most important thing a writer should have," O'Dell replied, "Anthony Trollope, the great English storyteller, said that the most important thing was a piece of sealing wax with which to fasten your pants to a chair. And I agree with him" (Commire, p. 163). Like many writers, O'Dell found it difficult sometimes to stay on task. Yet his many novels show that he managed to do so time and time again.

The Sea

The sea is a key element in O'Dell's books. *Isle of the Blue Dolphins, Zia, The Black Pearl, The 290* (1976), and *Alexandra* (1984) all show O'Dell's love of and respect for the sea, even though it is not always portrayed as a friend. In *The Black Pearl,* for instance, the ocean is the home not only of valuable pearls that sixteen-year-old Ramon's father collects for sale; it is also the home of the Manta Diablo, the "huge manta about which there are numerous legends and superstitions, especially among the Indians" (Usrey, *Dictionary of Literary Biography,* p. 282). Through his fierce battle with the creature Ramon learns a lesson about what it means to be a man.

The 290 is set on the Atlantic and the Caribbean. In this book, sixteen-year-old Jim Lynne develops from a shipbuild-

Ben-Hur (1926) was one of the greatest silent films ever made. Production of the film took years and cost $4 million—a staggering amount of money at the time.

When asked to name "the most important thing a writer should have," O'Dell replied, "Anthony Trollope, the great English storyteller, said that the most important thing was a piece of sealing wax with which to fasten your pants to a chair. And I agree with him."

Anthony Trollope (1815–1882) wrote forty-seven novels.

manta also called a giant devil ray; a huge, bat-shaped fish related to sharks

apprentice one who learns by experience under the direction of skilled workers

ing apprentice in England into a member of the crew on the ship he helped build. To his great disgust, Jim becomes involved in the distasteful business of transporting slaves.

The Hawk that Dare Not Hunt by Day (1975) takes place in sixteenth-century England during the turbulent conflict between the Church of England and the Roman Catholic Church. Readers interested in the Protestant Reformation will enjoy this first-person story about sixteen-year-old Tom Barton, who illegally smuggles William Tyndale's translations of the Bible into England during a time when freedom of religion was very restricted.

first-person the position or perspective of someone inside the story

Other Settings

Not all of O'Dell's books involve the sea. As a boy, he went to West Virginia with his mother to visit relatives. He became fascinated by the coal mining culture and touched by the poverty of the people. *Journey to Jericho* (1966), which is set in West Virginia, is based on what he learned there.

Sing Down the Moon explores the U.S. Army's forced dislocation of the Navajo people to Fort Sumner. *Streams to the River, River to the Sea: A Novel of Sacagawea* takes place along the trail of the Lewis and Clark expedition from 1804 to 1806.

In his later years, O'Dell lived in New York State and became interested in colonial America. *Sarah Bishop* (1980) is based on the true story of a girl whose father sided with King George at the beginning of the Revolutionary War. Sarah's life is complicated by the fact that her brother joins the colonial forces against the British. Thus, both her country and her household are entangled in a war that divides even members of the same family.

The Serpent Never Sleeps: A Novel of Jamestown and Pocahontas (1987), set in Virginia, combines colonial history with O'Dell's interest in Native Americans.

Native Americans, Hispanics, and Chicanos

As an adult, O'Dell traveled with his wife throughout Mexico and the American Southwest. They became acquainted with the Tarascan culture in Mexico. He became very interested in the history of those areas, and in the ways the lives of Native Americans and Chicanos were influenced by the arrival of European settlers. This interest is obvious in *The King's Fifth, Sing Down the Moon, Streams to the River, River to the Sea: A Novel of Sacagawea, The Treasure of Topo-El-Bampo* (1972), and in the trilogy made up of *The Captive* (1979), *The Feathered Serpent* (1981), and *The Amethyst Ring* (1983).

Criticism

Although *The King's Fifth, Sing Down the Moon,* and *Streams to the River* all received high honors, some of O'Dell's books about the Southwest and Mexico did not. For example, Jean Fritz wrote in the *New York Times Book Review* that *The Treasure of Topo-El-Bampo* is "almost impersonal . . . so that we are never inside one character long enough to feel anything" (p. 148). Reviewers have also been critical about the trilogy. Michael Usrey calls it "a failure" (p. 291) because O'Dell fails to show the reader how it felt to be involved in the fall of the Aztec and Inca powers. Usrey also says that O'Dell stereotypes the Europeans as greedy and heartless and the natives as unintelligent and peaceful. Others are particularly critical of what they believe are O'Dell's inaccurate and insensitive portrayals of Mayan, Aztec, Inca, Mexican, and Spanish cultures, especially in the trilogy. In *The Journal of Reading,* Isabel Schon writes that O'Dell dwells "on only negative aspects of the Mayan culture" (p. 323). She says that he should not use the words "barbarian" to describe the Mayans, "brutality" to describe pre-Columbian civilizations, "sleepy" to describe the Mexicans, or "absurdity" to describe Spanish people and their customs because such words give readers a one-sided impression of the people they describe. Schon believes O'Dell should "portray other people and cultures with a certain degree of authenticity and objectivity" (p. 323).

stereotypes portrays characters that are not original or individual because they conform to a preconceived category

Main Characters' Gender Roles

Some of O'Dell's characters may be stereotypes, but many of them are not. In a number of his books, the main character is a strong and intelligent girl who does not fit the stereotype of the helpless female who must be rescued by a strong male. One such character is Karana in *Island of the Blue Dolphins.*

Karana stays on the island to rescue her brother and survives there without help from anyone. In that novel's sequel, *Zia,* the title character shows the strength of her determination as she persuades the sailors to rescue Karana from the island. In *Sing Down the Moon,* Bright Morning is put in charge of keeping her mother's sheep and helps her Navajo family and neighbors as they are forced from their homes by an unrelenting government. The title character in *Sarah Bishop* shows great determination in her search for her brother when he is captured by enemy soldiers. In *Alexandra,* the title character faces a difficult choice of keeping her family safe or turning in a group of drug smugglers, and Bright Dawn in *Black Star, Bright Dawn* faces the challenge of the Iditarod race in Alaska with intelligence and skill.

The boys are also often atypical. In *The King's Fifth* (1966), Esteban de Sandoval is a gentle boy who would rather make maps than fight in battles. Even when he finds gold, he ultimately realizes that it can bring more pain than joy, and he abandons it for the greater satisfactions of friendship and integrity. Like Esteban, Jim Lynne in *The 290* does not approve of the blustering cruelty of many of his shipmates. He uses a nonconfrontational approach in his clever plan to free the slaves who are held by his uncle. In *The Black Pearl* Ramon discovers that manhood involves the bravery of love and unselfishness.

Unlike Esteban, Jim, and Ramon, Manuel in *Child of Fire* never grows out of his immature impulsiveness and cannot overcome his habit of using violence to solve problems. As a result, he does not survive.

All of these protagonists except Manuel meet hardship with an inner strength that serves them better than the brute strength of violent confrontation. In his novels, O'Dell provided examples of people who use their heads and their hearts more than their biceps to overcome adversity.

> *In his novels, O'Dell provided examples of people who use their heads and their hearts more than their biceps to overcome adversity.*

O'Dell and Dogs

In a number of O'Dell's books, dogs are loyal companions to the main characters. In *Island of the Blue Dolphins,* Karana befriends and takes care of a wild dog named Rontu, whom she has seriously wounded with an arrow. This episode in the book probably comes out of O'Dell's own experience with animals. When he was a boy he often went hunting, but later in his life he deeply regretted killing animals when he was younger (Collier and Nakamura, *Major Author and Illustrators for Children and Young Adults,* p. 1792).

In *Sing Down the Moon,* Bright Morning has a dog that helps herd the sheep and even accompanies her on a long journey after she is kidnapped. He remains a friendly companion to her throughout the book.

Bright Dawn trusts her safety to the loyalty and skill of her Siberian husky, Black Star. The husky is based on O'Dell's own dog, who, as he says in *Speaking for Ourselves,* "roams through the pages of *Black Star, Bright Dawn* in a continual state of excitement" (Gallo, p. 155).

In his young adulthood O'Dell owned a German shepherd named Eric, who traveled with him. "I took him everywhere," said O'Dell. "I stayed only in hotels that would accept him. He never saw a kennel." When Eric became ill, O'Dell took care of him. Eric's death was very similar to the account of Rontu's death in *Blue Dolphins.* In his later years, O'Dell owned poodles who slept in his study as he wrote.

Themes

The themes of O'Dell's novels are universal. Even though some of them were written many years ago, they still illustrate basic human challenges and emotions that young readers can understand today. As O'Dell explains, "Many of my books are set in the past, but the problems of isolation, moral decisions, greed, need for love and affection are problems of today as well" (Collier and Nakamura, p. 1792).

When he received the John Newbery Medal for *Island of the Blue Dolphins,* O'Dell wrote that Karana "learned first that we each must be an island secure unto ourselves. Then, that we must 'transgress our limits,' in reverence for all life" ("Newbery Award Acceptance," p. 104). These themes also appear in many of his other books. Malcolm Usrey summed up the purpose of O'Dell's books this way: "O'Dell writes for children to make them aware of man's inhumanity but also of the possibilities for endurance, resourcefulness, and moral courage" (p. 295).

A major reason for the survival and endurance of O'Dell's characters is that their healthy self-confidence gives them

theme   central message about life in a literary work

resilience the ability to easily recover from change or misfortune

hope. They have a resilience that keeps them from being destroyed by the challenges they face and that will not let them give up. Rather than seeing life as a series of problems they cannot solve, they feel confident that they can recover from tragedy and loss and still live meaningful lives.

Another reason for their survival is the resourcefulness that helps them solve problems in very clever ways. When they need something that is not readily at hand, they create it out of what nature offers them.

Finally, many of O'Dell's main characters summon up great courage as they face uncertainty and danger. Anne Devereaux Jordan writes that they face their fear "and have their

irreparable not able to be repaired

lives irreparably shaped by the actions their courage has engendered. Their actions, however, have no great public or historical ramifications. These books portray young people changing only the course of their personal history. Necessity and circumstance have dictated courage rather than a call to glory or a desire for heroism" (*Triumphs of the Spirit in Children's Literature,* p. 17). The main characters in Scott O'Dell's books show how young people can prevail in difficult circumstances when they use their inner strength and resilience, take charge of their own actions, and turn tragedy into triumph.

If you enjoy O'Dell's books, you might also enjoy Avi, Paula Fox, Ernest Hemingway, Gary Paulsen, Robert Louis Stevenson, and Theodore Taylor.

Selected Bibliography

WORKS BY SCOTT O'DELL

Novels for Young Adults

Island of the Blue Dolphins (1960)

Journey to Jericho, illustrated by Leonard Weisgard (1966)

The King's Fifth, with decorations and maps by Samuel Bryant (1966)

The Black Pearl, illustrated by Milton Johnson (1967)

The Dark Canoe, illustrated by Milton Johnson (1968)

Sing Down the Moon (1970)

The Treasure of Topo-El-Bampo, illustrated by Lynd Ward (1972)

The Cruise of the Arctic Star, maps by Samuel Bryant (1973)

Child of Fire (1974)

The Hawk That Dare Not Hunt by Day (1975)

The 290 (1976)

Zia (1976)

Carlota (1977)

Kathleen, Please Come Home (1978)

The Captive (1979)

Sarah Bishop (1980)

The Feathered Serpent (1981)

The Spanish Smile (1982)

The Amethyst Ring (1983)

The Castle in the Sea (1983)

Alexandra (1984)

The Road to Damietta (1985)

Streams to the River, River to the Sea: A Novel of Sacagawea (1986)

The Serpent Never Sleeps: A Novel of Jamestown and Pocahontas, illustrated by Ted Lewin (1987)

Black Star, Bright Dawn (1988)

My Name Is Not Angelica (1989)

Thunder Rolling in the Mountains, with Elizabeth Hall (1992)

Other Written Works

Representative Photoplays Analyzed by Scott O'Dell. Hollywood, Calif.: Palmer Institute of Authorship, 1924.

Woman of Spain: A Story of Old California. Boston and New York: Houghton Mifflin, 1934.

Hill of the Hawk. Indianapolis: Bobbs-Merrill, 1947.

Man Alone, with William Doyle. Indianapolis: Bobbs Merrill, 1953.

Lifer, with William Doyle. London: Longmans Green, 1954.

Country of the Sun: Southern California, an Informal History and Guide. New York: Crowell, 1957.

The Sea is Red: A Novel. New York: Holt, 1958.

"Newbery Award Acceptance." In *Newbery and Caldecott Medal Books: 1956–1965.* Edited by Lee Kingman. Boston: The Horn Book, 1965, pp. 99–104.

The Psychology of Children's Art, with Rheda Kellog. San Diego: Communications Research Machines, 1967.

"David, an Adventure with Memory and Words." In *Psychology Today,* January 1968, pp. 40–43.

"Acceptance Speech:. Hans Christian Andersen Award." In *Horn Book.* October 1972, pp. 441–443.

Organs in Mexico, with John T. Fesperson. Photos by Scott O'Dell. Raleigh, N.C.: Sunbury, 1979.

"The Tribulations of a Trilogy." In *The Horn Book Magazine,* April 1982, pp. 137–144.

"Scott O'Dell." In *Speaking for Ourselves: Autobiographical Sketches by Notable Authors of Books for Young Adults.* Edited by Donald R. Gallo. Urbana, Ill.: National Council of Teachers of English, 1990, pp. 154–155.

Venus Among the Fishes, with Elizabeth Hall. Boston: Houghton Mifflin, 1995.

Manuscripts

Scott O'Dell's manuscripts can be found at: Free Library in Philadelphia, Univ. of Oregon Library in Eugene, Pamona Public Library in Pamona, Calif., and Walter Library at the University of Minnesota in Minneapolis.

WORKS ABOUT SCOTT O'DELL

Collier, Laurie, and Joyce Nakamura. *Major Authors and Illustrators for Children and Young Adults: A Selection of Sketches from* Something About the Author. Detroit: Gale Research, 1993, vol. 5.

Commire, Anne. *Something About the Author.* Detroit: Gale Research, vol. 12.

Fritz, Jean. *New York Times Book Review,* 23 April 1972, p. 8. In *Children's Literature Review.* Edited by Ann Block and Carolyn Riley. Detroit: Gale Research, 1976, p. 148.

Horovitz, Carolyn. "Only the Best." In *Newbery and Caldecott Medal Books: 1956–1965.* Edited by Lee Kingman. Boston: The Horn Book, 1965, p. 156.

Jordan, Anne Devereaux. "Of Good Courage." In *Triumphs of the Spirit in Children's Literature.* Edited by Francelia Butler and Richard Rotert. Hamden, Conn.: Library Professional Publications, 1986.

Lovelace, Maud Hart. "Biographical Note: Scott O'Dell." In *Newbery and Caldecott Medal Books: 1956–1965.* Edited by Lee Kingman. Boston: The Horn Book, 1965, pp. 105–108

Schon, Isabel. "A Master Storyteller and His Distortions of pre-Columbian and Hispanic Cultures." In *The Journal of Reading*. January 1986, pp. 322–325.

Usrey, Malcolm. *Dictionary of Literary Biography: American Writers for Children Since 1960: Fiction*. Edited by Glenn E. Estes. Detroit: Gale Research, 1986, pp. 278–295.

The Santa Barbara Mission in California is closely associated with the events of *Island of the Blue Dolphins* and *Zia*. Built in 1786, the mission is located at:

2201 Laguna Street
Santa Barbara, CA
93103

Zibby Oneal

(1934-   )

by Susan P. Bloom

In each of her three books for the young adult reader Zibby Oneal charts the territory of the traditional family as she imaginatively reconstructs from her own experience the unfinished work we all struggle with in the process of growing up. At the center of each of her books a troubled adolescent female seeks direction in her life.

A Writer's Beginnings

Born on 17 March 1934, Oneal grew up in a middle-class nuclear family like many others in the 1930s and 1940s in America: her father James Bisgarden, was a thoracic surgeon; her mother, Elizabeth (Dowling) Bisgarden, a talented housewife, and her only sibling, a sister two years younger than herself. Oneal herself has spoken repeatedly about her typical childhood—a nuclear family of two parents, two children, a home on a quiet street in Midwest America. It was

nuclear family father, mother, and at least one child

thoracic surgeon doctor who operates on the upper chest

433

staid serious and restrained

ordinary within the constraints of what she knew as the daughter of a physician who had economic advantages—her surroundings were upper middle class. Like other families at that time, they knew the war and the depression as distant realities. Their Omaha, Nebraska, household, while typical, was neither staid nor entirely ordinary. With "volumes in her head" (Bloom and Mercier, *Presenting Zibby Oneal,* p. 7), her mother provided the girls with a love of books, reading and reciting to them from early childhood and enlarging their game playing with the imaginative lives of characters from the classics. Oneal's father, an amateur painter, was responsible for creating an artistic awareness in the girls.

These dual interests, the literary and the artistic, are apparent both in Zibby Oneal's life and in her novels. While her sister went on to pursue an artistic life, Zibby Oneal followed a literary path, a direction that began in her earliest years as a teller of tales. Oneal recalls entertaining herself beneath a tree in her backyard with childhood stories, composites of known fairy tales and childlike fears, pretense, and longings. It was not until she had her own family—like her mother, she married a physician (Robert M. Oneal); like her parents, she had two children—that these tales, first spoken, began to take shape as the novels of a maturing writer.

pretense ambition

In *The Language of Goldfish* (1980), Oneal's first important book, the art teacher Mrs. Ramsay speaks of pictures in her student Carrie's sketch pad as "marking-time pictures . . . what you're drawing until you find what you're looking for" (p. 115). Oneal's earliest published works, written while her children were young, were similar "marking-time" works as she struggled to find her own voice. *War Work,* published in 1971, replicates Oneal's family with a winsome tale of adventure, set during the summer of 1944, featuring two young daughters of a physician. Oneal hoped that this book would help her own children, growing up during the unpopular Vietnam War, to understand better the spirit of America at home during World War II. Even though her next novel, *The Improbable Adventures of Marvelous O'Hara Soapstone* (1972), continues to explore issues of sibling love and jealousy in another household like Oneal's own, its fantastic story upstages development of character as its plot-driven predecessor did. While these early books feature the family as the primary setting, suggesting that all important stories take Oneal back to relationships with parents and siblings, there is a sense in which Oneal was still writing not at this point about what truly inspired her.

When her daughter and son, for whom she wrote these early volumes, reached their twenties, Oneal returned to the childself who composed stories about characters in conflict, stories that continued to possess her and that offered unfinished pieces of business she had more leisure to tackle. In each of her novels for young adults she went back to the child-parent interaction that she had romanticized in her childhood mythic imaginings. She was able to do this honestly with the accumulated weight of her own living—as daughter, sister, wife, and mother—behind her. Freed from having to work around her children's schedules, Oneal developed her own schedule for writing.

Although she admits to being a morning writer, Oneal freely concedes to being a procrastinator, taking advantage of the distractions a home affords. An avid rewriter, Oneal often begins her day reworking her manuscript from the day before. While others agonize over revision, she revels in this process; it is getting down the first telling that exhausts her. She enjoys working with her editor, eliminating, reshaping, rethinking whole sections of her original handwritten manuscript.

The Language of Goldfish

No longer a creative child musing beneath the tree but an adult working in the garden, Oneal recalled in a 1987 speech being interrupted by a "skinny, lonely, troubled thirteen-year-old . . . trying to attract [her] attention" ("Metamorphosis," p. 7). This young girl would not allow Oneal to get on with her gardening; she insisted on sharing her story, demanding it be written down. Oneal remembers with affection the summer she wrote *The Language of Goldfish*. In a borrowed house surrounded by a garden of blooming flowers, she was never happier; she believes the charged summer atmosphere was essential to the book. With the creation of Carrie in *The Language of Goldfish,* Oneal truly found her forte: her interest in writing about the dramatic process of becoming a separate individual apart from one's parents and protectors, a process acutely realized in adolescence.

Young Carrie, like Oneal's earliest childhood creations, has idealized her childhood, seeing there a perfection that

forte strength; what one is good at

nostalgic homesick or desiring to return to a past way of life

Oneal acknowledges her fascination with islands, real and imagined.

Oneal wants "to make children understand that adolescence is a self-absorbed world—this may be why I always have islands in my books—but it's not a place you can stay forever."

did not exist. Fearful of the changes that adolescence promises, Carrie resists growing up. She reminisces nostalgically about her family's past life in a Chicago apartment. Even in their new home in the suburbs, Carrie cleaves desperately to a single comfortable image of childhood. In their new backyard, there is a goldfish pond at whose center is an island of rocks to which she and her sister retreat; there they invent a language with which they call the goldfish to them.

Oneal acknowledges her fascination with islands, real and imagined. In an interview with Wendy Smith (*Publishers Weekly,* 21 February 1986), she speaks of her "responsibility to make children understand that adolescence is a self-absorbed world—this may be why I always have islands in my books—but it's not a place you can stay forever" (p. 98). While Carrie's older sister Moira effortlessly dismisses their secret language and embraces the culture of adolescence, Carrie clings to their childhood invention. Oneal crafts the novel concentrating on the tension between holding onto and letting go of childhood.

At the opening of the novel, Carrie, needful of perspective and help, travels by train to see her psychiatrist following her suicide attempt almost a year earlier. Images of movement that propel Carrie forward toward health war with the autumnal season and the stasis it brings. Oneal's artistic sensibility attunes her always to color; indeed, reading her novels opens the world not only of sight but of the other senses as well. As Oneal draws word pictures of Carrie's world for us, Carrie's sense of isolation and alienation is relieved somewhat through her own art. Carrie first draws abstract designs executed without color, miming its absence in the dying season of winter that ushers in her illness. As Carrie moves, with the help of her therapist and her art teacher, Mrs. Ramsay, to greater acceptance of herself and her family members as they are, Oneal liberates Carrie's art as well. The only colors that appear in Carrie's troubled and tumultuous world occur during her frightening and disorienting panic attacks: "colors—queer colored shapes—beg[i]n to tumble around like the colored glass in a kaleidoscope" (p. 12). In her art and in her life Carrie floats and drifts in whiteness, allowing only for what is "neat and certain and clean" (p. 33). Carrie's challenge is to accept change, the messiness and uncertainty of life that terrifies her, and she must do it despite her parents' refusal to acknowledge the severity of her illness. This is not the daughter they expected, and they make little effort to understand the daughter they have.

Carrie moves from drawing the shadows of things to drawing the things themselves. She begins to create drawings of an island, the island that inhabits her panic attacks, aware of but not fully understanding its meaning to her. The first such drawing surprises Carrie and delights one of Mrs. Ramsay's children, who wants it for her own. When Carrie asks Saskia why she likes it, the child replies that even though there are no people in it, "there could be" (p. 117). Saskia's perceptive comment foreshadows drawings that will give way to both color and people as Carrie makes room for them in her life as well as in her art. Everything that Carrie knows now includes her awareness that the island of her panic attacks and her subsequent paintings is the tiny pile of rocks at the center of the pond, the site of her childhood idyll. She sees it for the "very small island" it is, one "she could easily reach . . . with the handle of a broom" (p. 179). This novel, which opens with movement, also closes with movement as the slowly recovering, more confident, emotionally open Carrie turns and walks toward the lighted house of her neighbors.

foreshadow suggest events yet to come

subsequent following

A Formal Feeling

Having dealt with the transition from childhood into adulthood and the related struggles with family and peers from whom one feels excluded, Oneal returned to this familiar terrain with *A Formal Feeling* (1982). A descending plane, not a train, defines the initial movement of this novel as sixteen-year-old Anne Cameron returns home for Christmas vacation. Just as Carrie is filled with misgivings of self and embraces the certainty of structured art rather than face life's ambiguities, Anne feels a distrust that she thinks she understands. Both of her parents have abandoned her: her mother unexpectedly died a year earlier, and her father, a professor, has married a woman totally unlike Anne's perfect mother. With icy composure Anne isolates herself from everyone, including her older and more comfortable brother, who reaches out to her. Oneal sustains the imagery—anticipated in the cold formality of the Emily Dickinson poem from which the title derives—throughout, as Anne views the world "always

composure self-control

There is an article about Emily Dickinson in volume 1.

foot unit of rhythm in poetry

repressed kept down, hidden, or forgotten

looking through windows" (p. 137) "enclosed . . . in a shell of crystal" (p. 15). Her running and skating provide movement but no direction; they echo Dickinson's mechanical feet that go around. Other movement interrupts Anne's sense of control; the song refrain "Over the river and through the woods to grandmother's house we go" "occupie[s] Anne's mind like an uninvited guest" (p. 100). When an early morning skating accident on an island patch of ice compels Anne to stop her frantic activity, she is forced to confront repressed events in her life from which she has been unconsciously running.

As Carrie has been afraid to grow up and has romanticized her past, Anne has been afraid to look back at a past she also idealized. If Anne sees her mother as less than perfect, then she might have to face truths about herself. Anne relives her terror of feeling responsible for her mother's first abandonment of the family when she was eight. Angry at her mother's insistence that she perform her best at the piano, Anne had secretly wished for her mother's disappearance. Perhaps then, as in Oneal's earliest childhood stories, she could have her father for herself. Beneath the terror of her mother's early disappearance and return lies the question of how her mother could leave her if she loved her. For Anne, at the deepest level resides the "unspeakable . . . Did I ever love my mother at all?" (p. 155). But remembering her mother as controlling and exacting, remembering "years of trying to please her mother, of trying not to be angry and to be in control" (p. 156), Anne learns, is only part of the truth. When she remembers "other memories, as real as the anger," Anne frees not only her mother but also herself. Loving her mother, Anne has to make room for imperfect feelings for herself as much as for her mother. She learns that perfection is a dangerous illusion that prohibits the more realistic ambivalence of human relationships.

ambivalence uncertainty

Anne "outlive[s] her 'Hour of Lead'" and freely mourns her mother's death for the first time. She can leave her family—her father, her new stepmother, and her brother, all of whom she sees with greater truth and acceptance—to return to school. The plane, whose landing at the beginning she distrusted, begins an ascent, symbolic of Anne's own climb. The hopefulness that concludes this young adult novel does not strike a false or sentimental note. Oneal's ability to craft her books with restraint, grace, and elegance distinguishes her work from the more obvious, less reflective problem novels that flood the market.

In Summer Light

Kate Brewer completes Oneal's young adult trilogy of introspective heroines. In *A Formal Feeling,* Anne's greatest unease is with her perfectionist mother. Kate Brewer, the seventeen-year-old protagonist of *In Summer Light* (1985), must come to some accommodation with her father, a demanding and difficult famous artist. Back at her island home for the summer to recuperate from mononucleosis, Kate encases herself in her hatred of him

Once again, Oneal crafts precise imagery that juxtaposes the warm summer colors of Martha's Vineyard and the colors that define her artistic home against the "monotone" (p. 15) that defines Kate, who feels "she ha[s] had enough of color" (p. 17). Kate bitterly resents her father's dismissal of her art at the very moment when her talent is most apparent. Although her artistic temperament and sensibility literally color her essence, Kate opts to reject not only her father but her art as well. Like the talented Carrie and Anne in the other novels, Kate must undergo a period of quiescence before she can awaken to her fullest potential. All three young woman "sleep" for a time: Carrie's suicide attempt induces sleep and a stay in the hospital; Anne's sprained ankle forces rest; Kate's mononucleosis brings on slumber. In her acceptance speech for the Boston Globe–Horn Book Award for *In Summer Light,* Oneal acknowledges her debt to the classic fairy tale of *Sleeping Beauty*. Although young men play minor roles in Oneal's two previous novels, the gentle and kind graduate student Ian, who has come to catalog her father's work, arrives on the scene as a "prince [with] neither wealth nor title [who] . . . succeed[s] in awakening Kate" (p. 33). In loving him as an appropriate male figure, Kate moves beyond paralysis. She can return to her stalled English paper on Shakespeare's *Tempest,* viewing the magician Prospero, so like her father, as more than simply selfish and self-serving. Like Anne's acceptance of her mother, Kate's acceptance of her father as he is, an imperfect man and an aging artist, releases Kate to finish her paper and return to the art that sustains and energizes her. With health and perspective

introspective self-absorbed; literally, looking inward

protagonist main character of a literary work

mononucleosis disease caused by an increase in the number of white blood cells in the blood; it makes a person very tired and can last for weeks or months

quiescence inactivity or calmness

There is an article about William Shakespeare in volume 3.

renewed, she can leave her island behind. Oneal writes: "The movement away and out into the world, into concern for other people, has to happen; you aren't adult until you make that move. Sure, explore your feelings . . . but then get into the world" (*Publishers Weekly*, p. 98).

Conclusion

Since she began writing in 1971, Oneal has produced a limited but important and critically praised body of work. Only two pieces follow *In Summer Light*. While neither deals with adolescent angst nor returns Oneal to a younger audience, both reveal her skill in drawing sensitive portraits of women, young and old: one of the real artist Grandma Moses, the other of a fictionalized granddaughter of a suffragette. Each woman acknowledges her father and his importance in her life as dreamer and painter to be emulated or head of the household to be honored and obeyed. Each woman finds her own way as she struggles to define her unique self.

Oneal sets her readers on a course of self-discovery, inviting them to attend, through her characters, to their own evolving selves. Readers recognize themselves in Carrie, Anne, and Kate and can transfer that sense of "always becoming," of never fully resolving the fundamental questions about family and self, to their own lives.

angst anxiety or anguish

suffragette woman of the nineteenth or early twentieth century who fought to win the right of women to vote

If you like Zibby Oneal, you might also like Paula Fox and Cynthia Voigt.

Selected Bibliography

WORKS BY ZIBBY ONEAL

Picture Books

Turtle and Snail, illustrated by Margot Tomes (1979)

Maude and Walter, illustrated by Maxie Chambliss (1985)

Novels

War Work, illustrated by George Porter (1971)

The Improbable Adventures of Marvelous O'Hara Soapstone, illustrated by Paul Galdone (1972)

The Language of Goldfish (1980)

A Formal Feeling (1982)

In Summer Light (1985)

Other

Grandma Moses: Painter of Rural America, illustrated by Donna Ruff (1986)

A Long Way to Go, illustrated by Michael Dooling (1990)

Speeches

Acceptance speech for the 1986 Boston Globe–Horn Book Award for *In Summer Light.* In *Horn Book,* January/February, 1987, pp. 32–34.

"Metamorphosis." Unpublished manuscript of talk delivered at the Center for the Study of Children's Literature, Simmons College, Boston, 16 July 1987.

WORKS ABOUT ZIBBY ONEAL

Bloom, Susan P., and Cathryn M. Mercier. *Presenting Zibby Oneal.* Boston: Twayne, 1991.

Brodie, Deborah. Letters to Zibby Oneal. 25 October 1984 and 26 February 1985. Kerlan Collection, University of Minnesota, Minneapolis.

Commire, Anne, ed. "Zibby Oneal." In *Something About the Author.* Detroit: Gale Research, 1983, vol. 30, pp. 166–167.

Glastonbury, Marion. "Missing Persons." *Times Educational Supplement,* June 1983, vol. 3, p. 41.

Greelaw, M. Jean. "Zibby Oneal." In *Twentieth Century Children's Writers.* 3rd ed. Edited by Tracy Chevalier and D. L. Kirkpatrick. Chicago and London: St. James Press, 1989, pp. 741–742.

Kelso, Dorothy H. "Stories: Hard Fact and Deft Fantasy." *Christian Science Monitor,* 8 November 1972, p. 84.

Locher, Frances C., Martha G. Conway, B. Hal May, and David Versical, eds. "Zibby Oneal." In *Contemporary Authors.* Detroit: Gale Research, 1982, vol. 106, pp. 381–382.

McHargue, Georgess. "Coming of Age." *New York Times Book Review,* 14 November 1982, p. 48.

Senick, Gerald J., and Melissa Reiff Hug, eds. "Zibby Oneal." In *Children's Literature Review.* Detroit: Gale Research, 1987, vol. 13, pp. 153–160.

How to Write to the Author
Zibby Oneal
501 Onandaga Street
Ann Arbor, MI 48104

Smith, Wendy. "Working Together." *Publishers Weekly,* 21 February 1986, pp. 97–98.

Stine, Jean C., and Daniel G. Marowski, eds. "Zibby Oneal." In *Contemporary Literary Criticism.* Detroit: Gale Research, 1984, vol. 30, pp. 279–281.

Katherine Paterson

(1932-)

by Gary D. Schmidt

Soon after her novel *Lyddie* was published in 1991 I asked Katherine Paterson why she was so unrelentingly hard on the novel's main character. Lyddie is a young girl whose father abandons the family; her mother takes her youngest siblings away and apprentices Lyddie to an innkeeper. Lyddie eventually finds a job at a mill in Lowell, Massachusetts, where she nearly works herself to death trying to earn enough money to pay for her farm, which is still lost. Her mother dies penniless along with younger siblings. For a time Lyddie has the love of her brother Charles, but he grows away from her. For a time she has her sister Rachel, but Rachel leaves Lowell for her health. For a time Lyddie has two close female friends, but she loses these relationships also. Then Luke Stevens offers to marry her, bringing her the farm, a warmhearted extended family, and all his love. But she rejects him.

apprentice to set at work as an apprentice, or one who learns by experience under the direction of skilled workers

Quotations from Katherine Paterson that are not attributed to a published source are from a personal interview conducted by the author of this article on 5 August 1992 and are published here by permission of Katherine Paterson.

Paterson does not see it that way. "Oh, she comes back and marries him," she says.

I look at her blankly. Has she forgotten how her own novel ends?

"I know it's not in the book," she continues. "But that's what happens. She returns, marries Luke, and perhaps founds a library. Lots of girls did do that after coming back home from the mills of Lowell."

For Katherine Paterson, characters have a life and history beyond the pages of her books. In fact, when you come to the end of a Katherine Paterson novel, you have a sense that a path has been pointed out but that the characters have just started down that path. They may be like Gilly in *The Great Gilly Hopkins* (1978), who is just learning how to live by giving love, even when her dreams are shattered. Or they may be like Jess in *Bridge to Terabithia* (1977), who is learning how to use, among other things, his imagination to expand the lives of others. Or they may be like Takiko in *Of Nightingales That Weep* (1974), who must get past her own superficiality so that she can learn how to establish a home. All these characters have hard lessons to learn under circumstances sometimes as hard as Lyddie's, or even harder.

What is remarkable about Paterson's characters is that they learn to hope. In the middle of dreadful circumstances, characters hope. And it is that hope, rooted not merely in sheer blind optimism but in a real understanding that the world can be a difficult and bitter place, which enables Paterson's characters not only to keep going but in some measure to triumph over circumstances. In *Rebels of the Heavenly Kingdom* (1983), Wang Lee and Mei Lin find at the end of the novel that their dreams have been shattered. Not only has the utopian community of which they were a part turned sour and even deadly, but much of China has been ravaged by those whom they had followed. Indeed, Wang Lee and Mei Lin have played a part in that destruction. But now, when all seems lost, they return together to Wang Lee's destroyed farm and find the seed rice that he has hidden. It will bring a crop, and with it will come hope for a new life together. That is hope in a Katherine Paterson novel: the pain is still there, and the hardship is not minimized, but there is hope for a better life.

superficiality lack of deep or sincere character

utopia ideal of a perfect society

The Years in the Orient

It is hard not to see some of this same pattern in Paterson's own childhood, which was constantly filled with moves, fresh starts, and new attempts to adjust to a new and different world. She was born in Tsing-Tsiang Pu, in Jiangsu Province on China's eastern coast on the Yellow Sea. Her parents, George Raymond Womeldorf and Mary Goetchius Womeldorf, were missionaries, and unlike some missionaries of this period, they believed strongly in becoming a part of the culture in which they worked. So the family learned Chinese and, instead of living in the British quarter of the city where many missionaries lived, they lived in a neighborhood where most of their neighbors were Chinese. Paterson's father worked most closely with a Chinese minister, and Paterson remembers him riding from village to village with food and medicine, often having to sleep on flea-ridden straw in a barn because there was nowhere else to sleep.

missionary a person sent to a foreign country on behalf of a religious organization in order to promote its faith or to carry on humanitarian work

Most difficult of all, however, was that this was a time of war and conflict in China. The seat of the Guomindang (or Kuomintang) government led by Chiang Kai-shek was in Nanking, not far from this missionary family. Several years before Paterson was born, the Guomingdang violently purged all the Communists from the government, but under Mao Tse-tung the Communists grew in strength and numbers, and the two parties fought all around Jiangsu Province for five years during Paterson's early childhood. The Communists called an uneasy truce with the Guomingdang only to fight the Japanese, who invaded China in 1937, when Paterson was five years old. This fighting lasted until World War II. Paterson's family rarely saw China at peace.

Her family became refugees in 1937, when they left China for Virginia, remaining there for a year. They returned to China in 1938, hoping that conditions would allow them to stay, but they did not. In 1940 the family was forced to flee again, never to return to China as a missionary family. Paterson herself would not return to China for more than forty years, when she went back to do research for *Rebels of the Heavenly Kingdom,* her only novel set in the land of her birth.

refugees people who flee to a foreign country in order to escape danger

Despite the hardships, her early childhood years gave Paterson a love for and understanding of the Orient. She would come to think of its culture as incalculably older than her American culture, with a people whose language and sense of beauty she might come to understand but could never be completely a part of. When it came time for her to be a missionary, from 1957 to 1962, she returned to the Orient, but this time to Japan. When she came to write her first three novels—*The Sign of the Chrysanthemum* (1973), *Of Nightingales That Weep*, and *The Master Puppeteer* (1976)—she set them all in Japan and placed in each of them a wise, thoughtful, and (sometimes) gentle figure who seems to embody the character of the culture.

Early Years in America

Returning from China, Paterson found herself coming to a homeland that had never been her home. She also found herself to be something of an outsider. During her year in Richmond, between the two flights from China, she was the only student in her class who received no valentines at all, a sign of rejection that she would never forget. In fact, she once told her mother that all her stories were about the time she received no valentines, a comment suggesting that her tales are about characters who find themselves separate and different from those around them.

> *In fact, Paterson once told her mother that all her stories were about the time she received no valentines, a comment suggesting that her tales are about characters who find themselves separate and different from those around them.*

It is this very difference in Paterson's characters that causes many of their difficulties. In *Come Sing, Jimmy Jo* (1985), it is James's supreme musical talent that sets him apart from the rest of his family and almost threatens to split the family into fragments. In *Bridge to Terabithia*, Jess is set apart by his artistic and sensitive soul; in *Park's Quest* (1988), Park is set apart because of how little he knows about his father, an ignorance shared by Muna in *The Sign of the Chrysanthemum*. The same pattern appears in Paterson's retold folktale, *The Tale of the Mandarin Ducks* (1990), in which the samurai Shozo and the kitchen servant Yasuko are set apart from a cruel and cold court by their tender and loving hearts. In each case, characters are different from those around them, and although these differences create real difficulties, they also lead to hope.

When Paterson was a child, her family did not settle down long enough for her to overcome the sense of constantly being new and different; she was always the outsider.

samurai a Japanese warrior

Between 1937 and 1950, when she turned eighteen, the family moved fifteen times, from China to Virginia to North Carolina to West Virginia to Tennessee. She particularly remembers her reception in North Carolina, after the family fled China for the second time. There, at the Calvin H. Wiley Elementary School, she felt that she had been dropped into a different world. She spoke English with a British accent. She wore clothes that had been handed down from others and thrown into a missionary barrel. She was suspected of being some sort of Oriental spy and was referred to as a "Jap," even though at that time she had never set foot in Japan. She had few friends. The only thing Paterson could do about this situation, she did: she abandoned the British accent that had marked her language and cultivated a North Carolina accent, with which she still speaks today.

This background may explain in part why so few of Paterson's characters have close companions; often they are very alone. Lupe in *Flip-Flop Girl* (1994) seems to cultivate this loneliness by wearing strange clothing and holding herself apart, but Leslie and Jess in *Bridge to Terabithia* both sense the same kind of isolation—Leslie because her ideas and lifestyle are markedly different from the others in her community, Jess because he has to work hard at being like everyone else. Lyddie loses each of her friends one by one. She eventually must stand completely on her own for a time, much as Louise in *Jacob Have I Loved* (1980) seems to lose the Captain and Call and finds that she must leave home to find herself.

Even characters who find friends seem to find them only painfully: Park, who lives uneasily with his half-sister Thanh; Jimmy Jo, who finds the king confusing and in some ways fearful; and Gilly, who lands among three friends but cannot accept their love until she must leave them. One wonders how these characters' lives might have been different if Paterson had lived in one place for all her childhood.

One result of Paterson's sense of separation was her love of reading and writing. If she found ostracism at the Calvin H. Wiley Elementary School, she also found the library. In China she had read children's literature such as *Winnie the Pooh, The Wind in the Willows,* and the sentimental Elsie Dinsmore books. Now she read books by Robert Lawson, Rachel Fields, and Kate Seredy, encouraged by a stern yet understanding librarian at her school. Paterson began to write plays and act in them. And as a writer she found what she had not had before: the respect and admiration of other children around her.

Apprenticeship of a Writer

In 1950, when Paterson went to Bristol, Tennessee, to attend King College, she did not go with the idea of becoming a writer, but she did immerse herself in the works of poets such as John Donne and Gerard Manley Hopkins; dramatists such as Sophocles and William Shakespeare; and novelists such as C. S. Lewis, whose Narnia Chronicles were being published during these years. Although she would not develop a voice like any of these writers, she later believed that an apprenticeship in them had indeed affected her own sense of the writer's craft.

After graduation, Paterson still had not seriously considered becoming a writer. Like Louise in *Jacob Have I Loved,* she was looking for the choices that would determine her life. When a former professor asked her if she had thought of becoming a writer, she replied that she would not add another mediocre writer to the world. His response was telling: he suggested that perhaps God was calling to her to be just that. One hears here the voice of Joseph Wojtkiewicz in *Jacob Have I Loved,* telling Louise that perhaps God has been preparing her for this valley all her life. Paterson was not yet ready to take up this vocation, although she had considered it enough to realize that doing so would mean risking mediocrity.

She turned instead to teaching. After she traveled to Lovettsville, in northern Virginia, to teach in a small elementary school, the next year she went to nearby Richmond to attend the Presbyterian School of Christian Education. She earned her degree and then went to Japan, where she enrolled at the Naganuma School of Japanese Language and began work as a teacher and missionary. She worked for eleven pastors in the rural areas of Shikoku Island, the smallest of Japan's major islands. After four years she returned home to a familiar situation: she had been changed by her time in Japan, with new ideas to express and new ways to express them, and once again she was an outsider in an alien culture.

There is an article about William Shakespeare in volume 3, and an article about C. S. Lewis earlier in this volume.

After her return to Virginia, she moved to New York and accepted a fellowship at Union Theological Seminary, where in 1962 she earned a degree that prepared her for her first writing assignment: three works of church school curriculum titled *Who Am I?* (1966), *Justice for All People* (1973), and *To Make Men Free* (1973). It was also in 1962 that she married John Barstow Paterson, a Presbyterian minister. The couple had four children, and Paterson tried to balance her work as a mother and as a writer doing curricula for the National Council of Churches and the Presbyterian Church, U.S.A.

The Life of the Writer

With the encouragement of her husband, Paterson had also been writing for a broader audience, even though none of her work had yet been published. A series of Christmas stories she had written for their church, Tacoma Park Presbyterian, would not be published until 1979 as *Angels and Other Strangers*. The breakthrough came in 1973. After two years of rejections, *The Sign of the Chrysanthemum* was accepted and published. It inspired three novels written in four years, all set in Japan. That rapid pace continued as Paterson wrote a series of books for children that were to win some of the field's highest awards: *Bridge to Terabithia,* winner of the Newbery Award; *The Great Gilly Hopkins,* winner of the National Book Award and a Newbery Honor Award; and *Jacob Have I Loved,* winner of her second Newbery Award. Paterson seemed to have taken children's and adolescents' literature by storm. During the next decade she published only three novels but a spate of essays and book reviews on young adult literature.

In 1981 Paterson tried her hand at translation and produced *The Crane Wife*. It was a sign of things to come. She began to try a variety of literary forms, but she continues to write a novel about every three years. In *The Tale of the Mandarin Ducks,* she retold a Japanese folktale. In *The Smallest Cow in the World* (1991) she wrote a controlled-vocabulary book. In "Asia in 1492," a selection in Jean Fritz's *The World in 1492* (1992), she composed a history. And in *The King's Equal* (1992) she penned an original fairy tale. In the 1992 edition of *Who Am I?* Paterson rewrote her first book for a new generation. It is not surprising that in each of

In 1989, a film adaptation of *Jacob Have I Loved* was shown on PBS's *Wonderworks* series as *Jacob I have Loved*. Bridget Fonda played the lead role of Louise.

these books, with the exception perhaps of her historical works, Paterson continues to explore the themes of the outsider and, most especially, of hope.

When she accepted the National Book Award for *The Great Gilly Hopkins* in 1979, Paterson said that she wanted to be known as "a spy for hope." She wanted to be like the two Hebrew spies who went into the Promised Land and came back to report that it was a land truly flowing with milk and honey, and that the people should go forward into it. Paterson's work holds out the hope of milk and honey. But it does not say that there will be no giants to tangle with, that there will be no hardship and heartache to endure. That is not the way of this world.

When I think back upon my interview with Katherine Paterson at her home in Barre, Vermont, I think of stories. I think of sitting back on the sofa and listening to her laugh and tell tales. The time passed, and my series of questions was forgotten in the stories. Any writer must first be a storyteller. Any reader must first come into a book because of the story and the world of the story. Whether that world is China or Japan, the island of Rass on Chesapeake Bay, an estate in Virginia, the mills of Lowell, Massachusetts, or the fairy-tale realm of a prince who demands a princess equal to himself, Paterson tells a story to say, with Trotter of *The Great Gilly Hopkins,* that yes, life is hard. No denying that. But, as Paterson says, there is "nothing to make you happy like doing good on a tough job, now is there?"

If you like the works of Katherine Paterson, you might also enjoy the works of Cynthia Voight and Lois Lowry.

Selected Bibliography

WORKS BY KATHERINE PATERSON

Fiction

The Sign of the Chrysanthemum (1973)

Of Nightingales That Weep (1974)

The Master Puppeteer (1976)

Bridge to Terabithia (1977)

The Great Gilly Hopkins (1978)

Angels and Other Strangers: Family Christmas Stories (1979); published in Great Britain as *Star of Night* (1980)

Jacob Have I Loved (1980)

The Crane Wife, translated by Paterson as retold by Sumiko Yagawa (1981)

Rebels of the Heavenly Kingdom (1983)

Come Sing, Jimmy Jo (1985)

Consider the Lilies: Plants of the Bible, with John Paterson (1986)

The Tongue-Cut Sparrow, translated by Paterson as retold by Momoko Ishii (1987)

The King's Equal (1988)

Park's Quest (1988)

The Tale of the Mandarin Ducks (1990)

Lyddie (1991)

The Smallest Cow in the World (1991)

Flip-Flop Girl (1994)

Nonfiction

Who Am I? (1966; 1992)

Justice for All People (1973)

To Make Men Free (1973)

Gates of Excellence: On Reading and Writing Books for Children (1981)

The Spying Heart: More Thoughts on Reading and Writing Books for Children (1989)

"Asia in 1492." In *The World in 1492.* Edited by Jean Fritz et al. (1992)

WORKS ABOUT KATHERINE PATERSON

Biographical Studies

Buckley, Virginia. "Katherine Paterson." In *Horn Book,* August 1978, pp. 368–371.

Haskell, Ann. "Talk with a Winner." In *New York Times Book Review,* 26 April 1981, pp. 52, 62–68.

Jones, Linda T. "Profile Katherine Paterson." In *Language Arts,* February 1981, pp. 189–196.

"Katherine Paterson Named Recipient of the 1983 Medallion." In *Juvenile Miscellany,* winter 1983, pp. 1–3.

Namovicz, Gene Inyart. "Katherine Paterson." In *Horn Book,* August 1981, pp. 394–399.

Critical Studies

Baer, Elizabeth R. "Books as Bridges: The Tradition of the Child Reader in Katherine Paterson's *Bridge to Terabithia*." In *Literature and Hawaii's Children. Imagination: A Bridge to Magic Realms in the Humanities*. Edited by Christina Bacchilega and Steven Curry. Honolulu: Literature and Hawaii's Children, 1990, pp. 63–71.

Bell, Anthea. "A Case of Commitment." In *Signal,* May 1982, pp. 73–81.

Chaston, Joel D. "Flute Solos and Songs That Make You Shatter: Simple Melodies in *Jacob Have I Loved* and *Come Sing, Jimmy Jo*." In *Lion and the Unicorn* (1992), pp. 215–222.

———. "The Other Deaths in *Bridge to Terabithia*." In *Children's Literature Association Quarterly,* winter 1991–1992, pp. 238–241.

Curry, Steven. "Fate and Friendship: Lessons of Loss in *Bridge to Terabithia* and *Charlotte's Web*." In *Literature and Hawaii's Children. Imagination: A Bridge to Magic Realms in the Humanities*. Edited by Christina Bacchilega and Steven Curry. Honolulu: Literature and Hawaii's Children, 1990, pp. 96–100.

Goforth, Caroline. "The Role of the Island in *Jacob Have I Loved*." In *Children's Literature Association Quarterly,* winter 1984–1985, pp. 176–178.

Gough, John. "*Bridge to Terabithia:* The Subtlety of Plain Language." In *Idiom,* summer 1983, pp. 19–22.

Huse, Nancy. "Katherine Paterson's Ultimate Realism." In *Children's Literature Association Quarterly,* fall 1984, pp. 99–101.

Jameson, Gloria. "Developing Self-Identity through Religious Consciousness in Stories of George MacDonald, C. S. Lewis, Madeleine L'Engle, Katherine Paterson, Ursula Le Guin, and Laura Adams Armer." In *Hawaii 3: Literature and Hawaii's Children*. Honolulu: Literature and Hawaii's Children, 1988, pp. 143–147.

Kimmel, Eric A. "Beyond Death: Children's Books and the Hereafter." In *Horn Book,* June 1980, pp. 265–273.

———. "Trials and Revelations: Katherine Paterson's Heroic Journeys." In *New Advocate,* fall 1990, pp. 235–245.

McGavran, James H., Jr. "Bathrobes and Bibles, Waves and Words in Katherine Paterson's *Jacob Have I Loved*."

In *Children's Literature in Education,* spring 1986, pp. 3–15.

Mills, Claudia. "Children in Search of a Family: Orphan Novels through the Century." In *Children's Literature in Education,* winter 1987, pp. 227–239.

Nist, Joan. "Archetypal Strands in Katherine Paterson's Novels of the Orient." In *Literature and Hawaii's Children. Imagination: A Bridge to Magic Realms in the Humanities.* Edited by Christine Bacchilega and Steven Curry. Honolulu: Literature and Hawaii's Children, 1990, pp. 25–29.

Powers, Douglas. "Of Time, Place, and Person: The Great Gilly Hopkins and Problems of Story for Adopted Children." In *Children's Literature in Education,* winter 1984, pp. 211–219.

Rees, David. "The Wound of Philoctetes." In *What Do Draculas Do? Essays on Contemporary Writers of Fiction for Children and Young Adults.* Metuchen, N.J.: Scarecrow Press, 1990, pp. 222–234. (First published as "On Katherine Paterson, Alexander Pope, Myself, and Some Others." In *Children's Literature in Education,* autumn 1983, pp. 160–170.)

Smedman, M. Sarah. "'A Good Oyster': Story and Meaning in *Jacob Have I Loved.*" In *Children's Literature in Education,* autumn 1983, pp. 180–187.

———. "Not Always Gladly Does She Teach, nor Gladly Learn: Teachers in *Kunsterinroman* for Young Readers." In *Children's Literature in Education,* September 1989, pp. 131–149.

———. "Out of the Depths to Joy: Spirit/Soul in Juvenile Novels." In *Triumphs of the Spirit in Children's Literature.* Edited by Francelia Butler and Richard Rotert. Hamden, Conn.: Library Professional Publications, 1986, pp. 181–197.

———. "The Quest for the Father in the Fiction of Katherine Paterson." In *Literature and Hawaii's Children. Imagination: A Bridge to Magic Realms in the Humanities.* Edited by Christina Bacchilega and Steven Curry. Honolulu: Literature and Hawaii's Children, 1990, pp. 30–39.

———. "The Quest for the Father in Katherine Paterson's *Of Nightingales That Weep.*" In *The Child and the Family: Selected Papers from the 1988 International Conference of*

**How to Write to
the Author**
Katherine Paterson
c/o HarperCollins Publishers
10 East 53rd Street
New York, NY 10022

the Children's Literature Association. Edited by Susan R. Ganon and Ruth Ann Thompson. New York: Pace University, 1990, pp. 59–64.

———. "Springs of Hope: Recovery of Primordial Time in 'Mythic' Novels for Young Readers." In *Children's Literature,* 1988, pp. 91–107.

———. "When Literary Works Meet: Allusion in the Novels of Katherine Paterson." In *Where Rivers Meet: Confluence and Concurrents, Selected Papers from the 1989 International Conference of the Children's Literature Association.* Edited by Susan R. Ganon and Ruthe Anne Thompson. New York: Pace University, 1989, pp. 59–65.

Gary Paulsen

(1939-   )

by Gary M. Salvner

Like most authors, Gary Paulsen enjoys talking about his books, and one story he likes to tell concerns his famous survival stories about Brian Robeson, *Hatchet* and *The River*. It seems that after *The River* was published in 1991, a reporter from *National Geographic* magazine contacted Gary Paulsen and wanted to know where the real Brian Robeson lived. "You know, it's a novel," Paulsen explained. "Yeah, but he's a real kid," the man replied. "You changed his name, but he's a real kid."

How did Gary Paulsen learn to write survival books so believable that even adult reporters think his main character is real? What makes *Hatchet* (1987) so convincing that it has become one of the best-selling young adult books of all time? Successful books do not come easily, but they do become possible with a writer like Paulsen, whose own life has been an adventure story and whose books are often based upon his own life experiences. "I don't make stuff up much," admits Paulsen. "Most of the things I write about are based

Quotations from Gary Paulsen that are not attributed to any other published source are from *Presenting Gary Paulsen* (1996) by Gary M. Salvner.

> *"Most of the things I write about are based on personal inspection at zero altitude, and I have scars pretty much all over my body to prove those things."*

autobiographical relating to the author's own life

odyssey journey of adventure, growth, and discovery

on personal inspection at zero altitude, and I have scars pretty much all over my body to prove those things." A reader interested in Gary Paulsen's novels first has to know something about his life.

A Life of Adventure and Struggle

Gary Paulsen was born on 17 May 1939 in Minneapolis, Minnesota, and his childhood and teenage years were difficult for him. His father, Oscar Paulsen, was a career military officer who, before Gary was three, was sent to Europe at the beginning of World War II to serve under the famous general George Patton. Gary and his mother, Eunice Paulsen, moved to Chicago, where she went to work in an ammunition factory, and he spent many lonely days with a very unreliable baby-sitter.

Some of Paulsen's experiences as a young child appear in his books. His adult "autobiographical odyssey," *Eastern Sun, Winter Moon* (1993), for example, reveals the loneliness and instability of these years. His book *A Christmas Sonata* (1992), however, tells of a happy time: a trip to northern Minnesota when four-year-old Gary and his cousin saw a "real" Santa Claus and discovered the magic of Christmas. *The Cookcamp* (1991), a book that Paulsen says is "almost straight nonfiction," tells about a boy who goes to live with his loving grandmother for a summer in northern Minnesota, where she cooks for a crew cutting a road through the woods into Canada.

When World War II ended in 1945, Paulsen's father was sent to Manila, in the Philippines, and Paulsen and his mother moved there also. Unfortunately, life in the Philippines was also unhappy for the boy. Both his parents began drinking heavily, and he spent much of his time wandering around the bombed-out city with the Paulsens' houseboy

Returning to Minnesota in 1949, the Paulsens continued to have a tragic family life, and Gary Paulsen was sent on several occasions to live with relatives. Because he moved around so much, his school experiences were not very happy either, and he was not a good student. Paulsen became a reader, he explains, only because of a friendly librarian who coaxed him into signing up for a library card and found enjoyable books for him to read. Paulsen remembers reading all the time after that to escape, hiding out in the basement of his apartment building while his parents drank and fought upstairs.

The other escape for Paulsen was to the woods and rivers near his home, and he grew to love the outdoors. As he explains in the book *Father Water, Mother Woods* (1994), these adventures gave him a way to endure his hard life, and they gave him knowledge he would later use in writing *Hatchet* and *The River.*

In 1957, Paulsen graduated from high school with "probably a D— average," tried college for two quarters, and eventually joined the army. After his stint in the army, which he did not enjoy very much, he went to work in the satellite-tracking business in California. One night at work, Paulsen suddenly decided that he wanted to be a writer. Almost instantly, he quit his job and moved to Hollywood to learn the writing business.

As any writer will tell you, wanting to write and actually making a living as a writer are two very different things. For several years, Paulsen worked at his writing while moving around from California to Minnesota, New Mexico, and Colorado. Slowly he started to sell a few adult novels and how-to books.

Sadly, the alcoholism that had afflicted Paulsen's parents during his childhood also caught up with him during these years, and by the late 1960s he had given up writing. By 1973, married to Ruth Wright Paulsen and the father of their son, Jim, and two children from a previous marriage, Paulsen realized finally what alcoholism was doing to him. He got help and was able to stop drinking. A short time later, back in Minnesota, he tried to start writing again while he eked out a living by running a trapline to capture small game for the state of Minnesota.

These were not easy years for Paulsen, but eventually he put them to good use. When a friend gave him an old dogsled and four dogs to help him expand his trapline, Paulsen almost immediately fell in love with dogsledding. He spent long hours running his sled and entered a few local races. Then in 1983 he entered the famous Iditarod dogsled race, the 1,200-mile run across Alaska that has been called "the last great race on earth." Voted by his fellow mushers "the least likely to get out of Anchorage," Paulsen managed to finish the grueling race, and it forever changed him as a

musher dogsled driver

grueling exhausting and difficult

person. "The Iditarod makes you not normal," explains Paulsen. "It becomes so weirdly possessive of you that it ruins your life."

What Paulsen means is that running dog teams somehow became everything to him. He bought a whole kennel of dogs and began spending eighteen hours a day on his sled. In 1985 he entered the Iditarod a second time. All told, Paulsen estimates that he has put in more than 22,000 miles on a dogsled.

Partly to pay for his dogsledding, Paulsen also wrote a lot during these years, turning out popular books such as *Dogsong* (1985), *Hatchet,* and *The Crossing* (1987). But in 1990, while training for a third Iditarod, he experienced heart problems. Told by his doctor that he could no longer run dogsleds, he sold his equipment and dogs. To keep himself from despair over the fact that he had to give up something he loved so much, he poured all of his energies into his writing. He has been writing at a furious pace ever since.

Paulsen's Survival Stories

A number of patterns are visible in Gary Paulsen's books for young adults. Some, for example, are almost totally nature adventure stories, and it is these books, particularly *Hatchet* and *The River,* that his young readers know best. *Hatchet* is the story of thirteen-year-old Brian Robeson, who, while flying to visit his father in Alaska, survives a plane crash into a small lake in northern Canada and has to live for fifty-four days in the wilderness with only a small hatchet. In the book's sequel, *The River,* Brian returns to the wilderness to help a psychologist, Derek Holtzer, learn about human survival techniques. The trip goes awry when Derek is struck by lightning during a terrible storm and falls into a coma. Once again, Brian must depend upon only his wits and his understanding of the natural world as he builds a crude raft and uses it to float Derek and himself down a river to a remote trading post.

awry not as planned

Paulsen has written other popular survival stories. In *The Voyage of the Frog* (1989), for example, fourteen-year-old David Alspeth survives an amazing sea adventure alone in the Pacific on a twenty-two-foot sailboat. In *The Haymeadow* (1992), another fourteen year old, John Barron, survives storms, attacks by wildlife, and loneliness while tending six thousand sheep for a summer in a mountain meadow in Wyoming. Paulsen himself is the protagonist in *Woodsong* (1990), a nonfiction book that tells of his early adventures on dogsleds in northern Minnesota and his first Iditarod race in 1983.

A review of *Woodsong* in the 27 July 1990 issue of *Publishers Weekly* refers to Gary Paulsen as "the best author of man-against-nature adventures writing today." There are, perhaps, two reasons for this acclaim. First, having spent so much time in the wilderness himself, Paulsen knows how to bring his natural setting to life in his books. Everything about his stories seems authentic. Second, Paulsen respects nature. His characters learn to survive, not because they conquer the natural world but because they learn to adjust themselves to it.

Coming-of-Age Stories

If Gary Paulsen has a deep love for nature, he has an equal admiration for young people, which may be why he has spent so much of his career writing for them. "I feel that we've dramatically let our youth down," Paulsen explained in a *Los Angeles Times* interview (31 July 1994). "Look at us—we've somehow managed to design nuclear weapons. We've polluted one jewel of a planet. We're overbreeding at a rate that's frightening. We've generated all these problems, and we're not giving them the tools to survive with. We simply don't tell them the truth."

Many of Paulsen's books for young readers attempt to tell the truth about our world and about the problems of growing up. At the beginning of *The Island* (1988), Wil Neuton, having just moved with his parents from the city of Madison to northern, rural Wisconsin, finds a small island on an isolated lake in the woods. He returns to the island day after day to examine, draw, and write about what he sees there.

Like Henry David Thoreau's retreat to Walden Pond, Wil's relocation to his remote island teaches him about nature, about people, and about himself. At the end of the book, when his encampment on the island comes to an end, he finds that he is more in harmony with himself and with the world in general.

Henry David Thoreau (1817–1862) lived alone at **Walden Pond** in Massachusetts and wrote *Walden*, in which he recorded his thoughts while living a simple life in harmony with nature.

protagonist main character of a literary work

Other Paulsen protagonists develop understanding not by retreating from the world but as a result of adventures in it. The unnamed main character of *Tiltawhirl John* (1977), for example, runs away from home for a summer, works on a farm, and joins a traveling circus (something Paulsen himself did when he was fifteen). In doing so he sees "so much of the wrong side of people that I'm not sure I want to be a person" (p. 9).

Russel Suskit, a fourteen-year-old Inuit Eskimo boy in the book *Dogsong,* wakes up one day and realizes, "I am not happy with myself" (p. 9). He goes to live with the village shaman, Oogruk, learns his people's "old ways," and eventually takes a dog team on an extended run that puts him in touch with nature, his heritage, and himself. He learns to sing a "Dogsong" expressing this new understanding of himself and his world.

shaman traditional healer and spiritual leader

Brennan Cole, the main character of the novel *Canyons* (1990), also goes on a journey of self-discovery. After finding the skull of an Apache youth in a remote New Mexico canyon, Brennan becomes somehow linked to the spirit of this ancient warrior, Coyote Runs, and he travels to an old Apache place of worship to release Coyote Runs's spirit and, in a sense, his own spirit as well.

John Borne, in *Tracker* (1984), goes deer hunting alone for the first time because his beloved grandfather is dying of cancer. Instead of killing the beautiful doe he spots, he tracks her for two nights and a day until he finally, miraculously, gets close enough to touch this magnificent wild animal. The tracking experience teaches him some profound lessons about life and death.

Adult Teachers and Guides

An interesting pattern in Gary Paulsen's books of self-discovery is the use of flawed but kind adult mentors who offer young people lessons about life. Carly, in *Popcorn Days and Buttermilk Nights* (1983), goes to live with his Uncle David, a blacksmith who decides to build a whole set of carnival rides from old machinery so that the children of the town can feel the magic of the circus. Carly comes to admire and love this man, who "could tame joy and hammer it into the shape of living, the way he hammered steel into the shape of a hoof" (p. 4).

Another Uncle David, this one a great-uncle in the story *The Winter Room* (1989), teaches young Eldon and Wayne that the old stories he tells around the stove on the farm on winter nights are more than stories; they contain truth and are filled with life. In *The Monument* (1991), the artist Mick Strum comes to a small town, Bolton, Kansas, to create a monument to the town's war dead. In the process, he teaches Rachel (Rocky) Turner about art and life by showing her how to "watch and learn and work and live and be" (p. 104). In *Dancing Carl* (1983), war veteran Carl Wenstrom tends the ice rinks in the small northern town of McKinley, Minnesota, and reveals to two boys, Marsh and Willy, the pain and the love of a fragile spirit as he "dances" on the ice.

Other war veterans teach young people about life in *The Car* (1994), in which two Vietnam veterans, Waylon Jackson and Wayne Holtz, take Terry Anders on a journey of discovery across America; *The Foxman* (1978), in which a reclusive World War I veteran is befriended by a fifteen-year-old boy and his cousin; and *The Crossing*, in which an army sergeant, Robert Locke, helps Manny Bustos escape a horrible life in Juarez, Mexico.

The Moods of Gary Paulsen

Although many of Paulsen's books are about survival or growing up, and many contain interesting adult guides, some of his works are effective largely because of the moods they create. At times Paulsen's writing is very funny, as it is in *The Boy Who Owned the School* (1990), a story about shy Jacob Freisten's comical adventures in high school; *Harris and Me* (1993), about the hilarious adventures of two young boys on a farm in the 1950s; and the Culpepper Adventures books for very young readers.

Paulsen is also occasionally angry in his books. One place to hear this angry voice is in his 1993 work *Sisters/Hermanas*, a story of two fourteen-year-old girls—one of them a popular student who is trying out for cheerleader, the other an illegal Mexican immigrant who makes her living on the streets. Anger is also heard in *Nightjohn* (1993), the story of a slave in the 1850s who escapes from his master, is captured and tortured, escapes again, and secretly returns to the plantation to teach the young slave children to read. Finally, there is a subdued anger in one of Paulsen's own favorites among his works, *Sentries* (1986), which weaves the stories of four young people together with "battle hymns" that reveal how war disrupts people's lives and destroys life as well.

Whether angry or happy, whether writing about survival or growing up, Gary Paulsen is always a hopeful writer, for he believes that young people must be respected as they are guided into adulthood. And he continues to write enthusiastically, commenting that he has "fallen in love with writing, with the dance of it." Taken together, Gary Paulsen's sense of purpose and love of writing ensure that he will continue to write enjoyable and effective books for young adults for years to come.

Readers who enjoy Gary Paulsen's works might also enjoy the works of Jack London and Robert Newton Peck.

Selected Bibliography

WORKS BY GARY PAULSEN

Mr. Tucket (1968; 1994)

Winterkill (1976)

Tiltawhirl John (1977)

The Foxman (1978)

The Night the White Deer Died (1978)

Dancing Carl (1983)

Popcorn Days and Buttermilk Nights (1983)

Tracker (1984)

Dogsong (1985)

Sentries (1986)

The Crossing (1987)

Hatchet (1987)

The Island (1988)

The Voyage of the Frog (1989)

The Winter Room (1989)

The Boy Who Owned the School (1990)

Canyons (1990)

Woodsong (1990)

The Cookcamp (1991)

The Monument (1991)

The River (1991)

A Christmas Sonata (1992)

The Haymeadow (1992)

Harris and Me (1993)

Nightjohn (1993)

Sisters/Hermanas (1993)

The Car (1994)

Father Water, Mother Woods (1994)

Call Me Francis Tucket (1995)

The Rifle (1995)

The Tent (1995)

WORKS ABOUT GARY PAULSEN

Chevalier, Tracy, ed. *Twentieth Century Children's Writers,* 3d ed. Chicago: St. James, 1989.

Commire, Anne, ed. *Something About the Author.* Detroit: Gale Research, 1993, vol. 54, pp. 76–82.

Garrett, Agnes, and Helga P. McCue, eds. *Authors and Artists for Young Adults.* Detroit: Gale Research, 1989, vol. 2, pp. 165–173.

Lewis, Randy. "He Owes It All to Librarians and Dogs." In *Los Angeles Times,* 31 July 1994, pp. E1, E6.

Miller, Kay. "Suddenly Fame and Fortune." In *Minneapolis Star-Tribune Sunday Magazine,* 10 July 1988, pp. 5–12.

Nelms, Elizabeth D. and Ben F. Nelms. "Gary Paulsen: The Storyteller's Legacy." In *English Journal,* January 1992, pp. 85–88.

Review of *Woodsong.* In *Publishers Weekly,* 27 July 1990, pp. 234–235.

Salvner, Gary M. *Presenting Gary Paulsen.* New York: Twayne, 1996.

> **How to Write to the Author**
> Gary Paulsen
> HC 72 Box 5051
> Tularosa, NM 88352